# RAISING JESUS

## THE SKEPTIC'S GUIDE TO FAITH IN THE RESURRECTION

E.J. Sweeney

WESTBOW
PRESS®
A DIVISION OF THOMAS NELSON
& ZONDERVAN

WestBow Press books may be ordered through booksellers or by contacting:

WestBow Press
A Division of Thomas Nelson & Zondervan
1663 Liberty Drive
Bloomington, IN 47403
www.westbowpress.com
1 (866) 928-1240

ISBN: 978-1-9736-3758-5 (sc)
ISBN: 978-1-9736-3760-8 (hc)
ISBN: 978-1-9736-3759-2 (e)

Library of Congress Control Number: 2018910013

Print information available on the last page.

WestBow Press rev. date: 10/25/2018

# DEDICATION

To my wife Cherie, who believed in this project, and
in me, even when I didn't. None of this would have
been possible without your love and support.
I love sharing this adventure of life with you!
And to my Risen Lord, whose radical love makes life so much more
challenging,
but also, so much more exciting and fulfilling.
And infinitely worth it!

# CONTENTS

Introduction ............................................................................ix

Part I: Virtual Certainty— The Historical Evidence

Chapter 1   The Scandal of It All .................................................1
Chapter 2   In the Eye of the Beholder....................................34
Chapter 3   You Complete Me ...................................................77

Part II: An Uncanny Fit—The Resurrection
and the Historical Jesus

Chapter 4   Junk Scholarship..................................................... 139
Chapter 5   Will The Real Jesus Please Stand Up! .................... 162
Chapter 6   Who Cares Who Rises?........................................... 182

Part III: Life Is Hard...Then You Die!—
The Philosophical Question

Chapter 7   Dead Men Don't Walk............................................. 193
Chapter 8   The Great Intruder .................................................206
Chapter 9   The Logic of the Universe....................................232

Appendix I: The Bright Light of Eternity or Just the
        Operating Table? ......................................................289
Appendix II: Shrouded in Mystery.............................................295
Acknowledgments ...................................................................305

# INTRODUCTION

I T WAS A BEAUTIFUL Easter Sunday afternoon. Church that morning had been exhilarating. The music was inspiring, the sermon moving. Flowers adorned the sanctuary and Spring was in the air. The entire service was a rousing celebration of resurrection hope. I left on a high.

But then my wife showed me something that totally rained on my parade. Someone had posted a video on Facebook that claimed Christianity had "plagiarized" the resurrection from pagan mythology, that the idea of Jesus' resurrection was stolen from the many pagan myths of dying and rising gods. The video presented itself as a scandalous new discovery revealing that the Christian faith was based on a hoax.

My joy turned to anger. Not because my faith was in a shambles. Not because I felt betrayed by the Church which had deceived me with what it knew to be a lie, a fable.

No, I was angry because this "bombshell discovery" now making the rounds on social media *wasn't new at all*. The objection was first raised in the 1890's! Even back then it failed to gain much traction. By the 1940's, after scholars had a chance to thoroughly analyze all the evidence, it had been completely refuted.

No major scholar today takes this argument seriously.[1]

And yet, thousands of people were being duped. They were being misled by outright misinformation that presented itself as legitimate scholarship. Like my wife, who knows a lot about her faith but still had to ask whether there was any truth to this video.

Many think that it's naive to believe Jesus rose from the dead. That it's childish, like believing in Santa Claus or the Tooth Fairy. Completely irrational. Anti-intellectual. Unscientific. Even delusional.

I would too...if I hadn't seen the evidence.

A die-hard skeptic, *I need to see to believe.*

Hard facts. Compelling proof. Rigorous logic.

*This* is what I believe in.

I don't blindly believe "because the Bible tells me so." I accept evolution as the best scientific account of how we got here. Without objective data to back it up, I don't trust personal experience, especially personal religious experience. I categorically reject "alternative facts."

I am fully a child of our modern, scientific worldview.

In fact, my overriding bias is to *deny the miraculous.* My running assumption is that there must be some rational explanation to every so-called "miracle." Unless some detached, objective authority—like an unbelieving doctor—can verify a miracle, I won't accept it. And even then, I only tentatively commit. I'm never surprised when it turns out that a supposed miracle can later be explained naturalistically. I even expect it.

Where others see divine intervention, I only see coincidence.

I'm also not a conspiracy theorist, seeing things that aren't there. I don't believe the United States government was responsible for 9-11 or "Tower 7," whatever that means. I don't believe in UFO's, ET's or any other assorted acronymed alien invaders. I always look for the simplest and most rational explanation for any phenomena.

I seek and want to find a naturalistic answer to *everything.*

This is especially true of Jesus' resurrection. Not only is it the most farfetched, fantastic, and unbelievable event ever reported (a dead man coming back to life utterly transformed to the transcendent sphere), it's the one event—if true—upon which everything else turns, our entire worldview, everything we think and believe.

If Jesus isn't risen, then he is simply a tragic figure, *a mere mortal*, perhaps even fraudulent or self-deluded. He can add nothing to our understanding of ultimate reality—why we're here and what happens when we die. Only a fool would orient their life around him and his teachings. As Paul says, if Christ is not risen, then Christian faith is in vain. Christians are the most pathetic lot of people the world has ever known. (I Corinthians 15:12-19)

But if Jesus is risen, then he is everything he claims to be: the Lord of All. In him we encounter the living God, *Ultimate Reality itself.* He is the answer to life's most perplexing questions, to the meaning of life and the secret of true happiness. Only a fool would refuse to stake their whole life, and eternal destiny, on him.

No other event of history has such profound implications.

And on top of all of this, when I first began examining the evidence, *I didn't want it to be true.* I was much more attracted to several other religions I was studying at the time: Buddhism, Islam, and especially Taoism. They made a whole lot more sense. And they were far more reasonable to follow. But if Jesus really rose, then I would have to accept that Christianity—all of it—was true.

If Jesus really rose from the dead, I would have to believe in things I found totally absurd at the time, things like the Incarnation—Jesus is fully human and fully divine; the Trinity—God is Three Persons, yet One God; and the Atonement—Jesus' death on the cross saves us from sin and death. Huh???

If Jesus really rose from the dead, I would have to radically change my life. I would have to live an impossible—not to mention totally insane—ethic: turning the other cheek, loving my enemy, forgiving without limit, and so on.

If Jesus really rose from the dead, I would have to become part of the Church with all its hypocrisy, archaic teachings, and mind-boggling ways; an institution I often found, and still often do find, infuriatingly self-righteous and out of step with reality.

Yes, if there is anything I am disposed to doubt, it is the resurrection of Jesus.

It's the stuff of *fantasy.*

And I *really* didn't want it to be true.

But, when I first confronted the evidence, I was forced—on purely rational, scientific, and historical grounds—to conclude that it is far more difficult not to believe it happened than to believe it did. Over the past thirty years, as I've continued to probe the evidence and arguments more deeply, both pro and con, historical and metaphysical, the reality of the resurrection has only become more and more undeniable.

Despite my skeptical nature, my bias, my doubts, my preference, my desire, my will, I have to admit that the facts make it *virtually certain* that Jesus rose from the dead. This book is designed to show you that evidence in a clear, unfiltered, and systematic way.

## Resurrection 3.0: Three New Takes on an Old Question

So, how is this book different from the many other fine books on the resurrection?

Three distinct ways.

First, I will rely on the most *balanced* and *up-to-date* scholarship. I've found that most of the popular (i.e., non-academic) books on the resurrection tend to slant toward one extreme of scholarship or the other. In other words, they are either liberal and tend to be prematurely dismissive of it—and anything miraculous for that matter—or they are conservative and tend to be credulously simplistic—they fail to rigorously apply the scientific criteria to their investigation of it.

When I first began my quest, I read every book I could on either end of the spectrum and everything in between. It was a long and arduous process. But I eventually discovered the mainstream, where the best, most balanced, and most *trustworthy* scholarship is found. That's what I present here.

Over the past four decades there has been a flurry of popular books questioning the historical facts surrounding the life of Jesus, including the resurrection. These books present themselves as mainstream scholarship, as if they represent the consensus of modern biblical scholars. From Reza Aslan's *Zealot* to Bart Ehrman's *How Jesus Became God*, John Dominic Crossan's *Jesus: A Revolutionary Biography* to Elaine Pagel's *The Gnostic Gospels*, The Jesus Seminar's *The Five Gospels* to Dan Brown's *The DaVinci Code* (I know it's only fiction and Brown is not a biblical scholar, but so many have accepted the "facts" he presents about Jesus as representing the current scholarly consensus that it's necessary to include him here), the impression is given that among scholars it is a *forgone conclusion* that most of what the gospels record, especially the resurrection, is the stuff of legend.

I've read most of these books. Many of them are great reads.

Unfortunately, they *aren't* the best or most balanced scholarship. Not even close.

I used to own a truck. A big, beautiful Dodge Ram 4x4. Fast and powerful, it sat up high, giving you a great view of the road and a rock-solid feeling of safety. Originally, I bought it for the snow—as a volunteer firefighter I needed to get to the firehouse quickly and my rear-wheel-drive Ford Crown Victoria wasn't cutting it. I loved my truck, especially the way it looked, with its shiny black finish and chrome alloy wheels.

Wherever I went, I always parked in the furthest space I could find so that nobody would park near it. My greatest fear was someone denting it. My wife thought it was crazy that we'd have to walk hundreds of feet across empty parking lots. I didn't care. I loved my truck.

I remember the day it got its first scratch. I cried.

I only took my truck out in good weather. If it was raining or snowing, I left it home and drove my old rear-wheel-drive car instead. I didn't want it to get dirty or be in traffic when road conditions weren't optimal. Yes, I did say I bought it specifically for the snow. But I didn't have the heart to take it out in bad weather. I couldn't risk someone losing control and crashing into it. I loved my truck.

On a good day, my truck got about twelve-and-a-half miles to the gallon. I bought it right around the time Al Gore's movie

*An Inconvenient Truth* hit the theatres. Global warming was just beginning to come into popular consciousness. I didn't want global warming to be true. I loved my truck. But, if global warming was real, my truck was destroying the environment and I'd have to give it up: *a very inconvenient truth indeed.*

So I looked into the science. I tried to find every scholar I could who denied global warming so I could justify keeping my truck. But instead, I found that the overwhelming majority of scientists agree it's real. It's not even close. Those who deny it are on the fringe. They represent an *extreme* position that few of their peers follow. As much as I want the deniers to be right, I can't deny the majority consensus and the science behind it.

I own a car now.

Like those who deny global warming, the biblical scholars cited above and the very popular books they've written are at the fringe, representing an extreme position. They don't represent the mainstream of modern scholarship at all. This book does.

And while most books on the resurrection aren't that extreme, as mentioned above, the readable ones tend to tip to one side or the other. For example, on the conservative side, they simply presuppose that the biblical reports are accurate. I won't do that. For me, it was never good enough to blindly accept that Scripture is historically true. It had to be substantiated on other grounds.

In fact, my belief in the trustworthiness of Scripture rests upon the truth of the resurrection. I only came to believe in the inspiration of Scripture because I *first* believed Jesus rose from the dead. If he didn't, I wouldn't. So, I don't take the biblical accounts of the resurrection at face value. Instead, I show how aspects of them can be verified by the tools of historical scholarship, and I explain why most scholars now believe that, in substance, they can be trusted as fairly accurate.

Of course, this approach might eliminate some things that may actually be true in the biblical report. But if it can't be verified independently, it won't be part of the evidence I use. For example, I don't presume that the story in Matthew's Gospel of the guards placed at Jesus' tomb is true—though it may be—because it can't be substantiated by the historical criteria normally used by scholars.

In addition to using the most balanced scholarship, I will also use the most up-to-date as well. In the last twenty years or so, there has been a dramatic shift within mainstream scholarship itself and this has radical implications for any study of the resurrection.

When I was in divinity school, one of my professors told us a story about one of his predecessors, a venerable Yale scholar who was writing a book about the historical Jesus. Every morning, this professor was in the habit of getting up early and taking a walk down the hill from the divinity school to the main campus and back. During his walk, he would be deep in prayer, communing with God. And so, in his book, *without any shred of evidence* from the gospels, this venerable Yale scholar concluded that Jesus got up every morning and *took a long walk,* usually in *the hills* of Galilee, where he communed with God his Father *in prayer.* Just like this professor did!

My professor's point was that most books about Jesus tell you more about the author and their agenda than about the historical Jesus. In fact, the sheer volume of different—and often contradictory—portraits of Jesus scholars have produced over the last century betrays this fact. It has been a source of great embarrassment for the field.

However, within the past two decades a consensus has begun to emerge. For the first time, mainstream scholars are coming into basic agreement about the historical contours—the bedrock facts—of Jesus' life. And the implications this has for the resurrection are huge, implications, as far as I'm aware, no one has drawn out. I do, especially in Part II where I also provide a detailed explanation of this recent trend in scholarship.

Second, the best and most balanced books on the resurrection fall into two camps. Either they are very academic and hard to follow—N.T. Wright's *The Resurrection of the Son of God* is the best recent book but it's also *seven hundred pages* of heavily footnoted text and technical, scholarly argument—or they are easy to read, but lack the substance many hard-core skeptics are looking for—Lee Stobel's well-known *The Case for Christ* is a good case in point, as an number of skeptics I've given the book to have told me after reading it. (Lest anyone think I'm being overly critical, I have great admiration for both books—they are two of my favorites and I recommend them all the time.)

One of the main things that makes this book unique is that it *balances substance with readability.* The evidence is laid out in an easy-to-follow, systematic fashion. And complex arguments are illustrated with concrete examples that reveal the power of their unfiltered logic, especially in Part I where things can get very confusing.

Unfortunately (or fortunately, depending how you look at it), there is *so much* evidence that it is impossible to include every detail in a (relatively) short book. I've tried to reserve the intricate nuances for the endnotes (that's why there are so many) and recommend resources for those who want to pursue them in greater depth.

On the one hand, I don't want you, the reader, to get lost in a dizzying myriad of information. Therefore, I've tried to be as concise as possible without losing the substance of the argument.

On the other hand, I do want you, the reader, to know that there is so much more to each piece of evidence presented here, and in the endnotes you can go deeper and find other resources to explore further if you wish.

I've also included a number of quotes by some of the most critically adept scholars on the subject, not only to reinforce how substantial the evidence is, but also to show how it has won acceptance among many intellectual heavyweights who tend to be quite skeptical. They demonstrate that believing in the resurrection isn't naïve or anti-intellectual at all!

Third and most important, for the majority of skeptics the great obstacle to belief in the resurrection is a philosophical one: *people just don't come back from the dead!* They can't even begin to consider the historical evidence without addressing the apparent absurdity of such a claim, and rightly so.

How is a *rational* person supposed to believe this stuff?

This was the biggest obstacle for me. And it's where people usually get stuck.

Part III is devoted to this question. In fact, what might make this book most unique is the way it puts all the metaphysical and historical evidence together.

A word of warning: the resurrection is a *self-involving* question. It isn't something you can remain detached about. Like the question of global warming, if true, it requires a commitment, a radical change of lifestyle. And as with global warming, the will is often the dominant factor in determining what we believe. We often only see what we want to see. The technical term for this is "confirmation bias." Recent studies show how powerful and pervasive it is. In the Conclusion, I will talk about what all this means for evaluating the evidence presented here and how we can overcome our biases, *if we want!*

## Knowledge is Power

So why bother reading this book? Why spend the time and effort?

Well, if the resurrection is true, then it's *the most important thing you can know.* Nothing in all of history is more significant. Nothing is more life-changing. It is the key to ultimate reality, to the meaning of life, to our eternal destiny, to the deepest longings of the human heart.

The potential payoff makes it more than worth the effort.

But even if you don't come away convinced, you'll have only wasted a few hours—hopefully you were entertained along the way! And then you'll be able to impress your friends at parties by using Christians' best arguments against us!

One last thing: yes, the title is a play on a recent, best-selling book about Jesus' crucifixion. Because of people like this well-known author and former talk show host, Christianity is often thought to be based on a simplistic worldview, on flimsy scholarship of a decidedly biased and conservative bent—otherwise known as "alternative facts"—or on no scholarship, no reason or logic, at all.

The impression is that, to follow Christ, you have to leave your brain at the door.

Moreover, rightly or wrongly, this book's author is associated with a version of Christianity that appears bitter, angry, self-righteous, judgmental, and emphatically aligned with a specific brand of partisan politics.

Who'd really want this version of Christianity to be true?

*Raising Jesus* is meant to be an antidote to this kind of mean and joyless Christianity. The Jesus I and many others believe rose from the dead—the REAL Jesus—isn't mean and joyless at all. Quite the opposite, he is *the* source of the greatest joy, love, mercy, and grace this world—and the next—offers.

And he's not a Republican (or a Democrat) either.

Most of all, *Raising Jesus* is meant to be an antidote to this kind of simplistic Christianity.

*You don't have to get a lobotomy to believe Jesus rose from the dead!*

In fact, based on the evidence, I—along with many other skeptics—have found, and hope to show, that it is the *most reasonable* conclusion you can make.

# COMING ATTRACTIONS

## An Overview for Those Who Like to Know What's Coming

**Part I** examines the historical evidence surrounding the empty tomb and appearances of Jesus. The empty tomb and appearances are considered separately in chapters 1 and 2, respectively, and then together in chapter 3.

**Part II** looks at the larger historical context of Jesus' life. Chapter 4 outlines the state of modern biblical scholarship. Chapter 5 gives an overview of the emerging consensus of scholars regarding the historical Jesus—who they think the *real* Jesus was. And chapter 6 shows how this affects the case for the resurrection.

**Part III** dives into the philosophical question. Chapter 7 discusses the problem and reveals why it isn't insurmountable. Chapter 8 presents four philosophical arguments that suggest the resurrection. And, after examining the present state of the God debate, chapter 9 demonstrates why, metaphysically, the resurrection is a logical necessity.

**The Conclusion** evaluates the evidence in light of the limitations of our subjective horizons—how we can overcome them in searching for the Truth—and explains what resurrection faith actually involves.

# PART I: VIRTUAL CERTAINTY

## *The Historical Evidence*

# CHAPTER

# 1

# The Scandal of It All

## *The Empty Tomb*

I T'S A WELL-KNOWN STORY. According to the biblical accounts, early on the Sunday morning following Jesus' crucifixion, several of his women followers went to the tomb he was buried in and found it empty. Immediately, they returned to tell the other disciples. In disbelief, several of the men ran to the tomb and saw for themselves that it was empty.

But why should we trust these accounts?

There are significant *discrepancies* in key details of the story.

And even if they turn out to be reliable, there are far more *plausible* ways to explain the tomb being found empty.

How do we know that Jesus' body was actually buried in the first place? And if buried, in a tomb everyone knew?

How do we know that the women didn't just go to the wrong tomb?

Or that a few of Jesus' disciples didn't remove his body to pull off some kind of hoax?

Or that grave robbers didn't steal the body?

Or that someone else, for some unknown reason, didn't move it?

# 1. Who's on First? Discrepancies in the Gospel Narratives

At first glance, the different gospel stories of the empty tomb remind you of the famous Laurel and Hardy skit, "Who's on First?" No matter how hard they try, the writers can't seem to get their stories straight.

For example, they don't agree on *which women* actually went to the tomb, a simple, but critically important detail.

To make it worse, they include some *farfetched, legendary details*, particularly the presence of angels, the number and location of which they also can't agree on.

Right off the bat these stories are suspect.

Look at the variations in the list of women who visit the tomb. In Matthew, Mark, and Luke, two similarly named women appear: Mary Magdalene along with another Mary, whom Mark and Luke go on to identify as the mother of James. There is a third woman in Mark and Luke: Mark calls her Salome; Luke, Johanna. John only mentions one woman, Mary Magdalene.

So what is it: one, two, or three? And which ones?

Let's start with the most problematic, the mention of only one woman in the Gospel of John. In his highly-regarded commentary on this gospel, Raymond Brown, who was one of the foremost scripture scholars of the twentieth century, has shown that, as a literary device, John has a tendency to make an individual representative of a larger group or attitude. For example, Thomas is singled out to personify the doubt of all the disciples when they are first confronted with the risen Jesus. In this way John dramatizes both the trait and the larger group who holds it.[2]

So, in the story of the empty tomb, John simply chooses Mary Magdalene to represent and, thereby, *dramatize* the experience of the other women. In fact, 20:2 betrays the fact that he knew the original story included several women visiting the tomb: Mary responds to Simon and the Beloved Disciple with the plural "we" instead of "I", clearly indicating the presence of at least one other person beside herself. In other words, John is fully aware that there were several women who discovered the tomb empty.

Moving on to the other three gospels, the variation among the lists is not as significant as it first appears. Mary Magdalene and another Mary, possibly the mother of James as Luke and Mark specify, are *consistently named*. Most likely, this other Mary is alluded to anonymously in John as part of the "we".

It is really only the presence and identity of the third woman that is in question.

Still, this is a significant discrepancy.

However, as scripture scholar Richard Bauckham shows, once you understand the cultural context, this discrepancy actually reveals how careful and scrupulous the gospel writers were in naming the different women eyewitnesses. Given the norms of ancient historiography, the pressure on the gospel writers to harmonize their lists would have been enormous. A good historian was supposed to smooth things out. Not only was this an accepted practice, it was expected.[3]

But the gospel writers refused. Instead, they remained *completely faithful to the eyewitness testimony they inherited.* Despite the problem it created, the gospel writers only included the women they knew for sure were eyewitnesses to the event. If a particular gospel writer *wasn't certain* for himself that the lesser-known figures—namely, Salome and Johanna as the third-named woman—were present at the tomb, he omitted them.

> the Evangelists were careful to name precisely the
> women who were well known to them as witnesses
> to these crucial events in the origins of the Christian
> movement [which] explains the variations among

the lists of women…The omission of Salome by both Matthew and Luke shows that the Evangelists did not retain the names of women who had become obscure. Those named by each Evangelist were, like their stories, still fresh in the memory of that Evangelist's informants, if not in the Evangelist's own memory.[4]

In fact, these accounts don't read like a carefully crafted tale where every detail is consistently ironed out. They read like genuine eyewitness testimony that contains exactly the kind of discrepancies we would expect to see as different people recount the same event. It would be far more suspicious if they were perfectly harmonized. As psychologist and retired Notre Dame theologian Morton Kelsey explains:

> If all the descriptions were identical I would believe that they had been cut down to size and harmonized. Like true eyewitnesses, those who describe the events are struck by different aspects of the drama they lived through. A forgery of a signature can often be detected because it will be identical to one other example of the person's handwriting. But no two genuine signatures are identical. Similarly, no two reactions to a drama or to history are identical.[5]

This is one of the major problems for those who argue that the empty tomb stories are just later legends with no basis in historical fact: why *aren't* they more harmonized? If, as the argument goes, the church was simply making these stories up to defend the mythology of the resurrection, they certainly would be far more polished. They certainly would have gotten their facts straight. They certainly would have agreed on such a basic detail as which women went to the tomb!

Moreover, these stories are told in a way that's far too muddled to be an effective defense for the resurrection. Confronted with the empty tomb, the disciples turn away totally perplexed, full of doubt.

Even after the angelic interpreters explain that Jesus has been raised, they still don't know what to make of it. To us, this reaction in the story might look like a dramatic touch, put there to highlight the astonishing reality of the resurrection. But in that historical context, it would have had the opposite effect, undermining any effort to convince others it's true—if the eyewitnesses themselves weren't sure what the empty tomb meant, how can anyone else be? (More on this below in Chapter 1.3)

If invented, the empty tomb stories would have eliminated all confusion and doubt, making the fact that Jesus had risen explicit. That's exactly what happens in the Gnostic gospels. Written many years after the four biblical gospels, the resurrection narratives contained in the Gnostic gospels *are* full-blown legends. (See the example from the Gospel of Peter in Chapter 2.1) In vivid contrast, the empty tomb narratives retain just that kind of raw and unpolished quality found in eyewitness testimony.

But what about the angelic interpreters who explain that Jesus has risen? Even if the gospel narratives aren't full-blown legends, how can we take stories that exhibit this kind of legendary detail seriously?

In his book *The Virginal Conception and the Bodily Resurrection of Jesus*, Raymond Brown has thoroughly analyzed the narratives of the empty tomb. Based on the agreement of certain details across the four gospels, he shows that the earliest account ran something like this: "On the first day of the week Mary Magdalene and some other women went to the tomb of Jesus and found the stone rolled away from the entrance. A young man (or angel) explained: 'He is raised; he is not here.' The women left the tomb fearful."[6]

Brown then goes on to show that Jewish Apocalyptic literature of that period often contained angelic appearances which served to interpret divine mysteries. Putting it all together, he suggests that *the angels are introduced into the story to explain what the discovery of the empty tomb meant.*

So the simplest account of the story probably had Mary Magdalene and some women going to the tomb, finding the stone rolled away, and thinking the body had been stolen. No angels. No legendary detail.

> The real explanation of why the tomb was empty would have become apparent only after Jesus had appeared to his disciples...In order for Christians to develop a narrative of the empty tomb that they could pass on, they had to include the explanation as part of the story; and the way to do this was suggested by the patterns of apocalyptic literature, a literature that dealt with explaining God's eschatological mysteries. An angel or angels could be supplied to interpret the emptiness of the tomb...[7]

In other words, the angels are a *literary device*, already in vogue in some of the Jewish literature of the day, to explain the meaning of the empty tomb.

Brown passed away in 1998. But in the eyes of his peers, he remains one of the most highly esteemed and influential biblical scholars of our time. This is his assessment of the information contained in the empty tomb narratives: "The tradition that the tomb was known and was empty is considerably older than the Gospel narratives that have been built around the discovery of the empty tomb. It deserves preference to the poorly supported hypothesis that the place of Jesus' burial was unknown." And in a footnote to this remark he observes: "This tradition has been judged historical by one of the most critically adept contemporary Church historians, namely H. von Campenhausen."[8]

Despite the discrepancies and legendary accretions, at their *core* it is highly likely that the gospel narratives pass on *trustworthy eyewitness tradition* about the empty tomb.[9]

But even if the narratives weren't reliable, the best evidence for the empty tomb is found in the many details these stories contain, details which can be shown to be historically true whether or not the entire narrative is. To these we turn.

## 2. Say It Ain't So, Joe: the Embarrassing Role of Joseph of Arimathea

If Joseph of Arimathea did, in fact, bury Jesus' body in a tomb he owned, he is a key figure. Besides the women disciples, he is the most credible link to the exact location of the tomb and the fact that Jesus' body was placed there immediately following his crucifixion.

So how do we know he really buried Jesus' body?

As Brown says: "Many have pointed out that the normal procedure following the execution of an accursed criminal (Deut 21:23; Gal 3:13) would have been to dump the corpse into a common burial place reserved for malefactors. A few adventurous scholars have suggested that the very idea that the body of Jesus could not be found sprang from the impossibility of correctly identifying his body in such a common burial ground." If Jesus' body were dumped into a common burial site, his remains could have just decomposed in anonymity among the many others that littered the place.

But Brown continues: "However, an almost insuperable obstacle to such theorizing is raised by the person of Joseph of Arimathea who appears in all four Gospels. It is virtually certain that he was not a figment of Christian imagination, that he was remembered precisely because he had a prominent role in the burial of Jesus, and thus that there was someone who knew exactly where Jesus' body had been buried."[10]

Joseph plays no other role in the New Testament. So it is incomprehensible why the early church would connect him of all people, this obscure character from an insignificant town, with such a crucial piece of the story if he didn't play this role historically.[11]

But far more remarkable, Joseph was a member of the Sanhedrin. As a member of this council, *he agreed to sentence Jesus to death.* The scandal this would have caused the early church cannot be overstated: the man who buries Jesus, who plays such a pivotal role in the story, *had voted to have him crucified!*

Making it even worse, the Sanhedrin was actively persecuting the early church. They were bitter enemies. The fact that Jesus hadn't been buried by his own beloved family and friends, as was custom, but left to a member of the church's bitter enemy because his followers were no where to be found, would have been an enduring disgrace.

So why would the early church have given someone who was a member of the group responsible for Jesus' crucifixion and which was so hostile to their movement such an honorable role, especially in such stark contrast to the disciples' shameful absence, unless it was true?

Joseph's role in the story is far too scandalous to have been invented.

This scandal is obvious in the way the gospels treat the incident. In Mark, the first gospel written, Joseph is simply called "a respected member of the council, who was also himself waiting expectantly for the Kingdom of God." (Mk 15:43) Mark crudely states the embarrassing fact: the same Joseph who buried Jesus in his own tomb had earlier that day taken part in his crucifixion.

Each subsequent gospel writer tries to give it a better spin. In Luke, Joseph is said to disagree with the decision. And in Matthew and John, he becomes a disciple. As a matter of fact, his favorable portrayal in the developing tradition suggests he may very well have become a disciple later on: if it was his tomb that was found empty, it is conceivable that this may have convinced him Jesus really rose. Regardless, being such an embarrassment, Mark's scandalous portrayal of Joseph's participation in Jesus' death is undeniably more accurate and historical.[12]

But if Joseph participated in the sentence against Jesus, why would he offer to bury him?

First-century Jews believed that an unburied corpse was a curse on the land. A violation of Torah, it put all the people in jeopardy. While it may be hard for us to understand this taboo and the extraordinary compulsion associated with it, as a pious Jew, Joseph couldn't allow a dead corpse to remain exposed. *So Joseph didn't bury Jesus out of any kind of respect for him, but out of compulsion for honoring the Law.*

The way he treats Jesus' body confirms that this was his motive. It was common practice to wash the body before burial. It would be a terrible offense not to. But Joseph doesn't do this for Jesus, even though his body would have been covered with blood from the scourging and crucifixion. He fails to perform the customary honor due a beloved family member.

Instead, he only does what is minimally required for a *common criminal*.[13]

This, too, would have been an awful embarrassment for the early church, a poignant reminder of the *shameful burial* Jesus received. But to the point, the lack of proper preparation for burial in Jesus' case is fully consistent with the portrayal of Joseph as a pious member of the council.

Again, it is hard for us to imagine how outrageous and offensive all this would be for first-century Jews. As Brown remarks: "Annointing and spices surely were features of an honorable burial. Those are not mentioned in the Synoptic accounts of Jesus' burial…Thus Mark's account is singularly lacking in elements that would suggest an honorable burial for Jesus…The only burial preliminary reported by Mark is that Joseph 'tied up' Jesus' body in the linen material, i.e., the absolute minimum one could do for the dead. This frugality puzzles many who think that the Marcan Joseph was a disciple of Jesus."[14]

*No disciple would treat Jesus so disrespectfully*. If the story of Joseph was invented, it certainly would have included the proper reverence performed for a loved one. The fact that Joseph treats Jesus' body so shamefully, as that of a common criminal, vividly corroborates the other evidence above that shows he played this embarrassing role historically.

One last thing. The fact that Joseph is said to have placed Jesus in a *new* tomb adds to the credibility of the story. The "newness" of the tomb is an incidental detail. It serves no purpose and has no symbolic significance for the church telling the story. It's just a throwaway remark: "By the way, the tomb happened to be new." As Brown says:

Three of the Gospels (Matthew, Luke, and John) mention that Jesus' tomb was a new one, with Luke and John specifying that it was one "where no one had ever been buried." The latter detail may be an apologetic touch...But the "newness" of the tomb is neutral and may reflect an authentic memory that, although buried privately, the corpse of Jesus, accursed as it was under the Law, could still not be allowed to contaminate other corpses in a family grave. Since there was an element of hurry in the burial of Jesus, the choice of a hitherto unused tomb close to the place of execution is quite plausible.[15]

There's absolutely no reason to include such an unimportant descriptive detail unless it was *actually the case* that Joseph placed Jesus in a tomb that happened to be new; a detail that makes perfect sense because his body couldn't be allowed to contaminate the other remains found in a used tomb.

The vast majority of scholars agree that Raymond Brown's magisterial *The Death of the Messiah* is the most thorough examination of the crucifixion, including Jewish burial practices, done to date. In it, Brown reaches this conclusion:

How much of that is history? That Jesus was buried is historically certain. That Jewish sensitivity would have wanted this done before the oncoming Sabbath (which may also have been a feast day) is also certain, and our records give us no reason to think that this sensitivity was not honored. That the burial was done by Joseph of Arimathea is very probable, since a Christian fictional creation from nothing of a Jewish Sanhedrist who does what is right is almost inexplicable, granted the hostility in early Christian writings toward the Jewish authorities responsible for the death of Jesus. Moreover, the fixed designation of such a character as "from Arimathea," a town very difficult to identify and reminiscent of no scriptural symbolism, makes a thesis of invention even more implausible. The very fact that the later Gospels had to ennoble Joseph and to increase the reverence of the burial given to Jesus shows that Christian instincts would not have freely shaped what I have posited for the basic account.[16]

Brown also notes that even the venerable Rudolf Bultmann, perhaps the most influential scripture scholar of the twentieth century and an extreme skeptic about historical data in the gospels—he thinks they are largely myths—admitted, "This (Jesus' burial by Joseph in Mark) is an historical account which creates no impression of being a legend apart from the women who appear again as witnesses..." (He's referring to the women who witness Joseph placing Jesus in his tomb.)[17]

Joseph's embarrassing role makes it virtually certain that, immediately after being crucified, Jesus was buried in a tomb that was known and could be readily identified.[18]

# 3. Dumb and Dumber: The Disciples' Initial Reaction

In the volunteer fire department I belong to, we've fought many fires over the years. When we retell the stories of those fires, as we're in the habit of doing, it's amazing how much more heroic we become!

It's just human nature to embellish, to make yourself look better.

That's why the disciples' reaction to the news of the empty tomb and later appearances is so baffling. The way *they* tell it, they were gutless fools who doubted the whole thing. Even as they worshiped the resurrected Jesus and were about to receive his commission to proclaim to the world all that they'd experienced, Matthew's gospel tells us that "some doubted." (Matthew 28:17) Not exactly what you'd expect from faithful followers. Or from those trying to tell a story that would convince others to believe.

Morton Kelsey states the obvious:

> Had most of us been making up this story we would have written it quite differently. We would have probably concluded it something like this: "And when the women saw the shining divine messenger sitting in the tomb they were astonished, but the holy being spoke to them and told them that Jesus had risen from the dead and they were to go and tell the disciples and go to Galilee to meet him. At these words the women wept for joy and threw their arms around each other. For a few moments they were silent in their joy, and then cries of joy and exultation broke forth from their lips: 'He is risen, He is risen. The Lord is risen indeed.' Then they dashed forth from the tomb with light steps and ran down the hillside calling out to everyone they met: 'He is risen. He is risen indeed, alleluia.' They found the disciples and they rejoiced at the good news the women brought; soon afterward they all set off for Galilee."
>
> But this is not the way the Gospel tells it. The women were terrified and ran off, telling no one because they were afraid…they were torn between doubt and fear.[19]

And the reaction of these women disciples is *far* better than their male counterparts. At least they didn't abandon Jesus at the cross, cower in fear for their lives, and then deny it's Jesus when he appears right in front of their faces—they think he's a ghost!

If the disciples were making the whole thing up, there is little chance they would have portrayed themselves so badly. They would have made themselves look heroic. They would have depicted themselves faithfully standing by Jesus at the cross and courageously anticipating his resurrection.

Instead, *according to them*, they hide in fear. Completely clueless. *They even continue to doubt after he appears to them.*

The only way to explain how the disciples are portrayed in the gospels is as historical fact: this is the shameful and embarrassing way they reacted when confronted with the surprising and disturbing reality of the empty tomb and appearances that followed.

From our perspective, admitting doubt might seem like a clever tactic. A way to show that the disciples weren't credulous. That they had a healthy dose of skepticism.

This might work in our age, but not theirs.

In their context, introducing doubt into a story that contained none would only alienate prospective believers. It would only raise unnecessary questions about their already startling claim: "If his disciples had doubts, if they aren't even sure about what they saw, how is anyone else supposed to be?" To the ancient mind, doubt wouldn't demonstrate the disciples' healthy skepticism, but rather, their confusion. It would create an element of uncertainty about what they actually experienced. It would demonstrate a glaring weakness in their claim.[20]

The gospels tell us that Peter, chief among the apostles, denied Jesus in his time of greatest need.

They also tell us that Judas, another member of his intimate inner circle, betrayed him.

Because these two events are so embarrassing to the early church, virtually no scholar today would deny they happened. They are simply too scandalous and counterproductive to its mission for anyone in the church to have invented them. We can know with certainty that Peter denied Jesus and Judas betrayed him.

The same can be said of the disciples' doubt. This must have been their actual reaction because it is simply too embarrassing and counterproductive to have been made up. We can know with certainty that, in the face of the startling events surrounding the tomb, their reaction, a reaction such potentially cosmic-altering events would naturally arouse, was fear and doubt.[21] They were reeling from the stupefying fact that the tomb Jesus' body had been placed in lay empty three days later.

## 4. Feminism First-Century Style: Women as the First Eyewitnesses

You've probably heard the stats. Even in the second decade of the twenty-first century, some fifty years since the women's liberation movement began in earnest, women in America doing the same job as men still don't earn the same pay as their male counterparts.

It's outrageous.

If you're like me, it probably makes your blood boil. Equal pay for equal work! As modern Americans, we fundamentally believe that everyone, regardless of gender, race, religion, or anything else, should be treated fairly and equally.

But this pay disparity is nothing compared to the shockingly low status of women in Jesus' day. Back then, women were seen more as property than people. They had no rights, dignity, or identity apart from those male figures in their lives who defined them as a mother, daughter, wife, etc.

It's no wonder that Martha, as she performs the customary duties of waiting on her male guests, is so irate at her sister Mary for sitting at Jesus' feet listening to him teach. (Luke 10:38-42) A woman's place was in the kitchen serving the men, not entering into their sophisticated discussions.

It's no wonder that the disciples are so shocked when they return to find Jesus speaking to the Samaritan woman by the well. (John 4:27) Women weren't allowed to speak to men in public.

It's no wonder that Jesus caused such scandal by calling women disciples. (Luke 8:1-3) This simply wasn't a role they were supposed to play. (One of the reasons Jesus was considered so radical and subversive was his attitude toward women—he took them seriously as full equals.)

Second-class citizen doesn't even begin to describe it.

Women in Jesus' day, at least in public, were practically invisible.

A major reason women were treated this way, as inferior, is because they were considered to be *weak-minded*. Since they couldn't keep it together emotionally, so the thinking went, they were hopelessly irrational.

In fact, as numerous ancient sources attest, in the Judaism of ancient Palestine, women were understood to be *too fickle* and *too emotional* to be trusted as objective observers—how could they be expected to keep the facts straight? As a result, a woman's testimony was *utterly useless*. Women weren't considered valid witnesses, especially in legal proceedings. Even if several women were witness to a crime, their testimony wouldn't be accepted in a court of law.

This is feminism first-century style.

Given all this, who in their right mind would ever make up the story of women discovering the empty tomb? No one would accept their testimony. It was totally useless. Actually, they make things worse. *Their critical role in the story only serves to undermine it.* To make it even more suspect and unbelievable.

As good first-century Jews, this was exactly how the male disciples reacted. To them, the women's tale was utter nonsense, the irrational delusions of emotionally-wrought women who can't keep it together in their grief.

And that's why no one in that day would ever think to invent the story of the women discovering the empty tomb: their presence in the story is completely counterproductive. It makes absolutely no sense to have women as the first eyewitnesses to the resurrection.

*Unless they actually were!*

The *only way* to account for them in the story is if that's how it happened. Is if the women *actually did discover the tomb of Jesus empty.*

Commenting on the women's presence in the story, scholar Frederick Bruner puts it this way:

This is particularly remarkable because the testimony of women was not received in first-century Jewish law courts. As we have noted earlier, if the resurrection story had been invented and was not historical, the evangelists would surely have inserted male witnesses at the grave site. But all four Gospels, with all their other discrepancies, unite at least in testifying that *women* were, in fact, the first commissioned witnesses of the empty tomb and its message...

Davies and Allison...remind us of women's low place and legal non-competence in Israel at that time by citing Josephus, *Ant.* 4.219: "From women let no evidence be accepted, because of the levity and temerity of their sex"; and they recall Celsus's mocking the church's earliest testimony to the empty tomb, in Origen's *Contra Celsum*, 2:59, as testimony from "a half-frantic woman."[22]

Even more remarkable is the fact that the first appearance of Jesus was to a woman. As scholar Ben Witherington notes: "C.H. Dodd once said that John 20 was the firsthand and most self-authenticating of all the Easter narratives because who would make up the notion that Jesus appeared first to a little-known woman from Magdala?"[23] Given feminism first-century style, no one in the early church would ever dare invent such a thing.

In fact, the tendency in the early church was to do the exact opposite, to *suppress and discard* the women's role precisely because of the embarrassment it caused. This is on full display in Paul's first letter to the Corinthians. Scholars generally agree that the creedal formula he is passing along in I Corinthians 15:3-7 is one of, if not the, earliest traditions reflecting the way the early church proclaimed the resurrection.

And yet, this tradition *completely omits the women.*

A stunning fact. *Their presence in the story is considered such a liability that it is left out of the basic creedal formula and never mentioned by Paul or any other New Testament writer outside the gospel narratives.*

As one of the leading scholars of our generation, N.T. Wright, points out, the church's early opponents seized on the women's embarrassing role, mercilessly. It was one of their major arguments against the resurrection. Clearly, the gospel writers would have loved to have been able to avoid this embarrassment by naming some "fine, upstanding, reliable" men as the first witnesses. If they were making the whole thing up, they certainly would have.

But they had no choice. Despite the terrible liability it presented, everyone familiar with the story knew that Mary Magdalene and a few other women were first to find the tomb empty and—at least in the case of Mary Magdalene—first to see Jesus appear.[24]

Given feminism first-century style, the presence of women in the story is one of the surest indications of its historical reliability.

## 5. Plausible Deniability: The Opponents of the Early Church Never Deny the Empty Tomb

In the fall of 2014, following the heroic leadership he demonstrated in the wake of Hurricane Sandy, New Jersey Governor Chris Christie was thought by many to be a shoe-in as the Republican nominee for president in 2016.

Then came "Bridgegate."

As an act of retaliation against his political opponents, members of Christie's leadership team allegedly ordered tolls closed on the George Washington Bridge to create a massive traffic jam. The ensuing scandal over Christie's role in Bridgegate undid all that good feeling about him and any real hope he had to be president in 2016.

Plausible deniability.

This was the term pundits bandied about when commenting on the whole fiasco. If it was plausible that Christie might not have had any knowledge of what his cronies did, then he could survive the scandal. As it turned out, the majority of Americans believed he had to know. His team couldn't do something like this without Christie's awareness and permission.

If a politician has good reason to claim no knowledge of a potentially embarrassing event, he or she can claim plausible deniability and escape indictment. This would have been the perfect and most natural position for the church's opponents to take in the wake of Jesus' resurrection: to deny any knowledge of an empty tomb.

*But they do the exact opposite—they freely admit the tomb is empty.*

The way they explain it is by charging that the disciples stole the body.

However—and here's the critical point—they can't "plausibly deny" the empty tomb because they know it's empty.

*Everyone knows it's empty!*

No one familiar with the circumstances surrounding the tomb can deny the fact that while it contained Jesus' corpse immediately following his crucifixion, it lay empty ever since. Even though many have intense motive to produce his dead body, no one can. And that's why, instead of pointing to a corpse, they offer a much more convoluted explanation.

This is how Brown frames it:

> How did the preaching that Jesus was victorious over
> death ever gain credence if his corpse or skeleton lay
> in a tomb known to all? His enemies would certainly
> have brought this forward as an objection; yet in all the
> anti-resurrection argumentation reflected indirectly in
> the Gospels or in the 2nd-century Christian apologists
> we never find an affirmation that the body was in the
> tomb. There are Christian arguments to show that the
> body was not stolen or confused in a common burial,
> *but the opponents seem to accept the basic fact that*
> *the body can no longer be found.* Even in the Jewish

legend that a gardener named Judas took the body only to bring it back, there is a recognition that the tomb was empty.(my italics)[25]

As far back as we can trace, those first-century Jews who denied the resurrection never denied the reality of the empty tomb. Locked in a heated debate with the early church over the resurrection, the simplest and most decisive way to refute it would be to produce the body.

But they don't. *Because they can't.*

Instead, they admit that the tomb in which Jesus was buried is empty.

Some scholars have challenged this point by asserting that the empty tomb story is a late legend invented by the church many years after Jesus' death. Therefore, the opponents of the church couldn't challenge the empty tomb by producing Jesus' body because *too many years would have passed before the claim was ever made.* At that point, it would be impossible for them to go back and identify the exact tomb and/or produce his corpse.

However, claiming the tomb was empty many years later, for the first time, would have been worthless. It proves nothing. If the opponents of the early church could point out how late this claim was first being made, then everybody would know that the reason they can't produce the body is because *it's too late to be able to do so.* Too much time would have passed for them to accurately locate the tomb and identify any decomposing corpse found in it as Jesus. All the opponents would have to say is: "You just came up with that! It's too late now to verify whether it's true or not."

This would render the empty tomb claim meaningless.

But the opponents of the early church never attempt to make this argument either. Instead, they challenge the emptiness of the tomb in other ways, tacitly admitting that it was widely known to be empty and known to be this way early enough that they *can't simply dismiss it as a late claim.*

In fact, it is highly likely that the disciples "went public" with their claim that the tomb was empty within *fifty days* of Jesus' death (see Chapter 1.7 below). And if so, the opponents—along with everyone else—would have had ample opportunity to examine the exact tomb for themselves.

N.T. Wright has shown that the story of the guards placed at Jesus' tomb in Matthew's Gospel—a story which may not be historical, at least in all its parts—is, nevertheless, based on a real charge by the church's earliest opponents to explain the empty tomb by claiming the disciples stole his body. Traces of this charge are contained in the story, and the story itself is one way the Christians attempted to answer it. As such, it reflects a lively debate between the early church and its opponents over what happened to cause the tomb to be found empty.

*But nowhere is there any hint of challenge to the basic fact of the tomb being known and found empty.*

If the rumor that they stole the body wasn't already out there, the disciples would have been utterly foolish to answer it. Why put potentially damaging ideas into people's heads? Their attempt to answer it through stories like the guards at the tomb indicates that the rumor was so widespread that they had no choice but to deal with it. However, by creating this rumor, their opponents, at least implicitly, are acknowledging that the tomb is empty. They are trying to explain a brute fact they cannot deny some other (less problematic) way.

So, while the story of the guards may not be historical, "...this sort of story could only have any point at all in a community *where the empty tomb was an absolute and unquestioned datum.*"(my italics)[26] Without exception, the opponents of the early church never deny the basic fact of the empty tomb.[27]

But what about their accusation that the disciples stole the body? Could it be true?

If the disciples did steal the body, they would have known that Jesus didn't rise. What reason would they have had to pull off such a hoax? If they received acclaim and adulation, got wealthy or famous, became powerful and influential, or gained some other benefit, it would make sense. Then they would have had good motive to lie.

But what they got instead was persecution, torture, and in many cases, martyrdom. True, they are now famous figures and have been throughout history. However, during their lifetimes, their position in society was made significantly worse and less secure by proclaiming the resurrection. They mainly came to be revered for the heroic way many of them suffered and died for the faith, a legacy they never could have foreseen: the incipient church was a small band of marginalized misfits—no one back then could have ever predicted the prominence it would have centuries later.

If the letters they write are any indication, even in the communities where they held leadership positions, where they potentially could have had some honor and prestige, their lives were made far more complex and burdensome by the many challenges of trying to hold these fragile and often fragmented communities together against immense pressure from the outside world. In other words, it would have been far better for them if they remained fishermen and tax collectors!

Why would they suffer and die for a lie?

A lie whose only promise lay beyond the grave.

A promise they would have known to be patently false.

As a matter of fact, the remarkable courage they displayed in the face of danger and persecution was based squarely on the belief that Jesus' resurrection assured them of an eternal reward with him who had conquered death. Which is absurd if they knew he was dead![28]

No, they had no motive to lie about the empty tomb. And therefore, we have to take the explanation they offered to their deaths seriously: that the tomb was empty because they believed with all their hearts that Jesus had indeed conquered the grave.

The Kennedy assassination has probably attracted more conspiracy theories than any other event in history. Thirty years after the assassination, CBS ran a special reexamining the evidence. The host was Dan Rather. He was a reporter in Dallas the day Kennedy was killed. For a long time, Rather believed there was a conspiracy.

But during the show he made a telling admission. After so much time had passed, he concluded it simply couldn't be a conspiracy. The reason? Based on his vast journalistic experience, he knew that *no group of people can keep a secret that long.* If there'd been a conspiracy, especially as vast as many were speculating, someone, somewhere, sometime, would have given up the ghost. A deathbed confession; a braggadocious remark; a slip of the tongue; a leak to the press.

It would have come out by now.

Conversely, consider the Watergate cover-up. As Chuck Colson admitted: "With the most powerful office in the world at stake, a small band of hand-picked loyalists, no more than ten of us, could not hold a conspiracy together for more than two weeks."[29]

If the resurrection was a hoax, it involved dozens if not hundreds of people—the early tradition handed on by Paul indicates there were at least some five-hundred witnesses. While the match was lit to burn them as human torches, or the cage prepared to feed them to the lions, or as the nails were about to be driven into their arms for crucifixion, someone, somewhere, at some point would have called time out and given up the lie.

But no one ever did.

Instead, they suffered intense persecution and went to early deaths based on the sure knowledge that *because Jesus had risen, so would they.*

Plausible deniability.

Yes, it is absolutely incredible that the opponents of those first proclaiming the resurrection didn't simply say Jesus was buried somewhere else, or like some modern scholars have suggested, that he wasn't buried at all. That his corpse just rotted away. (There will be more on this kind of speculation below.)

The fact that they admit the tomb is empty and come up with a far more elaborate theory to explain it is astonishing. Couple this with the evidence surrounding Joseph of Arimathea, the disciples' doubt, and the women as first witnesses, and the bare fact of the empty tomb is nearly impossible to deny.[30]

## 6. Fashion Matters: Jesus' Burial Clothes

But what if someone else stole or moved the body? Finding the tomb empty, could the disciples have *mistakenly* believed this meant Jesus was risen? (This may be the strongest challenge to the empty tomb, and for that reason I will also consider the possibility the body was inadvertently moved in several other places and in much greater depth, especially when considering the appearances.)

While the evidence already presented makes this highly unlikely and the evidence for the appearances will virtually rule it out, there is one detail in the discovery of the empty tomb, judged by many scholars to be authentic, that corroborates the larger body of evidence.

In the primitive story of the male disciples going to the tomb to check out the women's report (Luke 24:12, 24), the mention of Jesus' clothes is an incidental detail. Nothing is made of it. It doesn't lead to belief or provide any kind of proof. So, as with the newness of the tomb (see Chapter 1:2 above), it is likely a *genuine memory* that had no significance in the story other than that this is what they saw and they didn't know what to make of it.

It's only later in John, the last gospel written, that it is infused with meaning. The beloved disciple believes because he knows that if the body were stolen or misplaced, the clothes would have gone with it. Grave robbers wouldn't bother to remove them before taking the body. This would be the main thing of value in the tomb. They didn't care about the body, just the valuables placed with it. Usually, the clothes or other articles of value were stolen and *the body was left behind.*

Similarly, someone moving the body to another tomb wouldn't bother to remove the burial clothes. If, for whatever reason, they chose to move the body, they would have moved it burial clothes and all. In keeping with Jewish purity rites, no one would dare risk direct contact with the decaying flesh of a dead corpse.

Since the presence of the burial clothes seems to be an authentic detail in the earliest form of the story, and since there would be no reason to steal the body by itself because it held no value, the possibility that someone else stole or misplaced the body can practically be ruled out.[31]

## 7. Extreme Dating: The First Day of the Week vs. The Third Day

In the Judaism of Jesus' time, "the third day" was a symbolically loaded image. When referring to the general resurrection in the age to come, the prophet Hosea exclaims: "On *the third day* he will raise us up." (6:2) Later in the Talmud, there is evidence of a swirling popular expectation that the general resurrection of the dead would occur on *the third day* after the world ends.[32]

"The third day" was probably the most popular metaphor for the bodily resurrection.

In the New Testament, there are two ways the discovery of the empty tomb, and therefore the day of Jesus' resurrection, are dated. One is "on the third day" and the other is "the first day of the week." Because of its rich symbolism, "the third day" would quickly become the preferred dating.

Even though Paul writes First Corinthians in the mid-50's—about twenty years after Jesus' death—the vast majority of scholars, the most skeptical included, admit that the tradition he passes on in I Corinthians 15:3-7 is early, probably formulated within five years of Jesus' death, some even putting it within two years of the crucifixion. Because this creedal formula uses "on the third day" to date the resurrection, it clearly attests that this had become the preferred dating quite early, within five years of the event at the latest.

Why, then, do the gospels, written much later, refer to "the first day of the week"? As Brown explains: "...the basic time indication of the finding of the tomb was fixed in Christian memory before the possible symbolism in the three-day reckoning had yet been perceived."[33]

In other words, the "first day of the week" designation was widely in use before it occurred to anyone to use the more powerful metaphor of "the third day" language. Once this occurred, the original designation would naturally drop out of use in favor of the more evocative one. So, the empty tomb story must have originated prior to this usage: a later legend obviously would have used the much more meaningful "on the third day" language. As scholar and resurrection expert William Lane Craig points out, it must go back to at least within five years of Jesus' death, and likely much closer.[34]

And, because it has no symbolic value and is quickly replaced by a more prominent metaphor, this primitive detail is best explained as the neutral time indicator that marked the actual date the empty tomb was discovered: early on the first day of the week—which also happened to be the third day—following Jesus' crucifixion. Incidentally, such a short time frame would leave little room for confusion about the tomb, especially since the intervening day was the Sabbath where activity and movement were severely restricted.

All this indicates that the original story of the empty tomb must have been circulating at a time when those familiar with the events could challenge and/or verify the claims being made—for example, object that Jesus was never buried, speak to the women witnesses, go see the tomb for themselves, produce his dead body, and so on. If the basic details of the story could be upended—if Joseph of Arimathea denied he ever buried Jesus; if someone could show that Jesus' body was stolen or moved to a different grave; if someone produced evidence that his body was placed in a common burial place instead or simply left at Golgotha to decompose—then faith in the resurrection would come undone, something many at the time had a powerful motive to see happen. Because the story was circulating so close to the event, there was *ample opportunity to discredit it,* if possible.

In fact, the time frame can probably be narrowed down even more.

Most scholars agree that Pentecost, fifty days after Passover, that is, fifty days after Jesus' crucifixion, marked a significant moment in the early church. While many question elements of the story Luke tells in Acts 2, they admit that it was likely the first large-scale, public proclamation of the early "kerygma"—the primitive outline of the saving events of Jesus' death and resurrection. This public proclamation of the kerygma happens in Jerusalem, the very place where Jesus was crucified and allegedly buried. And, it happens within fifty days of these supposed events. This suggests that the last possible date the church went public with the resurrection, *the last possible date before the facts surrounding the empty tomb would begin to be scrutinized*, was fifty days after the discovery of the empty tomb.

While the story probably went "public" soon after the discovery of the empty tomb—three days after Jesus' death or thereabouts—that first Pentecost is still plenty of time for those in Jerusalem to discredit the story of the empty tomb if they had a reason or way to do so; in other words, if they could credibly claim Jesus was never buried and/ or produce his decaying corpse.[35]

## 8. Location, Location, Location: The Persistent Memory of the Site

Jerome Murphy-O'Connor is well known as a biblical scholar with special expertise in the archaeology of Jerusalem. He is usually quite skeptical about the many sites in the city venerated by Christians throughout the centuries. In his judgment, most of them are legendary and speculative. But he believes there is every reason to think the site of Jesus' tomb is authentic.

"'The most important argument for the authenticity of the site is the consistent and uncontested tradition of the Jerusalem community, which held liturgical celebrations at the site until ad 66.' That's *until* ad 66, as early a date as you can imagine for a site in the Holy Land."

He also believes that there had to be directions to the tomb for the many pilgrims flocking to Jerusalem to venerate it. The inhabitants of the city would *have grown tired of having to direct them to the tomb*. In addition, pilgrims must have left graffiti on the tomb, just as they did with the catacombs, to mark their visit to this most holy of sites. "As with the tomb of Peter in Rome, graffiti most likely identified the tomb of Jesus."[36] This graffiti would then help other pilgrims identify the spot.[37]

The spot in question is found under the Church of the Holy Sepulchre. In 40 A.D., long before the church was built, Hadrian's Temple was erected over the site. This was probably a deliberate move by the emperor to show the superiority of the Roman gods to the Christian God. As Murphy-O'Connor suggests, early Christians had to tell visitors on pilgrimage to Jerusalem, "It's under here." Eventually, there would be written directions around the pagan temple to identify it.

In the fourth century, the emperor Constantine demolished Hadrian's Temple. The church historian Eusebius reports: "As layer after layer of the subsoil came into view, the venerable and most holy memorial of the Saviour's resurrection, beyond all our hopes, came into view."[38]

Many scholars suspect that Constantine destroyed Hadrian's Temple in order to build the Church of the Holy Sepulchre, not because he found any vestige of evidence for Jesus' tomb, but simply to make a political statement. He was replacing the Roman pagan religion represented by the temple with the new religion of Christianity.

However, the archeological evidence suggests otherwise. Eusebius says that when it was unearthed, Constantine saw clear evidence that the tomb was that of Jesus. What did he see that would allow Constantine to identify the tomb?[39]

> Perhaps the strongest argument in favor of the authenticity of the site, however, is that it must have been regarded as such an unlikely site when pointed out to Constantine's mother Queen Helena in the fourth century. Then, as now, the site of what was to be the Church of the Holy Sepulchre was in a crowded urban location that must have seemed as strange to a fourth-century pilgrim as it does to a modern one.

But we now know that its location perfectly fits first-century conditions.

By the fourth century this site had long been enclosed within the city walls. The wall enclosing this part of the city (referred to by Josephus as the Third Wall) had been built by Herod Agrippa, the local ruler who governed Judea between 41 and 44 A.D. Thus, this wall was built very soon after Jesus' crucifixion—not more that 10 to 15 years afterward. And that is the crucial point.

When Jesus was buried in about 30 AD, this area was outside the city, in a garden. Corbo tells us, certainly in a cemetery of that time. These are the facts revealed by modern archaeology. *Yet who could have known this in 325 AD if the memory of Jesus' burial had not been accurately preserved?"*(my italics)[40]

By the fourth century, the common assumption would be that the tomb was outside the walls built in the early 40's. No one would believe the tomb was within them unless there was clear evidence to the contrary. What that evidence was we can only speculate. But the consistent memory of the site along with the likelihood that it was marked with graffiti left by pilgrims is a good guess.

Either way, the memory of the tomb seems to have been accurately preserved for the four centuries after Jesus' death, which is remarkable since this would require that it was well known in the *first decade* after his death, prior to the construction of the new wall and Hadrian's Temple in the early 40's.

## 9. Deja Vu All Over Again: Lack of Second Burial

Corpses decompose and decay. (You can thank me later for stating the obvious.) It was Jewish custom after a year's time to gather the remaining bones, place them in an ossuary, and perform a second burial. An ossuary is a stone box used for this "second burial" of the collected bones after the flesh had decomposed.

In the case of Jesus, as Wright explains, there is absolutely no hint of this. And the fact that there isn't is significant. Naturally, if Jesus' body was still in Joseph of Arimathea's tomb, he would want to use it again—recall that, because Jesus was considered a criminal and thus ritually impure, no one else could be buried there until his body was removed. At the same time, members of Jesus' family would have had a sacred obligation to give him this required final burial.

So just as the church was getting off the ground, frenetically proclaiming Jesus' victory over the grave, boldly announcing to the world that he is Lord, prominent figures in Jerusalem—Joseph as a member of the Sanhedrin and Jesus' brother James who became the leader of the Jerusalem church—would have been transferring his bones to an ossuary, placing him in his final resting place.[41]

An obviously impossible situation.

Of course, every so often some scholar will claim to have made a "new discovery" by finding the ossuary of Jesus, thereby proving the resurrection never happened. For the better part of a century, scholars have been aware of ossuaries bearing the name of Jesus. As Joseph Fitzmyer, a biblical scholar who is known by other scholars for his expertise in Aramaic (the common language spoken by Jews in Jesus' day), points out: "In the 1930's a first-century ossuary turned up in Jerusalem bearing the name of the deceased, *Yeshua bar Yehoseph*, "Jesus son of Joseph."...The Jewish Scholar who discovered the ossuary and published the inscription, E.L. Sukenik...drew no conclusions from it about any New Testament personage, realizing that "Jesus" and "Joseph" were commonly used names for Palestinian Jews of the first century. Such a discovery scarcely invalidated the story of the empty tomb."[42]

If someone today came across a gravestone bearing the name John, the natural question would be which John? It is such a common and popular name that no one would assume it was John Kennedy or John Adams or some other specific John. The names Jesus, Joseph, James, and Judas were so popular in that period that the discovery of a tomb bearing these names, even in combination, means nothing in terms of identifying who they were. In light of all the other solid evidence for the empty tomb, this is a desperate attempt to refute it.[43]

And the lack of any hint of second burial is fully (and provocatively!) consistent with the claim of an empty tomb.

## 10. The Common Grave Isn't All That Common

A few modern scholars have seized on the idea of a common grave to explain how a mythology about the empty tomb could have arisen. They argue that ordinarily criminals, like those who were crucified, were placed in a common grave. As Jesus' corpse decomposed, therefore, it would be impossible to identify him among all the other skeletal remains. Hence, no one could produce the body to refute the empty tomb story.

It is true that this, as far as we know, was *ordinarily* the case. But much of the solid historical data we already looked at—Joseph of Arimathea, the women as first witnesses, and so forth—shows that Jesus' burial was one of the rare exceptions to this rule.

However, even in the case of a common grave provided by the court for criminals and other violators of the Law not afforded burial in a separate tomb, remains were distinguishable. The Mishna, which records the custom of that period, provides clear evidence of this fact: "Once the flesh of the deceased criminal had decomposed, the bones could be gathered and buried in the ancestral burial place (Mishna *Sanhedrin* 6.6)."

And the Maccabean martyrs provide a case in point. Despite being put to death as criminals and therefore placed in a common grave, the tradition said that they received an honorable burial: in other words, second burial in a family grave. Thus, their bodies must have been identifiable. Even if the story of their burial is just a tradition, it could only be told if this was known to be a common practice at that time.[44]

So, both the Mishna and the tradition about the Maccabean martyrs show that remains in a common grave *could* be identified for second burial. Which is an insurmountable problem for those who want to argue Jesus' body couldn't be identified because it was buried in a common grave. Perhaps that's why the majority of scholars have not followed this line of thought.

## Conclusion: A House Without Foundation—No Resurrection without an Empty Tomb

Jews in Jesus' day were familiar with several notions of life beyond the grave.

They were familiar with the largely non-Jewish idea of a disembodied immortality—that the soul was liberated at death from the body, which remained in the grave.

They accepted the reality of Sheol—the mirky underworld where the dead went even while their body lay rotting in the tomb.

But when they spoke of resurrection (an event reserved for "the age to come"), they had one thing clearly in mind—the body was raised along with the soul. No corpse remained. That's what resurrection meant. So, to believe and then claim that someone had been resurrected *required* that their body had come back to life. No matter what was said about someone's soul or spirit being alive, if their body was still dead, rotting away somewhere, they most definitively weren't *resurrected*. It's as simple as that.

Therefore, it would be absolutely impossible for the early church to believe and then proclaim, as they did, that Jesus was resurrected if his body remained in a tomb somewhere, or if it was decomposing in a common grave. If anyone could produce his body, if anyone could point out the common grave it was rotting in, the whole thing would fall apart.

N.T. Wright, who has done the most exhaustive study of Jewish and non-Jewish beliefs about life after death in the biblical period, makes this abundantly clear. Based on his massive survey, Wright's conclusion is that, to both Jews and non-Jews of Jesus' day, the term "resurrection" always meant *embodiment*. It always involved some kind of new bodily life. This could be a good thing, as it was for Jews who looked forward to the general resurrection to come. Or it could be a bad thing, as it was for the pagans who longed for a disembodied immortality. But it never simply referred to a life or exaltation beyond the grave that didn't include the body.

This may be difficult for us to imagine since we routinely think in terms of our souls being liberated from our bodies at death. But without an empty tomb, no one could call what happened to Jesus a resurrection. They may have formulated other beliefs about him being alive again, other forms of life beyond the grave. But the specific belief in resurrection was only possible if his body had come back to life. And that, specifically, is what the earliest Christians were insisting happened with Jesus.

In fact, Wright points out, this is why some prominent non-Christian historians have concluded the tomb must have been empty.[45] As one of these leading non-Christian scholars, Geza Vermes, admits:

> When every argument has been considered and weighed, the only conclusion acceptable to the historian must be that the opinions of the orthodox, the liberal sympathizer and the critical agnostic alike—and even perhaps of the disciples themselves— are simply interpretations of the one disconcerting fact: namely that the women who set out to pay their last respects to Jesus found to their consternation, not a body, but an empty tomb.[46]

Scholars didn't always see it this way. There used to be lively debates about what the concept of resurrection meant. A number of scholars argued that the early Christians could have believed Jesus was resurrected even if his body was still in the tomb or rotting away somewhere. But, largely because of Wright's work, this is changing. And throughout Part I of this book, we'll see that this yields profound new insights into any study of the resurrection.

In fact, given what resurrection meant in that world, there is no way to explain the phenomena of the early church—how it could ever get started; how it could ever have come to believe Jesus was "resurrected"; how it could ever make such a claim publicly—without the empty tomb. This is the *only way* the kind of early Christian belief we know surfaced *could have ever surfaced*: if the tomb was well known and known to be empty, and no one (and there were plenty who had strong motive to) could produce Jesus' body or point to his rotting corpse.

Whatever else people want to say about what happened, at the very least there had to be an empty tomb.

# In the Eye of the Beholder

*The Appearances*

A FTER DISCOVERING THE EMPTY tomb, Jesus' disciples claim he appeared to them, risen from the dead.

But the appearance stories contain *even more* discrepancies than the empty tomb narratives. How can we trust them?

And even if we can, how do we know the disciples actually saw *Jesus* risen from the dead and weren't just having some kind of *delusionary* experience?

Confronted with an empty tomb—maybe, unbeknownst to them, the body was inadvertently moved by someone else—how do we know that these grieving disciples didn't just *imagine* seeing what they *so desperately wanted to see*?

How do we know the whole thing isn't just a *hallucination* of some kind?

# 1. Three's a Crowd: Discrepancies in the Appearance Narratives

Nowhere else do the four gospels vary so widely as they do with the stories of Jesus' appearances:

--In Matthew, Jesus appears first to the two women as they leave the tomb, then in Galilee to the eleven disciples gathered on a mountain. There they worship him, but some doubt. Finally, Jesus commissions them to make disciples of all nations and baptize in the name of the Father, Son, and Holy Spirit.

--In Mark, there is no appearance narrative in the original text, just the story of the empty tomb. Because it ends so abruptly, three *different* endings are eventually added in order to complete the story. But most scholars agree that, even though these appended endings may contain some early and reliable traditions, they were composed at a later point. However, the end of the original text *hints* at an appearance of the risen Jesus: the angel at the tomb instructs the women to tell Peter and the other disciples to go to Galilee where they will all see him.

(A good number of scholars believe that the reason Mark doesn't have a resurrection appearance is because his audience would already have been very familiar with this part of the story. Many of them would have become Christians precisely because they heard those original eyewitnesses, or their followers, narrate the appearances of Jesus these eyewitnesses personally experienced. As newer converts, what they needed, and what Mark provides, was to fill out the rest of the story, namely Jesus' public ministry and crucifixion.)

--In Luke, Jesus appears first to two unnamed disciples on the road to Emmaus, an encounter none of the other gospels record. When they return to Jerusalem to tell the eleven remaining disciples (minus Judas, obviously) and those gathered with them what they saw, Jesus appears in the midst of all of them. He shows them his hands and feet (the wounds of crucifixion) and then eats a piece of fish before explaining that the Messiah had to suffer in order to come into his glory. Then he commissions them to go and preach repentance and forgiveness of sins to all nations beginning in Jerusalem. Finally, he ascends to heaven.

--In John, he appears to Mary Magdalene while she is weeping by the tomb, then to the disciples, minus Thomas, gathered in the upper room in Jerusalem. He breathes the Holy Spirit upon them and commissions them to announce the forgiveness of sins. A week later he appears to "doubting" Thomas, inviting him to touch his wounds and see that he is truly risen. Finally, he appears in Galilee to seven disciples as they come ashore from an overnight fishing expedition. There he cooks a meal of fish and bread and eats it with them before having a conversation with Peter and leaving some additional instructions.

These are *vast* discrepancies. They give the impression that these stories are complete fabrications.

But upon deeper examination, these discrepancies actually provide good evidence for the trustworthiness of the accounts, and in three critical ways.

First, the most natural thing for the disciples to do when they first started proclaiming the resurrection was to relate the specific appearance or appearances each *personally experienced*. When you tell someone about your favorite restaurant, you probably don't pull out all the reviews it's been getting or tell them why your friends like it. Instead, you talk about all the great meals *you've* had there. When you see your favorite rock band in concert, you don't tell people how much the person next to you enjoyed it. You talk about how awesome it was *for you*. How amazing it was for you to see them "rock out" live. It's just human nature to focus on our own personal experience of events, especially the more powerful it is.

In the same way, the disciples didn't report every appearance of Jesus in sequence, but only the one or ones they had firsthand knowledge of—exactly what we'd expect them to do with such a life-transforming experience. In fact, firsthand, personal experience is the most effective way to attest to something. It's what other people find most compelling. As any good marketer knows, especially in this age of social media, the most effective way to market a product is through personal testimony. I've heard it called "product evangelization." It's why those corny infomercials feature so many personal testimonials. It's also why a person is far more likely to check out a restaurant, for example, if one of their friends, whether by post, tweet, or good old face-to-face conversation, shares a positive personal experience of it with them. It's just human nature to find firsthand, personal experience most compelling.

Naturally then, the disciples would have focused on what *they themselves* saw and experienced as the most effective way to convince others that Jesus was truly risen. Their personal witness to the events would be far more vivid and compelling.

All of this accounts for the wide variety of appearance stories: the witnesses to the resurrection were quite naturally focused on sharing *their* specific encounter with the risen Jesus, not systematically rehearsing the narrative of *all* the appearances he made. So, unlike other sections of the gospels, the appearances of Jesus were never told or recorded in order, as a complete narrative.

As Raymond Brown explains:

> The details of the passion would be meaningless unless from the start they were fitted into a sequence leading from arrest to crucifixion. One could scarcely tell of the arrest of Jesus without telling of the outcome; the sentencing had to precede the execution, etc. But the resurrection appearances were first reported to root Christian faith in the risen Jesus and to justify the apostolic preaching. To do this it would be enough to report one or two appearances of Jesus and not necessary to supply a chain of these appearances.[47]

When the gospel writers, in turn, put these stories into their appearance narratives, they were using the ones they were familiar with, the ones associated with the disciple or disciples they knew. The discrepancies, therefore, actually point to them being the product of authentic, eyewitness testimony, *representing the varied first-hand encounters different disciples had.*

At the same time, these discrepancies also reveal how many unique encounters with the risen Jesus there must have been. There wasn't just one powerful, formative experience, but *many different ones.* The wide variety among them shows that, whatever it was the disciples actually saw, there were numerous "appearances."

In fact, the early tradition Paul passes along in I Corinthians 15:3-7 provides evidence of other appearances no gospel writer includes: an appearance to James, the brother of the Lord, and another to five hundred at once—further proof of the large number and variety of appearances.

Second, the discrepancies in the narratives are exactly what we would expect from such a *transhistorical* event. *If* Jesus really rose, then the disciples encountered someone who had transcended the finite realm. How do you capture the reality of someone who has broken through to eternity, who now possesses infinite qualities, in finite words? All attempts to describe it are necessarily going to be feeble. So it's no wonder the disciples would struggle to articulate what they experienced, and do so, at times, in such divergent ways. In fact, it would be far more problematic if we didn't find discrepancies. Then we would rightly suspect they *weren't* describing something that transcended ordinary experience.

A good example of this is the failure of some of the disciples to recognize Jesus at first: Mary thinks he's the gardener; the two on the road to Emmaus assume he's a stranger; the disciples coming in from a long night of fishing have trouble identifying the stranger cooking them breakfast as Jesus. (I'll explain later why this lack of recognition had to be historical and wasn't fabricated.) In each case, they eventually come to recognize it is Jesus, but he is somehow *radically different, and in a way they can't quite put into words.* Because he is now endowed with transcendent qualities, they struggle mightily to comprehend him. We'll see an even better example of this below (Chapter 2.5) in the maddening paradox of their attempts to describe him. So, as the many different witnesses *groped* for ways to express the mind-blowing, transhistorical reality they were reeling from, we would naturally expect discrepancies to emerge.

Third, even though they are describing the most spectacular event in history, the appearance narratives are *remarkably restrained*. They don't sensationalize it at all. While commenting on the resurrection narrative of John 20, Ben Witherington observes: "Notably, the portrayal of the Easter events involves real restraint on the part of the Evangelist….[I]n a culture hungry for miracles, he avoids describing the greatest miracle of all—the resurrection of Jesus. [This] attest[s] to the integrity of this narrative."[48]

Just one look at the second century Gnostic Gospel of Peter, which doesn't resist describing the *actual* resurrection and in *fantastic detail*, and you get a sense of just how restrained the gospel writers are: two figures descend from heaven; the huge stone, which took numerous men to roll in place, now *automatically* rolls away so they can enter; three figures emerge with the first two assisting the third to stand up; the heads of these first two reach to the sky but the third *extends above the heavens*; a cross that is *floating in the air* follows them; a heavenly voice asks if he preached to "those who are sleeping" and *the cross* responds "yes." (Gospel of Peter 34-42) This is a far cry from the four gospels! But it represents the tendency all around them. And it illustrates how credible the gospels are: without any significant embellishment or elaboration, without any attempt to give it more "pizzazz," the appearance narratives *simply report* the basic encounters with the risen Jesus, *inconsistencies and all*.[49]

After thoroughly analyzing them, N.T. Wright concludes that these traditions faithfully represent the "different ways in which the original astonished participants told the stories."[50]

## 2. Have You Seen Elvis Lately? The Transformation of the Disciples—Part I: The Secret of Life

Do you remember the day Elvis died? I do. For his many fans, it was a sad and tragic day. Over the years since, a fair number of people have claimed that Elvis is alive. That they've "seen" him, back from the dead.

But how many of them do you think would stake their lives on this claim?

How many of them would suffer and die for this belief?

As much as these Elvis fans might wish, conjecture, or even insist he's alive, they wouldn't stake their life on such a claim unless it was *verifiably* true. No one would. No one dies for a conjecture or wishful thought.

According to Roman historical accounts, the emperor Nero used to light the path in his garden at night by using Christians as human torches. He would smear them with pitch and then use their flesh as fuel for the fire.[51] This is the kind of treatment those early Christians received for their belief in the resurrection. They were willing to stake everything, including their lives, on the belief that Jesus was alive.[52]

What Elvis fan would do that?

One of the great mysteries of history is how these selfish, skeptical, cowardly dimwits who abandon Jesus at his crucifixion are transformed almost instantaneously after his death into fearless, wise, grace-filled witnesses who are willing, even joyfully, to die for their crucified master. Christians were the most detested and marginalized group in that society. They were subjected daily to extreme hardship for their loyalty to someone who was long gone and, even worse, thought to be a disgraced messianic pretender.

And yet, *they were envied by those around them for the love they showed and the joy they possessed.* No circumstance could take this joy away, even death. In fact, they looked forward to death. It was, for them, *supreme gain*: life on high with Christ.

Again, these are the same disciples who fled in terror when Jesus was taken to his death.

How do you explain such an immediate and total transformation?

*Where else in the annals of history has any group been so instantaneously and completely transformed, especially in the wake of the tragic death and unconditional defeat of their charismatic leader?*

Huston Smith was the preeminent scholar of world religions during the last half of the twentieth century. For a scholar to dominate his field this long is a remarkable feat and a clear indication of how well respected he is. Listen to what Smith says:

> The people who first heard Jesus' disciples proclaiming the Good News were as impressed by what they saw as by what they heard. They saw lives that had been transformed—men and women who were ordinary in every way except for the fact that they seemed to have found the secret of living. They evinced a tranquility, simplicity, and cheerfulness that their hearers had nowhere else encountered. Here were people who seemed to be making a success of the enterprise everyone would like to succeed at—that of life itself...Outsiders found this baffling. These scattered Christians were not numerous. They were not wealthy or powerful. If anything, they faced more adversity than the average man or woman. Yet, in the midst of their trials, they had laid hold of an inner peace that found expression in a joy that seemed exuberant. Perhaps radiant would be a better word. Radiance is hardly the word used to characterize the average religious life, but none other fits as well the life of these early Christians. Paul is an example. Here was a man who had been ridiculed, driven from town to town, shipwrecked, imprisoned, flogged until his back was covered with stripes. Yet here was a life with which joy was the constant refrain: "Joy unspeakable and full of glory." "Thanks be to God who giveth us the victory." "In all things we are more than conquerors." "God who commanded the light to shine out of darkness has shined in our hearts." "Thanks be to God for his unspeakable gift." The joy of these early Christians *was* unspeakable. As the

fifth chapter of Ephesians suggests, they sang not out of convention but from the irrepressible overflow of their direct experience. Life for them was no longer a matter of coping. It was glory discerned.[53]

But it wasn't just profound peace and unspeakable joy that they acquired. In the wake of his death, the disciples also acquired an *instant comprehension* about Jesus and his mission. They were equipped with a wisdom and eloquence that defied their meager education, temperament, and abilities prior to his death. It's as if something suddenly clicked and they finally "got it." They finally understood what Jesus was all about in a way they had utterly failed to see (much to his continual consternation!) while he was alive.

These are the same blundering simpletons who kept asking Jesus for places of honor in the kingdom and to call down fire from heaven on their enemies. *Now they were gladly willing to sacrifice everything to serve others and lay down their lives for him.* They even prayed for him to *forgive those who were putting them to death.* And their preaching ignited a fire that would eventually win over the Roman empire.

Generally speaking, we know that crisis doesn't transform a person's character. It reveals it. When something like 9-11 happens, people don't somehow instantly become different people, better people. They simply show more fully who they really are.

As a group, the disciples were embarrassingly incomprehending, fearful, and self-seeking. (Once again, such a negative portrait is not something they would have invented—it had to be the reality.) The crisis of Jesus' death, however, doesn't intensify these qualities.

Instead, in each and every case, *it radically reverses them.*[54]

Take, for example, the impulsive "rockhead," Peter. Prior to Jesus' death he suffers from a chronic case of "foot-in-mouth" disease. He constantly says the wrong thing. He even tries to talk Jesus out of the cross, to which Jesus is forced to respond, "Get behind me *Satan!*"(Mark 8:33) (You know you're having a bad day when Jesus calls you the devil!) And, of course, despite bragging about how he would lay down his life to defend Jesus, during the climactic moments of the Passion, Peter famously denies Jesus three times.

And yet, shortly after the crucifixion, under the threat of death, he is publicly preaching to and converting hundreds with newfound wisdom and eloquence. (In the Acts of the Apostles, Luke may be exaggerating the number of converts, but few scholars deny that Peter was a leading force in the dynamic growth of the early church.) When persecuted for boldly proclaiming the gospel, Peter counts it joy to be able to suffer for his Lord. And when it is his turn to be put to death, he asks to be crucified upside down because he says he is *not worthy to die the same death as his Master.*

Peter's request to be crucified upside down has long been thought to be the stuff of legend, a fictitious embellishment designed to make him seem far more courageous than he was. But Richard Martin, a Jesuit priest and popular writer, points to some remarkable archeological verification of Peter's martyrdom:

> Religious legends sometimes have a strange way of turning out to be true. The best-known example may be the discovery of what is now almost universally accepted as the tomb of St. Peter. It was reputed to lie directly underneath the great dome of St. Peter's Basilica in Rome, though many scholars had judged this location doubtful and most likely inauthentic.
>
> It was believed that the Galilean fisherman ended his earthly life in the great city in AD 64 after being martyred by the Roman authorities. St. Peter is said to have asked to be crucified upside down, considering himself unworthy of ending his life as Jesus had. The basilica in his honor was also known to have been built atop a site—the Vatican Hill—occupied by a church since the time of Constantine in the fourth century. But whether the actual remains of Peter lay there was an open question.

43

In the 1930's and 1940's, however, a series of archeological finds under St. Peter's Basilica led to the discovery of the tomb of a man in his late sixties, near graffiti that included the word *Petrus.* Over time, the Vatican examined sufficient evidence to conclude that the bones of St. Peter had been located. The collection of the man's bones was largely intact, except for the feet, which were missing—not surprising given that the easiest way to remove a body crucified upside down would have been to chop off the feet first.[55]

The transformation of these disciples, especially their willingness to suffer persecution and die, can only be explained if they truly believed, beyond doubt, they had seen Jesus risen from the dead.

## 3. Check It Out! The Resurrection is a Public, Verifiable Event

But many people have died for their beliefs.

How is belief in the resurrection any different?

Here's resurrection scholar Gary Habermas's response: "Many of the apostles were willing to die specifically for this message, which differentiates their transformation from those, then or today, who are willing to die for an *ideology* that often is not linked to events, and for which the convert is not in a position to check out the nature of the claim."[56]

This is a critical point. The resurrection claims to be a fact of history, an external, objective event that could be examined in a public, verifiable way.

Those who die for a belief are trusting in the *interior, subjective experiences* of a leader or founder who claims to have received some revelation or attained some insight which generates that ideology. In many cases, the personal charisma of a leader is enough to persuade people to die for them and all that they stand for or claim to have experienced. But there is *no way to verify this kind of internal experience.*

Islam is a good case in point. As philosopher J.P. Moreland explains:

> Muslims might be willing to die for their belief that Allah revealed himself to Muhammad, but this revelation was not done in any publicly observable way. So they could be wrong about it. They may sincerely think it's true, but they can't know for a fact, because they did not witness it themselves.

> However, the apostles were willing to die for something they had seen with their own eyes and touched with their own hands. They were in a unique position not to just believe Jesus rose from the dead but to know for sure...

> While most people can only have faith that their beliefs are true, the disciples were in a position to know without a doubt whether or not Jesus had risen from the dead. They claimed that they saw him, talked with him, and ate with him. If they weren't absolutely certain, they wouldn't have allowed themselves to be tortured to death for proclaiming that the Resurrection happened.[57]

It wasn't Jesus' powerful experiences of the Divine, profound insights, or personal charisma that convinced the disciples to die for him. (Remember, the disciples abandoned Jesus at his death—when he was crucified, they *no longer* believed in him, a fact that is far too embarrassing to be made-up and that is unique in the annals of religion where belief in a founder is present and often peaking when they die.) It was the very public events surrounding his resurrection.[58] Events they were in a position to know happened, to verify.

But what about those who didn't witness these events for themselves?

According to the earliest written source for the resurrection, I Corinthians 15:3-7, the appearances of Jesus were historical events that a person living at that time could verify for him or herself by asking those who saw them. This tradition even says that there were some 500 such witnesses to an appearance of Jesus.

As William Lane Craig points out, Paul then adds something truly remarkable to this tradition. He says that most of these 500 witnesses are still alive, even though he notes that some have died. Clearly, Paul was familiar with many of these witnesses—they weren't just a number on a list. It's likely he had heard many of them talk about their encounter with the risen Jesus. But what's so remarkable is the reason he's mentioning they're alive at all: to make it clear that *they are still around to be questioned*. In effect, Paul is saying that they are available for anyone who wants to check out their testimony for themselves, who wants to know what they *actually* saw and experienced, who wants to *verify* what happened.[59]

Pastor Timothy Keller adds:

> Paul's letter was to a church, and therefore it was a public document, written to be read aloud. Paul was inviting anyone who doubted that Jesus had appeared to people after his death to go and talk to the eyewitnesses if they wished. It was a bold challenge and one that could easily be taken up, since during the *pax Romana* travel around the Mediterranean was safe and easy. Paul could not have made such a challenge if those eyewitnesses didn't exist.[60]

Paul's conversion took place within three years after Jesus' death, and he must have received the tradition he is handing on in I Corinthians 15:3-7 shortly thereafter, at the latest by A.D. 36 when he visits with Peter and James to learn about Jesus' public ministry from them. That means this tradition must have been circulating throughout the church prior to Paul's visit.[61]

So at most just a few years after Jesus' death (and most likely right from the start), the church was already boldly challenging all who doubted the resurrection to *verify it for themselves* by talking to the original eyewitnesses. And this challenge *was only possible because the appearances were objectively public events fresh in the memory of those who witnessed them.*

Christianity is based on a historical event. There's obviously more to it than this, but the foundational event upon which it stands or falls is the resurrection. If Jesus rose, then Christianity is true. If he didn't, then it's not. It's as simple as that.

You can explain every other major religion's origins, and virtually all other philosophies and worldviews, especially those that have a large number of adherents, as a product of human genius. They rest on the internal experiences, insights, and charisma of their founder or founders. You can't test whether what they claim has been revealed to them really has been or is just the result of human ingenuity. The leaders themselves might sincerely believe they've been divinely inspired, but how are we to know? Maybe they're just self-deluded.

To be sure, you can test how well their insights answer life's ultimate questions, and then make a judgment about whether you think it's divine revelation or not—indeed, many have attempted to show just how completely and compellingly Christianity itself does this, and how it is, therefore, *the* ultimate revelation of God. (I will flesh out this argument in Chapter 9 when discussing the philosophical questions surrounding the resurrection.) Still, there is no way to *objectively verify* that they aren't simply human in origin.

But Christianity is unique. It rises or falls on the very open, public and verifiable event of the resurrection, which is an event that either happened or it didn't. Unlike the inaccessible subjective experience of a charismatic founder, it is open to objective, historical verification.

And, if true, it has an *objectively supernatural character.* The divine origin of such a spectacular miracle—the greatest ever recorded, one that turns the cosmos on its head by reversing the most immutable law of nature, death itself—can't be denied. That can't be said for the rest. For example, Islam claims that the divine character and origin of the Quran is self-evident. If you read it, at least in Arabic, you will clearly see its supernatural origin. However, many have read it, even in Arabic, and yet, sincerely don't see its divine character.[62] The content of the book doesn't clearly prove it's supernatural. It depends on your individual perspective. It's a personal judgment call. You might accept the Quran as the definitive revelation of God or just as easily dismiss it as the musings of Muhammad. The resurrection doesn't give you this option.

If it happened, it is unequivocally supernatural.[63]

With all due respect to Shirley MacLaine, reincarnation provides a good contrast. How can you demonstrate claims to have lived previous lives are true? Even when people claim to know something of those lives they cannot ordinarily know—like the case I once heard of a woman who claimed to have been a civil war nurse in a previous life, and who could describe her experience in exquisite detail, which historians later confirmed to be accurate—there are ordinary ways to explain how they might have arrived at that knowledge. *The knowledge they claim to have from a previous life must also exist in a historical source, including oral or family traditions; otherwise, their claim to know something outside the normal course of things couldn't be verified.* But how can anyone be sure they didn't intentionally or unintentionally derive that information from such a source?[64]

For example, clairvoyance is a phenomenon where someone supposedly gains knowledge through extrasensory perception. But so far, scientific research into this type of phenomena has shown that such knowledge is the result of natural factors, such as sensory leakage or the failure to appreciate the rate of chance occurrences, among other things. People mistakenly believe they've attained information through extraordinary means when, in reality, it came to them in quite ordinary ways they just didn't realize. To date, despite numerous experiments, the scientific community has not been able to demonstrate that clairvoyance or any other paranormal acquisition of information is valid.[65] Reports from people who claim to be reincarnated are vulnerable to the same kind of confusion. It's impossible to tell whether it's all just in their minds or they actually lived a previous life. There is no way to verify it.

Unfortunately, so called "near death" or "life after life" experiences, where someone is clinically dead for a short time and then after being revived claims to have had an experience of heaven, provide another good example. They have become very popular and I wish they could be shown to be objectively true. They would provide dramatic and irrefutable confirmation of life after death.

But how can this personal, subjective experience ever be verified? It may simply be the euphoria caused by the adrenaline shooting through the body during the dying process. The bright light many report seeing might just be the large light in the emergency or operating room, where a bulk of these experiences happen. Even in the cases where someone claims to discover something they couldn't have otherwise known while "in heaven," there's no guarantee they didn't access this information in some other natural way.[66] Popular accounts, even ones that claim to have received extraordinary knowledge, such as in the book and movie based on the book *Heaven is for Real*, all rely on the personal testimony of the subject involved. For them it is powerfully real. But how do we verify it's objectively real, and not just all in their head?

Recently, Robert Spitzer, the former president of Gonzaga University who specializes in the philosophy of science—astrophysics in particular—has compiled some compelling evidence that at least some near-death experiences can be objectively verified. He points to three types of phenomena: what he calls "veridical reported data," where people are aware of objects or things happening around them during the death experience they could not ordinarily perceive; "visual perception of the blind" who are able to accurately describe realities they've never physically been able to see; and "personal information about deceased individuals" which could not otherwise be known.[67] (See Appendix I for more)

Let me be clear. I want Spitzer to be right. And I think he probably is. But this evidence doesn't have the same probative value as the resurrection. Near-death experiences remain in the domain of the subjective experience of those who have them. Though to date no one has successfully challenged the evidence Spitzer presents, it is still subject to the same kind of critique offered for other so-called paranormal experience. *Whatever knowledge a person claims to have been revealed has to exist in some other source in order to be verified. And there is no way to know for certain that this information hasn't gotten to them in some other ordinary way.*

But, unlike near-death experiences or reincarnation, the resurrection is open to public scrutiny and can potentially be established as a fact of history. It claims empirical, measurable effects, like, for example, an empty tomb, numerous eyewitness accounts to an external event that can be tested for veracity, a rapid worldview transformation the likes of which has never been seen before or since (see Chapter 3.3 below) and so forth.

And among the major religions of the world, this is absolutely unique. Abraham's call; Moses' encounter at the burning bush (no one else was there to verify the bush was actually burning); the great Hebrew prophetic oracles; Hindu philosophy; Confucius's ethics; Siddhartha's path to Nirvana; Muhammad receiving the visible Quran; Lao Tzu's discovery of the Tao; all are interior revelations or inspired insights, *the completely internal phenomena of a single individual who then testifies to the veracity of his or her solely subjective experience.*

The only possible exception to this is the Exodus, which is surely a public event and which is foundational for Judaism. But there are so many questions as to whether the biblical story is based on a real event or is pure legend. The quality and quantity of historical evidence is lacking. This is in striking contrast to the evidence for the resurrection.

And in any event, if it could be verified with the same degree of certainty, it wouldn't provide a rival claim undermining the historical reality of the resurrection. Instead, as part of the great Christian narrative that culminates in the resurrection, it would only serve to validate its authenticity.

Unlike all the other major world religions, Christianity rises and falls on one historical event. *An objective, publicly verifiable event.*

## 4. Back To The Future: The Unprecedented Depiction of Jesus' Resurrected Appearance

So far, it's clear that the disciples sincerely believed Jesus appeared to them from the dead. It was no hoax or deception. Hundreds were convinced they had actually seen the risen Lord. Many were willing to suffer and die for it.

But how do we know this wasn't just a figment of their imaginations; the product of a psychological defense mechanism for the profound grief they felt over the loss of Jesus; a case of mass hysteria, autosuggestion or group hallucination? Perhaps discovering an empty tomb, they were so overcome with grief, they so desperately wanted Jesus to be alive, that they "dreamed" or imagined they saw him.

So, how do we know the appearances weren't produced by some psychosocial phenomenon, a collective delusion of their minds? What evidence is there that the disciples saw something they could not have conceived on their own? That it truly was Jesus risen from the dead, and not something their psyches sincerely, but mistakenly, subconsciously manufactured?

At the beginning of the second *Back to the Future* movie, there is a scene where the main character's future son, Marty MacFly Junior, both played by Michael J. Fox, is talking on a phone. He's been sent via time machine thirty years into the future, to October 26, 2015. Since the movie was made in 1989, the writers had to imagine what thirty years in the future might look like. When it came to phone technology, they were *slightly* off. Marty isn't talking on a smartphone, or even a cell phone. No, he's in a *phone booth.*

How many phone booths have you seen lately?

You can't blame them. How could anyone in the mid-1980's ever imagine where technology would take us? Phone booths were everywhere back then and nothing indicated their subsequent demise. (Here's a short list of other things they got wrong: flying cars, Jaws 19, the abolishment of all lawyers, the Cubs winning the 2015 World Series—though, remarkably, they were only off by one year on this last one!)

In fact, what was all the rage back then was the phone card. That's right, the *phone card*. It was like a debit card for the pay phone. If you were stuck somewhere and didn't have enough money for the pay phone and couldn't make a collect call—remember what that was?—you could use your phone card to pay for the call. Of course, there was no chip to read the card's data or magnetic strip to swipe. You had to *call* the operator and tell them the code printed on the card. My, how times have changed.

The writers of the *Back to the Future* movies couldn't even begin to fathom the smartphone. Given all they knew about phones and phone technology, *the smartphone was utterly inconceivable.*

This is exactly the position the disciples were in. *The kind of resurrected body they claim to "see" is as farfetched and unimaginable as the smartphone was to the writers of the "Back to the Future" movies.*

People in Jesus' day had several clear ideas of what life after death might look like. If the stories of his appearances were the product of their imagination, the result of some kind of psychological trauma or autosuggestion, they would resemble the images they already had in mind.

But they don't. They are *radically* different.

*As radically different as the smartphone is from the phone booth.*[68]

This is crucial. If the disciples were mistaken about the empty tomb—someone did steal the body, it was misplaced, or it was left in a common burial ground—and then imagined they "saw" Jesus risen; if the appearances were just a figment of the disciples' imagination, they would conform to the widespread beliefs held at the time.

In fact, there were two well-known precedents that would have *undoubtedly shaped* the way they interpreted their experience.

According to the Old Testament, the prophet Elijah did not undergo a natural death but instead was taken up into heaven at the end of his life. According to subsequent tradition, he would return in similar fashion. In his "assumption" into heaven, the disciples had a ready-made model for conceiving Jesus' return from the dead: appearing pretty much as he was before, in a space- and time-bound body. A good example of this expectation, current at the time, is II Baruch 50:2: "For the earth shall then assuredly restore the dead… It shall make no change in their form; but as it has received them, so it shall restore them."[69]

The other well-known precedent was found in contemporary Jewish apocalyptic and mystical depictions of immortality. The righteous dead are often depicted as dazzlingly bright heavenly figures, and in some cases, are said to be shining like the stars.[70] This is similar to the way Jesus is portrayed in the story of the Transfiguration. (Mark 8:2-9; Matthew 17:1-8; Luke 9:28-36) As the revelation of his divine glory, he becomes dazzlingly radiant. Indeed, because this story is shaped by Old Testament allusions, many scholars would argue that it *was* largely shaped by the gospel writers', or their sources', imaginations. Jesus is also depicted as bright, shining, and radiant by the author of Revelation (1:12-16) in the prophetic vision of him given to John, and by Luke when he appears to Paul in Acts (9:3-5). And in Matthew (13:43), Jesus himself depicts the righteous dead shining like the sun in eternal life. Undoubtedly, this notion was alive and well.

These are the two major ways the disciples would naturally have conceived Jesus' appearance. But they don't.

They depict him in a radically different way:

--He is the same Jesus who walked the earth, but he appears in such a different form that *a number of his disciples fail to recognize him at first.* For example, Mary Magdalene thinks he's the gardener. The two on the road to Emmaus think he is a stranger. Peter's companions in the boat don't recognize the man calling them from the shore. (By the way, this failure to recognize Jesus has to be an authentic memory, not something the gospel writers invented, because it introduces an element of doubt that is damaging: if his own disciples were confused about his identity, maybe they were also mistaken about seeing him alive again. Maybe they were so overcome by grief they weren't thinking straight or mistook him for someone else. Either way, it undermines their claim.)

--He can be seen, heard and even touched, but his body is now so transformed that it exhibits qualities never before imagined for a resurrected person. *Though thoroughly physical and embodied, he transcends space and time, appearing and disappearing at will.*

--He bears all the wounds of his passion in his body, the marks of the nails in his wrists and feet, the wound in his side, but his body is now *immortal; utterly immune to pain and decay; no longer vulnerable to anything. Bearing the marks of corruption, it is incorruptible.*

--He can cook and consume food, yet *his "body" is thoroughly spiritual; no longer bound by the constraints of the physical world. He is so tangible, food is really consumed, but so immaterial, he can pass through walls and locked doors.*

In short, he has a "spiritual body." One that retains all the characteristics of two *mutually exclusive realms*: the physical, space-time-bound world, and the ethereal, transcendent, unlimited heavenly sphere.

I know this is an *oxymoron*—a finite physical body that has all the qualities of an infinite spirit—but *that's the point! The Jesus who appears in the gospels is so far from anything imagined up to that point, so paradoxical and full of contradiction, that it would be impossible for the disciples to conceive all of this on their own.*

N.T. Wright explains that the gospel descriptions are unlike anything that preceded them, or, for that matter, anything since. While they can't seem to find adequate language to describe him, they depict Jesus with many of the same properties a normal body has—it can be touched, it can consume food and drink, it can speak audible words, etc. However, it also defies the limits imposed on normal bodies—it can appear and disappear, pass through locked doors, ascend to the heavens before them, etc.

Nothing in Jewish literature or imagination had prepared for a portrait like this. If the gospel writers had made something up to fit a preconceived notion, the one thing they would certainly have done is describe the risen Jesus shining like a star. According to Daniel 12:3 (a very influential passage in Jewish thought at the time), this was how the righteous would appear at the resurrection. But Jesus didn't. His body seems to have been transformed in a way for which there was neither precedent nor prophesy, and of which there remains no second example.[71]

No psychological phenomena, no figment of the imagination, no delusion or hallucination of the disciples could conjure up such an unprecedented and totally bizarre notion.

Their minds simply couldn't have innovated so wildly.

For example, as Craig notes, and other leading skeptical scholars such as John Dominic Crossan acknowledge, nothing new or innovative is experienced during a hallucination. Hallucinations are projections of a person's mind and, therefore, can't go beyond the content of that person's mind. However, Jesus' resurrection "involved ideas utterly foreign to the disciples' minds." Ideas they couldn't possibly have come up with on their own through a hallucination.[72]

As human beings, we interpret our experiences through the lens of our own worldview. Despite groping for language, mystics (those who claim to have had profound visionary experiences of the divine) describe their experiences in remarkably similar ways. But each processes and articulates what they've experienced according to what they know. Muslims say they've encountered Allah; Christians, Jesus; Buddhists, Nirvana; and so on. Each interprets what they "see" through the lens of their prior knowledge, experience, and expectations.

I once counseled a woman who had a terminal condition. Even though she had been brought up in the Christian tradition, she always spoke about God in a very generic, even dismissive, way. But then one night she had a powerful and vivid vision of God. When she described her vision to me, she talked about seeing Jesus at the foot of her bed coming to comfort her. In this "divine encounter," whoever it was she actually saw she understood to be Jesus. I don't know whether Jesus was actually appearing to her or not, but I do know that she was interpreting her experience through the conceptual framework familiar to her.

The same holds true for the disciples. If the Jesus they "saw" was simply a product of their imagination, his appearance would have been interpreted through the lens of their prior experience—the only conceptual framework available to them at the time—*closely resembling what they expected to see.*

However, *the depiction of Jesus' resurrected body is such a radical departure from every other understanding of immortality they held, they couldn't have conceived it on their own.* This "transphysicality," as Wright calls it[73], is a complete and total innovation.

And nothing—*nothing!*—in the available notions of life beyond the grave at the time prepared for this.[74]

## 5. You Can't Make This Stuff Up: The Maddening Paradox of Jesus' Appearances

But that's not all. Not only is there no precedent for Jesus' "transphysicality," the paradox it involves is maddening.

Raymond Brown summarizes what many other scholars have noted: in the way it depicts Jesus, the New Testament evidence is lucidly clear that his risen existence is glorious and eschatological, transported completely beyond the limitations of finite existence. Even though he is tangible and corporeal, his body is transformed into the eschatological sphere, endowed with transcendent powers.[75]

In the Jewish mindset of first-century Palestine, bodies are spatial entities, bound by space and time. A body that suddenly appears in a room even though the doors to that room are locked and then vanishes the same way *is a spirit, **not a body**. Spirits appear and disappear. Bodies do not!*

The disciples could easily imagine Jesus appearing as a spirit in a vision.

Likewise, they could imagine Jesus returning with an ordinary physical body much as he was before, and as he would be at the general resurrection, even though that event belonged in the future when all would be raised at once.

They could even imagine Jesus residing in bodily form in the heavens, like Elijah, and then ethereally appearing to them from heaven in a vision.

But a real, tangible, spatial body that possessed qualities which transcended the earthly dimension was an *intolerable contradiction*.

*You can't make this stuff up.*

In I Corinthians 15 Paul is trying to describe the transformed body believers will receive when they share in Jesus' resurrection life. Because he bases this on what he saw and experienced when he claims Jesus appeared to him, it gives us a clear idea of what he thinks Jesus' resurrected existence consists of.

Paul maintains that Jesus has a real, tangible, corporeal—i.e., material—body, but rejects the idea that it is natural or physical.[76] Huh? What other kinds of "bodies" are there? The essence of bodily-ness is physicality.

But wait, it gets worse.

As absurd as it sounds, while he says that Jesus' risen body isn't physical, he also says it's more real, more incorruptible, more "bodily." In other words, it's more *robustly physical* than the physical body—whatever that means!

Confused yet?

And at the same time, this "more robustly," more *intensely physical* body completely transcends the physical realm, defying the limits of space and time.[77] It's a finite body which is essentially transcendent. Wait, what?

*You can't make this stuff up.*

Paul wants to have his cake and eat it too! Clearly, he's encountered something his mind can't quite absorb. As Fitzmyer observes: "When Paul brings himself to say something about the risen body, he indulges in oxymoron and identifies the one and the same "body" with all that is not body, viz. with spirit. Though he may know as little as anyone else about the constitution of the risen body, Paul is struggling, perhaps not too successfully, to preserve the reality of it."[78]

"Indulging in oxymoron" is *not a flattering way* to characterize Paul's attempt to describe the risen Jesus. But it does capture the impossible challenge Paul and the other disciples faced in trying to find something intelligible to say about the reality they experienced.[79]

As one famous, modern philosopher remarked in quite an understated way: "I find the idea of a spiritual body very peculiar in that, after all, when you say something is spiritual, it's rather like saying it's immaterial."[80] In other words, a "spiritual body" is a complete contradiction of terms.

*You can't make this stuff up.*

Perhaps the most telling indication of just how strange and unintelligible this reality is, is the abject failure of most Christians to comprehend it. Most Christians, now and throughout the ages, hold to a view of life after death that *barely resembles Jesus' resurrected appearance.*

Even with the New Testament, even with two thousand years of church tradition and teaching, Christians overwhelmingly imagine life beyond the grave in a way more akin to the disembodied immortality of the Greek world than that of the resurrected Jesus portrayed in the gospels. Even though they should know better, they've opted to conceive of death as the soul being liberated from the body, freed from its decrepit, limited, earthly bondage. The paradoxical depiction of Jesus' resurrected body, a body that is spatial, tangible, and earthbound, and, at the same time, transcendent, unlimited, and heavenly, is simply too hard to comprehend.

Can you imagine a compassionate axe murderer? A kind terrorist? A loving serial killer? Of course not. Yet this is the kind of *oxymoronish absurdity* those who claim to have seen the risen Jesus are trying to maintain. Why?

Based on his massive survey—the most thorough to date—of notions about life beyond the grave in Jesus' time, N.T. Wright argues that the only way to explain how Jesus' followers could have ever conceived such a paradoxical depiction is by actual appearances of a shockingly transformed Jesus.[81]

As he puts it: "...in their strange portrait of a Jesus who is definitely embodied but whose body has unprecedented, and indeed hitherto unimagined properties...it is impossible to explain these pictures as fictional projections from early Christian theology."[82]

*You can't make this stuff up.* This is what we often say about something that is just so far-fetched, so bizarre, no one would ever think to invent it. It has to be true.

When it comes to the depiction of Jesus' resurrected body, this applies tenfold. It is simply too outlandish, too preposterous to have occurred to those claiming to have seen him, even if they were sincerely deluded, overcome by grief or experiencing some other kind of psychological phenomena.

If, even with some modification, they depicted Jesus pretty much as he was before death, or as a dazzlingly bright heavenly figure appearing before them, or as a disembodied spirit, or as shining like a star in the heavens, we would rightly suspect it was simply the work of their imaginations.

They could easily conceive these things.

But what they say is so *maddeningly paradoxical, so unintelligible that it would be impossible to invent, either overtly or subliminally.*

This couldn't be the result of some mind trick.

If, however, the disciples had a genuine encounter with a reality that utterly transcended all prior expectation, if they saw in Jesus' risen form something of another realm, their groping, bumbling failure to capture and relate it in comprehensible terms makes perfect sense.[83]

*You can't make this stuff up.*

# 6. If You Can't Think Straight, You Can't Innovate

As a volunteer firefighter, I can tell you that some of the most intense training we do involves trying to get out of situations where you, the rescuer, find yourself trapped. I attended a class once called "Getting Out Alive." The instructor had done extensive research on incidents where firefighters, police officers, and military personnel found themselves in life or death situations.

Some survived. Others didn't. The difference?

Those who routinely trained on similar scenarios while under simulated stress were able to get out alive. The reason?

In situations of extreme stress, the mind freezes. You can't think straight. You simply react based on your training, falling back on the way you've conditioned yourself to respond. Under extreme stress, the mind defaults to what it's been conditioned to think.

To make his point, the instructor told us this true story. An off-duty police officer was held up at gunpoint one day. Under the stress of looking down the barrel of a gun, he froze. In the heat of the moment, he couldn't think of a way to take the gun away. After it was over, he vowed to come up with a way to disarm a perpetrator if he ever found himself in that situation again. So he and one of his cop buddies devised a way an unarmed victim could defend himself. Then they practiced the maneuver over and over and over again until it became second nature, a reflex reaction.

They even bought a toy gun to practice with and would try to catch each other off guard with surprise attacks. One day his friend even burst into his shower! But they had honed the maneuver so well, he executed it without a hitch: with your left hand, strike the perpetrator's forearm, swiping it down and away, turning your body into his; then with your right hand, grab his arm and use the left to snatch the gun away; hand the gun back and repeat.

Remarkably, this same officer was held up again about two years later. (I wouldn't want to live in his neighborhood!) But this time he was ready. He performed the maneuver expertly and it worked, just as they had practiced: swipe with the left, knock the perpetrator's arm down and away; turn in and immobilize his arm; take the gun away; *hand the gun back and repeat.*

Yes, under the stress of the situation he did everything exactly as he had practiced, including *giving the gun back.*

Under the pressure of stress, the mind can't think clearly. It freezes. It defaults. It can only react the way it's been conditioned. It can't innovate.

*If you can't think straight, you can't innovate.*

Frequently, people argue that the appearances of Jesus are the result of the disciples' fragile state of mind. Reeling from inconsolable grief, ashamed and guilt ridden for the way they abandoned Jesus in his time of need, and running in fear for their lives (they thought the authorities were going to treat them the same way they treated Jesus), their minds create the wildly innovative illusion of the appearances as some kind of psychological defense mechanism.

However, the extreme stress they were under could only have the *opposite effect.* It could only produce what they were conditioned to think already. The kind of life after death they already expected.

I've been with many people in the immediate aftermath of losing a loved one. They often experience such immobilizing grief that they can't make the simplest decisions. In shock and consumed by emotion, they have trouble focusing. Many go through the whole process—from the death of their loved one, to notifying family, to making arrangements, to the wake, funeral, and burial—with very little awareness of what's happening. Later on, they have trouble remembering most of it, including the things they said and did. It's all a blur.

*If you can't think straight, you can't innovate.*

Overwhelmed by shock and grief, and in abject fear for their own lives, the disciples were under tremendous psychological and emotional stress. If the trauma of losing their beloved friend wasn't enough, running for their lives created the perfect storm of mind-numbing shock and disabling fear. In the wake of Jesus' crucifixion, they were in no position to think clearly.

Yet this is the exact time they claim to have seen Jesus. If the appearances were simply a figment of their imagination to soothe their inconsolable grief and tame their fear, they would naturally resort to their default position, the notions of immortality they had been conditioned to imagine and which were deeply ingrained in their psyche. Notions that would bring them comfort; notions that were *safe and familiar.*

But instead, they innovate, and wildly so—*unsettlingly so!*—when describing Jesus. Given the incredible stress they were under, this would *only be possible if what they saw actually was Jesus appearing in a way that defied all they had been conditioned to think about life beyond the grave.*

*If you can't think straight, you can't innovate.*

The Jesus of the appearances is not the product of the disciples' reflex reaction, the only reaction possible under such extreme stress.

## 7. Who Forgot the Stage Props? The Amazing Lack of Supernatural Symbolism

The depiction of Jesus in the appearance narratives is striking because, as we've seen, it includes things never previously imagined, in particular, the impossible paradox of a tangible body that is fully endowed with transcendent qualities.

But just as striking are the things it doesn't include. There are none of the supernatural stage props that normally accompany a heavenly vision:

*No chariots of fire. No cherubim and seraphim.*

*No four-headed beasts. No dazzlingly radiant light.*

*No earthquake, wind, or fire. No thundering voice.*

*No heavenly throne with angelic multitude trumpeting the glory of God.*

*No clouds coming down out of heaven.*

*No blinding flashes of lightning or peals of roaring thunder.*

This is quite extraordinary since in Jewish imagination, some or all of these "apocalyptic" stage props normally accompanied revelatory visions, interventions, or manifestations of divine glory.[84]

And, if ever there was an apocalyptic event, *this was it.* This was God's decisive intervention into history, the miracle of all miracles. You would think it deserved a cherubim or two! Talk about stealth— aside from Jesus appearing and disappearing, there is absolutely no fanfare.

A glaring oversight. None of the things you would expect to be there are there.

Yet, as we've already noted, there is one fantastic item no one can miss and no one could ever anticipate—a real body exhibiting transcendent qualities impossible for a real body to possess. It is difficult to underscore enough how exceedingly odd and improbable this whole picture is.

What should be there isn't there.

But, what no one could previously or possibly conceive is. And it's front and center, the proverbial elephant in the room.

For the Jewish imagination of Jesus' day, *the way this story is told is so strange and out of place.*

If the appearances were just the result of the disciples' imagination, a psychological delusion, then many of these stage props would be present. This is just how these things go down in the Old Testament and parts of the New, like the Transfiguration. This is how their imaginations were conditioned to work. This is what people saw and reported when they had such visions. This is how they told their stories.

So naturally you would expect at least some of these props to be present.

But they aren't. The story isn't embellished this way at all.

And the one thing that is "apocalyptic," Jesus' transcendent qualities, is the furthest thing from their imagination.

## 8. The Ill Will of Paul and James

In my college Introduction to Philosophy class many years ago, our professor argued very persuasively that the resurrection appearances were the result of some kind of autosuggestion. That the disciples' visions of Jesus reflected a deeply-felt psychological need for him to be alive.

At the time I wasn't aware of the arguments presented here, so I thought he might be right. All psychological explanations of the appearances, like the one he presented, are based on the idea that the mind can subconsciously create the realistic illusion of what it desires most to be true, especially when placed under the kind of duress the disciples were experiencing.

Then I asked him about Paul.

Paul didn't want Jesus to be alive. In fact, he wanted the exact opposite. He vigorously persecuted the early church. I asked my professor to explain that. He couldn't. He was stumped. It was a painfully awkward moment. He was actually stuttering trying to think up a response, but none came. I felt so bad for him, I wished I had never asked the question!

But it showed that at least one of the people who claimed Jesus appeared to him wasn't doing it as a result of autosuggestion. It was the *last thing* in the world Paul wanted. A bitter enemy of the church intent on its destruction, he wasn't disposed to have a visionary experience of Jesus. (In fact, a clear majority of scholars now acknowledge this point, accepting it as part of the historical bedrock and noting how unusual the appearance to Paul is. Attempts to explain Jesus' appearance to Paul merely as a visionary experience stemming from his guilt over persecuting the church, or something along these lines, have failed to convince most scholars, mainly because visionary experiences don't work this way.)

And he wasn't alone.

Certainly James, "the brother of the Lord," and possibly his other brothers weren't disposed to believe either since *they thought Jesus was crazy.* They even tried to pull him out of his public ministry.

People often wonder why Jesus didn't appear to nonbelievers. Great question. The answer: he did. Just look at Paul, James, and possibly the other "brothers" of the Lord.

So there are at least two, and probably more, who independently "see" Jesus despite a very strong desire not to. Each, for very different reasons, is an ardent skeptic: Paul is a zealous Pharisee persecuting the early church; James thinks his brother is "out of his mind." (Mk 3:21, 32; 6:3)

James' story is not as well known as Paul's, but it is equally compelling. James became a leading figure in the early church. Eventually, he even died for the faith. But during Jesus' lifetime, James, along with the other brothers of Jesus, clearly wasn't a disciple. Instead, he was deeply suspect about what Jesus was doing—whether out of concern for his brother or embarrassment for the family, he even went so far as to try and remove Jesus from his public ministry and take him back home.

Because James was so venerated in the early church, the gospel writers never would have depicted him being so skeptical of Jesus during his public ministry unless he actually was.[85] It was quite an embarrassment that, prior to Jesus' crucifixion, *the pillar of the Jerusalem church thought Jesus was out of his mind.* That's why, as Gary Habermas says: "...the majority of recent scholars concede that James was an unbeliever until he experienced an appearance of the risen Jesus." (See I Corinthians 15:7 where he is specifically named in the primitive list of appearances.)[86]

Craig reiterates that we are on solid historical ground in saying that, while skeptical before, after Jesus' death James and probably his brothers became zealous believers (even unto death, at least in the case of James). Craig then goes on to ask:

> How can that be? Though their brother's crucifixion
> might pierce their hearts, it certainly could not have
> caused them to worship Him as Messiah and Lord,
> as the early Christians did. When I think about this,
> I sometimes shake my head in amazement. Many of

us have brothers. What would it take for you to *die* for the belief your brother is the Lord, as James did? Even Hans Grass exclaims that one of the surest proofs of Jesus' resurrection is that His own brothers came to believe in Him. This remarkable transformation cannot be explained, except by the fact that, as Paul says, "then he appeared to James."[87]

The fact that James and Paul, and perhaps others not disposed to believe, claim to have seen Jesus resurrected means the appearances can't be the product of any kind of autosuggestion or similar delusion.

## 9. Doing the Impossible: the Resurrection of an Individual Before the Age to Come

In the 1988 NBA finals, the Detroit Pistons were considerable underdogs against the Los Angeles Lakers. Isaiah Thomas, the inspirational leader of the Pistons, suffered a severe ankle sprain in the third quarter of the critical game six. Team doctors concluded he would have to sit out the rest of the game and hope against hope to be able to play in game seven. But to everyone's astonishment, Thomas insisted that he give it a shot (no pun intended!) and play the rest of game six.

His foot was so swollen, somebody nearby exclaimed: "Play? *How's he gonna get his shoe on?*"

Not only did he manage to get his shoe on and actually play the rest of the quarter, he did the impossible. Barely hobbling around the court with a severe limp, he proceeded to put in what is judged by experts to be *one of the top five all-time best performances in NBA history*, scoring twenty-five points in the third quarter, a Final's record. Anyone who saw how much pain he was in following the sprain, how badly his ankle was swollen, thought it was impossible that he'd be able to play, let alone put in the performance of a lifetime.

Jewish belief about the resurrection of the body was *strictly an end-time event.* It would happen in the "age to come" *to all people, all at once.* The resurrection of an individual before the final age wasn't even on the radar screen. It *wasn't possible.*

Furthermore, at the general resurrection in the "age to come," God would initiate His kingdom of perfect peace and justice. Resurrection was *inextricably tied* to this perfected world. If the kingdom hadn't come, then the resurrection hadn't either. Period.

Obviously, the kingdom hasn't come. The world is still full of strife and injustice. And obviously, the general resurrection hasn't occurred either. Cemeteries are still littered with dead, decaying corpses. So, according to Jewish belief, it is simply out of the question that *anyone* could be resurrected.

*The resurrection of an individual prior to God's end-time reign of perfect peace and justice, prior to the general resurrection in the "age to come" when all would be raised at the same time, would be **absolutely inconceivable** for Jews in Jesus' day.*

Yet, this is exactly what the disciples were running around proclaiming: that an individual *had been* resurrected. This would have been thought as impossible as Isaiah Thomas setting a Final's record with a foot so swollen he could barely get his shoe on.

Impossible, *until you saw it for yourself!*

The *only* way the idea of an individual being resurrected prior to the general resurrection in the age to come could even *occur* to the disciples, let alone be something that transformed their worldview and, even more impressively, be something they would stake their lives on, is *if they actually witnessed the impossible.*

And, given what resurrection meant—the body was raised, brought back to life *physically*—the only way they could have ever come to believe Jesus was actually *resurrected*, and not just some spirit, apparition, or vision, is if they were confronted with a *physical body.* Without seeing a body, even if his disciples believed Jesus had somehow conquered death and was alive, they could never conceive his victory over the grave as a resurrection. Exaltation to the heavenly sphere; sitting at the right hand of God; appearing as a spirit in a vision—all well within the realm of possibility.

Bodily resurrection—totally impossible!

This cannot be emphasized enough: unless Jesus appeared to the disciples with a *real—albeit radically transformed—body*, one so real *they could see and touch it*, the idea Jesus was resurrected *could never* occur to them. *Only a tangible body could generate the previously inconceivable belief that Jesus was **resurrected as an individual before the age to come.***

But not only the disciples.

Even Jesus himself.

It's absolutely astounding that his own view of the resurrection seems to have been vastly different from what the gospels describe happening to him. When he talks about how he will "return" after being crucified, he frequently describes himself coming as the Son of Man on the clouds of heaven in his Father's glory to judge the world and bring about the final restoration of all things, the fulfillment of God's reign—the "age to come."

This is how he saw himself being vindicated: not three days after his death, but *at the general resurrection in the age to come.*

In other words, his view was perfectly in line with the prevailing view of his day.

In fact, the gospels record him teaching his disciples at length about how they should handle the indefinite period of time between his death and his return, instructions to remain prepared and not be misled if there is a long delay. He indicates this period could last months if not years.

One of the strongest arguments that this had to be Jesus' view is that it was a major embarrassment that he spoke about his vindication in a way that was *so clearly wrong.* No gospel writer would have included this unless it was well known that Jesus didn't think he would be resurrected before anyone else, that *he didn't foresee his own resurrection.*[88]

Instead, Jesus himself accepted the dominant worldview that resurrection was a universal event only conceivable in the age to come. Which goes to show just how entrenched Jewish ideas about resurrection were. And, just how inconceivable the resurrection of an individual was.[89] [90]

*The resurrection even takes Jesus by surprise.*

So, how *did* the disciples ever conceive the inconceivable: that Jesus, contrary to how everyone—including Jesus!—believed it could happen, rose three days after being put to death?

If they were simply looking for ways to express Jesus' vindication by God, and in a way that would be far more comprehensible and appealing to those they were trying to convince, they would have talked about Jesus' victory over death *the very way he did*. In line with Jesus' own prediction, and the way everyone else saw things, they would've said he was coming back on the last day to establish his reign. But instead, *in direct opposition to Jesus' own teaching*, they *insist on the impossible*: that he, an individual, was resurrected ahead of the age to come.

It cannot be emphasized enough that to generate this *specific belief* in *that context*, the disciples had to see a real, tangible, physical body, and not just a purely "mental" vision. *It is only when faced with **incontrovertible evidence** of an actual **bodily** appearance that they could ever speak of Jesus being **resurrected**.*

# 10. Anticipating the iPhone: A Radically Modified, yet Perfectly Uniform Picture of Resurrection

There's one more thing in that context that is equally stunning: what the disciples were now claiming resurrection involves. As we've seen, it's a *radical modification* of Jewish belief, adding qualities of transcendence that were previously unimaginable and are maddeningly paradoxical. However, despite being such a drastic and totally unexpected departure from the prevailing belief, their concept is *completely uniform*.

The Old Testament concept of resurrection wasn't. Even though there were common assumptions, there was a lot of speculation about the details of what the resurrected body would actually look like. But the New Testament presents *one specific and perfectly consistent view of what it entails.*[91]

As N.T. Wright asks, how do we account for such a rapid, radical, and specific modification arising out of such a multifaceted understanding of life beyond the grave? And how do we account for it being made so consistently across such a wide range of (New Testament) texts?[92]

Everybody today knows what an iPhone is. We see people using them all the time. If you took a hundred people and asked them to describe one, you'd get a very consistent picture. But if you could go back just twenty years and ask the same question, no one would have any idea what you're talking about. And if they guessed, those hundred people would come up with a wide and dizzying array of ideas.

The iPhone is a *significant and specific modification* of the cell phone. Even if a group of people were familiar with the cell phone, unless they actually *saw* an iPhone, they couldn't guess the modifications made to it, and certainly not in a consistent way.

This is exactly the position all first-century Jews were in. Since the resurrection hadn't taken place, no one knew for sure exactly what it would look like.

All, that is, except the early church.

They claimed to know *exactly* which aspects of the Old Testament concept were accurate and which weren't. And exactly how the actual thing would *wildly exceed* all these concepts.

How could they be so sure?

How could they ever come up with such a consistent, yet radically modified view of the resurrected body?

*It's as if they'd already seen what it looks like.*

In fact, coming up with all this on their own in such a consistent way without actually seeing Jesus resurrected, without seeing him *physically,* is as likely as a hundred different people twenty years ago all coming up with the exact same idea for the iPhone.

## 11. The Edsel of Immortality: Who Would Want It?

In the late 1950's, the ailing Ford Motor Company introduced the Edsel to the market. It was supposed to be the car of all cars. To put Ford back on the map. But it turned out to be a colossal failure. A marketing disaster. Why?

Ford failed to understand the market. As Edsel scholar Jan Deutsch says, "It was the wrong car at the wrong time." The Edsel has become the quintessential example of how *not* to market a product.[93] Nobody wanted it.

The appearances of Jesus contain a view of immortality that is completely *unmarketable*. The Gentile world would find it repulsive—they were looking forward to liberation from bodily existence, with all its enslavements. Jews would find the resurrection of an individual impossible and a spiritual body unintelligible. Craig comments: "... physical appearances would have been offensive to potential converts in both Judaism and paganism. Jews would tend to reject Jesus' physical appearances because they held only to a physical resurrection at the end of history. Pagans would tend to reject physical resurrection because they held to the immortality of the soul alone."[94]

Not only is it impossible to explain how the early church could come up with all of this, the bigger question is, *why would they want to?*

In their world, *it doesn't sell.*

It is so unappealing, so unmarketable, that they would have been under enormous pressure to modify this notion—if they could. The only possible reason they don't is because, as distasteful as it may be, this is precisely how Jesus appeared.

The other notions of immortality found in the world's major religions are entirely predictable and desirable. For example, reincarnation is a vision of immortality that is very popular and easily imagined. Even though it contradicts Christian faith, I've heard many a Christian express belief in or at least the desire for reincarnation. We naturally gravitate toward what's most familiar and long for a chance to do it all over again. Reincarnation provides both. It's safe and comforting.

Similarly, disembodied immortality, release from all the pain of this world and all the limitations imposed by these all too frail bodies that weigh us down, is quite attractive and easy enough for us to imagine. While it may be a leap into the unknown, the tremendous benefit of being liberated from this angst-ridden, earthbound reality is well worth the risk.

Even something like the general resurrection, a return to earthly existence, minus, of course, all the strife and injustice we experience here, is deeply alluring and no problem at all to conceive. In fact, in one form or another, it remains a popular view among many today, notably Jehovah's Witnesses.

All these visions of life after death are entirely predictable and desirable, infusing many cultures and belief systems.

The transphysicality suggested by Jesus' resurrected appearance is *not*.

It's a foreign, bizarre, and unsettling reality.

When you play out the implications of Jesus' resurrection, it isn't pretty. What the resurrection body will be is so mystifying that we are left with little idea of what eternity will "look" like. All we know is that our embodied existence matters, and matters eternally. A fact many of us lament. Our bodies and what we do in them is often a source of great pain, regret, and limitation. The only upside of our physicality is that it is familiar. But we won't simply get back all we know and are comfortable with. It will be so radically transformed as to be barely recognizable.

Liberation from bodily existence is comforting, freeing.

Envisioning eternity on a perfected earth, a paradise, a return to Eden, is also comforting, safe and familiar.

But transphysicality requires trusting in an incomprehensible reality that, as Paul says: "No eye has seen, nor ear heard, nor the human heart conceived, what God has prepared for those who love him." (I Corinthians 2:9)

We prefer knowing what we're in for. We want the security of predictability where we can feel in control. Transphysicality promises none of this.

By the way, this is why it's ridiculous to suggest that the empty tomb stories or depictions of Jesus appearing with a real, tangible body were invented by the later church or gospel writers; in other words, that features which play up Jesus' physicality (e.g., leaving an empty tomb behind, being capable of being touched, cooking and eating food, etc.) were invented to defend the faith and appeal to potential converts. Over the years, a variety of scholars have argued just that: for apologetical purposes, there was a tendency in the tradition to turn a spiritual experience of Jesus into a physically embodied appearance, to put "flesh and bones" on a purely visionary phenomenon. Being a product of this later development, the appearance narratives and/ or their sources have added physical features to what was originally understood to be a purely spiritual and ethereal encounter with Jesus in order to convince people of the reality of this encounter.

But this has it completely *backwards*.

If anything, the tendency would have been to downplay these features, not place them front and center; to de-emphasize the physical nature of Jesus' appearances; to make it more palatable by spiritualizing the whole thing.

A purely spiritual appearance would have been a far easier sell.

*Because it was so unintelligible and unappealing, transphysicality would have been a major stumbling block to potential converts, not an apologetical advantage.*

In fact, I Corinthians 15 reveals just how undesirable transphysicality was. It was even a problem *in* the church, with many Corinthians preferring a more spiritual view. Grounding his argument in Jesus' own transphysical appearance, Paul works hard throughout this passage to persuade the Corinthian church that a glorified *body* is an essential part of eternal life and that it's a *good* thing. But the fact he has to make this argument *to converts* shows how primitive, crude, and repulsive the gospel portraits of Jesus would appear in that context.

If transphysicality wasn't there from the beginning, if it wasn't an undeniable part of the historical record, it would make no sense to invent something that was so problematic and offensive to the audiences the early church was trying to appeal to.

This view of immortality is not comforting. It's not desirable.

*It's the Edsel of immortality.*

And that's why no one, not even the disciples, would invent it; or even think to invent it; or least of all, delude themselves by subconsciously inventing it in the deepest recesses of their minds.

Especially if such a "delusion" was meant to bring comfort, satisfy their deepest longings or assuage their greatest fears.

Especially if they wanted their message to change the world.


## Conclusion: Ghostbusting—So What Did They Really See?

Whether or not it really happened, the story of Jesus' Transfiguration (Mark 9:2-8 and pars.) gives us a good idea of what first-century Jews were thinking. According to the story, both Moses and Elijah appear alongside Jesus as he's transfigured. They appear and then disappear but in *bodily form.*

There is, however—and this is key—*absolutely no hint of resurrection.*

In fact, as everybody knew, Moses' body was still buried in its grave in Moab awaiting the general resurrection at the end of time. (Deuteronomy 34:1-8) And after being "assumed," Elijah's body was still thought to be residing in heaven until it would return at that same end-time. (2 Kings 2:1-12)

So, they are appearing from heaven in a *purely spiritual way.* In a vision.

Even though they can somehow appear in a recognizable form resembling their earthly bodies, they are *pure spirit.* There is absolutely no suggestion the general resurrection has happened or that they have been resurrected. In fact, according to the prevailing worldview, a *body* can't appear and disappear. Any "body" people saw appearing and disappearing like this would necessarily be visionary; in other words, ethereal and immaterial, and most certainly not a real, tangible body.

So what drove the early church to insist that Jesus hadn't just appeared from glory like Moses and Elijah, but was actually resurrected? That it was *physically* him, albeit dramatically transformed?

This further step is totally unnecessary and nonsensical. Actually, it's absurd.

A *vision* of Jesus would be enough to establish God had vindicated him. And it would have fit comfortably into their worldview. It would've been intelligible.

The answer has to be that Jesus' actual bodily appearance was so overwhelmingly real, those original eyewitnesses were forced to talk about it as a resurrection and not simply a visionary appearance. He must have been so tangible, so real for all to see, hear, and touch, that their entire worldview was rocked to its core, compelling them to speak in a way that was total jibberish in their context.

*The disciples had to have seen a real, physical body; otherwise, they never would have insisted on the utter nonsense of resurrection.*

But if physical, then external. Something "out there" in the real world.

And definitely not a visionary delusion produced by the internal dynamics of the mind.

Yet at the same time, bodies this real are, by nature, bound by space and time. Even the Jewish understanding held that the resurrected body, though no longer subject to death and decay, wouldn't be able to transcend space and time. This is simply how it is with bodies that exist in the physical realm. It's what it means to have a body.

But Jesus can and does. His very real, very tangible body is able to appear and disappear; to utterly transcend the physical realm; to do what physical bodies are not, by their very nature, able to do.

Where did the early church get all of this?

The only way to explain this kind of resurrection faith is if Jesus appeared to them with *an actual body they could see and touch and which, astonishingly, possessed previously unimaginable, transcendent qualities.*

# CHAPTER

# 3

## You Complete Me

*The Empty Tomb and Appearances Together*

OR BELIEF IN JESUS' resurrection to have emerged, there had to be both an empty tomb *and* "transphysical" appearances. One without the other would have led to all kinds of other conclusions or beliefs. But the only way *resurrection* faith is possible is if those first disciples believed they witnessed both.

There are a number of significant phenomena that only the reality of an empty tomb and appearances, together, can account for.

## 1. Bad Ancient Historiography: The Character Flaws in the Resurrection Narratives Reveal Their True Character

Have you ever embellished a story? You know, added some dramatic details to make a point or for added emphasis? The vice principal at the first school I taught in had the reputation of being a strict disciplinarian. The story around school was that he once threw a misbehaving student out of the second-floor window of his classroom.

As you would expect, the kids were terrified of him.

But truth be told, he never threw anyone out of a second-floor window. That was just part of the legend that grew around the fact that he was really strict; something that naturally happens as people try to make their point. Facts are embellished. Legends grow. In fact, the more powerful our experience, the more we tend to exaggerate to emphasize our point.

Ancient historiography not only allowed for this kind of exaggeration and embellishment, *it demanded it.* In a way that seems disingenuous to us, the good historian not only reported the facts, he or she interpreted them with lavish symbolic details and prolific literary allusions to tease out the meaning of the event, to dramatically make the point.

But the narratives of the empty tomb stories and appearances of Jesus exhibit a striking lack of embellishment. Despite recording an event that begs for this kind of symbolic interpretation, they show very little of it.

They aren't good ancient historiography!

A quick comparison with the passion narrative reveals how striking this is. As Richard Bauckham observes:

> There is an intertextual network that serves to interpret the passion of Jesus by setting it within the experience and the expectation of Israel. But when we read on to the accounts of the empty tomb and the resurrection appearances there are hardly any such allusions. The stories show little sign of following literary precedents, and standard narrative motifs, the building blocks of many an ancient story, are rare. For all the ingenuity of scholars these stories remain strangely *sui generis* and lacking theological interpretation. None of the

standard Jewish formulas or images of resurrection occur. We seem to be shown the extraordinary *novum*, the otherness of resurrection, through the eyes of those whose ordinary reality it invaded. The perplexity, the doubt, the fear, the joy, the recognition are those of deep memory, mediated, to be sure, by literary means, but not entirely hidden behind the text.[95]

We know how vitally important it was for the gospel writers to show that the events of Jesus' life *fulfill scripture*. Either through direct citation, allusion, or echo, the rest of the gospel narrative is at pains to show how all that Jesus does and all that happens to him fulfills the Old Testament.

But why not here? Why not with the most important event of his life?[96]

For one thing, there was no expectation something like this would, or even could, happen. Not even close. Both Luke and John, for instance, each insist in their own way that the resurrection fulfills scripture, but they are at a total loss to find one precise Old Testament passage that would back this up. They are desperate to show how, but can't. In other words, there is nothing in all of scripture that could have ever anticipated, predicted, or shaped the way this story is told.

For another thing, they don't seem to be the slightest bit free to modify the tradition in order to fit Jesus' resurrection into the larger narrative arc of salvation history. This is something they would have felt essential: *surely the central event in salvation history would be found prophesied in the Old Testament!* Yet they make no attempt to connect the two. No attempt to subtly adjust the story so that there might be some vague resonance with Old Testament prophesy. These stories are apparently too set-in-stone, too foundational, to allow for modification, even for the very best of reasons.

This glaring omission, made deliberately but reluctantly for sure, shows the story to be entirely original and essentially unaltered.[97]

One other thing is conspicuously lacking. In the wake of 9-11, there were numerous stories of people quitting their jobs, or leaving bad relationships (getting divorced, etc.); in short, making drastic changes they were reluctant or unwilling to prior to that tragedy. In fact, the events of that day caused just about every American to reflect profoundly on their own life, even if it just meant going home and hugging your loved ones a little tighter. Inevitably, it's a natural and powerful human instinct to ask what a major event like this means to us personally.

But this doesn't happen in the resurrection texts. Not at all. No one says, "Alleluia, Jesus is risen, and now *that means we will rise too.*" Nowhere does the text say, "And Jesus ascended to heaven, having defeated death once and for all *so that all might live forever.*" The emphasis, instead, is on Jesus' vindication and now fully revealed divine identity. The personal meaning of his resurrection for human beings after death isn't really mentioned at all. The rest of the New Testament will mention it, often. It's a major theme. But not the resurrection narratives.

When people watched those planes fly into the towers on 9-11, they were horrified at what they had just witnessed. If you could freeze that moment in time, that would be the focus: the event itself and what it meant for America, that we were under attack. But after a little time passed, those same people began to think about what that event meant to them, personally. Now they see it through the prism of how it affected their lives.

However, the raw image of what they witnessed, what it meant to the country and those directly affected—their grief and loss—was the more *primitive reaction.*

Lacking the dimension of personal meaning, the resurrection narratives exhibit this more primitive quality.[98]

One last thing must be said about these narratives. In the final analysis, it must be said that, despite all their differences, the resurrection narratives do consistently agree in the *basic details* of the story: Jesus was crucified on a Friday and buried before sunset by Joseph of Arimathea in a tomb near Jerusalem; that Sunday, several women went to the tomb and found it empty; after which, Jesus appeared a number of times to different disciples, raised from the dead in his crucified but strangely transformed body; finally, during one of these appearances he commissioned a large group of them to go and preach the good news to the world. Overall, they agree on far more than they differ.

This leads Wright to conclude:

> The stories exhibit…exactly the surface tension which we associate, not with tales artfully told by people eager to sustain a fiction and therefore anxious to make everything look right, but with the hurried, puzzled accounts of those who have seen with their own eyes something which took them horribly by surprise and with which they have not yet fully come to terms.[99]

Good ancient historiography they are not!

## 2. A Dead Messiah is a Non-Starter!

If I told you Benedict Arnold was the greatest hero of the American Revolution, you'd think I was crazy, right? He was a traitor who got what he deserved, dying an infamous death for his treacherous act. George Washington was the real hero of the revolution.

Though there are obvious differences, Jesus' contemporaries would have thought of him as a Benedict Arnold rather than a George Washington.

As a traitor rather than a hero.

In Jesus' time, many would-be messiahs came and went. If you wanted to claim you were the true Messiah, there was only one way to prove that you were the real deal. *All you had to do* was liberate Israel from the Roman Empire in a decisive military victory that would establish God's reign of peace and justice over the world through your kingship.

The wolf living with the lamb.

People beating their swords into plowshares.

In short, the messianic age. Make this happen, and you clearly are the Messiah.

In fact, this was the tactic virtually all would-be messiahs embarked on. Believing God was raising them up as His annointed, they started revolutionary movements (some more successful than others) designed to gain Israel's independence. None of these worked, of course, and in each case, not only was the would-be messiah put to death in some kind of humiliating defeat, but the very fact their movement failed to secure the expected results proved they weren't the real deal.

*A dead messiah is a non-starter.*[100]

Jesus was crucified by capital punishment at the hands of the Romans. A shameful, humiliating, and total defeat. His revolution never really got off the ground, militarily speaking at least. In fact, he didn't seem interested in such a revolution—a very strange approach to messiahship indeed.

And nothing had changed as a result of his movement. Israel was still living under Roman oppression. Clearly, God's reign of peace and justice, the messianic age, had not begun. By every measure, Jesus was most certainly *not* the real deal. As Shabir Ally, a modern Muslim apologist puts it, "a crucified Messiah is as self-refuting as a square circle, a four-sided triangle, or a married bachelor."[101]

To the Jews of his day, Jesus was the anti-Messiah, the ***anti-Christ!***

This is precisely what the crucifixion proved: God's utter rejection of Jesus. He might have had delusions of grandeur about being the Messiah, but this was, *for all to see,* God's decisive judgment on that.

*A dead messiah is a non-starter.*

And yet, in the face of his obvious and total defeat, the early church was proclaiming not only that Jesus was Messiah, but far more outrageously, the world's True Lord. That he was *on par with Yahweh Himself.*

For Jews fully immersed in this worldview, Jesus hadn't done enough to qualify as Messiah. Of all would-be's, he was the most pathetic. Others had at least come close to leading a successful rebellion. Jesus didn't even seem interested, spending his time teaching and healing, not in the power center of Jerusalem, but mostly in the boondocks and backwoods of Palestine, "heathen Galilee."

To claim Jesus as Messiah was laughable. To say he was also God in the Flesh, at Whose Name every knee shall bow and every tongue confess as Lord of All, was *a quantum leap of insanity*. No human, not even the true Messiah himself reigning supreme, could ever dare make this claim.

How could anyone seriously consider *him* to be Lord of All?

After all, *a dead messiah is a non-starter.*

So, how does a hick Galilean, working-class-Joe carpenter, become the Son of God?

How does a crucified, death-penalty convict, charlatan messianic pretender, become the Lord of the Universe?

How does a group of Jews watching this man die the death reserved for slaves, traitors, and blasphemers come to publicly proclaim *to their own deaths what no Jew could ever conceive possible*, that he is God incarnate?

And how does this group of Jews who would rather die than commit blasphemy by worshiping anything or anyone other than Yahweh, worship *this man* as they worship Yahweh Himself and rather die than *blaspheme **His Name**?*

Other than the resurrection, what could account for such a mind-boggling claim?

N.T. Wright underscores the essential question:

> Why then did the early Christians acclaim Jesus as
> Messiah, when he obviously wasn't?..Faced with his
> death, why would any of his followers have dreamed of
> saying that he was Messiah—and…of reordering their
> worldview around this belief, so that Christianity was

launched precisely as a messianic movement, albeit with significant differences?

Indeed, they could have done what every other messianic group had done in the wake of their leader's very public and tragic execution: give up their dreams and go home, happy to escape alive. Or, they could go find another messiah. Wright points out how James, Jesus' brother, would have made an ideal candidate. But instead, James gives his life for his belief that Jesus was the Messiah (and so much more!).[102]

In Jesus' day, there were many who claimed to be the Jewish Messiah, the real deal. They've come and gone in complete anonymity because their movement failed and they were put to death.

Jesus suffered the same fate. So why didn't he die in the same anonymity?

A *dead-messiah is a non starter*. A non sequiter. A complete contradiction in terms. A dead messiah is *no messiah at all*. And this isn't even the most outrageous claim the early Christians were making. They were insisting that *this dead man*, this obvious-for-all-to-see messianic pretender, was *Yahweh in person, the eternal God!*

How do people who knew Jesus as a man just like them, who saw him suffer a scandalous and humiliating death at the hands of a foreign oppressor, people who would die for their belief that Yahweh is Lord alone, come to worship him as the creator of all that is (including them!), and come to be willing to die for this belief instead?

Ben Witherington drives this home:

> The real sticking point for Jesus' followers is that the culture of the Middle East at that time (and still today) was an honor and shame culture, and crucifixion was the most shameful way to die in that world. It was not seen as a noble martyrdom of any sort. People in that world believed that the manner of your death most revealed your character. On that

basis, Jesus was a scoundrel, a man who committed treason against the state, a man who deserved the punishment used for slave revolts. The Romans called it 'the extreme punishment' and no Roman citizen would be subjected to it.

It wouldn't make sense to create a story about a crucified and risen man being the saviour of the world—*unless* you really believe it is historically true—because the instinctive reaction to such a message is exactly what Paul, the earliest New Testament writer, said it would be: It was a stumbling block or scandal to the Jews, and sheer nonsense to Gentiles. (I Cor 1:23) If you have seen the famous graffito from the pagan catacombs in Rome, the drawing of a donkey hanging on a cross, with a Roman kneeling below it with a sarcastic remark about 'a man worshipping his god,' you realize how such a message must have come across, at least initially, to those being evangelized in the Roman world...If you are interested in myth making, or creating a saga that could be received and believed in those first-century cultures for the sake of evangelism, the early Christian approach is certainly not the way to go about it...Martin Dibelius, the famous old German father of form criticism of the gospel, once admitted that you have to posit a historical "X" big enough to explain the rise of Christianity after the ignominious death of Jesus on a Roman cross. He was right.[103]

That "X" big enough could be none other than the resurrection.

Why did Christianity *wildly succeed* where all other messianic movements utterly failed? The Romans were still in charge. The world was still full of strife and injustice. God's reign was nowhere in sight. Nothing had changed.

But here was this little band of followers, themselves fully immersed in Jewish messianism, claiming in the face of all the overwhelming evidence to the contrary, that *Jesus was the real deal*: that he was the true Messiah; that he *had* ushered in the messianic age (still, of course, to be fully realized in the future, but for them, undeniably begun nonetheless); and that he was immeasurably more than any Jew ever dared imagine the Messiah—or any human for that matter—could be: *the Lord of All.*

And the reason they give for making such an outrageously counterfactual claim? Because Jesus' tomb lay empty and he, utterly transformed yet thoroughly embodied, had appeared to them risen from the dead.

There are two monumental steps the early church makes that are fully incomprehensible without the resurrection: that a dead man is the Messiah. And far more remarkable and shocking than the first: this dead man is the world's True Lord, God in the flesh. Given that a dead messiah is a non-starter, the only possible way to explain how Christianity ever got started in the first place—you really can't explain its existence any other way—is the fact of the empty tomb, followed by transphysical appearances of the risen Jesus.

Many would-be messiahs have come and gone.

But *only Jesus, the dead-messiah, remains.*

And only the resurrection can explain that.

# 3. What's In a Worldview? The Transformation of the Disciples—Part II: A Quantum Leap of Cosmic Proportions

"Hear, O Israel: The Lord is our God, the Lord Alone. You shall love the Lord, your God with all your heart, and with all your soul, and with all your might." (Deuteronomy 6:4-5) "The Lord *Alone.*" Or, as the Hebrew can also be rendered, "The Lord is *One.*" Devout Jews would recite this prayer, the Shema Israel, several times a day: often first thing in the morning, once during the middle of the day, and as the last thing before going to bed. It was the first thing a Jewish child learned and the last prayer a dying Jew uttered. The Shema embodies the central truth that defined first-century Judaism: God is One.

In other words, the Lord *alone* is God.

*Alone* the creator and sustainer of the universe.

*Alone* holy, eternal, and transcendent.

*Alone* worthy of worship.

Nothing was more precious, sacred, or true for first-century Jews. It was the unshakable foundation of their worldview. The lens through which they saw everything else.

However, almost immediately after Jesus' death, the disciples, *a group of devout first-century Jews*, began to proclaim that Jesus was Lord. *That this man had the same status and deserved the same worship as God.*

This was blasphemy in the highest. It deserved immediate death. Nothing could be more repulsive.

But this willingness to boldly blaspheme what they had held to be most sacred isn't the most stunning part of it. The truly astonishing thing is how *utterly inconceivable* this claim would have been in the first place. It required two *quantum leaps* of thought that would have been *impossible* in first-century Palestinian Judaism:

First, that God could be more than one.

These thoroughly Jewish disciples who faithfully prayed the Shema three times a day are now running around proclaiming that God is *two*: Father and Son (the third person, the Holy Spirit, would soon be added to the equation). To say God is two persons means you're no longer talking about the *One* God of monotheistic Judaism. You're talking polytheism, what the detested pagans believed. It's an intolerable contradiction to believe in two (and eventually three) divine persons and still believe in the one true God of Israel.

The second quantum leap was that a human being could be God.

That the transcendent Lord, the utterly Other, could somehow assume frail and fallen humanity.[104] That the infinite could become finite; the Creator, one of His creation; the Eternal God, mortal; the Holy One, tainted by sinful flesh. How can this be?

God in human form? Unthinkable.

In fact, claiming God was more than one and had taken on human flesh denied the very *essence* of who God is. Modern monotheists—Jews and Muslims—totally get this. That's why they think Christianity is idolatrous, blasphemous, a fundamental denial of the one true God. Not to mention, unbearably illogical.

Try to imagine how stupefying the early church's belief in Jesus' divinity was. This was a human being, just like them. Someone they walked the dusty roads of Palestine with. Someone they ate and drank with. They saw him in all his human frailty. They saw him get tired and (sorry to be crude but it's true) have to go to the bathroom. They saw him get angry and cry. And above all, they saw him suffer— horribly—and die.

And here they were—not long after his *death*—claiming that this man who they knew in all his human vulnerability is the *eternal* creator and sustainer of the universe. That he is the one *who created them*. That he *transcends space and time*. That he *is ultimate reality itself.*

What would it take for you to think of a human being you knew this closely—or any human being for that matter—to be the eternal God? The one who created you!

The quantum leap involved in all of this requires a catalyst of equal or greater dimension to launch it. Because it so radically transformed the disciples' worldview, their most basic belief about the cosmos, the catalyst had to be earth-shattering, an event of *cosmic proportion*.

By reversing the most fundamental law of nature, death, the resurrection happens to be such an event. In fact, it's hard to think of another event that could qualify.

The resurrection is the only "X" big enough.

The Japanese novelist Shusaku Endo writes that if we reject the resurrection, we will be "forced to believe that what did hit the disciples was some other amazing event different in kind yet of equal force in its electrifying intensity." Implying that, to explain this quantum leap any other way would require far more faith than believing in the resurrection itself.[105]

Moreover, the *speed* at which this quantum leap occurs is utterly breathtaking. No worldview, especially one so vital and entrenched as this one, has ever been so rapidly transformed. In every other case, it takes at least several generations to achieve such a dramatic transformation of worldview. As Timothy Keller observes:

> After the death of Jesus the entire Christian community suddenly adopted a set of beliefs that were brand-new and until that point had been unthinkable…in every other instance that we know of, such a massive shift in thinking at the world-view level only happens to a group of people over a period of time. It ordinarily takes years of discussion and argument in which various thinkers and writers debate…That is how culture and worldviews change.[106]

A good example of this is race in America. During slavery, African Americans were thought of as sub-human, literally and, in some ways, legally: according to the Constitution, three-fifths the worth of a white person (see Article 1, Sec 2, Par 3). After slavery ended in the 1860's, it took another one hundred years—roughly *four generations*—before the civil rights movement gave people of color true equality under the law. It's been two generations since the civil rights movement and, while there has been substantial progress in race relations, whatever you may think of Black Lives Matter, it is clear that racism still exists in America. Transforming the worldview of slavery continues to be a long process taking multiple generations to achieve.

This is just how worldviews change.

So how is it that the worldview of these early disciples is so *rapidly and radically transformed, and in a direction that would have been impossible for them to conceive prior to Jesus' death?*

There is simply no other way to explain such a rapid "explosion of worldview" except as the result of the resurrection. It is the only thing that could account for both the magnitude and speed in such a quantum leap of worldview.

But what about *The Da Vinci Code?*

It claimed that belief in Jesus' divinity didn't take shape for three hundred years, at the Council of Nicea. And then only by political fiat. I know, I know, *it's only fiction.* But so many people have assumed this claim is factual that it has to be dealt with as a historical assertion.

Admittedly, if this claim is true, or even if, as a number of older scholars have argued, belief in Jesus' divinity took several generations to evolve, then the entire argument presented here falls apart: there was no immediate quantum leap that can only be explained by the resurrection.

So, how do we know that this quantum leap happened right away, that those first-generation Christians actually believed in Jesus' divinity?[107]

Roughly twenty-five years ago, a scholar named Larry Hurtado wrote a book that changed the way his colleagues look at this question. Prior to Hurtado, scholars were divided as to whether belief in Jesus' divinity happened right away or, under the influence of Hellenistic culture, evolved in a non-Jewish context over several generations. But in *One God, One Lord,* Hurtado has effectively put the question to rest. He's shown that those first Jewish disciples *worshiped* Jesus as only Yahweh could be worshiped.

(Hurtado has also put to rest another claim that has been made less frequently, namely that, by Jesus day, pure Jewish monotheism had been *compromised* by the surrounding pagan culture's polytheistic beliefs and robust concept of "the divine man." Scholars point to a multiplication of intermediary figures (e.g., angels) in the literature of that period who act on behalf of Yahweh and seem to share in His authority, and the personification of traits that mediated God's presence and activity in the world (e.g., Wisdom). As a result, they argue strict monotheism would have been "softened." In this context, it wouldn't have been that big of a leap for those first Christians to see Jesus as divine. They could easily assimilate belief in Jesus' divinity alongside Yahweh.

Hurtado convincingly shows that the exact opposite was actually the case: at that time, Jewish monotheism was as fierce as ever and wouldn't tolerate—or even *think* to entertain—another rival to Yahweh or the slightest hint of a person being divine.)[108]

After thoroughly critiquing Hurtado's argument, scholars now generally agree that the first Christians understood Jesus to be fully divine. In fact, given the conceptual framework of first-century Judaism, many argue that those very first disciples couldn't have exalted him any higher, as Yahweh's own equal. In other words, they had come to believe that the divine identity includes the Father and the Son, who form a perfect unity or oneness.

The evidence that this happened rapidly, virtually instantaneously, is found throughout the New Testament, including in its earliest-recorded parts. In fact, in one of the earliest passages from the New Testament, one that easily goes back to the first-generation disciples and reflects their thinking, we find one of the clearest and most exalted affirmations of Jesus' divinity.

(Hang in with me here—it gets a little technical, but if you have any doubt about this question it's worth it!)

Scholars agree that Paul wrote his letter to the Philippians sometime in the mid-50's AD. (Some would say slightly earlier in the decade and others slightly later, but practically all agree it was in the 50's.) This is roughly twenty years after Jesus' death, well within the first Christian generation. In Chapter 2, verses 6-11, Paul seems to be quoting a hymn that was used in worship and/or as a short confessional formula.[109] Most scholars would say that Paul is borrowing this hymn—he didn't compose it at that time—which means it actually goes back to an earlier period, perhaps the 40's or even the 30's AD. So it clearly expresses what those first-generation Christians thought about Jesus, *some of whom knew him personally.*

The hymn itself borrows a line from the prophet Isaiah (43:22-23), which says that every knee shall bow and tongue confess that Yahweh is Lord. Scholars call this part of Isaiah the most fiercely *monotheistic* section of the Old Testament. It jealously defends the absolute oneness and transcendence of Yahweh and magnifies the infinite difference and distance between him as Creator and his creatures.

Yahweh *alone* is worthy of having every knee bow and tongue confess in worship and adoration that he is God.

But in a revolutionary move, the hymn applies all this to Jesus! It says that *he now shares the same status and power as Yahweh and therefore deserves the same worship and adoration.*

The hymn also calls Jesus LORD. This was the title reserved for Yahweh alone. Jews maintained that the divine name, Yahweh (YHWH), was too holy to be pronounced except in the most sacred contexts. By Jesus' time, only the high priest was allowed to pronounce it when he entered the sanctuary once a year to offer atonement for the people's sins on the feast of Yom Kippur. As a result, when referring to Yahweh the rest of the time, they used a substitute name: Adonai. When this Hebrew term was translated into Greek, it became Kyrios, which in English translates as Lord.

The upshot of all this is that this text, which is one of, if not, the earliest fragments in the New Testament and can be traced back to the earliest Christians, some of whom undoubtedly knew Jesus during his public ministry, *unequivocally gives Jesus the divine name*. Since names indicated identity in that culture, and since the divine name indicated that the one who bore it also bore the divine identity, i.e., was God, and since the divine name was reserved for Yahweh alone, there is no doubt these earliest Christians were thinking of Jesus as having the same identity and being on the same level as Yahweh.

Another expression used by the earliest Christians is "Maranatha." (I Corinthians 16:22) The New Testament is written in Greek, but Jesus and his disciples spoke Aramaic. There are a few Aramaic words and/or phrases preserved in the New Testament. This is one of them. It means "Our Lord, Come," and scholars agree it was spoken by those earliest Aramaic-speaking Jewish disciples as they expressed their longing for Jesus, *the Lord*, to return in glory. Again, as early as we can trace, the church was calling Jesus "Lord," *giving him the divine name (and, therefore, identity) reserved for God alone.*

As Harvard-trained agnostic turned priest and later Cardinal Avery Dulles says:

> The Gospels clearly exhibited the faith of first-century Christians that Jesus was a divine being, Son of God...Already in the sermon attributed to Peter on Pentecost, Jesus is identified with the Lord—the Adonai of the Old Testament—of whom it had been written that he would send forth His spirit upon all flesh before manifesting Himself as a universal judge at the end of time.
>
> *In terms of the theological vocabulary available to Jewish Christians at the moment the Church was born, we could scarcely hope for, or even conceive, a more forceful affirmation of Christ's divinity.*(my italics)[110]

In Galatians 1:13-24, Paul provides indirect evidence of how extremely early and widespread this affirmation was. He's confessing—to his great shame—that he violently persecuted the early church. As a zealous Pharisee, a faithful Jew out to protect God's honor, he admits that he sought to destroy the church (unto death) until, on the road to Damascus, God revealed to Paul that Jesus was indeed His Son, and, remarkably, Paul came to share the very faith he was trying to destroy.

But why was Paul so driven to persecute this particular group of Jews? There were other groups of fellow Jews he, as a Pharisee, had significant disagreements with: the Sadducees, Essenes, and those who would later be known as Zealots, among others. He doesn't seek to destroy any of them. What was it about the early church that would cause such fierce, and even deadly—at least in the case of Stephen, the first martyr—opposition from so zealous a Jew?

Because it was deserving of death, it had to be a capital offense. In that period, the only capital offenses punishable by death were murder, adultery, and blasphemy. And since the early church doesn't seem to have been engaged in any systematic scheme to commit murder or adultery, the only possibility is blasphemy. Which is completely consistent with what Paul himself indicates: the major change at the center of his conversion experience (he doesn't mention anything else), turning him from dogged persecutor to faithful adherent, was the revelation that Jesus is *God's Son*—utter blasphemy to a Pharisee, or any other faithful Jew for that matter, but, apparently, the *bedrock* belief of the early church.

So prior to his conversion, which virtually all scholars agree was only a few years after Jesus' death, the faith Paul was trying to destroy, the faith he came to adopt, was the faith that said Jesus is the Son of God. Thus, Paul's intense persecution of the early church indirectly shows that *within a few years of Jesus' death,* at the very latest, this *entire group of Jews* was *exalting Jesus to divine status.*

One of the most impressive ways to see how pervasive this understanding of Jesus' divinity was among the first-generation Christians is the way that Paul, in all his writings, can simply *assume* Jesus' divine identity. As a member of that first Christian generation, writing to other first-generation Christians, he didn't have to argue that Jesus was divine.

He had to argue many other points, but not Jesus' divinity.

It was universally accepted. It was *a given.*

As N.T. Wright observes: "Paul can, in fact, assume his (very 'high') view of Jesus as a given. He never says, even to Corinth, 'How then can some of you be saying that Jesus was simply a wonderful human being and nothing more?'"[111] Which leads Wright to conclude:

> *None of this seems to have been a matter of controversy within the earliest church.* This indicates...that this Christology must have been well established even sooner, since if it had only been accepted, say, in the late 40's we might have expected to catch some trace of anxiety or controversy on this point in Paul's early letters at least. And we do not. The identification of Jesus with YHWH seems to have been part of (what

later came to be called) Christianity from more or less *the very beginning*. Paul can refer to it, and weave it into arguments, poems, prayers and throwaway remarks, as common coin. Recognizing Jesus within the identity of Israel's One God, and following through that recognition in worship (where monotheism really counts), seems to have been part of 'the way' from the start.[112]

Belief in Jesus' divinity was a firmly-embedded truth for the earliest church. Within the first generation, if not virtually right away, *it wasn't even a point of controversy.*

Paul even applies the *Shema Israel* to *Jesus*. (I Corinthians 8:6) As *the* core identity marker of monotheistic Judaism, the Shema captured better than anything else the bedrock belief that God is One. But, writing I Corinthians in the early 50's, Paul fundamentally revises the Shema to include Jesus alongside the Father as *together* the One True God. [113] It's impossible to imagine a more radical revision of Jewish monotheism; or a more explicit affirmation of Jesus' divinity.

There was a time when scholars simply assumed that the later texts of the New Testament contained a fuller, more developed understanding of Jesus' divinity. No more.[114] From a first-century Jewish perspective, these earliest texts present his divinity in as high and explicit a way possible.[115]

So, contra *The Da Vinci Code*, the Council of Nicea didn't invent Jesus' divinity!

In fact, if anything, *Nicea is a step backwards.*[116]

As Richard Bauckham explains in *Jesus and the God of Israel*, as early as we can trace, the earliest Christians maintained that Jesus shares the attributes unique to the divine identity: creation, sovereign rule, eschatological lordship and exaltation, and eternality. At Nicea, when the very clear Jewish understanding is translated into the concepts of Greek philosophy, categories of nature and essence, this is diluted by separating out what he does and who he is; which in turn, opens the door to understandings that actually diminish the full divine identity Jesus has in the New Testament. Nicea actually dilutes and diminishes what those first Christians, including those who knew Jesus personally, were saying about him soon after his death. Their belief in Jesus' divinity was as high and exalted as it could be, right from the beginning.[117]

Avery Dulles brings us back to the obvious conclusion:

> The fervent conviction of the primitive Church, so bravely and powerfully heralded, stands out as a true miracle. Whence would the apostles have drawn their faith in Jesus' divinity if not from a revelation? How else can one explain that a group of pious Jews became so suddenly, so unanimously, and so unshakably convinced of a doctrine which to Jewish ears could only sound like blasphemy? It would be quite impossible to conceive that they would have exalted a mere man, one that many of them had known in the flesh, to divine honors.

Dulles then quotes P.L. Couchoud:

> [the Jews] adored Yahweh, the one God, the transcendent and ineffable God, whose image they did not portray, whose name they did not pronounce, who was separated from every human creature by abyss upon abyss...The Jews honored the emperor but they let themselves be cut to pieces rather than profess even in a whisper that the emperor was a God; and they would also have let themselves be cut to pieces if they had been obliged to say the same thing of Moses himself.[118]

And yet, this, and so much more, is precisely what that first band of Jewish disciples was saying about Jesus. Only the earth-shattering events of an empty tomb and transphysical appearances could cause such a complete, radical, and rapid upheaval in their worldview.

The quantum leap they make can only be explained one way: the resurrection.

## 4. The End Is Here! A Bad Case of Apocalyptic Fever

Imagine you are those first disciples. You've been taught to believe in the general resurrection of the dead at the end of the age. But now you're convinced someone has actually been resurrected. What's the natural conclusion?

The "age to come" has arrived. *The end is here!*

You'd be freaking out.

And that's exactly what happened. *They freaked out.*

They think the apocalypse is going to happen at any moment.

The fervent prayer of those first Christians was "Maranatha," "Our Lord, come." (I Corinthians 16:22) It reflects their belief that Jesus' return was imminent, right on the horizon.

One of the earliest crises in the church takes place in Thessalonica. A number of believers were distraught because their loved ones had died. Mistakenly, they thought their loved ones couldn't be saved now because they wouldn't be alive to meet Jesus when he returned. In other words, they were so convinced the end was upon them, *they believed none of them would die before Jesus came back.*

When Paul addresses this crisis, he assures them that when Jesus does come, their loved ones will rise from their graves and actually be saved first, even before they will. But he also cavalierly presumes that he and those he is writing to *will still be alive when all this happens.*

As a matter of fact, the Thessalonian Christians were so sure Jesus was about to come back at any moment that a number of them just stopped working—what sense does it make to work if the world is about to end? (I Thessalonians 4:11, II Thessalonians 3:6-13)

Writing to the Corinthians, Paul counsels those who are unmarried to follow his example and remain single. (I Corinthians

7:25-31) Paul wasn't opposed to marriage. In this same chapter, he commands those who are married to live their conjugal life to the full. However, since he thinks the earth as we know it is about to pass away, getting married doesn't make any sense: there's no point starting a family if the world's about to end.

Many people wonder why it took two generations before the bulk of the New Testament was written down. The reason? Why write for subsequent generations *when there won't be any*. It was only as the apostles began to die off and the church realized the end wasn't as imminent as they thought it was that they began to put the oral tradition into writing.

In fact, the greatest crisis in the early church was sparked by the apparent *delay* of Jesus' return. People were so sure it would happen at any moment, certainly within the first generation of disciples, that when the apostles started dying off it caused a major crisis of faith.

Rarely, if ever, in the annals of history has there been such a bad case of *apocalyptic fever*. Other Jewish movements at the time looked forward to God's imminent intervention. Many were eagerly hoping for the Messiah to come, or for God to act decisively to liberate Israel from Roman rule. The Essenes are the closest example. But even they existed for generations without any real crisis over the delay of their expectation.

No other group came close to the *intensity* and *focus* found in the early church. Each had a relatively loose expectation about exactly when and how this intervention of God would take place. They weren't *consumed* with it the way the early Christians were. Moreover, they expected *Yahweh* to intervene somehow; they didn't expect a human being—Jesus—to return, as the church so clearly did. And, the general resurrection only figured into *some* of these expectations, but even when it did, *it wasn't a prominent feature*. In stark contrast, the early Christians believed the general resurrection was actually dawning upon them, so much so that it didn't make sense to work, or marry and have children, or put anything down in writing.

It's as if the early church thought the "age to come" *had come*.
Actually, it's not as if. They truly did.

That's why, without any of the necessary signs Jews expected to signal its arrival, the early church spoke and acted as if the "age to come" was already here. Even though the pagans ruled the world, injustice and oppression were rampant, and people still died, they steadfastly maintained the "age to come" was upon us. Time wasn't just marching along. The world wasn't just blindly continuing on its tragic trajectory. It had all been transformed. The final consummation had begun. Everything had changed, even though nothing apparently had.

Talking about the writer of the Christian Apocalypse, the Book of Revelation, revered Yale scripture scholar Brevard Childs says this: "The whole apocalyptic scenario which he inherited has now been reinterpreted as completed action. It does not lie in the future, but in every apocalyptic cycle described, God now rules his universe and the kingdom has come."[119]

Unlike every other Jewish end-time scenario, unlike every end-time scenario period—which all look forward to some decisive, divine intervention, some cosmic, reality-altering event, an event which has yet to occur—the early Christians believed that the decisive divine intervention, the cosmic, reality-altering event, had already happened.

*That the apocalypse had already begun.*

In a world filled with so much pain and suffering, who would be so foolish, so deluded, so callous to claim the "age to come," the age of God's perfect peace and justice, had already arrived? More to the point, how could anyone possibly maintain this fiction in the face of all the overwhelming evidence to the contrary?

Although easily overlooked, this is one of the most remarkable features of early Christianity. Within the Jewish worldview, the claim the church was making about what age we are in is only possible, only intelligible, if the early Christians had *experienced an apocalyptic event, an actual resurrection*—if they had encountered Jesus come back from the dead bodily. In that period, nothing other than Jesus' resurrection, his *physical* appearance, could trigger such an intense degree of apocalyptic fever combined with such a specific focus on the imminence of the general resurrection.

But what's even more remarkable is that when this apocalyptic fever wanes, when Jesus doesn't return in the disciples' lifetime, *the church doesn't fall apart.*

Instead, it grows. And *it grows explosively.*

About fifteen years ago, my wife Cherie and I were driving down to Washington, D.C. for vacation. Around 11:30 p.m., we were channel surfing and came across a radio evangelist who was fanatically proclaiming that the world was going to end that very night. According to his calculations, the end would come at midnight. He and his radio flock were huddled together waiting for Jesus to arrive.

As we listened, a thunderstorm erupted. I don't know if thunderstorms in Maryland are always so much more spectacular than they are in Connecticut, but this was the most violent thunderstorm I've ever seen. Blinding lightning and peals of thunder so loud they shook the car. Even though we were admiring the beauty of the storm and laughing at this evangelist, I started to get a little scared.

Maybe he was right. Maybe this was it. The end. Jesus' second coming.

Then I thought, am I ready for this? Am I ready for the final judgment? I have so much more life to live, so much more to experience. And besides, did he have to come back right at the beginning of our trip and *ruin our vacation?*

Well, as you can plainly see, that July midnight came and went and the world didn't come to an end. A little after midnight, the radio evangelist conceded to his audience that his calculations may have been off by a few weeks. He even proposed a new date for "the end" a few months later. Of course, that date came and went too. I wonder how many of his little cult stuck around to see if he was right.

Jim Jones. David Koresh and the Branch Davidians. Heaven's Gate.

Many groups have had similar expectations about an end-time scenario. They fervently believe in some kind of cosmic event ushering in the end of the world as we know it. However, when their expectation goes unfulfilled, these groups inevitably lose momentum. Most of them fall apart and disappear. Those that remain have to find a way to rationalize their mistaken belief, but even then, they usually don't last over time.

The fact that the second coming didn't happen in the disciples' lifetime just as they expected is often used as a reason to argue that Christianity is a fraud. Proof that Christianity, like many a cult, is built on an end-time scheme that its founder was mistaken about. Indeed, Jesus himself most likely *did* mistakenly believe and teach his disciples he would return in judgment during their lifetime. And this is why it is so astounding that early Christianity didn't fall apart as a result of this expectation going completely unfulfilled.

*It should have shattered the early church.*

But it didn't. Despite the crisis it caused, the church thrived.

That's because its faith wasn't based on this expectation. It was based on something that had already happened; something they believed, no matter what, was sure and certain; something nothing could shake, even something as fundamental and upsetting as the delay of Jesus' return.

Only a cosmic event like someone rising from the dead could trigger such an intensely-focused apocalyptic fever. Only the resurrection could convince the early church they were already living in the "age to come" despite all the staggering evidence to the contrary. And only the resurrection could keep the infant church from imploding, as end-time cults inevitably do, when this expectation went unfulfilled.

That the church not only endured, but actually thrived through this crisis, is due to the fact that it is based on a historical event, not an eschatological hope. If there was no resurrection under-girding Christian faith, it wouldn't have survived the first generation.

As Raymond Brown summarizes it:

> Christianity is a religion of hope, and what God has yet to do in and through Jesus remains an important component of its theological outlook. Nevertheless, the substance of the Christian proclamation to the world is what God *has done* in Jesus. If the gospel or

good news is put on the scales, that aspect outweighs insistence on what God *will do.* "Who, in faith's eye, Jesus already is" outweighs in the balance "Who, in hope's anticipation, Jesus will be."[120]

For Jews, as well as virtually the rest of humanity through time, God's decisive intervention into history is an event on the future horizon. But the Christian community was claiming it had *already occurred.* In Jesus' resurrection, God's climactic intervention had shifted from future apocalypse to past historical event.

And this can only be explained by an empty tomb combined with actual bodily appearances of Jesus.

## 5. The Chutzpah It Takes to Change the Sabbath

If you're a Catholic who experienced Vatican II or know someone who did, you might understand how disruptive and disturbing change can be. When the Church relaxed its requirement of not eating meat on Fridays, it put many a pre-Vatican II Catholic into a tailspin. It created a real crisis of faith.

See, for them the issue wasn't proper cuisine. It was about worldview, what ultimately matters. If what the Church had taught for so long was changeable, what else was up for grabs? Does this mean that God changes? And if God changes, then what can you depend on?

But not only was abstaining from meat on Fridays profoundly connected to their understanding of God, it also provided a sense of identity. It distinguished you as a Catholic and all that means in terms of belief and behavior. It was a social marker revealing what community you belong to, what makes you unique, who you are. For many Catholics of this era, not eating meat on Fridays was so viscerally connected to what matters most that they just couldn't do it. They continued abstaining.

The central institutions of Judaism—Torah, Temple, Monarchy, the Sacred Calendar which includes the Sabbath, Passover, Yom Kippur, etc.—were vital to its worldview, social structure, daily life and, most of all, identity. These were the "markers" which distinguished Jews from pagans. They went to the very heart of what it meant to be Jewish. And they were understood to be divinely ordained. In other words, unchangeable. They couldn't be tampered with by anyone but God.

Yet, how quickly these immovable institutions are transformed in the early church, even to the point of becoming unrecognizable! Within a few years after Jesus' death, this small band of Jews, who believe themselves to be completely faithful to the God of Israel, make drastic changes to these institutions.

Changes that overturn all they hold dear.

Changes that undermine their entire sense of identity.

Changes that upset everything that gives them security and meaning.

*Changes they believe only God can make.*

The most striking example is the Sabbath. Not only do they move it from Saturday to Sunday—the first day of the week in their calendar—they also regularly perform what is an abomination according to Jewish law: they eat the flesh and drink the blood of Jesus, a profanation of indescribable horror. For Jews, the Sabbath was exponentially more significant, sacred, and unchangeable than not eating meet on Fridays was for Catholics.

So where did they get the chutzpah to do this?

According to them, it's because Jesus rose from the dead *on the first day of the week*, and he told them to do this very thing in memory of him.

Other changes were just as shocking: circumcision (*the* sign of the covenant, established by God all the way back with Abraham, the Father of faith) was replaced by baptism; the kosher food laws were basically set aside; the moral teachings of Torah, God's unchanging law, were radically modified (for example, "an eye for an eye" becomes "turn the other cheek"); and the entire understanding of messiah was transformed to include heretical notions, especially the idea that suffering is integral to who the messiah is and what he accomplishes.

Again, where did they get the chutzpah to do all this?

*These changes arrogantly presumed to modify what only God could.*

*And they upset everything that gave them security, their entire sense of identity.*

What would permit, let alone motivate, them to so radically reshape their God-ordained worldview in these ways? To discard their most sacred institutions; to discard what mattered most to them?

The reason they cite, the resurrection (on the first day of the week), also happens to be only thing that could provide the chutzpah for such a total upheaval of what they held to be most sacred.


## 6. How Dare They? The Absolute Uniqueness of This Claim

The ancient Egyptians and Greeks had robust beliefs about dying and rising gods, such as the goddess Isis. But nobody ever actually thought these gods had come back from the dead. They understood it as it was: pure mythology.

As Wright makes clear: "Nor was it the case, as some writers are fond of saying, that the idea of 'resurrection' was found in religions all over the ancient Near East. Dying and rising 'gods,' yes—corn kings, fertility deities, and the like. But—even supposing Jesus' very Jewish followers knew any traditions like those pagan ones—nobody in those religions ever supposes it actually happened to individual humans."[121]

But with Jesus, this is distinctly different. Even though there are many people we would like to see return from the dead, *there is only one person in history about whom the claim is ever seriously made.* As the world-renowned Catholic theologian Karl Rahner once wrote:

> This uniqueness exists although there are enough
> people, including the murdered "prophets," whom we
> would like to experience as alive. Does not the reason

for this uniqueness lie in the fact that the reason itself is unique and simple and thus "true," and hence that it is not that accidental combination of disparate experiences and reflections which represents the cause of errors? Anyone who denies the resurrection of Jesus...would have to ask himself this question— that is, he would have to answer the question why the error he is asserting does not occur more frequently, even though the causes it presupposes are continually present.[122]

Why *isn't* the claim made more often?

The only instance where it is seriously entertained, where it has enough credence that people would even bother to argue about it, is in the case of Jesus. If in other cases the claim could be credibly made, it would.

But it can't.

No sane person seriously believes any other human being has come back from the dead. Even though there are plenty of candidates we'd like to see return—JFK, MLK, Elvis, to name a few—there is no credible evidence they have. Despite the strong urge to see them alive, no one would ever dare risk his or her life for such a claim or structure his or her worldview around such a belief.

The evidence generated by the empty tomb and appearances is absolutely unique in the annals of history. Only in the case of Jesus is there *enough evidence to allow the claim to go forward*. And this uniqueness suggests that the evidence might just be compelling enough for it to be true.

# 7. Thou Protesteth Too Much: The Curious Relief Afforded by the Alternative Explanations

During the presidential campaign of 2016, the media pressed Donald Trump to respond to legitimate questions about his taxes.

Instead of giving a direct answer, he talked around the question, indignantly and incoherently railing against the media and the "establishment," who, he claimed, were out to get him. This left the lingering suspicion that he didn't have a good answer.

He protested too much.

When people protest too much, it's usually a good indication they don't have a leg to stand on.

When you look at all the other ways people try to explain the resurrection and the mental gymnastics they have to perform to make their case, you see just how solid the evidence for it actually is: the resurrection is *by far* the simplest and most rational explanation of the evidence. The alternative explanations for the resurrection are so vacuous, far-fetched, convoluted, and/or just plain desperate, they leave the strong suspicion that *they are protesting way too much*.

To demonstrate, I'll showcase the most popular and forceful of these alternate explanations:

--*Jesus was never actually crucified*. There are several variations to this theory. One asserts that Jesus escaped at the last minute and Simon of Cyrene was mistakenly crucified in his place. This argument first surfaces in the second century. According to Irenaeus, the Gnostic Basilides argued that Jesus did not suffer but, "Rather a certain Simon of Cyrene was compelled to bear his cross for him... and through ignorance and error it was he who was crucified." This reflected his own Gnostic belief that Jesus couldn't suffer because he was pure spirit.

By and large, this is also how Islam comes to explain the resurrection. In Surah 4.156-7 the Quran criticizes Jews for saying "'we killed the Messiah, Jesus son of Mary, the messenger of Allah' when they did not kill or crucify him; but he/it was counterfeited before their eyes...and certainly they did not kill him."

There are still others who claim that Judas pulled off a grand deception by pointing out the wrong man, thereby duping the Romans to mistakenly crucify him instead.[123]

Of course, all of these theories fly in the face of what is clearly the most accepted historical fact about Jesus, that he was crucified at the hands of the Romans. In fact, if Roman soldiers made such a mistake, they could be put to death themselves—certainly a powerful motive to make sure they crucified the right person! And, these theories utterly fail to explain all the other aspects of Jesus' resurrection, especially the transphysical nature of his appearances.

--*Jesus didn't actually die*. While Jesus was indeed crucified, he only appeared dead. Raymond Brown cites one of the most clever of these theories:

> Thiering (*Qumran* 217-19) maintains that the high priest Jonathan kindly offered Jesus wine mixed with poison so that he would not suffer further. After tasting it, he lost consciousness and appeared to die. Simon Magus (a doctor) who had been crucified with Jesus and whose legs had been broken was put in the cave tomb with him (along with Judas). She assures us: "Within the tomb, Simon Magus worked quickly, despite his broken legs. He squeezed the juice from the aloes and poured it with myrrh down the throat of Jesus. The poison that was not yet absorbed was expelled, and by 3 A.M. it was known that he would survive."

While not quite as ingenious as this, others maintain Jesus fell into some kind of coma that fooled everyone into thinking he was actually dead.[124]

There are so many problems with this kind of explanation that very few scholars pursue this tack anymore. Wright notes that even those adamantly opposed to the resurrection have given up on this argument. Roman soldiers were experts at execution, and not just for the fun of it. As noted above, if they didn't do the job right, they could be put to death![125]

Besides, even if Jesus was somehow revived in this way, who would believe he had been resurrected? He would still look like every other human being walking the face of the earth. In fact, he'd be far more frail and vulnerable. His body would be badly bruised and beaten. Who'd seriously believe that a man hobbling around Jerusalem with gaping wounds in his hands, feet, and side had conquered death? And at some point, he would die (again).

Most now recognize how ludicrous this whole line of argument is.

--*Jesus' body was left to rot on the cross.* John Dominic Crossan is one of the most prominent and popular scripture scholars today. (He is frequently featured in biblical documentaries). Perhaps the strongest argument against the resurrection offered to date is his theory that Jesus' body, like the majority of those crucified by the Romans on Golgotha and elsewhere, was left to rot on the cross until the next crucifixion or was buried in a shallow grave (barely covered by dirt) where the wild dogs and other animals would eventually eat whatever remained of the flesh. This would make it impossible to identify his skeletal remains. Subsequently, driven by grief and guilt, Peter and the others had powerful visions where they truly believed Jesus was appearing to them. If no one could point out Jesus' body, or the bones that remained, it would be impossible to deny the empty tomb stories, which, Crossan argues, emerged much later when people both in and outside the church were no longer familiar with the details. Hence, in all sincerity, the "myth" of the resurrection was born.

As we saw above, the evidence that the empty tomb stories are very early and that Jesus' body was buried in a tomb that was well known is substantial and practically irrefutable. Crossan, however, thinks any evidence derived from the gospels is unreliable and points, instead, to a hypothetical "Cross Gospel," which he claims preserves earlier material. Much of his theory is built on this hypothetical construct.

But, scholar Charles Quarles responds: "Even without reliable Gospel testimony, Jewish legislation regarding the treatment of corpses, and evidence of Jewish burial practices from archeology, Josephus and Philo create difficulties for the theory that Jesus was left unburied."[126] Writing sometime in the last third of the first century, the Jewish historian Josephus records what was the prevailing practice of the time: "They [the Idumeans] actually went so far in their impiety as to cast out the corpses without burial, although the Jews are so careful about funeral rites that even malefactors who have been sentenced to crucifixion are taken down and buried before sunset.[127]

This evidence, derived independently from the gospels, makes Crossan's theory untenable. In fact, as the long track record of unrest in first-century Palestine attests, leaving bodies unburied, especially around feast days like Passover, especially in the holy city of Jerusalem, would undoubtedly spark riots. The Romans couldn't have cared less about Jewish sensibilities. But they did make all kinds of provisions to prevent unrest, often conceding to Jewish religious practices in order to keep the peace, which included allowing for the immediate burial of crucified corpses. And as we saw above (Chapter 1.10), even when buried in a common grave, the remains could still be identified for second burial.

However, there is a much more basic problem with the view that Jesus went unburied. It fails to explain the nature of the appearances. Had this been the practice, the disciples would have been fully aware that Jesus' body had been left to rot away or been eaten by wild animals. Yet they portray him risen in bodily form. Wright explains that had not Jesus' body been buried—had his body been left to decompose—no one seeing visions of him would or could have concluded he was resurrected.[128] Instead, they only would have concluded Jesus was alive in a non-bodily, spiritual sense.

Most problematicly, Crossan bases his theory on the very speculative reconstruction of a hypothetical source for the second-century Gospel of Peter. If his source is unreliable, as the majority of scholars agree it is, then his whole theory falls apart. Even though it is the *best contemporary explanation* of the empty tomb, it turns out to be a *desperate reach*. This is why, as William Lane Craig points out, the vast majority of scholars do not follow Crossan in this: "Here I simply register my agreement that attempts to explain the empty tomb and postmortem appearances apart from the resurrection of Jesus are hopeless. This is precisely why skeptics like Crossan have to row against the current of scholarship in denying facts like the burial and empty tomb."[129]

*--Jesus body was mistakenly placed in a different tomb.* Since the evidence that Jesus' body was buried is so strong, others propose that it was accidentally placed in the wrong tomb; or that the disciples went to the wrong tomb; or that the body was somehow innocently moved for some unknown reason, and this accounts for the belief that the tomb was empty.

However, had the body simply been misplaced somehow, this alone can't account for the kind of resurrection faith that emerged among those first disciples with all its radical modifications. Again, how do you explain the transphysical appearances?

And in any case, if the body was moved or misplaced—an extremely remote possibility—it would not go undiscovered for long. People were careful about who was in their family tomb (recall the practice of second burial, which meant they would be in and out of their tombs with regularity) and certainly would not want the *cursed* corpse of a rebel blasphemer to contaminate the remains of their loved ones.

Besides, given the widespread antagonism toward the early church, once the rumor of Jesus' resurrection began to take hold, it is highly likely that those who knew where his body was would quickly want to debunk the myth. Since we know that the latest the disciples likely "went public" with the resurrection was at Pentecost fifty days after the discovery of the empty tomb (see Chapter 1.7 above), their claim about the tomb would be common knowledge among the populace of Jerusalem, which would most likely include anyone who might have moved the body.

In fact, rarely do scholars argue anymore that there was some kind of mistake regarding the tomb. With his extensive knowledge of first-century Palestine, Wright believes that any misunderstanding would have been quickly sorted out. Moreover, he observes that the disciples' frame of mind would not have disposed them to jump to the conclusion Jesus was raised, since no one was expecting anything remotely like that. Instead, they would be the first to believe there was some kind of mistake or malice (in the case of grave robbery) and, out of respect for their dead friend, been the first and most zealous in trying to locate his body in order to give it a proper burial.[130]

Moreover, there is good reason not only to think that the tomb was well known, but also that there was intense public interest in it during the immediate aftermath of Jesus' death. Philosopher Stephen Davis observes: "...the story of Joseph of Arimathea's involvement in the burial of Jesus seems so strongly supported and inherently trustworthy that it renders the argument for an unknown tomb quite implausible...And if Luke is correct (why doubt him?), the apostles' preaching *did* create a public stir almost immediately, and the authorities became involved immediately as well."[131] If all this is true, there is little chance the body could have been inadvertently moved without it quickly being located.

However, because I think this is the only alternative explanation that has any remote possibility of being true (it is the one I have wrestled with most), I will return to it twice (below and Chapter 3.9) in order to rule it out more decisively.

*--The appearances of Jesus are the result of some kind of psychological phenomena.* Other explanations bypass the question of the empty tomb and center on the appearances as some kind of psychologically-induced vision of the first disciples: mass hallucination, autosuggestion, or cognitive dissonance.

You've probably seen news reports like the one of large crowds flocking to see an image of the Blessed Virgin Mary in a tree, or, my personal favorite, the face of Jesus in a cheeseburger!

People are gullible.

And they often, sincerely, misinterpret the phenomena they encounter.

Mass UFO sightings often turn out to be some naturally-occurring astronomical event like a shooting star; or some human activity such as an airplane making an unusual maneuver; or a military exercise no one was alerted to. And we know that there are numerous documented cases of cognitive dissonance, hallucination, and autosuggestion where people prove to be stunningly out of touch with reality.

In fact, one of the strongest arguments mounted to explain the appearances has been the well-documented psychological phenomenon known as "cognitive dissonance": a fantasy produced by one's deepest longings that is completely divorced from reality. It often occurs in the wake of some traumatic event. In the disciples' case, so the argument goes, they were so overcome with grief that they were unable to accept the tragic reality of Jesus' death. As a result, they created the fantasy that he was still alive, appearing to them from the dead.

They so desperately wanted it to be true, their brain convinced them it was.

N.T Wright has examined the most popular and compelling parallels of this phenomenon used by scholars to explain the resurrection appearances. What he's discovered is an astounding *lack of parallel.*

The most revealing example is a 1950's flying saucer cult from the Midwest. One woman convinced a small group of "believers" she was receiving messages from outer space saying a massive flood was about to engulf America. At the appointed time, only these true believers would be rescued, by a flying saucer. When that date came and went, the "faithful" came up with an alternative explanation: God spared America because of the faith of this group.

Despite the obvious failure of their vision to prove true, they continued in their activities, trying to attract more and more members. They so desperately wanted it to be true that they believed the fantasy despite the obvious reality. Because they received quite a bit of publicity, a group of sociologists quickly launched an experiment to study the psychology driving this cult. These observations were then used to illustrate how the disciples could sincerely believe the fantasy of Jesus appearing to them from the dead.

The problems associated with using this parallel are manifold. The flying saucer group was significantly smaller than the number claiming to have seen Jesus—there were only about twelve "cultists." In fact, three of its members included the sociologists who infiltrated the group in order to study it. To conduct their "experiment"

112

successfully, they naturally had to act like they were enthusiastic adherents. But like the undercover government agents in the 1960's anti-war movement who inevitably agitated those groups toward more subversive activities, the sociologists were no doubt egging on their fellow cult members just by their mere presence in the group. Far from remaining detached observers, they contributed to the dynamic of the group.

Moreover, the cult fell apart only a month after the prediction of the flood failed to materialize. Everybody returned to their previous lives, never looking back. It didn't produce anything close to the conviction (even unto death), endurance and staying power of Christian belief in the resurrection.

The other "parallel" examples cited alongside this one, which are weaker illustrations of the same, only reinforce the point.[132]

There is also the problem of scale. Bearing in mind Paul's challenge to those who doubt to go interrogate the some five hundred or more witnesses, the number of people claiming to have seen Jesus makes such a large-scale delusion extremely improbable. And in the small number of cases where the masses have been "deluded," cases that bear little resemblance to the appearances of Jesus, the "fantasy" is inevitably exposed in due time. For example, when many Japanese refused to believe they lost WWII in the wake of government propaganda, the hard truth eventually came to light and the mass delusion ended.

The hundreds who witnessed Jesus could hardly have all suffered some form of cognitive dissonance. Moreover, at least in the cases of Paul and James, there were several eyewitnesses who had no desire for it to be true. All of these psychological projection theories strain (unsuccessfully) to explain this fact, especially how an enemy of the church, Paul, could have experienced such a delusion.

But what about mass hallucination?

According to psychologist Gary Collins, this is impossible: "Hallucinations are individual occurrences. By their very nature, only one person can see a given hallucination at a time. They certainly aren't something which can be seen by a group of people. Neither is it possible that one person could somehow induce a hallucination in somebody else. Since a hallucination exists only in the subjective, personal sense, it is obvious that others cannot witness it."[133]

A good example of this, recounted by resurrection specialist Michael Licona, is found among Navy SEALS during what is the most intense week of training they receive.

> About 80 percent of the guys hallucinate due to the lack of sleep. A lot of time they're out on a raft doing an exercise called "around the world," where they go out in the ocean, around a buoy, and they come back to shore. They're trying to be first because then they'll be rewarded with rest. It's at this time that many start seeing things.
>
> One seal told me he actually believed he saw an octopus come out of the water and wave at him. Another guy believed that a train was coming across the water toward the raft. He'd point to it and the others would say, "Are you crazy? There are no trains out here in the ocean." He believed it so strongly that before what he perceived as the train hit him, he rolled into the ocean and they had to retrieve him.
>
> A Seal told me about another guy who was waving his oars wildly in the air. When he was asked what he was doing, he said, "I'm trying to hit the dolphins that are jumping over the boat." I asked the Seal, "Did you see the dolphins?" He said, "No." I said, "Did anyone else see the dolphins?" He said, "No, they were busy having their own hallucinations!"
>
> You see, hallucinations aren't contagious.[134]

Clinical psychologist Gary Sibcy backs this up: "I have surveyed the professional literature…written by psychologists, psychiatrists and other relevant health care professionals over the last two decades and have yet to find a single documented case of group hallucination, that is, an event in which more than one person purportedly shared in a visual or other sensory perception where there was clearly no external referent."[135]

--*The disciples had a profound experience of grace and forgiveness.* In the wake of abandoning Jesus at the crucifixion and, especially in Peter's case, denying him, the guilt-riddled disciples, particularly Peter, are overwhelmed by an experience of his mercy. Somehow, in the deepest part of their psyche, they know all is forgiven.

This powerful experience generates "sightings" of the "risen" Jesus.

Besides pressing the question about what other than actual appearances themselves could have possibly *generated* such an experience of grace (Jesus' real appearance to them, assuring them he has indeed forgiven them, is by far the best explanation for this experience), this argument suffers the same fatal flaw that all the psychological explanations suffer: the Jesus who appears is not the figure they would in any way expect or imagine. *He is far too outlandish to be the fulfillment of their deepest longings.* (In this case, for forgiveness.) That's why they are initially *terrified* at the sight of him. Their fear and doubt make absolutely no sense if the vision was fabricated by their minds to provide *comfort.*[136]

Even as strong a skeptic as Crossan admits that visions can only contain concepts that reflect what is already known and expected.[137] They aren't innovative in any significant way, certainly not as innovative as transphysicality was for the disciples.

An overwhelming experience of grace alone can't generate this kind of innovation.

Furthermore, who says Peter and the rest had to feel guilt and shame? It would be just as likely that they would be angry at Jesus for deceiving them (as a false messiah), or disappointed in God for letting them down. Grief usually produces a confusing mixture of emotion, and guilt, even under these circumstances, is not necessarily the only or strongest response.

Ultimately, as William Lane Craig points out, any psychologically-induced visionary experience along the lines of cognitive dissonance, hallucination, or a profound experience of grace can't account for the fact that the disciples consistently describe *external, earthbound sightings of Jesus in bodily form.*

Suppose for a moment the disciples were unaware that Jesus' body had been moved and found the tomb he was buried in empty. Then, as a result of some kind of psychological process, they imagined they "saw" him somehow alive. In this event, they would have concluded that Jesus had been "translated" or "taken up" directly to heaven in the way Enoch (Gen 5:24, Heb 11:5) and Elijah (2 Kings 2:11-12) had been in the Old Testament. Stories like these are also found in Jewish writings outside the Bible; for example, Testament of Job 40, where the bodies of two children killed in the collapse of a house are not found, but later the children are seen glorified in heaven. However, as in these other cases, if the disciples had such an experience, they never would have concluded that Jesus had been *resurrected* from the dead.

For first-century Jews, a translation and a resurrection are categorically different. In their mind-set, translation—or "assumption" as it's sometimes called—is the direct transfer of a person, body and all, into heaven. As we've seen, resurrection, in contrast, is a return from the dead to physical, embodied life, and only possible in the "age to come" for all people at once.

So even with an empty tomb, the most hallucinatory visions of Jesus would produce is the belief that he had been translated or assumed into heaven. As Craig concludes: "Even if it were possible, therefore, that the disciples under the influence of the empty tomb projected hallucinatory visions of Jesus, they would never have projected Him as literally risen from the dead. They would have had a vision of Jesus in glory in Abraham's bosom. That is where, in Jewish belief, the souls of the righteous go to await the final resurrection. If the disciples were to have visions, then they would have seen Jesus there in glory."[138] (See the parable of Lazarus and the Rich Man in Luke 16:19-31 for a good example that reflects this belief: from his place of torment, the rich man sees Lazarus resting in the bosom of Abraham.)

This is a crucial point. Vivid heavenly visions (of Jesus) would have fit firmly within their conceptual framework. The Old Testament contains a number of them: Daniel, Isaiah, and Ezekiel, just to name few. A vision of Jesus would mean he had been vindicated by God. But it wouldn't mean he was resurrected. *Minus a physical body, that was absolutely impossible.*

No matter how real it seemed to them, if the disciples had some kind of vision of Jesus that was the result of their imaginative processes, it would have led them to talk about his *exaltation*, not his *bodily resurrection.*

However, they *unanimously* report a resurrection, a physical, bodily appearance. Recall that, as the many different witnesses to the resurrection began sharing their personal encounters of the risen Jesus with the world, the appearance stories likely circulated independently before they were put into a complete narrative. (see Chapter 2:1) This makes their unanimity on the physicality of Jesus' appearance all the more impressive. Were they all having merely visionary experiences, we would expect some trace of that in at least some of their stories; some trace of nonphysical appearances. But we do not.[139]

Moreover, the disciples were certainly sophisticated enough to know the difference between a vision and what they claimed to be appearances of Jesus. They wouldn't have confused the two. Craig again:

> Paul (and indeed all of the New Testament) makes a sharp distinction between an appearance of Jesus and a vision of Jesus. The appearances of Jesus were confined to a brief period at the beginning of the Christian Way; they soon ceased and were never repeated. Visions, however, continued and were repeated. Paul himself had visions (2 Corinthians

12:1-7), but what he saw on the Damascus road was no mere vision. That is very interesting, for it shows the appearances seen by the disciples were essentially different from visions, with which they were familiar.

Visions, even ones caused by God, were exclusively in the mind of the beholder, whereas an appearance involved the actual appearance of something "out there" in the real world.[140]

Since resurrection belonged to the end-time, the "age to come," when it would happen all at once to everyone, without indisputable evidence of a *real, tangible, external, physical body*—no matter how transformed—an empty tomb with visions alone would never be enough to generate the faith that an individual had been resurrected ahead of that event.

Once again, the real flaw in this type of "psychological" explanation is that, as Wright notes: "...whatever it was that the early Christians were expecting, wanting, hoping and praying for, this was *not* what they said, after Easter, had happened."[141] If the resurrection appearances were merely the product of mass hallucination, autosuggestion, cognitive dissonance or any other internal, subjective psychological experience, we would find a much different portrait of the risen Jesus, one much more in line with the expectations they held.

Certainly not an *embodied* Jesus.

How do hundreds, through some kind of internal operation of their mind, some vision, each *individually* imagine something so *completely foreign to their worldview* and do it with such *unrelenting consistency*? How does each *project in his or her own head* the *same* previously *inconceivable* yet vividly *uniform* reality?

That something so unimaginable could be reported so vividly and so uniformly by so many defies psychological explanation. The only explanation is that they are *collectively* seeing the same *objective* reality.

--*The resurrection was taken from pagan myths about dying and rising gods.* Many have pointed to the myths of dying and rising gods (e.g., Osiris, Isis, Adonis, Attis, Dionysius, Demeter and Persephone) as the source of Christian belief. Under the influence of such myths, resurrection faith was born. In other words, there was no unique encounter with the "risen Lord." Rather, the idea came to the disciples from the mythology saturating the surrounding cultures.

The resurrection isn't an innovation; it's a plagiarization!

Aside from the many other problems involved with these supposed parallels (see endnote 1 below), no one ever thought the god in question *actually* died and rose. They were simply tales. And these tales clearly didn't influence the Jewish view, which never thought in terms of Yahweh Himself dying and rising, and which remained entirely focused on the general resurrection, never imagining that an individual could rise outside of this end-time event.[142]

Moreover, there's a fundamental problem in using these kinds of parallels. Michael Licona proposes a poignant illustration that exposes the flaw:

> early one morning a plane took off from Massachusetts and after 9:00 a.m. flew into the seventy-eighth and seventy-ninth floors of one of the tallest skyscrapers in the world in New York City. The crash killed everyone on board. Of course, the event that comes to mind occurred on September 11, 2001, when a Boeing 767 flew into the South Tower of the World Trade Center. However, a similar event occurred on July 28, 1945, when a B-25 crashed into the Empire State Building. The similar details are stunning. However, there is no causal connection between the two events. They are completely unrelated.[143]

The parallels between the myths of dying and rising gods and Jesus' resurrection aren't nearly this striking. But even if they were, that doesn't necessarily entail a causal connection. Finding similarities isn't the same as showing that one influenced the other. And there is absolutely no evidence that these pagan myths had any influence on the stories of Jesus' resurrection.

*--The resurrection as recorded in the gospels is a late legend that was built up over many years.* Because naturalistic attempts at explaining the details of the resurrection as they stand in the gospels all inevitably fall short, the most common, contemporary scholarly rebuttal is the "legend" theory. Instead of trying to explain the empty tomb and appearances, these scholars argue that the gospels are legendary—most of the details they contain aren't historical, but made up; or at least embellished to the point of significant distortion. Thus, there was no empty tomb, and any appearances, if they happened, were merely hallucinations and/or experiences of Jesus' on-going presence among the community of faith.

It was only after many years, in the second and third Christian generations, that, under the influence of Greco-Roman notions of "divine men", belief in Jesus' divinity began to emerge. The resurrection narratives, replete with stories of an empty tomb and embodied appearances of Jesus, were *invented to under-gird this belief.* Because these stories are first told so many years after Jesus' death, no one can go back and challenge the claim of an empty tomb or question what the original disciples actually saw.

While this theory contains a number of flaws—most of which are addressed above with the alternative explanations that happen to incorporate different aspects of it—two, in particular, make it completely untenable. First, the legend theory depends entirely on the idea, prevalent in twentieth-century scholarship, that Jesus' divinity is a later development of the Hellenistic church. However, as we saw (Chapter 3.3), Larry Hurtado has definitively demonstrated that Jesus was worshiped as divine *virtually right away,* certainly within the earliest Jewish community of disciples:

> this reshaping of Jewish monotheistic devotion began
> among Jewish Christians of the first few years after
> Jesus' execution and cannot be attributed to some

later stage of the Christian movement and to the influx of converts from a pagan background. In short, we are dealing with a redefinition of Jewish monotheistic devotion by a group that has to be seen as a movement within Jewish tradition of the early first century C.E.[144]

And for Jesus' Jewish followers to have worshiped him as God almost immediately after his death could only mean that they found his tomb empty and believed they had seen him raised bodily. In which case, the gospel narratives are much more history than legend, history that could have been challenged—if they were able to—by those who were in close proximity to it.

Second, as we also saw (Chapter 2.11), any remnant of physicality was abhorrent to Greco-Roman notions of immortality. In death, they desired complete liberation from this earthly body. So, if the stories of Jesus' resurrection were later legends, if their authors felt free to write these stories any way they preferred, we can be sure that all traces of the physical would be eliminated: none of the crudeness of an embodied appearance; no need for an empty tomb. If anything, the overpowering inclination would be to *spiritualize* these stories as much as possible. They certainly would never add physical elements to an experience that was purely spiritual in the first place.

But the gospel narratives are replete with the physical.

In his immortality, the risen Jesus is thoroughly embodied— glorified to be sure, but nevertheless completely tangible, enough so that he leaves behind an empty tomb. Because the later gospel writers would feel enormous pressure to eliminate all traces of the physical, these elements must be *early* and *intractable*. Jesus' physicality had to be so entrenched in the original tradition that it couldn't be eliminated, even by later Hellenistic authors. In other words, the gospel writers and/or their sources weren't freely composing stories from scratch. Instead, they were passing on and recording early historical tradition.

As long as belief in Jesus' divinity and notions of physicality in the stories belong to the earliest manifestations of Christian belief, the legend theory has no basis. It turns out to be pure legend!

*The Upshot of These Alternative Explanations: Curious Relief*

It is a telling fact that John Dominic Crossan, who, as we saw above, has offered the strongest recent alternative explanation for the resurrection, refuses to debate the historical details with the major contemporary proponent of the resurrection, N.T. Wright. As William Lane Craig laments: "In previous exchanges on Wright's book, which I have been privileged to attend, Crossan has declined to engage Wright's argument on the historical level, preferring instead to dialogue about the theology of resurrection. This lack of engagement should be challenged..."[145] Crossan dances around the historical question, leaving the strong suspicion that he doesn't have a good response.

Many know Pope John Paul II. But do you remember John Paul I? Probably not. He was only Pope for little over a month. Tragically, he died shortly after being elected. His untimely death was surreal. And as a consequence, without a shred of evidence, all kinds of speculation sprang up about some kind of conspiracy to kill him. Elaborate theories—from a mafia plot to an "inside job" engineered by the Vatican—were spun out to explain his death.

Yet all the evidence pointed to natural causes. It was by far the simplest explanation.

The same is true with the resurrection: it is, by far, the simplest explanation of the evidence.

In *The Resurrection of Jesus: A New Historiographical Approach*, Michael Licona presents what I would call the most hyper-critical defense of the resurrection. He only allows himself to use what he calls the "historical bedrock," facts that the vast majority of scholars from every perspective, believer and non-believer, agree upon. This limits the effect of any bias in the interpretation of the evidence and gets as reasonably close to the objective historical reality as possible.

In the process, he thoroughly examines the strongest recent alternative explanations for the resurrection (all touched on in some way above), coming away with this conclusion: if you eliminate philosophical bias (i.e., stake a position of neutrality regarding the existence of God, miracles, the supernatural and such), the historical bedrock makes the resurrection "very certain." While I think the "objective" evidence is even stronger than this, his examination of the best alternative explanations to date is illuminating. They each require *more faith, more speculative leaps of imagination*, than the resurrection.

As Frederick Bruner concludes: "When one hears out the major opponents of the church's great convictions, there is curious relief"[146]

Curious Relief: these best alternative explanations are so weak, fanciful, convoluted and desperate that it only becomes *more apparent* that the resurrection is the most credible explanation. It is, by far, the most simple, rational, and coherent way to explain the evidence.

## 8. Chronological Snobbery: It's Not Naïve to Believe

C.S. Lewis was a classical scholar who knew how ancient people thought. He says we suffer from "chronological snobbery." People in the past, he points out, were often every bit as sophisticated and skeptical as we are. We may wonder how people in the past could believe all they did. But in reality, especially when you factor in their lack of modern, scientific knowledge, they weren't as naïve as we think. They may not have known about molecular biology or astrophysics, but that doesn't mean they were more gullible than us in ordinary matters.

In fact, there is abundant evidence of this kind of skepticism among those who would eventually come to believe in the resurrection. They initially sought a more likely explanation for the empty tomb (the body had been stolen) and thought reports of Jesus' appearances were nonsense; especially because they came from women, who they cynically dismissed as too fickle and emotional to provide trustworthy testimony. Some even doubted their own eyes when they first "saw" Jesus. They were well aware of magic and sorcery; they knew of those who claimed to have seen spirits and ghosts, especially of deceased loved ones—and they weren't having any of that!

So, riddled with doubt, seeking a more believable explanation for the tomb, many even struggling to believe it was actually Jesus they were seeing when he did appear, the disciples fit much better into our modern skeptical framework than the image we have of them. They weren't as naïve, credulous, and gullible as we think.

And when it comes to modern believers, *the one thing that can't be said* is that faith in the resurrection is naïve.

In *The Son Rises,* William Lane Craig cites Jacob Kremer, a German scholar who specializes in the study of the resurrection, who claims that the *majority of modern critical biblical scholars* hold that the empty tomb is firm historical data. They agree on:

> the fact that Jesus' tomb was actually found empty on Sunday morning by a small group of His women followers. As a simple historical fact, that seems to be amply attested. As D.H. Van Daalen has pointed out, it is extremely difficult to object to the empty tomb on historical grounds; those who deny it do so on the basis of theological or philosophical assumptions (like the assumption that miracles are impossible). But assumptions may simply have to be changed in light of historical facts. [147]

Kremer lists twenty-eight prominent scholars who accept the biblical accounts' accuracy in this regard. Craig then adds at least sixteen more he can think of.[148] He goes on to cite prominent German Biblical scholar Rudolf Schnackenburg who also agrees that "most exegetes accept the historicity of the empty tomb, so that this question is not the decisive point in the discussion about the resurrection." So, the majority of modern scholars believe the empty tomb is sound historical data.

Gary Habermas has done an extensive study of a wide range of over two thousand scholars' views on the resurrection. This is his conclusion:

> How do current scholars line up? In my own survey of recent resurrection sources...less that one-quarter of critical scholars who addressed the historicity question offered naturalistic theories...The almost three-quarters of remaining scholars hold either of the two views that Jesus was raised from the dead in some sense...
>
> ...Among the supernatural positions, we have the further subdivisions of those who prefer more visionary views (less than one-quarter of these particular scholars) and those who take the position that Jesus was resurrected in a real, though still transformed, body (more than three-quarters).[149]

If you do the math, this means that three-quarters of the three-quarters of this extensive sampling of scholars, some nine-sixteenths, over half (that is, over a thousand) think the appearances were a real manifestation of a risen, albeit transformed, Jesus. (Roughly three-quarters think it was a *supernatural* event!) And these are *highly intelligent, critical scholars* who have *intimate familiarity* with all the evidence and arguments mounted, pro and con. These are the people who've studied it most thoroughly.[150]

If it seems too simplistic or naïve to believe that a dead man could rise, consider this: *some of the most intelligent and critically adept people on the planet believe it's true.* In addition to the thousand plus critical biblical scholars noted above the following are all believers:

--Francis Collins, head of the Human Genome Project, director of the National Institute of Health, and one of the world's leading scientists known for his cutting-edge study of DNA.

--Michael Guillen, a theoretical physicist, former science correspondent for ABC news, and host of The History Channel's *Where Did It Come From?*, who taught physics at Harvard and has won awards for his work on *Good Morning America, World News Tonight,* and *20/20.*

--M. Scott Peck, Harvard-educated psychiatrist and best-selling author of *The Road Less Traveled.*

--John Lennox, University of Oxford professor of mathematics who is also known for his debates with the New Atheists, including Richard Dawkins and Christopher Hitchens.

--Alister McGrath, professor of historical theology at Oxford University whose background includes studying chemistry at Oxford and research in molecular biophysics that resulted in the development of new methodologies for investigating biological membranes.

--Nicholas Wolterstorff, highly-respected Yale philosopher and professor of philosophical theology.

--Armand Nicholi, clinical psychiatrist and professor of psychiatry at Harvard Medical School.

--Anne Rice, famed *The Vampire Chronicles* author who came to belief through a rigorous analysis of the historical evidence. (Rice subsequently "quit [institutional] Christianity" because of issues with the Church—a temptation I can relate to—but she is adamant that she hasn't quit Christ, in large part because of the historical evidence she discovered.)

--G.K. Chesterton and J.R.R. Tolkien, world-renowned authors and intellectual heavyweights.

In addition, some of the top scripture scholars quoted in this book, scholars who have gained widespread respect among their colleagues as tops in their field, such as Raymond Brown, N.T. Wright, John Meier, and Joseph Fitzmyer, believe in the resurrection.

From my own experience I can add a number of world-class scholars I met while in divinity school at Yale who also believe in the resurrection. I distinctly recall several memorable conversations where a couple of them shared their deep conviction about it despite having reservations about other Biblical data.

None of the people I'm citing here are naïve. They are profoundly skeptical, sophisticated, and critical thinkers, fully immersed in a modern, scientific worldview. And yet, they believe. I could add many more to this list.

Let me be perfectly clear: in no way am I saying this is proof, per se, of the resurrection. All I'm saying is that *it's not naïve to believe.*

It's also true that many intellectually astute people don't buy the evidence. But you can't rule out faith in the resurrection, as is often done, as something only a gullible simpleton would believe in. There is enough substantial and credible evidence to make belief in the empty tomb and supernatural appearances of Jesus something a skeptical, critical, rational person can accept.

It is a striking and undeniable fact that many intellectual giants have believed in it, with many of them coming to faith precisely through a rigorous examination of the evidence.

# 9. Stating the Obvious: The Corroborating Effect of Tomb and Appearances

At the risk of repeating myself, allow me to point out something that is probably obvious by now: the empty tomb and transphysical appearances provide powerful corroboration for each other. The reason this is so important, and therefore bears repeating, is that it *virtually eliminates the possibility that the disciples were somehow mistaken in what they claim to have experienced.*

For example, even though the evidence for the empty tomb is almost irrefutable, there still is the remote possibility it could be explained as the result of some kind of innocent confusion; maybe the body was accidentally moved. The evidence for the appearances, however, renders this practically impossible.

If the disciples were mistaken about the tomb and as a result "imagined" they saw Jesus, *they would have depicted him far differently.* The unprecedented and absurdly paradoxical way they depict him, and, moreover, as an individual resurrected prior to the end-time, is *only explicable by actual appearances of a tangibly embodied—albeit transcendently transformed—Jesus.* They never could have imagined him this way unless he appeared *physically.* In other words, with the *same body that was laid in the tomb.*

Conversely, an empty tomb gives objective verification to the appearances. The fact that no one ever could find or produce Jesus' body corroborates the disciples' bizarre claim to have seen him appearing, against all expectation, *bodily.* It verifies in a publicly observable way that they saw an actual body; that it was no mere vision or illusion. In other words, the empty tomb provides *objective* evidence to substantiate the eyewitness testimony of *embodied* appearances, *ensuring that they weren't just undergoing some kind of psychologically delusional experience.*

And so, the corroborating effect of the empty tomb and transphysical appearances significantly reduces the chances that the disciples were somehow mistaken.

## 10. You Complete Me: What Are the Chances of That?

On its own, the empty tomb doesn't lead the disciples to believe Jesus has been resurrected. Prior to the appearances, the disciples simply presume the tomb is empty because someone stole or moved the body. In that moment, no one concludes the "age to come" is upon them. No one believes Jesus is God. No one radically redefines the Jewish understanding of resurrection. Without appearances, the empty tomb is just, and would have remained, a perplexing anomaly.[151]

Likewise, on their own, appearances wouldn't produce the belief that Jesus had been resurrected. No matter how real a vision of Jesus seemed, no matter how physical the body may have appeared, if his corpse still lay in the grave, everyone would be forced to accept the fact he was still dead and buried. Without an empty tomb, the appearances would also have to have been interpreted as some kind of fantastic anomaly.[152]

Resurrection faith would not have been possible with just an empty tomb or with just appearances. Both are necessary to form a complete and coherent picture of what is going on. Resurrection faith is *only born* when, in tandem, in a tight sequence of several days, the tomb of Jesus is discovered empty and his disciples believe he has appeared to them risen bodily from the dead.

And this fact points to an ***astonishing improbability***. Let me explain.

By themselves, each is an *extraordinary* event. One of a kind. Miraculous. A dead body simply vanishes from its only known location without any naturalistic explanation; a person appears from the dead with a real body that paradoxically exhibits transcendent qualities. *Independently*, something strange happens at the tomb and in the appearances that, in the annals of history, is absolutely unique. So unique, in fact, that, if they truly happened, each might rightly be called a "super miracle."

Yet each stands *on its own* completely separate from the other as a *well-attested* event. As we've seen, based purely on the strength of the historical evidence, each of these two *extraordinarily unlikely* events is *highly likely* to have happened.

And, they happen in *tandem*. These two separate, very well-attested, absolutely unique-in-the-annals-of-history events, *just happen to have happened in a tight sequence together.*

But they don't just happen together. They happen together in a way that is *absolutely necessary to get a complete picture* of the larger reality of which each is an irreducible part. *They complete each other.*

What are the odds?

The legend of Santa Claus is a childhood myth. But suppose one Christmas a substantial number of rational, sober-minded parents claimed to have found presents neither they nor anyone else had purchased marked out for each of their children under their tree. And suppose further that, following an independent review of each case, all reasonable doubt that these parents might have been mistaken could be eliminated (for example, their houses were examined for signs of forced entry, interviews were done to insure that no one else who had access to their houses had purchased the presents for their children instead, none of the presents could be traced back to a known store or toymaker, etc.). This would be a highly unlikely, but truly remarkable thing. It might even cause you to doubt your Santa skepticism.

Then suppose you heard that a group of astronomers claimed to have seen an unusual occurrence in the night sky that same Christmas Eve. They observed a red sleigh being pulled by a team of reindeer and piloted by a rotund old man sporting a white beard and red coat. And suppose that this incident was also vetted so that you could be reasonably sure it was no hoax or delusion (it turned out these are some of the best-respected scientists in their field, they each described what they saw in great detail and with perfect consistency, they hadn't been imbibing in any egg nog that evening, etc.). On the basis of their observation, you might begin to entertain the possibility Santa Claus is real.

But when you took both events together, two completely separate and highly improbable events, each enjoying substantial evidentiary support and happening in close sequence, the probability that Santa Claus exists would reach a near certainty. The two well-attested, tandem events would reinforce and corroborate each other. Not only would each make the other more credible (hearing about the astronomers' observation makes the first report of presents just appearing under the tree believable and vice versa), but taken together, they would make the reality they represent—the existence of Santa Claus—that much more certain.

I don't want to press this analogy too far because there are major differences between the resurrection and this imagined "Santa sighting." However, it does begin to illustrate something that seems to have been missed in all the arguments for the resurrection.

In the empty tomb and appearances, we have two incredibly unlikely events, each happening independent of the other. They are totally separate and distinct occurrences arising out of their own unique set of circumstances. In other words, belief in the resurrection of Jesus is not based upon a singular event or experience, which could be the result of a mistake or misinterpretation, but upon *two categorically different* events.

And independently, each can be shown to have the highest historical probability of being true. Each stands on its own as a very well-attested event. Even though they end up corroborating each other, *the argument for one being true depends in no way on the argument for or existence of the other*—that's why the evidence for the empty tomb and appearances could be presented *separately* above.

Moreover, as we've seen, neither suggests the other. In other words, neither could generate nor account for the other: *each would naturally generate very different kinds of phenomena,* such as non-embodied visions of Jesus "translated" to heaven in the case of an empty tomb alone; and, though intensely more real, vivid, and unprecedented, "ghost-like" experiences of Jesus—still very much dead and buried—in the case of transphysical appearances alone.

*Separately, they each have a powerful claim to be historical.*

Yet at the same time they stand in close proximity and in a way that mutually interprets one another. Each requires the other to make a coherent whole. An empty tomb by itself would be remarkable. We might not know what to make of it—how a body could vanish like that—but it would be one of the most incredible events ever recorded.

Likewise, on their own, transphysical appearances would be spectacular. We might be totally perplexed by what it would mean that a person could appear from the dead physically even while his body lay decomposing in its tomb, but it would be one of the most unique and marvelous phenomena in all of history.

It's only when transphysical appearances of Jesus follow immediately upon the discovery of his empty tomb that an intelligible picture emerges. They don't make sense on their own.

They are totally interdependent for their meaning—*they complete each other!*

And here's the rub. Like a Santa Claus sighting, the probability of one of these events happening at all is extremely low. The probability of two such unlikely events happening at all is even lower. *But the probability that two such unlikely events would just randomly happen together in such a tight sequence—a matter of days—and in a way that is necessary to correctly and fully interpret the reality they both point to, is virtually nil.*

**How do two separate and distinct events that are so phenomenally unlikely yet so independently well-attested occur so closely together and in the exact sequence required to yield such a spectacularly unprecedented but perfectly cogent meaning?**

Given the improbabilities involved in such an astonishing confluence of circumstances, a "super miracle" is by far the most likely explanation.

# CONCLUSION TO PART I

THE HISTORICAL FACTS SUPPORTING the resurrection are so compelling that one Jewish writer, Pinchas Lapide, concluded that it is a "fact of history that cannot be denied." He made this conclusion after thoroughly reviewing the evidence in his book, *The Resurrection of Jesus: A Jewish Perspective*. Of course as a Jew, even though he admits the resurrection actually happened, he draws other conclusions about what it means. But this is a philosophical position (to be examined in Part III below) not a historical conclusion.[153] The historical conclusion is clear: the resurrection is the only satisfactory way to explain the evidence.

Unlike those disciplines of science that can observe recurring phenomena, history can never guarantee with one-hundred-percent certainty that a particular event happened. The most it can give is a judgment of high probability.

The resurrection enjoys this status. Listen to Timothy Keller's sober conclusion:

> Nothing in history can be proven the way we can prove
> something in a laboratory. However, the resurrection
> of Jesus is a historical fact much more fully attested
> to than most other events of ancient history we take
> for granted. Every effort to account for the birth of

the church apart from Jesus' resurrection flies in the face of what we know about first-century history and culture. If you don't short-circuit the process with the philosophical bias against the possibility of miracle, the resurrection of Jesus has the most evidence for it.[154]

The tandem realities of an empty tomb and appearances achieve the highest historical probability an event of ancient history can have.

This is what N.T. Wright, who is perhaps the most respected scholar of this generation, concludes:

> Nobody was expecting this kind of thing; no kind of conversion-experience would have generated such ideas; nobody would have invented it, no matter how guilty (or forgiven) they felt, no matter how many hours they pored over the scriptures. *To suggest otherwise is to stop doing history and to enter into a fantasy world of our own...In terms of the kind of proof which historians normally accept, the case...of the tomb-plus-appearances combination is what generated early Christian belief, is as watertight as one is likely to find.*

> We are left with the secure historical conclusion: the tomb was empty, and various 'meetings' took place not only between Jesus and his followers (including at least one initial skeptic) but also, in at least one case (that of Paul; possibly, too, that of James), between Jesus and people who had not been among his followers. *I regard this conclusion as coming in the same sort of category, of historical probability so high as to be virtually certain, as the death of Augustus in ad 14 or the fall of Jerusalem in ad 70.*(my italics)[155]

Virtual certainty.
History can't produce a higher judgment.

# SUGGESTIONS FOR
# GOING DEEPER

Bauckham, Richard, *Jesus and the God of Israel: God Crucified and Other Studies on the New Testament's Christology of Divine Identity*, Grand Rapids, MI: Eerdmans, 2008.

Brown, Raymond E., *The Death of the Messiah: From Gethsemane to the Grave, Volume II*, New Haven, CT: Yale University Press, 2010

_____, *The Gospel According to John XII-XXI: The Anchor Bible, Volume 29*, New York, NY: Doubleday, 1966.

_____, *The Virginal Conception and Bodily Resurrection of Jesus*, New York, NY: Paulist Press, 1973.

Craig, William Lane, *The Son Rises: The Historical Evidence for the Resurrection of Jesus*, Eugene OR: Wipf and Stock Publishers, 1981.

Hurtado, Larry W., *One God, One Lord: Early Christian Devotion and Ancient Jewish Monotheism, Third Edition*, London: Bloomsbury T&T Clark, 2015.

Licona, Michael R., *The Resurrection of Jesus: A New Historiographical Approach*, Downers Grove, IL: InterVarsity Press, 2010.

Olson, Carl E., *Did Jesus Really Rise from the Dead? Questions and Answers about the Life, Death, and Resurrection of Jesus*, Fort Collins, CO: Ignatius Press, 2016.

Stewart, Robert B. ed., *The Resurrection of Jesus: John Dominic Crossan and N.T.*

*Wright in Dialogue,* Minneapolis, MN: Fortress Press, 2006.

Wright, N. T., *The Resurrection of the Son of God: Christian Origins and the Question of God, Volume Three,* Minneapolis, MN: Fortress Press, 2003.

# PART II: AN UNCANNY FIT

## The Resurrection and the Historical Jesus

# CHAPTER

# 4

## Junk Scholarship

### *The Real Jesus of Real Scholarship*

### If It Doesn't Fit, You Must Acquit

"**I**F IT DOESN'T FIT, you must acquit." This was the famous refrain defense attorney Johnnie Cochran used in his summation at O.J. Simpson's murder trial. During the most dramatic moment of the trial, the prosecution produced the glove Simpson supposedly used while committing the gruesome murders of Nicole Brown Simpson and Ron Goldberg. They wanted him to try it on.

When O.J. tried, it wouldn't fit.

Throughout his closing argument, Cochran drove this point home by repeating the refrain: "If the glove doesn't fit, you must acquit!"

The way something "fits" the overall historical picture is one of the main ways scholars determine whether it's true or not. It's known as the "criterion of coherence." The more something "fits," or

139

coheres, with other historical data that is known to be true, the more likely it is to be true as well.

When O.J. was first accused of murder, much of the country was in disbelief. Most people thought he was innocent because it didn't "fit" with his character. He was the charming retired football star hurdling through the airport in those Hertz rental car commercials; the witty NFL color commentator; the affable character in the "Naked Gun" movies who had us laughing hysterically in the aisles.

Brutally stabbing his ex-wife and her friend didn't seem possible. It didn't *cohere* with everything else we knew about him.

But as time went by and the shocking information about the way he had abused Nicole Brown Simpson flowed in, the accusation seemed more credible. When people saw the pictures of her beaten and battered face plastered all over their TV sets, they immediately had a very different impression of O.J. And since his acquittal in the murder trial, the exploits that eventually landed him in jail—armed robbery, assault, and kidnapping (he held someone at gunpoint in an attempt to recover sports memorabilia)—make the whole idea of O.J. committing murder seem much more likely.

It *coheres* with all the evidence that has emerged in the intervening years.

## What's O.J. Got To Do With It?

The historical evidence for Jesus' resurrection is impressive. As we saw in Part I, it even rises to the level of virtual certainty. Ordinarily, this would be more than enough to conclude it happened. We accept most events of ancient history with far less.

But when it comes to the resurrection, too much is at stake.

Even with virtual certainty, there is still a *chance*, however small, that the historical evidence surrounding the event itself could be wrong. Personally, if I am going to stake my life on this, I need further corroboration. I need to see substantial evidence, beyond the events themselves, that confirm them. That show they are no fluke.

So, outside of the empty tomb and appearances, is there any corroborating evidence? Is there any way to verify that the strange events of that first Easter are what they truly claim to be? That they *cohere* with the larger historical context?

Actually there is—and modern scholarship is paving the way.

When it comes to Jesus, *it all fits.*

*And in an uncanny way.*

However, before I can demonstrate how this works, I need to do two things. First, explore the recent trends in modern scholarship in order to clarify the common misconceptions many have about where scholars stand on this question—this is the subject of the present chapter. And second, provide the sketch of the historical Jesus produced by this scholarship—the subject of the next chapter.

Then I will show how it all fits, like a glove!

## Duped by Junk Scholarship

A few years ago, I met a lawyer at a wake while we were both waiting in line to pay our respects. He shared how he was an avid reader and loved history. He also shared how, growing up Catholic, he listened intently to the homilies at church, homilies which routinely presented the events in the Bible as if they really happened. As a result, he believed the Bible was historically accurate. But then he began reading a number of books which claimed to reveal that the Bible is largely a myth. That it's not based on solid history at all. Since these books, some of them best sellers, presented themselves as legitimate scholarship, he accepted them at face value.

And, he felt duped by the Church. He was angry that it would have misled him so badly.

Sadly though, it wasn't the Church that was misleading him. It was *these books.* And the truly sad and infuriating thing is that they *continue to mislead so many more.* In fact, before I came across the far more legitimate scholarship, I was duped by a number of these books too!

As I mentioned in the introduction, there's been a deluge of popular books over the last thirty years or so which insinuate in one way or another that *the Jesus of the gospels is **not** the Jesus of history*. That instead of being the miracle-working Son of God come to save the world from sin portrayed in the gospels, the historical Jesus was nothing more than a revolutionary zealot, a political subversive, an egalitarian prophet; *or* an itinerant cynic philosopher, a proto-Gnostic sage, a wisdom-spinning teacher of timeless truth; *or* a charismatic holy man, a spirit healer, a mystic uniquely endowed with divine consciousness; *or* some hybrid of the above. In other words, these books present a *dizzying array* of alternative and in many ways contradictory portraits of the "real Jesus." In fact, as many scholars admit—including John Dominic Crossan, who happens to be one of the most prominent of these writers!—the sheer volume of different portraits is an embarrassment to the field and the integrity of the enterprise.

Despite the media's infatuation with these scholars (is it really any surprise the media would gravitate toward these sensational claims rather than report the more traditional and mundane findings of legitimate scholars?), giving them an inordinate amount of attention as the latest and greatest, *they hold extreme positions that the vast majority and most respected of scholars don't find persuasive at all.*

When these books are subjected to peer review, they are quickly shown to be seriously flawed, often because they rely on outdated tools and methods (see the discussion on form criticism below), are highly speculative, build their arguments on questionable sources, and/or tend to ignore relevant evidence that doesn't fit their presuppositions. Most of all, in each and every case, they fail to put *all* the data together in a coherent way; they leave large pieces unaccounted for.

A good example of this is one of the most recent best sellers of the genre, Reza Aslan's *Zealot*. It's a very well-written and engaging book. And it makes a number of accurate observations most contemporary scholars would heartily agree with. But, Aslan tends to conveniently ignore data that doesn't fit into his thesis.

For instance, scholars on all sides of the spectrum agree that Jesus' teaching "love your enemies" (Matthew 5:43-45; Luke 6:27) is one of the most certain things Jesus said and that he meant it in a universal way (i.e., to be applied to all people, Jew and non-Jew alike). However, Aslan argues that Jesus only meant "love your enemies" in a fiercely nationalistic way (i.e., it only applies to fellow Jews you might have some dispute with). Because a zealot would never teach something like this (love your non-Jewish enemy), he simply dismisses this universal application as the work of the later church without providing any evidence to refute the arguments that have led to this staggering agreement among scholars of every stripe.[156]

Other examples where Aslan fails to adequately account for the data are Jesus' practices of free forgiveness and teaching with divine authority (Aslan says Jesus taught with the authority of God, as His appointed agent, but doesn't tease out the implications). Not only do the vast majority of scholars agree that these were central features of Jesus' ministry, they also agree that they are completely unique to Jesus: no other messianic figure *dared* to do either. And for good reason. Both imply an outrageously blasphemous self-estimation. They are prerogatives that belong to God alone. You could get killed for behaving this way, acting as if you were God!

Aslan's main thesis is that Jesus—though in some ways unique, to be sure—was simply like a number of other revolutionary zealots of his time who sought to establish the *earthly* kingdom of God by gathering an army of disciples to challenge Roman occupation, believing that God, somehow, would miraculously come to their aid as He had done for others in the Old Testament, giving them the victory, and enthroning the leader as king. But the data he conveniently ignores, the data the majority of scholars readily admit into the historical record, suggests just the opposite: Jesus was *shockingly different.*

This is most apparent when it comes to Jesus' miracles. Aslan claims that he was just one of many wonder workers who littered the Galilean countryside in that era.[157] He bases this on an assumption scholars *used to* make: because they had discovered several apparent parallels to Jesus' miracle working activity a number of years ago, they thought there were many more. But as we'll see in the next chapter, this assumption turned out to be wrong. Not only weren't there that many wonder workers around the time of Jesus, those who did exist weren't like him at all. In his miracles too, Jesus proves to be absolutely unique, something Aslan gets completely wrong by relying on *outdated* scholarship.

Even more problematic, Aslan fails to put all the historical data together in a *coherent* way. If Jesus was just a zealot in the contemporary mode, a peasant nationalist looking to overthrow the Romans and establish the Jewish nation again, much of what the majority of scholars agree is solidly part of the historical record just doesn't fit. For example, Jesus' revolutionary understanding of a wildly and widely merciful God; the centrality of love in his teaching and praxis; and his all-pervasive and unrelenting focus on the "age to come," what scholars refer to as the "eschatological."

In fact, in a saying generally judged to be authentic, Jesus says: "I tell you, many will come from east and west and will eat with Abraham and Isaac and Jacob in the kingdom of heaven, while the heirs of the kingdom will be thrown into the outer darkness, where there will be weeping and gnashing of teeth." (Matthew 8:11-12; Luke 13:28-29) In other words, in the eschatological kingdom, the "new age" Jesus is about to usher in at the consummation of his ministry as the "eschatological" prophet, *pagans* will be welcomed in ahead, or even instead, of many Jews.

Why would a zealot intent on leading an earthly revolution against pagan oppressors focus so zealously on the radical love of God, a love that has no boundaries—it even includes pagan oppressors!—and on the imminent "age to come," an age that puts an end to the earthly order? (Incidentally, the way we know Jesus wasn't simply talking about an earthly kingdom in this passage is that Abraham, Isaac, and Jacob, long since dead, are now alive again. Moreover, one of the things scholars are now most agreed on is that Jesus presented himself as God's *eschatological*—as opposed to just earthly—prophet or agent.)

Furthermore, why would a rebel leader go so willingly and non-violently to his death? (Aslan seems to suggest that Jesus thought he and his followers would die for their sedition and that this would force God to intervene somehow—sedition implying *violent* resistance, which Aslan maintains Jesus was fully prepared for.) In the garden of Gethsemane, when Jesus pleads with his Father to avoid the cross, he is unlike all other Jewish martyrs or Greek heroes, who approach death with great courage and resolve. By contrast, Jesus is pathetic, which is why the early church would never invent this story, as most scholars agree. Most scholars also agree that Jesus' action at the last supper, identifying the bread and wine with his body and blood—the prophetic symbol he chose to explain what he was about to do by dying *sacrificially* on the cross—would never have been invented by anyone else because the idea of eating flesh and drinking blood was so horrifying to Jewish sensibilities.

Both clearly show that Jesus went *willingly* and *non-violently* to his death. And that he didn't die as a rebel leader, but rather, somehow saw his death as the climactic sacrifice that would establish the New Covenant, the restored relationship between God and humans, and thereby, defeat the real enemy which is sin and death.

For all of this, Aslan provides no explanation.

But the major flaw in Aslan's argument is the way he tries to explain the resurrection. He adopts a view which a number of older scholars advocated: that belief in Jesus' divinity originated, not with Jesus' original Jewish disciples, but with the later influx of Hellenistic Jewish and Gentile believers who imported pagan ideas. Jesus only came to be thought of as "god" because the pagan mythology of "divine men" distorted the original Jewish believers' understanding of him as a thoroughly human messiah.

The "legend" of the resurrection grows around this belief. As Aslan puts it: "The resurrection stories in the gospels were created to...put flesh and bones on an already accepted creed; to create narrative out of an established belief; and, most of all, to counter the charges of critics who denied the claim, who argued that Jesus' followers saw nothing more than a ghost or spirit, who thought it was the disciples themselves who stole Jesus's body to make it appear as though he rose again."[158] Thus, the emergent belief in Jesus' divinity generated the stories of resurrection, and not visa versa.

The first problem with this thesis is that, as we already noted in Part I, the narratives *aren't* carefully crafted tales. They are full of discrepancies (which scholars like Aslan are quick to point out) that render the notion they are a *systematic* effort to counter charges *ridiculous*. Moreover, as we also noted, there would have been immense pressure on the early church *not* to put flesh and bones on the creed, but to take them off. To make their creed seem less preposterous to a world that thought resurrection was ludicrous and/or repulsive, the overwhelming tendency would be to spiritualize the whole thing, the exact opposite of what Aslan suggests.

But the far bigger problem is this: if belief in Jesus' divinity happened right way, within that early community of Jewish disciples, it blows Aslan's entire thesis right out of the water. As I mentioned earlier, with the publication of Larry Hurtado's One God, One Lord, mainstream scholarship has arrived at a clear consensus about the origin of belief in Jesus' divinity. As Hurtado himself observes:

> It is also encouraging that over the years since the first appearance of OGOL [One God, One Lord] there has developed a groundswell of scholarly judgment that reflects some of the main positions put forth in the book. In particular, the remarkable Jesus-devotion reflected already in Paul's letters did not first emerge under the influence of a "pagan" environment in Diaspora cities such as Antioch, or in some incremental process largely driven by the influx of converted Gentiles. Instead, this Jesus-devotion erupted initially among *Jewish circles* of Jesus-followers in Roman *Judaea,* and *astonishingly early and quickly.*(my italics)[159]

Hurtado's now classic book showed that the very first Christians worshiped Jesus alongside Yahweh as God. And if Jesus was thought to be divine virtually right away, then Aslan can't dismiss the resurrection so easily. For those first disciples to conceive the inconceivable and commit what was for them the most outrageous blasphemy, they must have seen his crucified body somehow transformed to a glorified state.

Just as significant, as a number of scholars have shown, including Hurtado himself, Jesus must have been living a life consistent with the post-resurrection belief in his divinity. Otherwise, the resurrection *by itself* can't fully account for such a belief. Those original disciples must have seen Jesus say and do things in his public ministry that, in light of the resurrection, led them to believe he was fully divine— things like the gospels describe him doing. "This firm conviction of continuity between the man Jesus and the exalted heavenly figure of the post-Easter faith and visions can only mean that in his own lifetime Jesus had made a powerful and lasting impression."[160]

If Jesus was merely a zealot, his resurrection would have signaled something *entirely different* to them, such as vindicating him as the true rebel leader, an earthly messiah, and propelling them to take up arms and fight the Romans. In other words, for those who knew Jesus personally to worship him as God after the resurrection, he must have been much more like the gospels describe him, and not just a revolutionary zealot (more on this in chapter 6 below).

Anne Rice knows how historical scholarship works. For years now, she has been doing extensive research for her best-selling novels. In fact, even though they're fiction, she has become known for the historical accuracy of the background details. So she is intimately familiar with the discipline.

When she first began looking into the figure of Jesus, this was her experience:

> Having started with the skeptical critics, those who take
> their cue from the earliest skeptical New Testament
> scholars of the Enlightenment, I expected to discover

that their arguments would be frighteningly strong, and that Christianity was, at heart, a kind of fraud…

What gradually came clear to me was that many of the skeptical arguments—arguments that insisted most of the Gospels were suspect, for instance, written too late to be eyewitness accounts—lacked coherence. They were not elegant. *Arguments about Jesus himself were full of conjecture. Some books were no more than assumptions piled upon assumptions. Absurd conclusions were reached on the basis of little or no data at all.*

In sum, the whole case for the nondivine Jesus who stumbled into Jerusalem and somehow got crucified by nobody and had nothing to do with the founding of Christianity and would be horrified by it if he knew about it—that whole picture which had floated in the liberal circles I frequented as an atheist for thirty years—that case was not made. *Not only was it not made, I discovered in this field some of the worst and most biased scholarship I'd ever read.*

I saw almost no skeptical scholarship that was convincing, and the Gospels, shredded by critics, lost all intensity when reconstructed by various theorists. They were in no way compelling when treated as composites and records of later "communities."

I was unconvinced by the *wild postulations* of those who claimed to be children of the Enlightenment. (my italics)[161]

When fringe scholars present "alternative facts" that deny global warming, legitimate scientists call it what it is: "junk science." The same should be said about the stream of popular books written about Jesus in recent years—much of it *is* "junk scholarship." And for years now, this junk scholarship has been duping people into believing that the "real Jesus" bears little resemblance to the gospels.

Nothing could be further from the truth.

## Change is Coming

To a far lesser degree, however, even mainline scholarship has tended to be skeptical about the historical reliability of the gospels. Until recently that is. Despite not getting much play (it usually takes popular culture twenty to thirty years to catch up with the leading edge of mainstream biblical scholarship, especially when it isn't as sexy or scandalous as its junk scholarship counterpart), contemporary scholarship is now revealing that, in substance, the gospels paint a fairly accurate historical picture. In other words, *the Jesus of history is a lot more like the Jesus of the gospels than not.*

Allow me to explain.

Over the last twenty years or so, there has been a dramatic shift in biblical scholarship due to several key developments, starting with newfound attention being paid to the Jewish context of Jesus and the roots of the New Testament. Commenting on this new direction in historical Jesus scholarship, which he calls the "Third Quest," N.T. Wright observes: "The 'Third Quest'...has placed Jesus precisely within his Jewish eschatological context, and has found in consequence new avenues of secure historical investigation opening up before it...it locates him firmly within Judaism, though looking at the reasons why he, and then his followers, were rejected by the Jewish authorities."[162]

As a result, like never before, the pieces of the puzzle are coming together to paint a clear, consistent, and historically compelling portrait of Jesus, one that makes perfect sense in his first-century Jewish context. Many of the old enigmas have been solved, and fresh, new insights are yielding an emerging consensus among scholars that had been sorely lacking. It turns out that the Jesus of the gospels does fit comfortably and compellingly into his Jewish context, even if he stands out from it in a number of startling ways; and that, therefore, much of the historical data recorded in the gospels is reliable.

This is Wright's conclusion:

> As the late historian John Roberts, author of the monumental *History of the World* (1980), sums it up, '[the gospels] need not be rejected; much more inadequate evidence about far more intractable subjects has often to be employed [in writing history].' The portrait of Jesus we find in the canonical gospels makes sense within the world of Palestine in the 20s and 30s of the first century. Above all, it makes coherent sense in itself. The Jesus who emerges is thoroughly believable as a figure of history, even though the more we look at him, the more we feel once more that we may be staring into the sun.[163]

In addition to this new focus, there are more first-century sources available to scholars than ever before. These are shedding new light, though not without complexity and nuance, into the Palestinian-Jewish context in which Jesus lived. And the more this context is understood, the more the things Jesus said and did are finally making sense, especially his most perplexing sayings and deeds, the meanings of which have often mystified and eluded scholars for generations. We are finally getting a consistent and coherent picture of his goals and aims.

## Bad Form

At the same time, the primary reason for much of the scholarly skepticism about historical data in the gospels over the past century is being rethought. As Timothy Keller explains:

For almost a century biblical scholarship was dominated by a view called "form criticism." The form critics believed that the Gospels are folk literature, the product of oral tradition. Oral tradition was believed to be formed by communities that felt free to modify, embellish, and shape the stories to fit their own needs and to answer their own questions. It was believed that these communities did not care if the accounts were historically true at all. This was the form critics' answer to the question of how information about Jesus' life reached the Gospel writers.

In this kind of scenario, the oral tradition would be very fluid and unstable. It couldn't be trusted to preserve information accurately. Even if these communities didn't feel free to modify it, it was believed that they wouldn't be able to pass it on without significant distortion. Like the "telephone game," where one person whispers a secret into someone else's ear until it's gone around the room, the original information would barely be recognizable. By the way, when I learned how to interpret scripture, form criticism was one of the primary tools I was taught to use, and this is the approach I've taken most of my life.

Keller continues: "But in the last twenty years the very premises of the form critics have come under attack, and they should no longer be taken for granted." As it turns out, the transmission of oral traditions in ancient cultures, especially when "remembering some shared historical origin account" proves to be *very reliable*. Scholars have found that when it comes to foundational stories, oral cultures are very careful to preserve them accurately over long periods of time, even over multiple generations. And in the case of the Jesus tradition, the time between the events of his life and the recording of the gospels is much shorter, only a generation or two. In fact, much of it was passed down while many of the original eyewitnesses to the events were still alive to safeguard it from error or embellishment.[164]

With Paul we have good evidence of the care taken by the early church to preserve the Jesus tradition. In I Corinthians 7:10, Paul gives instructions about divorce that he says are not from him, but the Lord. Two verses later, he adds his own advice, which he makes clear is *not* from the Lord. He is careful to preserve what Jesus said and distinguish that from his own words.

And again, in I Corinthians 11:23 he says he received from the Lord the words spoken at the Last Supper. Paul doesn't mean he received them directly. He wasn't there. Rather, he means that they have been passed down from the Lord, basically in tact, through the witnesses who were. (As these words are preserved in four different places in the New Testament, there are slight variations in wording, but this doesn't affect their meaning at all—some variations are to be expected as the Aramaic Jesus spoke was translated by different people into the Greek used throughout the Roman Empire.)

Moreover, here and a number of times Paul uses a technical term for receiving and handing on these traditions which puts stress on the fact that they have been transmitted via a *thorough* process of teaching and learning—they aren't just casually communicated, but retained at a deep level of understanding.

The way Paul handles these traditions reveals how, by and large, the early church certainly treated them: with the utmost care and respect, diligently working to preserve them as faithfully as possible.[165]

# Mind Games

Modern neuroscience backs these findings up. Experiments show that we are very good at accurately remembering "emotionally charged events" over long periods of time. Events like Jesus' mesmerizing miracles, heated controversies with the religious leaders, spellbinding teachings, provocative parables, shocking association with sinners, poignant compassion for society's most marginalized, upsetting action in the Temple, or violent death. They make a *vivid imprint* on our memory.

In his book *Talk like TED*, Carmine Gallo elucidates the recent neuroscientific research:

"An emotionally charged event (usually called an ECS, short for emotional competent stimulus) is the best-processed kind of external stimulus ever measured," says molecular scientist John Medina. "Emotionally charged events persist longer in our memories and are recalled with greater accuracy than neutral memories."

...When you experience an emotionally charged event (shock, surprise, fear, sadness, joy, wonder), it impacts how vividly you remember that particular event. [For example, even though you may have forgotten where you put your keys this morning, you] can probably remember not only *where* you were on September 11, 2001, when terrorists hijacked planes and flew them into the World Trade Center, but you also vividly recall *what* you were doing, and *whom* you were with, the expression of their faces, what they may have said, and other small items in your environment that you otherwise wouldn't pay attention to. People remember vivid events, they forget mundane ones.

The University of Toronto psychology professor Rebecca Todd discovered that how vividly a person experiences an event influences how easily he or she can recall the event or the information later. Todd published her research in the *Journal of Neuroscience*. "We've discovered that we see things that are emotionally arousing with greater clarity than those that are more mundane," says Todd. "Whether they're positive—for example, a first kiss, the birth of a child, winning an award—or negative, such as a traumatic event, breakups, or a painful and humiliating childhood moment that we all carry with us, the effect is the same. What's more, we found that how vividly we perceive something in the first place predicts how vividly we will remember it later on. We call this 'emotionally charged vividness' and it is like the flash of a flashbulb that illuminates an event as it's captured for memory.

..."In the brain when you're emotionally aroused you produce higher levels of norepinephrine as well as stress hormones. We've known for some time that emotional arousal enhances memory. Our study was the first to show another effect of emotional arousal is that you actually perceive events more vividly at the time when they occur, and that, too, increases the likelihood you'll remember it.

..."It's as if the event is burned more vividly into our perceptual awareness...Part of the reason is that the amygdala, a brain region that is key for tagging the emotional importance of things, talks to the visual cortex—the part of the brain that allows sight—and ramps up its activity so that we are actually perceiving those events more actively."[166]

Because they were emotionally charged events, many of the things recorded in the gospels about Jesus are likely to have been *vividly burned into the perceptual awareness of those who experienced them, and therefore, remembered clearly and accurately.* And when they told these stories to others, they would have a *similar effect on the hearer.*

As Gallo goes on to explain, the mind can't tell the difference between what it imagines and what it actually experiences. "Neuroscientists have found that the visual cortex of your brain cannot tell the difference between what's real and what's imagined. If you can think of something vividly—really imagine it—the same areas are activated as if you were actually seeing the event. That's why metaphors, analogies, and rich imagery are powerful ways to paint a picture in the mind's eye, in some cases even more effective than the actual image."[167]

Those second- and third-generation Christians who never saw Jesus themselves, but who were responsible for writing the gospels, would still have had the emotionally charged events of his life vividly burned into their perceptual awareness when they first heard about them. In turn, they would be fully capable of recalling them accurately.

We commonly assume that memory is faulty. And it often is— just look at how many times eyewitness testimony in court turns out to be mistaken. But the latest psychological research on eyewitness memory tells a different story. It's not faulty in all cases. After doing a thorough investigation into this research, Richard Bauckham has shown that under certain conditions, memory is startlingly accurate and eyewitness testimony highly reliable.

These conditions include:

--*unique or unusual* events; what we consider *memorable.*

--*consequential* events; ones that are important to us.

--events in which we are *emotionally involved.*

--events that contain vivid imagery.

--events that are *frequently rehearsed* after occurring.

Most of the gospel narrative qualifies as uniquely memorable, consequential, and emotionally involved events. And clearly these events were frequently rehearsed soon after they occurred. For example, this is the only way to explain how Jesus' reputation spread while he was alive: the witnesses to these events had to be telling others what they saw and heard.[168] As Bauckham observes:

> The eyewitnesses who remembered the events of the history of Jesus were remembering inherently very memorable events, unusual events that would have impressed themselves on the memory, events of key significance for those who remembered them, landmark or life-changing events for them in

many cases, and their memories would have been reinforced and stabilized by frequent rehearsal, beginning soon after the event. They did not need to remember—and the Gospels rarely record—merely peripheral aspects of the scene or event, the aspects of recollective memory that are least reliable. Such details may often have been subject to performative variations in the eyewitnesses' tellings of their stories, but the central feature of the memory, those that constituted its meaning for those who witnessed and attested it, are likely to have been preserved reliably. We may conclude that the memories of eyewitnesses of the history of Jesus score highly by the criteria for likely reliability that have been established by the psychological study of recollective memory.[169]

So while the gospels might contain errors or omissions in peripheral details, the kind of detail required in courtroom testimony, for example, and which is often unreliable, by and large they contain the kind of memories that the psychological research reveals to be highly reliable, meaning that at least *in substance*, they possess a high degree of historical accuracy. While they are certainly imbued with the hindsight of faith—interpretive details, allusions, and embellishments—*at their core*, they contain reliable information.

In essence, they reveal the "real Jesus."[170]

In 1974 when I was nine years old and in fourth grade, my elementary school teacher showed us a short film that made a powerful impact on me. It was about the doctor who, in the 1950's, discovered how to transfuse blood. Before he discovered this procedure, if you were losing large amounts of blood, you would bleed out and die. There was no way to save your life. But because of his discovery, countless lives have been saved.

Ironically, several years after inventing the procedure that saved so many other lives, this doctor was in a terrible car accident and lost a lot of blood. He desperately needed a blood transfusion to save his life. When the ambulance rushed him to the closest hospital, the ER doctor took one look at him and *refused to treat him*. He told the medics they'd have to take him to another hospital. While en route, the doctor died.

The reason the ER doctor refused to treat him?

It was an all-white hospital in the deep South of the 1950's.

And the doctor who invented this procedure was *black*.

When I began teaching in 1987, some thirteen years later, I was trying to think of an example that would illustrate the unexpected twist Jesus uses to make his shocking point at the end of the parable of the Good Samaritan.[171] Even though I hadn't thought about the story of this doctor for years, it came to mind and I began using it in all my classes just as I had remembered it.

In 2001, as I was in the habit of doing, I told this story to another one of my classes. The next day a student brought in a book from home which documented the doctor's story. His name was Dr. Charles Drew, which I either failed to take note of when I saw the film or simply forgot. As it turns out, he didn't invent the procedure for transfusing blood, but he did develop a technique for the long-term preservation of blood plasma, which made the blood bank possible. His technique was put to the test during World War II, and he became the first Director of the American Red Cross Blood Bank. And the car accident occurred in 1950. None of which I remembered accurately.[172]

However, aside from these details, I got the gist of the story right. For thirteen years I had forgotten all about it. But it had so "imprinted" itself on my memory that *I could recall the substance of it accurately* and then *tell it over and over again with little to no variation* for another thirteen years, so that twenty-six years after first seeing it, I had *accurately preserved the essential outline* of what I had witnessed so many years before.

Jesus clearly affected the disciples far more profoundly than this film affected me. And they certainly began telling the stories about him far sooner than I ever did about Dr. Drew, practically right away. So it's not that much of a stretch to think that they were able to accurately remember the substance of their experiences of Jesus and communicate them to others. And that, in turn, their followers were able to do the same, even over the course of two or three generations, until the last gospel was finally written.

In fact, good evidence that the oral tradition was carefully preserved can be found in the texts themselves. In *The Jesus Legend*, Paul Eddy and Gregory Boyd show that many key features of the gospel accounts would have been highly *embarrassing* and even *dangerous* for the early church: the undesirable people Jesus associated with, the obtuseness of his disciples, the notion of a suffering messiah, the belief in Jesus' divinity, and the concept of individual resurrection. In both Jewish and pagan environments, the church would have suffered ridicule at best and persecution at worst for maintaining such ideas and including them in their writings.

Yet, they are featured prominently.

If they weren't an undeniable part of the historical record, what motive would the gospel writers have for including them? That the gospel writers, and the oral tradition before them, maintain such embarrassing and dangerous ideas means the form critics were surely wrong in thinking that these stories were liberally modified to suit the community's needs.[173]

Another indication that the texts are "substantially rooted in history" is the *lack of interpretation* given to a good number of the events they convey. If they were composed after Jesus' death, we would expect them to reflect a post-resurrection perspective. And in fact, many do. But many more don't. Many passages, incredibly many miracle stories, lack this kind of interpretation. (By the way, stories that are rooted in history may have been given a post-resurrection interpretation in the gospels simply as a result of the later insight Easter gave to the meaning of Jesus' words and deeds. A post-resurrection perspective doesn't necessarily mean they aren't substantially historical.)

According to Bauckham, as they stand in the gospels, the miracle and exorcism stories show few signs of interpretation, both in the way Jesus (minimally) interprets them in his teaching and the way the early church tended to interpret everything from this post-Easter perspective. Instead, largely they preserve the immediate impact and meaning such events would have naturally generated prior the resurrection, prior to way this event transformed the church's understanding of Jesus' life and ministry. The reason we're inclined to read more into them is because of their context in the gospel narratives, which are infused with this resurrection perspective. This strongly suggests that they retain eyewitness testimony.

> The relatively small extent to which the stories have
> been affected by post-resurrection interpretation has
> to be explained by the probability that it was the
> stories in the fairly fixed form already given them by
> the eyewitnesses during Jesus' ministry that survived
> the revolution in understanding consequent on the
> cross and the resurrection.[174]

So, both the external evidence, modern findings on how oral traditions and memory work, and the internal evidence, the texts themselves, show that the form critics got it wrong when they thought the oral tradition didn't accurately preserve the Jesus of history.

In substance, it did.

## What's in a Life?

One last major development. A large segment of scholars used to think that the gospels were a unique genre, an entirely new kind of writing, a complete innovation. And they simply presumed this genre was a type of mythology. In other words, that the gospels were primarily *fictions*, modeled on the "divine men" and supposed wonder workers of Greek and Roman mythology.

In the last twenty years, however, this has been completely overturned. As a result of groundbreaking work by several scholars, the consensus now is that the gospels fall into a genre known as "ancient biography." Although ancient biographies had an agenda and were to differing degrees, therefore, embellished in order to dramatize events, tease out their meaning, and/or persuade readers, they all built on a bedrock of historical fact.

Scholar David Aune sums it up this way: "While biography tended to emphasize encomium or the one-sided praise of the subject, it was still *firmly rooted in historical fact rather than literary fiction.* Thus while the Evangelists clearly had an important theological agenda, the very fact that they chose to adapt Greco-Roman biographical conventions to tell the story of Jesus indicated that they were *centrally concerned to communicate what they really thought happened."*(my italics)[175]

This is how it works. Suppose you had a favorite teacher growing up. That teacher made a deep and powerful impression on you. They changed your life, and in ways that you couldn't even put into words. Years later, you meet your future spouse. As you're getting to know each other, you want to share with him or her what this teacher meant to you, to your life, to the person you are now.

How do you capture the profound impact they had on you?

You certainly give examples of things they said and did that are rooted in real memory, "history" if you will. You might share how spellbinding their lectures were, or how they listened to you for hours while you were going through a hard time at home, or how one day they encouraged you to see something in yourself you didn't think was there.

But to adequately communicate to your future spouse how much they inspired you, you say things like: "He or she was the best teacher ever; the coolest person I've ever met; the smartest and wisest human being on the planet!" Obviously, others would make similar claims about their favorite teacher being the best ever, so your statement is an exaggeration to make a point. And obviously, they aren't as smart as Einstein or as wise as Buddha, so that's grossly overstating it.

Additionally, you might imbue some of the stories you tell about them with details that aren't precisely accurate. For example, maybe one day during class this teacher jumped up on a chair to illustrate a lesson. However, when you tell it, you say they jumped up on their desk, clearly stretching it. But it helps to make your point that they did dramatic things like this to keep the class engaged.

The way you embellish helps convey the impact they had. At the core, however, what you're saying about them is true. You didn't just make the whole thing up or significantly distort the essence of who this teacher was.

In a similar way, as ancient biography, the gospels, though embellished at times for effect, are, at their core, relating genuine history. The gist, or essence, of what they record can be trusted to give us a fairly accurate portrait of the "real Jesus."

So where does all this leave us?

As one of the leading scholars of this generation, N.T. Wright provides a good summary. He points out that, just as we saw with form criticism, the tools biblical scholars relied on in the past are proving to be fundamentally flawed and outdated. Since these tools were often used to justify presuppositions that led to rampant skepticism about the historical data, this shift in biblical scholarship is having a dramatic effect.

The new approach scholars are taking is, for the *first time*, creating a coherent picture of the historical Jesus which is attracting a growing consensus of scholars.[176]

# Will The Real Jesus Please Stand Up!

*The Emerging Consensus of Modern Scholarship*

S O WHAT HAS THIS new approach revealed about the historical Jesus? Essentially, this is the emerging consensus:

--Jesus believed that the Kingdom of God was breaking into the world through him, through his words and deeds. He wasn't just announcing it. He *embodied* it in his very person. He presented himself as history's central figure.

As a result, he demanded an all-consuming commitment from those who would follow him, the kind of allegiance and devotion *only God could require.* He spoke as if a person's response to him determined *their response to God* and therefore their eternal destiny. And as the one who was personally inaugurating God's kingdom by vanquishing evil itself through his own power, he presented himself as *Yahweh's personal presence among humankind.*

It's revealing that Jesus chose twelve disciples—matching the twelve tribes of Israel—to symbolize the fact that he was ushering in what scholars call "reconstituted Israel." This is what his Kingdom agenda was all about: establishing God's reign of perfect peace and love by making Israel the instrument of God's grace (the "light to the nations") it was always intended to be. But instead of including himself as one of the twelve, he sets himself apart, putting himself above them just as God is set above Israel. In other words, *he puts himself in the position of God vis-a-vis Israel!*

--Jesus forgave sinners. Only God could forgive sins. Only God had the authority to do so. As his enemies so irately pointed out, this was a clear case of blasphemy—*arrogantly presuming a prerogative of God for himself.*

As if this wasn't bad enough, Jesus offered what scholars call "free forgiveness." At that time, there was an intricate system set up in the Temple for people to atone for their sins. The Temple was the place of Yahweh's unique presence on earth. And the sacrifice performed in it was the way sinners could be reconciled to him. Jesus simply bypassed the whole thing! He declared people forgiven without having them do any of what the Law required. In effect, Jesus was saying that he was replacing the Temple. *That he is where the unique presence and mercy of God is to be found.* (By the way, his action in the Temple at the end of his life, a prophetic sign of its destruction, made this perfectly clear: now that he had come, it was no longer necessary.)

--Jesus spoke and acted with an authority that was properly reserved for God alone. Instead of saying, "thus says the Lord," he solemnly declared the truth of God with his well-known "Amen, Amen, *I* say to you" proclamations, speaking unlike anyone else ever dared, as if he knew *intuitively* the mind and will of Yahweh. He modified the eternal and unchangeable word of God, Torah—something only God could do—as if he knew its real intent. (e.g., "You have heard that it was said: 'You shall love your neighbor and hate your enemy.' *But I say to you,* 'Love your enemies...'" Matthew 5:43-45; Luke 6:27) And, as we just saw, he claimed the authority to forgive sins. In all of this he was flirting with outright blasphemy, treading on the authority that belonged *exclusively* to God alone

--Jesus spoke of God as his "Abba" (my own dear Father) and referred to himself as "*the* Son." In this way, he was implying that he saw himself as the *unique and therefore divine* Son of God the Father. (The Messiah could be called God's son in a merely human sense, but Jesus goes way beyond this kind of usage.) It's true that he taught others to call God "Abba" as well, but he understood his "Sonship" to be categorically different, to be special and exclusive.

In the parable of the Tenants in the Vineyard, which is clearly an allegory for God's dealings with Israel (Mark 12:1-12), Jesus depicts himself as the son of the vineyard owner (i.e., God), and therefore, the ontological (i.e., in his very being, the actual and hence divine) Son of God. This is a parable most scholars judge to be authentic because it ends *without any hint of the resurrection.* If it was merely a creation of the early church, it certainly would have included some reference to "the Son's" vindication, some allusion to his resurrection victory.

But it doesn't. Instead, it ends with his humiliating defeat.

Even the widely respected and very cautious John Meier, who in his recent book has gone against the longstanding grain of critical scholarship by claiming that only a handful of Jesus' parables can be definitively demonstrated to be historical, judges this parable to be authentic.[177] In other words, according to Meier, of all Jesus' parables, this is one of the few we can be most sure he told.

And in it, he clearly presents himself as God's absolutely unique, divine Son.

In another passage, speaking about the "age to come," Jesus warns against speculation about when it will happen by saying: "But about that day or hour no one knows, neither the angels in heaven, *nor the Son,* but only the Father." (Mark 13:32) The tremendous embarrassment this statement would have caused the early church cannot be overstated. Surely the *divine* Son should know the date of his return! In fact, his ignorance about such a critical event continues to create problems for believers to this very day: how could the fully divine Son of God not know this? *How can he be divine if he doesn't?*

And that's why no one in the early church would ever invent such a saying.

It could only have come from the mouth of Jesus.

But in the very same breath he claims ignorance about "the end," he clearly refers to himself as *the* Son of the Father, positioning himself on a plane higher than the angels; in other words, on a level with God, as the Father's one and only Son.

And in a saying that the majority of scholars judge to be a very early, probably going back to Jesus himself, he solemnly declares that only the Father *really knows* the Son and only the Son *really knows* the Father. (Matthew 11:27; Luke 10:22)[178] In context, Jesus is explaining to the disciples why he alone has the authority to reveal who God is. Whether or not, as some scholars think, he only meant this symbolically (i.e., he knows God the way a son uniquely and intimately knows his father and vice versa), at the very least, he's indicating in a veiled way that he shares such a loving, intimate union with the Father that *he has complete access to the mind of God.*

And if he meant it literally, then he's claiming to share the inner divine life, *to have the very mind of God himself!*

In addition to having this exclusive knowledge, he claimed to possess God's exclusive power and authority over all things. For example, he often spoke of himself as "the Son of Man" who would come to judge the world, another prerogative reserved for God alone.

All this implied that he was somehow on the *same level* as the Father, *as God.*

And that he was somehow *aware* that *he shared the divine identity.*

--Jesus presented a radical and in many ways scandalous image of God that *far transcended any concept up to that point* and, incidentally, has continued to profoundly challenge, mystify, and infuriate people ever since. His acts of free forgiveness and table fellowship enacted and embodied this image. He goes out of his way to hang out with sinners and society's most marginalized in order to signify their welcome into the Kingdom and the lavish love God has for them.

He taught in even clearer terms, scandalously depicting the utterly transcendent and holy God as a *"Dad"* (the sense of "Abba" in the Aramaic) who wants nothing more than *intimate fellowship* with his children; as a *prodigal father who loves to a foolishly extravagant degree.* In fact, the father in this, his most famous parable, the parable of the Prodigal Son, behaves in a despicably undignified way for that culture, a depiction his contemporaries would have found *utterly repulsive.*

But this is precisely the essence of who he said God is: reckless mercy, ridiculous grace, in short, unconditional love. And who he is! In many instances he taught this way in order to justify his own behavior, to explain what he was up to; why he associated with sinners and forgave them so freely; why he sought out the least and the lost.

His understanding of grace is so contrary to the way the world works. When we talk about loving someone, we usually mean there is something lovable about them, something of great worth or value that elicits our love: beauty, kindness, intelligence, etc. But Jesus says God's love isn't like that at all. It's qualitatively and *quantum*tatively different.

He doesn't love us because we're so good, but because *he's so good.*

Maybe that's why so many people, even today, find his message of grace so hard to take. It strikes at the core of our ego. We like to think there is something of great worth about us, that we deserve God's love, that we are entitled to it. After all, if there is, if there is something we can do to earn it, if it's something we're owed, something we have a right to, then we have control over it.

*We like being in control.* (It makes us feel like we're God!)

But Jesus says the only way we can have God's love is if we freely receive it.

If we *do nothing* but accept it.

If we completely lose control, because *it is* completely out of our control!

This paradigm of grace is totally unique among the major religions of the world. Even Christians struggle to "get it." Many still want to believe that it's about being a "good person." That life, in the end, is fair. What goes around comes around. Karma. We get what we deserve.

In other words, that it's up to us.

That we're at the center of things.

But Jesus is saying that the ultimate point of existence is to have a relationship with the God who loves you like a prodigal dad—which can only happen when you accept His love as pure gift, because *true love* can't be earned, owed, or presumed as an entitlement. It can only be freely received, when you lose your*self* in it.

And the fact that God could love those who "don't deserve it"— like Hitler, a serial killer, or those who've deeply wounded or wronged us—as much as He loves us, scandalizes us to the core, the way it did Jesus' first hearers. Our sense of justice, of fairness, is such an overwhelming impulse. Yet Jesus outrageously subverts this most profound and passionate of human sensibilities. We don't get what we deserve—and that's supposed to be good news!

We just can't seem to wrap our heads around Jesus' image of a God of pure grace. It's altogether too much for us. I can't count the number of people I know, Christians included, who either explicitly refuse to accept this paradigm of grace because it's "not fair"; understand it intellectually but, because it feels so unnatural, because their guilt and shame won't let go, because all the love they know—the only kind of love human beings are capable of—is conditional, just can't bring themselves to trust it could actually be true for them; or—as I often find myself doing—keep trying to add something to it, add some "good work" that will make us more worthy of it, in other words, turn it into something other than pure grace. It's just not in our nature to believe God would love us unconditionally.

Our inability, or *unwillingness*, to "get this" is one of the surest signs of how otherworldly it is.

Robert Spitzer points out how completely innovative this whole paradigm is: "Surprising as it may seem, great philosophers such as Socrates and Plato, and the world's great religions and sages, simply did not see these truths prior to the preaching and life of Jesus. After Jesus reveals them, the philosophical world catches the implication— namely...that God is unconditionally loving."[179]

Prior to Jesus, no one had presented such a radical image of God—or dared to!

In turn, Jesus told his would-be followers they must love their enemies, forgive without limit, turn the other cheek, judge not lest they be judged, and die to themselves if they were going to live his way.

In other words, love like God does; like Jesus does.

Jesus' ethic would also have shocked and repulsed his hearers. As a number of scholars of ancient history have pointed out, their world was rigidly hierarchical. It was an accepted fact that people at the top mattered far more than people at the bottom. This might be true in our world, too, but at least we give lip service to the idea that all people possess equal worth. They didn't. Indeed, those at the bottom were viewed more as a means to an end than ends in themselves; in other words, as objects to be used and abused.

There was no sense of the inalienable dignity of each person. No regard for individual rights. No ideal of equality. No concern for the poor and marginalized. "Giving back" wasn't the cultural rally cry it is for us. Power and position were prized; compassion and charity mocked. Humility was viewed as weakness. Forgiveness for fools. Sacrificial love the height of idiocy.

The closest thing to a sacrificial ideal was the "noble" death, which was as much about the bravado of the individual dying as it was about the ideal of giving one's life for another (think Socrates). That's why no one would ever imagine crucifixion, the most humiliating and degrading of deaths, could ever be noble. It was abhorrent. Jesus' call for his followers to carry their *cross* of self-denying love in imitation of him, the kind of love we see as most heroic, would have struck them as vile and shameful.

Equality and justice for all. The inalienable dignity of each person. We hold these ideals dear. We've internalized them. They're *sacred* to us. But prior to Jesus, they simply didn't exist. Instead, it was a cold, cruel, top-down world.[180]

In stunning contrast, Jesus identifies himself, *Godself by implication*, with the least.

In flagrant opposition to how the "great ones" of that world made their authority felt, he declares that he has come not to be served, but to serve.

In an *outrageous move*, he surrounds himself with women as well as male followers, treating them as full equals.[181]

He comes to establish a radically egalitarian Kingdom where people certainly have different gifts, roles, and positions, but where just as certainly *each individual* is infinitely cherished by the Absolute Power behind the universe.

He pronounces the last—the poor, the hungry, the marginalized— "blessed," promising that they will be first when his Kingdom comes in force. And he upsets the social order by associating with the excluded and forgotten, insisting that his Kingdom will be built on just such as these.

He declares that the Kingdom is only open to those who become like little children, who—in direct contrast to our culture's romantic notion of childlikeness—were *scorned* in Jesus' day because they were the most vulnerable and dependent members of society. Who accept the Kingdom, therefore, not on their merits, but as *pure gift*.

As "charity!"

He says that the one who makes him or herself least, who humbles him or herself and serves the rest, will not only be following his example, but will indeed be greatest in the Kingdom because this is what the Kingdom, what God, is all about: *self-denying love*.

If we're honest, as much as we've bought into many of his ideals— just look at how foundational they are to the Constitution: the equality and dignity of every person, for example—Jesus continues to offend.

His ethic, too, is altogether too much for us.

For instance, Jesus didn't say respect your enemy. Or be good to your enemy. He said *love* your enemy. In other words, look at them the same way you would look at your closest loved ones. Treat them *like your own dear family*. This is completely unnatural. Actually, it's repugnant. Besides, it's completely irrational and impractical. If you don't put your foot down and resist your enemy, they'll walk all over you.

They'll destroy and devour you.

And yet, when we see someone loving their enemy, like the Amish taking care of the family of the man who murdered their children in a school shooting; or the families of the Charleston church members forgiving the man who killed their loved ones in cold blood, we are *irresistibly captivated by the **sublime beauty** of such **reckless grace**.*

Even though we want to see these killers fry, *something deep inside wishes we could love like that.*

Even though it seems completely insane, there is something so right, so good—so *super*natural!—about it.

Something *so divine* about it.

And as "crazy" as this ethic is, it has a power to reconcile, heal, and transform like nothing else in this world can. This was vividly on display with Ghandi undoing British colonization in India and Martin Luther King during the Civil Rights movement. It was non-violent resistance—both Ghandi and King based their tactics on the Sermon on the Mount (via Tolstoy)—and not force, or legislation, or passionate appeals for justice, or anything else that ultimately transformed both societies.

In the wake of apartheid, peace and healing came to South Africa largely because of Nelson Mandela's and Bishop Desmond Tutu's insistence on the kind of radical forgiveness Jesus taught rather than the more natural desire for retribution and strict justice. And in Rwanda and other parts of Africa torn apart by tribal warfare and genocide, it is efforts aimed at enabling victims to forgive those who tortured them and killed their families that are achieving the only real and lasting peace.

On the face of it, this ethic is dangerously out of touch with reality—insane.

And yet, we can't deny the sublime perfection it embodies. We can't deny its unique power to transform hearts and minds, to overcome injustice, to reconcile and heal.

If Jesus' paradigm of grace doesn't rock us to the core, it's because we've become so jaded to it. We throw the terminology around so much, we think we "get it" when we really don't. We have no idea how radical, extravagant, extreme, and counterintuitive it is. A quick example: do you *long* to see Osama bin Laden in heaven? God does, according to Jesus. Ultimately, Jesus taught that it is up to him whether he accepted this offer of God's grace, or not—i.e., repented—which, based on what we know, isn't likely. But it *is* God's will to see him in heaven—and should be ours too, if we really "get it."

If this infuriates you; if you can't accept a God who would forgive the architect of the horror of 9-11; if you don't *rejoice*, as God does, at the thought that he might have repented in his last moments and is now in paradise, then you—like most of the rest of us—are jaded to how profoundly counterintuitive Jesus' ethic is.

People through the ages have alternatively praised and disdained Jesus' breathtakingly lavish ethic. His was an *otherworldly* paradigm. It truly is out of this world, either completely reckless—*crazy*—or, properly *divine*.[182]

--Jesus lived his own radical ethic to such a sublime degree that his disciples would later make the daring claim that he was like them in every way *but sin*. This is a bold assertion. And one not easily made if there isn't at least a grain of truth in it. As a public persona, it could easily be refuted, especially by his enemies.

As we so often discover with public figures, everyone has some "ghost" in their closet, some Achilles heal, some moral defect or weakness. Even the best people, who we'd never dare say were perfect in the first place, are frequently exposed as frauds. However, as Notre Dame professor Richard McBrien points out: "But neither do we have any evidence that Jesus *did* sin. Not even his gravest enemies could make the accusation, and even less make it stick. This is one of the most remarkable aspects of the belief in, and the claim of, the sinlessness of Christ. If the moral gap between Jesus' words and deeds had been apparent to anyone at all, it would have been brought to public attention, so threatening and so revolutionary was his message."[183]

While there are several New Testament references to Jesus' sinlessness, the earliest is found in Second Corinthians. Most scholars agree Paul wrote this letter in the mid to late 50's at the latest. In II Corinthians 5:21, he says that Jesus is able to save us because he—unlike the rest of humanity!—"knew no sin."

A ridiculously stunning statement.

Paul is writing within twenty five years of Jesus' public ministry, while some of those who knew Jesus personally, both friend and foe alike, *are still alive*. If this statement were false, even in the slightest way (someone saw Jesus do something sinful even just one time), it would be challenged, especially by Jesus' enemies.

Paul must have been fully confident that *no one could*.

And this is all the more remarkable because, in a Jewish context, where the defining attribute of Yahweh is His holiness, only God is sinless. There's a famous incident in the gospels where a rich young man approaches Jesus with the title "Good teacher." (Mark 10:17-22; Matthew 19:16-30; Luke 18:18-30) Jesus quickly takes him to task by saying, "Why do you call me good. No one is good but God alone." Whether, as the story's told, Jesus meant to deny he was God, or instead to challenge the man to see that he was indeed divine, is a hotly debated topic among scholars. But one thing is clear: in that context, true goodness—sinlessness—was equated with divinity.

God alone is good. And this is what people who knew Jesus were claiming about him.

Even if we can't know whether Jesus ever sinned or not—we don't have access to his private thoughts, for example—it betrays the kind of impression he must have made. People found him to be so breathtakingly good, so radically and perfectly loving, *that they actually entertained the idea he was sinless.*

He stood out in a way no other person in history ever has.[184]

--Jesus also performed miracles. In fact, in the sober judgment of some of the most critically adept scholars, *if there is anything that can be said about the historical Jesus, it is that he was understood by his contemporaries to be a healer, a miracle worker.* No one else has so many or such spectacular miracles attributed to them. In the evaluation of two highly respected historical Jesus scholars, Gerd Theissen and Annette Merz: "No where else are so many miracles reported of a single person as they are in the Gospels of Jesus."[185]

John Meier, who has done the most extensive and critically acclaimed examination of Jesus' miracles to date, has shown that many of his most extraordinary miracles—healing the blind, raising the dead—have the strongest evidence to support them. For example, in the case of Jesus raising Jairus' daughter from the dead, Meier points out six markers of historicity: the presence of personal names; the fact that Jairus is a synagogue ruler, which would be very objectionable to the early church because they had been expelled from the synagogue by the time the gospels were written; the embarrassment of Jesus being laughed to scorn; the Aramaic phrase "Talitha koum," which is grammatically incorrect and reflects an informal spoken context as opposed to a formal written one; a number of "Semitisms," Aramaic (the language Jesus and his contemporaries spoke) words or phrases scholars detect behind the Greek text; and the absence of Christological titles (e.g., Lord) attached to such a major miracle—he is merely referred to as "teacher" even though this is a spectacular demonstration of his divine power, something the church would not have missed if inventing the story.[186]

In Meier's typically cautious estimation, this is impressive enough evidence to conclude that the basic story is rooted in a historical event.

In fact, after meticulously analyzing each of Jesus' miracles in painstaking detail, Meier goes on to conclude that *the miracles are among the most solid historical data from Jesus' life*:

> To sum up: the historical fact that Jesus performed extraordinary deeds deemed by himself and others to be miracles is supported most impressively by the criterion of multiple attestation of sources and forms and the criterion of coherence. The miracle traditions about Jesus' public ministry are already so widely attested in various sources and literary forms by the end of the first Christian generation that *total fabrication by the early church is, practically speaking, impossible (my italics)*...

The curious upshot of our investigation is that, viewed globally, the tradition of Jesus' miracles is more firmly supported by the criteria of historicity than are a number of other well-known and often readily accepted traditions about his life and ministry (e.g., his status as a carpenter, his use of '*abba*' in prayer, his own prayer in Gethsemane before his arrest). Put dramatically but with not too much exaggeration: if the miracle tradition from Jesus' public ministry were to be rejected *in toto* as unhistorical, so should every other Gospel tradition about him.[187]

Jesus is not just the most prolific miracle worker in antiquity. He is thoroughly unique in the way he goes about it.

Years ago, a number of scholars speculated that Jesus was just one of many similar wonder workers wandering ancient Palestine and its environs. However, in all the sources that have been unearthed since, only a dozen or so such examples have been found. The three closest examples these scholars usually cite are Hanina, Honi the Circle-Drawer, and Apollonius of Tyana. But each of these "parallels" is riddled with all kinds of problems. For example, in the earliest and most reliable source, Honi seems to have only performed *one* "miracle"—he persisted in praying for rain (drawing a circle around himself, as a later source tells it, and refusing to leave until God made it rain, hence the name) and it rained.

That's it. That's the extent of his "miracle" working activity.

The life of Apollonius is written over one hundred years after he lived and appears to be largely legendary. It may even have been influenced by the gospel stories of Jesus' miracles. Moreover, Apollonius's miracles are designed to astonish and amaze, to *glorify him*. As Raymond Brown comments: "...one should be wary of the claim that Jesus was portrayed like the many other miracle-working teachers, Jewish and pagan, of his era. The idea that such a figure was a commonplace in the 1st century is largely a fiction."[188]

As it turns out, there *weren't that many* wonder workers roaming around.

As it also turns out, they *weren't really similar* to Jesus at all. He towers over them not only in the number of miracles attributed to him, but also in how he performs them. As opposed to the few other pagan and Jewish examples scholars have found, Jesus doesn't perform miracles for his own glory—he frequently heals people in private, taking them away from the crowds; he combines the miracles with his teaching ministry—legitimate teachers didn't want the reputation of being a miracle worker because "wonder workers" were often viewed with suspicion; and he requires faith from the recipient—his miracles always point to the larger reality of God's compassion and love.

Most importantly, in striking contrast to these other wonder workers, Jesus performs miracles *by his own authority*. He doesn't need to pray to God or use some kind of magical incantation or gesture. Instead, he performs them as one who is in full possession of divine power, as if it's *intrinsic to his nature*. He simply issues a command and they happen.

As Raymond Brown points out, this betrays what is most remarkable about his miracles: "The lines of demarcation between Jesus and God…are very vague. The kingdom comes both in and through Jesus. The power to do the healings and other miracles belongs to God but also to Jesus."[189]

Because the historical record is so clear that Jesus performed miracles in this unique way, Robert Spitzer concludes that: "Inasmuch as Jesus was aware of possessing divine authority and power, and aware that *possession* of this power was categorically different from *all* the Old Testament prophets, He must have also been aware of His divine status…that made His possession of divine power possible."[190]

However the miraculous is to be understood philosophically—supernatural event or not—historically, Jesus is reputed to be the most unique and prolific miracle worker who ever lived, *by far*. And he performed miracles as if he was doing them, *quite literally*, by the "finger of God."

--Through his ministry, Jesus claimed to be *vanquishing Satan, defeating evil itself.* Think how absurd and audacious that is. Jesus wasn't just lighting a candle instead of cursing the darkness. He wasn't just practicing random acts of kindness in an attempt to subvert the demonic powers and principalities. He wasn't just trying to overcome evil by being the perfect model of a life of love in the hope of inspiring the multitudes to do likewise. No, he was claiming to bring the reality of evil, Satan, all the cosmic power that opposes anything good, to its knees.

To the point of *unconditional surrender.*

That Jesus' performed exorcisms, proclaimed that the Kingdom of God was being established in and through him, and presented himself as God's eschatological (end-time) prophet/agent, rank among the most secure historical bedrock of his life. Together, they constitute *a mission to eradicate evil from the face of the earth,* a mission Jesus seemed to think would culminate in his death on the cross: his crucifixion would be the ultimate defeat of evil.

However delusional all this might appear, in his own mind at least, Jesus saw himself being uniquely charged with and completely capable of—*as only God can*—vanquishing evil *for good!*

--In a way that would be all too clear to his contemporaries, Jesus carefully orchestrated a nexus of prophetically symbolic actions during the last week his life that made his intentions and self-understanding explicit. (Past prophets often employed this kind of symbolic action to get their message across). Beginning with his messianicly-charged triumphal entry into Jerusalem, which signaled Yahweh's return to Zion (many Jews maintained that God had withdrawn the Shekinah glory of his presence long ago and that the main component of the "age to come" would be the return of this glory to the Temple sanctuary); his dramatic action in and prediction about the Temple, advocating its destruction and replacement; and ending with his words at the Last Supper, which interpreted his death as the true sacrifice that will once and for all reconcile God and humanity, Jesus was showing himself to be the long-awaited Messiah, but with a shocking and unthinkable twist: the Temple was no longer necessary because his body and blood was replacing it—and its atoning function—as the locus of Yahweh's presence on earth.

This was the interpretive key Jesus provided. Within the Jewish symbolic world of that day, it clearly communicated that he thought *he* was the dwelling place of God's Shekinah glory; that Yahweh *had* returned, *in* him.

In him, Yahweh had become present *in person.* [191]

--Jesus saw his death as the decisive event of history, the event that would establish a new and eternal covenant, i.e., relationship, between God and humankind. He didn't die as just another martyr like the Maccabees or the prophets of old, but as *the one upon whom history turned.* He saw himself standing at the climax of the Jewish narrative, fulfilling the story of salvation history.

*He believed his death would reconcile creation to its Creator.*

It was the reason he could forgive sin so freely. Somehow, he was taking sin upon himself and putting an end to the alienation it caused between us and God. This all comes together at the Last Supper as he tried to explain to his bewildered disciples all that was about to happen. We know his words over the bread and cup are authentic because they are so *repulsive* to Jewish sensitivities, far more intense than our disgust at cannibalism. Eating human flesh and drinking blood were absolutely taboo.

Not to mention grotesque!

But this was the prophetic sign he chose to *memorialize what he was doing.* And the words point to the fact that he saw his death as the vicarious, atoning sacrifice that would restore the divine-human relationship. That giving his body and shedding his blood would establish the new and eternal covenant between God and humankind.

In fact, one of the major reasons Jesus was put to death is that, in the eyes of the Jewish authorities, he had clearly committed blasphemy. And indeed, he had. He arrogantly presumed the prerogatives of God belonged to him. Which is totally consistent with the way he understood his death: as *the* event which would save the world.

--Jesus also predicted his death would lead to his ultimate vindication. He said he would return on the clouds of heaven with his Father's angels to judge the world.

On the eve of his death, he even blasphemed once more before the High Priest (Mark 14:62)—which insured his execution—by declaring that God would make it known for all to see that Jesus sits at the right hand of the Power, meaning that *he shares the power of God; that he truly is his divine Son.*

As explained above (Chapter 2.9), it is highly unlikely the early church would invent such a saying since Jesus was so clearly wrong about returning in this way, especially in predicting that the very High Priest and Sanhedrin he was standing before at that moment would see him in all his glory.

Obviously, they did not.

## The Real Jesus

This is the general scholarly consensus. Even if different scholars might challenge or qualify some of its parts, it is the overall picture recent scholarship has produced. And it points to an *astonishing self-estimation.*

Jesus thought of himself as the Son of Man who would judge the world.

As the unique Son of the Father sent to vanquish evil and bring about God's reign, ultimately through his own awful suffering and death.

As Yahweh's personal, embodied presence on earth, possessing in himself the divine power to heal and the divine authority to forgive sin.

It's important to point out that this is not exactly what the early church said about him. They called him Lord, Savior, the Son of God, the great I AM, teasing out the meaning of his more enigmatic self-designations. This is another reason to think that this portrait was how Jesus thought of himself. Otherwise, the gospels wouldn't have preserved an understanding and terminology the later church didn't adopt and continue to use.

Of course, there's a good reason why Jesus couldn't come right out and say he was the Lord, the Son of God, the great I AM. That was outright blasphemy, punishable by immediate death. He would have been stoned on the spot. His mission would be over before it ever began—that's probably why he waits until his trial to make what is historically likely to be the clearest public statement he ever made about his identity. (See this episode before the High Priest cited above.)

No critical scholar would ever say Jesus came right out and said he was God. The places in Scripture where this occurs, like when he uses the divine name ("I AM") for himself, are obviously post-Easter retrojections of what the church came to believe about him.

And no true scholar thinks he thought of himself the way later Christian faith would, as the eternal Son of God and Second Person of the Trinity. By every indication, he wouldn't have had what it meant to be divine worked out so fully.

But, even if he went about it in a cryptic way, even if he didn't have the full scope of his divinity all worked out, a growing number of scholars do believe that this, in some sense, is what he meant to imply. He certainly claimed a number of divine prerogatives as his own, especially in the way he behaved. In some of his parables and more enigmatic sayings made in public, he hinted at a divine identity. At times with his disciples in private, he was much more explicit, even though they lacked the conceptual apparatus to comprehend most of what he was saying—prior to the resurrection, no Jew could conceive that a human being was divine.

However, the best historical judgment is that this is, in one way or another, what Jesus understood himself to be—the divine Son of God.

# To Infinity and Beyond

One final puzzle: where did Jesus get all of this?

I once had a conversation with an Orthodox Jew. She was genuinely baffled that I could believe a mortal human being could be God incarnate, that the *infinite* could possibly take up residence in the *finite*. It was totally incomprehensible to her.

Try as she might, she just couldn't wrap her head around it.

As an orthodox Jew, this would have been just as true for Jesus. Jews were familiar with pagan gods who supposedly took human form, but it wasn't in the realm of possibility for the eternal, transcendent, true Lord of the universe to assume limited human flesh. That would be an untenable paradox, something they just wouldn't be able to wrap their minds around. If a suffering messiah, as we saw earlier, is as self-refuting as a square-circle, or married-bachelor, then exceedingly more so the idea of Yahweh in human form.

So where did Jesus come up with this? One answer is that he was delusional. Through the ages, other unstable and/or morally questionable people have made similar claims. But Jesus gave no impression of being an egomaniac. Quite the opposite. His character was impeccable, exhibiting sublime wisdom, humility, and goodness. Indeed, the combination of such a grandiose self-estimation and such radical humility is absolutely unique in history and is itself quite a paradox. As Keller notes:

> Jesus is one of the very few persons in history who founded a great world religion or who, like Plato or Aristotle, has set the course of human thought and life for centuries. Jesus is in that tiny, select group. On the other hand, there have been a number of human persons over the years who have implicitly or explicitly claimed to be divine beings from other worlds. Many of them were demagogues; many more of them were leaders of small, self-contained sects of true believers. What is unique about Jesus is that he

is the only member of the first set of persons who is also a member of the second.

The first group had a great impact on millions of people largely because of their brilliant teaching but also because of their admirable lives and characters, which, of course, included humility. Buddha emphatically said he was not a god, and Muhammad, of course, wound never, ever have claimed to be Allah, nor did Confucius identify himself with heaven. The second group consists of those who claimed to be God but never were able to convince anyone but a small number. Why? Because it is virtually impossible to live such an extraordinary life that most people would be forced to conclude you were not merely a human being. In the whole history of the world, there is only one person who not only claimed to be God himself but also got enormous numbers of people to believe it. Only Jesus combines claims of divinity with the most beautiful life of humanity.[192]

It's a provocative question: how did an apparently sane and faithful first-century Jew not only ever conceive that he could somehow be God's personal presence on earth, but then dare to go on and stake his whole life on it? It's comprehensible how the disciples might arrive at this conclusion *after* witnessing the resurrection. But prior to this earth-shattering event, such a stunning self-estimation, which is at the core of everything else Jesus said and did, defies the limits his historical context would have imposed.

So where'd he get it?

# CHAPTER
# 6

# Who Cares Who Rises?

## *Fitting Like a Glove*

J ESUS WAS CRUCIFIED ALONGSIDE two other criminals, sentenced, like him, to die by capital punishment. In their cases, however, the sentence was well deserved. But what if, instead of Jesus, one of the criminal's tombs was found empty and his friends had the same bizarre yet undeniable encounters with him? What if one of them rose from the dead?

What would you conclude?

That he was God, the savior of the world?

That his life was now the ultimate norm for human life?

*Of course not.*

What if it was John the Baptist or Mary Magdalene or Peter or Thomas or Caiphas or Pilate who was said to have died and risen?

Miraculous? Maybe.

Mystifying? Definitely.

The revelation of God in person? *No way!*

Nobody would ever conclude anything like what was claimed about Jesus.

N.T. Wright puts it this way:

> In the ancient Jewish world, as in the modern Western one, for someone who had been certifiably dead to become visibly alive again would mean that the world was indeed a stranger place than one had imagined; it would not at all justify a claim that the person to whom this odd event had happened was therefore the saviour of the world, the 'son of god,' Or anything else in particular...This forces us to ask: could the belief that someone had been raised from the dead, whatever precisely was understood by that, have produced the results it did—*unless certain things were known, and continued to be known, about the one who had thus been raised after having been crucified?*

> ...The cross and resurrection, in short, are clearly central to virtually all known forms of early Christianity. But the rise of that early Christian understanding is only comprehensible on the basis that certain things continued to be known, as history, about the one who (among so many others) was crucified outside Jerusalem and who (unlike any others before or since—a fact of some significance) was declared by his followers to be alive shortly afterwards. The resurrection thus vindicates *what Jesus was already believed to be;* it cannot be the sole cause of that belief which sprang up around it.[193]

The resurrection vindicates Jesus' divinity, but it doesn't fully account for it.

Without the other aspects of his public ministry outlined in the previous chapter, nobody would have concluded that he was the divine Son of God—the Lord—following the resurrection. This conclusion *presupposes* a life that was *already fully consistent with such a claim*; even if it wasn't completely clear, or clear at all, that he was divine until the resurrection.

*Unlike anyone else who ever lived,*[194] Jesus had to be doing and saying things that led those who knew him and now claimed to have seen him risen, to conclude he was God in the flesh. Otherwise, even seeing him risen, they never would have come to believe he was God. In other words, the resurrection makes explicit what was *already* implicit.

In fact, this is one of the strongest reasons to think the contemporary scholarly portrait of the historical Jesus outlined in Chapter 5 above is accurate: in light of the resurrection, those first disciples would never have concluded Jesus was divine *unless* he was saying and doing exactly the kinds of things that the best modern scholarship says he was. If he was just a rebel zealot, cynic philosopher, charismatic holy man, wise sage, teacher of timeless truth, wandering wonder worker, or subversive prophet, no one—*no one*—would have concluded he was the Lord, even if they believed with all their heart he had risen from the dead.[195]

And here's why this matters. It just so happens that *the one person in all of history about whom such a conclusion could be reached* is also the one person in all of history *who anyone has ever seriously claimed rose from the dead.*[196]

What are the odds of that?

Oxford philosopher Richard Swinburne has done a thorough statistical analysis of the probabilities involved in such a stunning coherence. This is his conclusion: "…there is no other prophet in human history, apart from Jesus, with whose life there is significant evidence of such a super-miracle [i.e., the resurrection] being connected…Yet, the coincidence of there being significant evidence for a super-miracle connected with the life of the only prophet for whom there is significant evidence that he satisfied the prior requirements for being God incarnate would also have been very improbable unless God brought it about."[197]

The "prior requirements for being God incarnate" he's referring to are, essentially, the remarkable pieces of data from Jesus' earthly career listed in Chapter 5.

But what's even more impressive is that each of these extraordinary pieces of historical data is completely independent from the others. For example, the impression Jesus made that he was without sin *depends in no way* on him performing miracles and vice versa. The fact that he introduced an otherworldly ethic can be verified historically *whether or not* he also spoke and acted with an authority that implied he was Yahweh's personal presence on earth.

What's more, each would stand on its own as true *even without the resurrection.* For example, as a historical datum, the fact Jesus performed numerous healings is true whether he rose or not. Likewise, offering free forgiveness to sinners, living his own radical ethic to a sublime degree, or believing he was dying as the vicarious sacrifice for sin, are in no way dependent on the resurrection. Each of these separate and unusual pieces of data can be isolated and *verified independently* as historical by themselves.

Yet astonishingly, all these remarkable pieces of disparate historical data *converge in this one life.* And when you put them all together, *they paint a **coherent picture** that is absolutely unique in the annals of history:* a person who speaks and acts as if he is God incarnate. No other major religious figure has ever made such claims or had such claims made about them.

But couldn't Jesus and/or his disciples have orchestrated all this to convince people Jesus was something he really wasn't? Or couldn't Jesus just have been insane, deluded, a megalomaniac who sincerely believed, as from time to time unstable people do, he was God?

Not really. Assuming Jesus, or his disciples, could even conceive something like this (as we've seen throughout, prior to the resurrection, it is historically implausible that any first-century Jew—unless he actually was God come in the flesh—could think of Yahweh as somehow taking on human form), it's virtually impossible to live a life so perfect people think of you as sinless (if you disagree, try it— you probably won't last the day!), especially if you are an unstable and self-absorbed, delusional megalomaniac. Moreover, all of Jesus' many miracles couldn't have been staged or faked. In fact, the ones scholars judge to be the most historically credible are also the most spectacular—e.g., giving sight to the blind, raising the dead—and therefore, most likely to be authentic miracles. Furthermore, Jesus' otherworldly ethic—an ethic he lived!—is so profoundly counterintuitive, self-denying, and yet unexpectedly sublime, that it not only defies being the mere product of human genius, it also defies any self-aggrandizing motive a person of unsound mind or group of questionable character might have.

Even if Jesus were deluded, a raging narcissist, or both, just believing you're God doesn't give you the ability to live a sinless life, perform miracles, or construct a supernaturally sublime ethic.

In addition, no first-century Jew would ever adopt such outlandish, scandalous, and utterly repugnant notions like, among other things, free forgiveness, which bypassed the central institution of Judaism—the Temple—and undermined what is most basic to Yahweh's nature—his holiness (not to mention that it made a mockery of any sense of justice: see the parable of the Laborers in the Vineyard (Matthew 20:1-16) or read the parable of the Prodigal Son (Luke 15:11-32) from the older brother's perspective); or like the self-refuting idea of a "suffering messiah" who idiotically goes to the *cursed* cross—the decisive public demonstration of God's utter rejection (that's why Paul, in I Corinthians 1:22-25, calls the cross a stumbling block, scandalous to Jews and foolishness to Greeks)—thinking that this will somehow "save" humanity; or like instituting a memorial meal that included the abhorrent ritual of eating flesh and drinking blood.

If Jesus and/or his disciples were trying to fabricate the whole thing to make people think he was in some way divine, this most certainly is not how they would have gone about it.

One of the sayings scholars most agree can be traced back to Jesus is his prohibition against fasting while he is alive. (Mark 2:18-10) The way he defends this questionable practice (pious Jews of the time regularly fasted) is by explaining that people don't fast while the bridegroom is around—weddings are a time for celebration, not fasting. But in the Old Testament and especially the symbolic world of first-century Judaism, the bridegroom represented Yahweh. Israel was his bride.

In effect then, Jesus is saying that the disciples shouldn't fast while he is with them because *he is the bridegroom. He is God, personally present on earth.* This is an outrageously arrogant statement, psychotically narcissistic. From the mouth of any other human being, we would dismiss him as a self-deluded, egomaniac. (Think David Koresh or the Reverend Sun Myung Moon, for example.)

But the thing about Jesus is that he is one of, if not the, most humble, selfless, and sane people who ever lived. Jesus clearly was not an egomaniac. He was the exact opposite. He was pure goodness incarnate.

Grandiose claims to divinity; a breathtakingly beautiful and self-denying life: this is *a stunning paradox that no one—especially in that day—could contrive.*

So here is this man who thought of himself as the personal presence of God among us, teaching with authority and forgiving sins; who introduced an otherworldly teaching about God's crazy love with its correspondingly radical ethic; who prolifically performed miracles unlike any other; who so impressed those around him with his goodness that they could claim he was without sin; who went to his death to establish the new and everlasting covenant that would definitively reconcile the divine-human relationship, all the while predicting he would come again to judge the world; and this man is *also the one person in all of history where the evidence is substantial enough to sustain the claim he actually rose from the dead.*

**That all of these extraordinary pieces of independent data which, when put together, point so clearly to a unique divine identity happen to coincide in the one person for whom there is significant evidence that he rose from the dead makes it exceedingly probable that he really did!**

Now it could be argued that the resurrection was invented for this purpose: the disciples were so impressed by this man they couldn't let him go; his remarkable life would be tragically incomplete without it, undoing all he seemed to be.

Except that, as we've seen, the evidence for the empty tomb and the appearances is *so complete on its own* as to be virtually certain. In fact, if the disciples invented or imagined the entire thing, it would've looked completely different. Not as radically unprecedented or paradoxically illogical.

So yes, if the evidence for the resurrection was flimsy, then admittedly we should suspect it was invented for this reason. But it's incredibly strong, and when you place it alongside the evidence for the historical Jesus, *it all fits, like a glove.*

The corroboration is staggering.

Back to the criterion of coherence. The more something fits with what is already judged to be historical, the more likely that is to be historical as well. The resurrection fits the historical evidence from Jesus' life and ministry in an uncanny and totally unique way.

Not only is there the astounding nexus of an empty tomb and appearances—a nexus that significantly increases the probability of each—there is also this *astounding nexus of historical data surrounding the life and ministry of Jesus,* which, when all combined, is absolutely breathtaking: otherworldly ethic, forgiving sins, teaching with authority, divine self-estimation, sinless, miracles, vicarious death, empty tomb, *and* appearances. All of which, also, amounts to a divine identity.

Historically speaking, the coherence is as total and complete as it could be.

Think of it this way. Belief in Jesus' divinity would not have occurred to the early church *unless* his life was somehow exceptional, already pointing in this direction. But the fact that his life was already pointing in this direction means that it fits with the resurrection as it would for no other person who has ever lived. In fact, his exceptional life begs for something like the resurrection to make sense of it. Without the resurrection, it would be tragically incomplete.

So if there is one life that the resurrection "fits" with, it is Jesus's.

And it just so happens that he is the only person in history for whom such a claim is ever seriously made.

It truly is an uncanny fit.

# SUGGESTIONS FOR GOING DEEPER

Bauckham, Richard, *Jesus and the Eyewitnesses: The Gospels as Eyewitness Testimony*, Grand Rapids, MI: Eerdmans, 2006.

Brown, Raymond E., *An Introduction to New Testament Christology*, Mahwah, NJ: Paulist Press, 1994.

Fitzmyer, Joseph A., *A Christological Catechism: New Testament Answers*, Ramsey, NJ: Paulist Press, 1982.

Meier, John P., *A Marginal Jew: Rethinking the Historical Jesus, Volume Two*, New York, NY: Doubleday, 1994.

Pitre, Brant, *The Case for Jesus: The Biblical and Historical Evidence for Christ*, New York, NY: Image, 2016.

Spitzer, Robert, *God So Loved the World: Clues to Our Transcendent Destiny from the Revelation of Jesus*, San Francisco, CA: Ignatius Press, 2016.

Strobel, Lee, *The Case for the Real Jesus: A Journalist Investigates the Current Attacks on the Identity of Christ*, Grand Rapids, MI: Zondervan, 2007.

Swinburne, Richard, *The Resurrection of God Incarnate*, Oxford: Clarendon Press, 2010.

Witherington, Ben III, *The Gospel Code: Novel Claims About Jesus, Mary Magdalene, and Da Vinci*, Downers Grove, IL: InterVarsity Press, 2004.

Wright, N.T., *Jesus and the Victory of God: Christian Origins and the Question of God, Volume Two*, Minneapolis, MN: Fortress Press, 1996.

# PART III: LIFE IS HARD... THEN YOU DIE!

## *The Philosophical Question*

# CHAPTER

# 7

# Dead Men Don't Walk

## *The Philosophical Objection*

A BLOG POST I ONCE read passionately exhorted people to THINK! It admitted that the historical evidence for the resurrection was there, but then went on to ask, what's more *reasonable*? That Jesus actually rose? Or that the whole thing is just a sincere mistake or misunderstanding? The point this post was making is that *reason* dictates we dismiss the historical evidence in light of the fact that there is nothing in our modern, scientific worldview that would justify thinking something like this *could* happen.

This blogger has it exactly right.

If there's no good reason—nothing in all our accumulated experience and/or logic—to think something like the resurrection could happen, then we should reject the historical evidence. No matter how compelling this evidence is, the resurrection is still extremely unlikely, if not impossible, to have happened.

Think about it this way. If a large crowd of people said they saw Superman fly by them one day, we wouldn't believe that a man can fly. Instead, no matter how reliable these witnesses seemed, we'd look for some other rational explanation for what they experienced. And even if we couldn't find one, we would still dismiss it because we know *people can't fly*.

However, if there is good reason to think the resurrection could happen, especially if there is good reason to believe there is a God who could intervene is such a way, then the *exact opposite* is true. The historical evidence makes it highly likely that it did happen, even to the point of virtual certainty.

But isn't this blogger right? All of the empirical evidence, all of human experience throughout the ages, all of the knowledge modern science has amassed, points to the simple fact that people just don't come back from the dead.

Life is hard...then you die.

Death is one of the most deeply entrenched and unrelenting laws of nature. And since no one has proven that God exists, there's no good reason to think there is a Being capable of intervening this way. (Christian proofs for the existence of God usually are inevitably grounded in the resurrection, which is a circular, and thus terribly flawed, argument: we can only know with certainty that God exists because of the resurrection, but we only know the resurrection is possible because God exists.)

*So how can any reasonable person possibly believe Jesus could have come back from the dead?*

Understandably, when it comes to Jesus' resurrection, the one final hurdle many people just can't get over is the *philosophical presupposition that people just don't come back from the dead*. Like Pinchas Lapide, they often admit that something strange happened there—the historical facts are too hard to deny—but whatever happened that first Easter, however compelling, it couldn't be a resurrection because things like that simply *can't* happen.

Modern science is often invoked to back this claim.

When I was a child, my parents told me that thunder was caused by God bowling in heaven. When I grew up, I learned the real explanation in science class. Maybe in the past, when, without the benefit of modern science, there were so many unexplained mysteries, the resurrection was something people with a "childish" worldview could think possible. But with all we now know about the universe and the way it works, it is absurd to think someone could defy such an inviolable law of nature and rise from the dead.

It turns out that this is the most common objection to the resurrection.

In fact, many people don't even bother to examine the historical evidence because they believe *a priori* (i.e., beforehand), as an established fact of our modern scientific worldview, that miracles, especially one as spectacular as this, simply don't happen.

For those who do bother, their evaluation of the evidence is often so influenced by this philosophical bias they aren't able to make a sober assessment of it: just look at how convoluted the alternative explanations are. They are so desperate to explain away an event they don't think is possible on philosophical grounds, they run roughshod over what they would otherwise accept historically.

But even if someone does admit the historical evidence is sound, they are still apt to doubt the resurrection happened. As R. Douglas Geivett observes:

> You might agree that good evidence exists for all sorts of things that, in principle, fall within the purview of historical investigation: many believed that Jesus had risen bodily (indeed, many believed that Jesus had been *raised* bodily from the dead *by God*), the tomb was found empty within a few hours of the burial of Jesus' body, Jesus was seen alive after these events by many people on various occasions, and so forth. But events are made more or less likely not only by circumstantial evidence susceptible of historical analysis but also by metaphysical possibilities

that fall outside the special province of historical investigation.[198]

This question of whether or not the resurrection falls within the realm of metaphysical possibility is *perfectly legitimate*.

Those who object to it on philosophical grounds are *right to do so*.

If it isn't *rational* to think something like this could happen in the universe we inhabit, it doesn't matter how much historical evidence is amassed.

The historical evidence, decisive as it may be, *isn't enough*.

The resurrection must also be a philosophical possibility.

So, is it?

## Strange Science

Surprisingly, the best place to start is modern science. In light of recent findings, the philosophical presupposition that something as anomalous as the resurrection just can't happen is being undermined by scientists themselves.

As Morton Kelsey pointed out several decades ago:

> There was a time when physicists thought that they really understood our natural world and what could and could not happen within it. This time has passed. There are so many loose ends, so many unanswered questions, so many accepted hypotheses that do not fit together...
>
> We have a tendency to believe what is most comfortable for us to believe, as T. S. Kuhn has shown with great clarity in his book *The Structure of Scientific Revolutions*. What we do not expect to see we simply do not perceive; what we don't want to see has two strikes against our perceiving it. The leading

edge of the modern scientific community is much more open to possibilities even though there is a rearguard action on the part of hidebound materialists and determinists that seeks to block us from understanding the mysterious nature of the universe that is opening up to us. Vital, transforming Christian faith is inevitably linked to the resurrection of Jesus. Those who wish to present the resurrection to modern people need to know the comforting humility of some of the greatest scientific minds. I have described this in several books. There was a time when science was a dogmatic adversary of religion and of Christianity in particular. However, with thinkers like Werner Heisenberg, T.S. Kuhn, and Robert Oppenheimer we find ourselves in an open universe, with some of the scientists themselves opting for a human soul and a God who can bring us to our full potential. Truly agnostic science can be a handmaid of Christianity and even of the resurrection faith, for it is agnostic about the conclusions of science itself.[199]

Werner Heisenberg is a good example of this trend. His Principle of Uncertainty (or Indeterminancy), first introduced in 1927, is based on the fact that with subatomic particles it is impossible to precisely measure the position and velocity of an object at the exact same time. Indeed, the very attempt to measure subatomic particles forces them to behave in unpredictable ways. This implies that the universe is more open than we previously thought possible: the immutable laws of the Newtonian-Enlightenment view don't hold true in all instances. In no way is this intended to be a defense of the miraculous. But it does demonstrate that there are anomalies in the physics of reality that defy precise measurement and predictable analysis, and that, though extremely rare, it may even be *reasonable* to anticipate finding other anomalies.[200]

There are other ways the universe is proving to defy predictable analysis. For example, within physics the two prevailing theories used to explain reality on a macro and micro level, general relativity and quantum mechanics respectively, *are incompatible with each other.* They don't fit together as a unified whole, yet they *succeed in explaining their respective domains better than any other theories.*

This is also true with something as basic as light. Physicists theorize that light consists of both particle and wave. Logically, light can't be both; but empirically, the theory that it is *works brilliantly* (pardon the pun!).

Similarly, in the field of medicine, epigenetics and neuroplasticity are challenging scientists to reevaluate a number of longstanding assumptions about how "fixed" our brains, bodies, and genes are. If you're worried you may have fried too many brain cells in college, it now appears that the mind has a previously unimagined plasticity that can "regrow" new ones!

It also now appears that we aren't doomed by our genetic profile to certain health conditions, like heart disease or cancer. We can actually "modify" our genes to some extent through lifestyle choices like diet and exercise.

All this *scientific discovery* points to the fact that the universe is a lot more unpredictable and mystifying than science used to think it was.

*Reality really is stranger than it seems.*

As Oxford mathematician John Lennox provocatively asks: "... in this advanced scientific age, how can one possibly believe that a physical body came through grave-clothes, and through locked doors into a room? But perhaps this advanced scientific age has made such a thing more conceivable, rather than less so. We know what the disciples did not know: matter consists largely of empty space; elementary particles can penetrate matter; some—like neutrinos—to immense depth."

In our "advanced scientific age," Jesus' resurrected body and the qualities it exhibited seem more logical than ever before: "In addition to that, there is the question of dimensionality. We are familiar with the four dimensions of space-time...Maybe nature itself involves more dimensions than we thought—string theory would suggest there may be more...

"The physics of matter...can help us at least to see that it might be very short-sighted and premature to dismiss out of hand the New Testament account of the properties of Christ's resurrection body."[201] On one level, at least, modern science might make the resurrection more, not less, intelligible.

And so, the great stumbling block to believing in the resurrection, that we live in a closed universe where something like this just can't happen, can no longer be an airtight objection.

Let me be totally clear: this is long way from establishing that something like the resurrection is likely or logical. These scientific anomalies are light years apart from a person returning from the dead.

The most this data suggests is that there are mystifying anomalies built into the structure of reality that make the universe more open and unpredictable than we ever thought imaginable. And in such a universe, it isn't *completely* irrational to think that an anomaly like a bodily resurrection could be a remote possibility.

## Pure Philosophy: Musings about Miracles

In addition to the findings of modern science, there are powerful philosophical reasons not to reject the resurrection *a priori*.

The famous philosopher David Hume was the major proponent of the view that miracles can't happen because they violate the fixed laws of nature, what he refers to as "uniform experience." Much of the philosophical objection to miracles is built on this very point. No historical evidence, Hume would argue, no matter how strong, can overcome the *staggering consistency* we observe in the natural order.

This *testable, provable, empirical "uniform experience" trumps any claim of past history.*

This sounds like an irrefutable argument. So irrefutable, in fact, that it has become the default position of our modern, scientific age. (It happens to be my default position too!) But Hume here commits a major logical fallacy. He is making a circular argument, *assuming what he is trying to prove.* Lennox exposes how:

> In anybody's book, miracles, by definition, are exceptions to what normally happens. If miracles were normal, they wouldn't be called miracles! What, then, does Hume mean by "uniform experience"? It is one thing to say "Experience shows that such and such normally happens, but there may be exceptions, although none has been observed, that is, the experience *we have had* has been uniform." It is an entirely different thing to say, "This is what we normally experience, and we must always experience it, for there can be no exceptions."

> ...What Hume does is to assume what he wants to prove, namely that there have never been any miracles in the past, and so there is uniform experience against this present instance being a miracle. But here his argument runs into very serious trouble. How does he know? In order to know that experience against miracles is absolutely uniform, he would need to have total access to every event in the universe at all times and places, which is self-evidently impossible... Therefore, Hume cannot know that miracles have never occurred. He is simply assuming what he wants to prove—that nature is uniform and no miracles have taken place!

The only real alternative to Hume's circular argument, or course, is to be open to the possibility that miracles have occurred. That is a historical question, and not a philosophical one, and depends on witness and evidence.[202]

Since no one has access to every event that ever has or ever will happen, miracles can't be ruled out *a priori*. Philosophically, it is an unjustified presupposition. "Uniform experience" may render miracles, especially one so spectacular as a dead man rising, *extremely unlikely*. But, a miracle should never be ruled out until the empirical historical evidence for such a claim is thoroughly examined.

And when you examine the historical evidence, *experience isn't as uniform as Hume suggests.*

There have been numerous scientifically documented "occurrences" that defy naturalistic explanation. Medically, examples abound. Many of us know of someone who has had a serious, even terminal, condition reversed in a way that defies explanation. I just met a man who told me he was given a diagnosis of terminal cancer with only months to live *seventeen years ago!* When he was re-examined, he was cancer free.

His doctors are still at a loss to explain how.

Perhaps the best example of these "medically inexplicable" cures is found in Lourdes, France, at the site where the Blessed Virgin Mary is said to have appeared in 1858. Years ago the Medical Commission of Lourdes was established to thoroughly investigate the many (over 1300) supposed healings that were associated with the site. It consists of twenty distinguished physicians and surgeons who come from various faith backgrounds, including a number who report having no faith at all. They are either agnostic or atheist. This commission has now documented sixty-nine cases where a *bona fide* physical condition was radically reversed or remedied, often instantaneously, but with, at present, no good medical explanation.

Please note, I'm not saying that these are miracles, in other words, caused by the intervention of some kind of personal God. But, unless science can eventually produce some other explanation, they certainly do constitute clear exceptions to uniform experience.[203]

A few scholars have even pointed to what may be an intriguing exception to uniform experience that pertains specifically to the resurrection, namely, apparitions of the dead. Dale Allison has done an in-depth study of these supposed apparitions. He's found that, while most reports by people claiming to have seen someone who has died are likely psychological in nature, some exhibit phenomena that, at least on the face of it, are *ontologically objective*: in an overwhelmingly physical way, individuals, and in a few instances, more than one person at a time, have reported seeing, hearing, and even, in a couple of rare cases, touching or hugging the deceased. (I am deeply skeptical about all this, but have to admit that the evidence these apparitions are legitimate is impressive.)

While there are radical differences between these veridical apparitions and the appearances of Jesus—for example, none involve an empty tomb (the body of the deceased remains buried), there are drastic differences in the quantity and quality of eyewitnesses (the vast majority only involve one person and none more than a handful, as opposed to the hundreds who witness Jesus); what they see is well within their conceptual framework (i.e., expectations, prior understanding of life after death, etc.); and virtually no one believes the person has been raised bodily from the dead (they are reported to be fleeting and merely suggestive visions/experiences, i.e., that the person is still somehow alive, not that they are witnessing an actual, permanent transformation to a specific, new mode of being)—if they prove credible, they challenge the metaphysical presumptions of modern materialism to the core and make the resurrection of Jesus much more plausible.[204]

One other thing needs to be challenged at this point. We are led to assume that modern men and women are too enlightened and sophisticated to believe in miracles. No intelligent person would accept them. And this is often used to simply dismiss the miraculous out of hand: since no modern rational person accepts them, why bother examining the evidence?

As I explained in the introduction, I'm very sympathetic to this presumption: as a modern, scientifically-minded person myself, *my* default position is to reject the miraculous. Simply out of hand. But philosophically, pre-empting a rigorous analysis of the question on the basis of what the majority of people believe isn't a valid move. At one point, the majority of people thought the earth was flat, that it was the center of the universe, and that it was only six thousand years old.

Moreover, a Gallup poll in 1989 revealed that 82 percent of Americans believed that miracles not only occurred by the power of God long ago but *continue to occur even in our own day*. Such a large segment of the population must surely include many highly educated, scientifically-minded people![205]

In 2010, a more recent Pew study put the figure of those who believe modern miracles occur at nearly 80 percent. And the 2007 Baylor National Religious Survey revealed that 23 percent of Americans even believed they witnessed a miraculous healing, with 16 percent saying they had received one.[206]

So it seems presumptuous, even wildly inaccurate, to say that modern, scientifically-minded people don't think the miraculous is possible. And yet, without any examination of the evidence, miraculous claims are routinely rejected in just this way.

In contrast, the soundest philosophical approach acknowledges that no argument to date has conclusively demonstrated that the miraculous is impossible. In fact, provided a healthy dose of skepticism, there are good reasons to remain open to the possibility of rare exceptions to uniform experience, and that some of these could be considered miracles, provided other evidence (i.e., that there is a God who is apt to intervene in human affairs) is introduced, a question that will be treated in chapters 8 and 9.

## One of These Things Is Not Like the Others: A One-of-a-Kind Event

But even if the scientific community was able to conclusively determine that we live in a closed universe; and even if no historical evidence of "miraculous" exceptions to our uniform experience could be produced, the possibility Jesus could rise from the dead still can't be ruled out.

Here's why. The resurrection is a one-of-a-kind event. It's absolutely unique. So unique, in fact, that, by overcoming death, it claims to be *the* great exception to "uniform experience." It's not just any ordinary miracle.

Miracles, of course, are *extra*ordinary by definition. But that's the point. This miracle so transcends all others, it's in a category by itself.

It's *the super-miracle*.

According to Christian faith, the resurrection is God's *decisive* supernatural intervention into history. Not only is it the most spectacular miracle ever; not only is it the one miracle that is indispensable to God's saving purpose for us—redemption hinges on it and the crucifixion—it's the entire basis of Christian faith: it reveals Jesus' divinity.

If it happened, Christianity is true. No other miracle is necessary.

But if it didn't, Christianity is false. No other miracle will suffice.

According to Christian faith, the resurrection is also *unrepeatable*. Only this man, the God-man, *can* defeat death. Only he is able to defy what is the most uniform end of our human experience.

Therefore, as a "one-off" event, it can't be rejected *a priori*. There is nothing in all our accumulated knowledge and experience that could rule out such an event because, *by its very nature*, nothing like it has ever happened (or ever will again). We wouldn't expect to see anything like it in the natural order. So, we don't need to live in a world infused with the miraculous for the resurrection to be true. Even if it could be shown that no other miracle had ever happened, the resurrection, being in a category by itself, would remain *logically possible*.

Still, these are meager results. Without a rational basis to think it's more than remotely possible, the blogger at the beginning of this chapter is right: despite the historical evidence, the resurrection is ridiculously improbable.

*No thinking person should accept it.*

So, is there any good reason to think it *would* happen? That it's not just logically possible, but supremely reasonable?

And, is there any philosophical justification for thinking the resurrection is a true miracle? That it's *the supernatural intervention of a personal God* and not just a random exception to uniform experience, an inexplicable anomaly?

CHAPTER

# 8

# The Great Intruder

*Without Presupposing God: Metaphysical*
*Serendipity Times Four*

L IFE IS HARD...THEN YOU die.

In Monty Python's classic movie *The Meaning of Life*, there is a scene where two unsuspecting couples are enjoying a dinner party. Suddenly, the Grim Reaper knocks at the door. Oblivious to the fact they are at literally at death's door, the couples gleefully invite him in to join the party.

As Grim points his bony little finger at the one he came to take, they laugh at him, as if he's merely an entertaining guest playing some kind of joke or party game. Caught off guard, Grim tries to convince them that he's serious. That he, death, is no joke. But the more he insists on the dreadful reality of his mission, the more the partiers mock him. And the more infuriated he becomes.

He gets so mad that he decides to take them all instead of just the one he originally came for. Even as he leads the partiers out of

206

the house to their deaths, they continue to laugh and joke with him. They're literally staring death in the face and go right along, acting as if it doesn't exist.

Like the partiers in the movie, we're a culture in denial. We worship youth. We act as if death will never come, and when it does come, we don't like to talk about it. Instead, we spend all our time hoping for some drug, some fountain of youth, some scientific discovery that will prolong life, even prevent the onslaught of death altogether: modern medicine, the latest diet or fitness craze, cryogenics, DNA extraction, cloning.

And when we can't get it, we search compulsively for some lasting testimony to our presence on this planet: wealth, fame, success, even something as simple as photographs. Anything to mark our tiny little stay on this planet, to leave some lasting and indelible sign that we were here and that our lives mattered. That they weren't lived in vain.

*We long for immortality.*

But the only guarantee in life is that we will die.

It is supremely painful to admit that no matter how big a mark we make, within a generation or two very few will know. And fewer still will care. No matter how much we try to deny, avoid, or make an end run around it, we are all mortal after all.

Life is hard...then you die.

When I was a child my dad died. For months after his death, I would have this recurring dream: It would be around dinner time when he came home from work. I'd hear a car, his car. The 65 Chevy would purr up the street and make its wide turn into the driveway. The door would open and my dad would get out. He's alive!

My heart would start racing, then my feet. I'd run out the front door and down the sidewalk and into his arms. He'd pick me up and carry me inside like he always did after coming home from work. And there we were, all together, a happy family again because he was alive.

Then I'd wake up with a feeling of total elation, sheer joy. And I'd run to my parents' bedroom...only to find that he wasn't there. That awful empty feeling in the pit my stomach, that suffocating grief, would return as reality set in again. It was only a dream.

Life is hard...then you die.

Although death is the most certain thing in life, *it feels so unnatural.*

It ruins everything. It is *the great intruder.*

Philip Yancey puts it this way:

> Nature treats death as a normal occurrence, the foundation of the all-important food chain. Only we humans react with shock and elaboration, as though we can't get used to the fact. We dress up our corpses in new clothes, embalm them, and bury them in airtight caskets and concrete vaults to slow natural decay. We act out a stubborn reluctance to yield to this most powerful of life experiences.
>
> [This]...'unnatural' [reaction] hint[s] at another world. In a way unique to our species, we are not fully at home here. As a symptom of that fact, we feel stirrings toward something higher and more lasting.[207]

Why can't we get used to death? Why does it feel so *wrong,* like an intruder?

Why do we resist it so?

It's such a natural part of life you'd think we'd just accept it and get on with our business. But we don't. *This mortal life begs for more.* Even though everyone who's ever walked this planet will die, we can't help thinking it's not supposed to be like this. It's not *supposed* to end. In one form or another it's *supposed to go on forever.*

People talk about a "god gene."

But really, the "immortality gene" is far more pervasive.

We have an insatiable thirst for immortality.

And right alongside this insatiable thirst for immortality is a relentless longing for *infinitely more than this life can provide.* Even in our best moments, we all have this aching sense that there has to be more than this. Even the best parties get old after a while! Nothing in this finite world can ever fully satisfy us. Our hearts are endlessly restless, looking for that missing piece that will complete us, that relationship that will make us happy and whole.

Life *is* hard. But against all our combined experience on this planet, against all the evidence to the contrary—the only evidence we have!—we think it *should* be different. We think it is somehow incomplete, not what it *ought* to be.

*Where* did we ever get such an idea?

Why can't we just be satisfied with this life? With all that it provides?

Why this aching sense that *we aren't home here.* That we aren't home *yet?*

What we really long for is not just endless life, but transcendence: infinite joy; perfect love. Somehow we are acutely and profoundly aware of an infinite horizon of possibility that exists beyond our reach. We can't simply accept our mortality and the imperfections of our existence and move on.

*We are wired for transcendence.*

And lo and behold, along comes this historical event *which just so happens to fulfill this longing perfectly.*

Karl Rahner, one of the greatest theologians of the 20th century, puts it this way:

> we hear this witness of the apostles with that transcendental hope in resurrection…Hence we do not learn something which is totally unexpected and which lies totally outside of the horizon of our experience and our possibilities of verification… the risen Jesus himself gives witness that he is alive in the successful and inseparable correspondence between transcendental hope in resurrection and the categorical and real presence of such a resurrection. The two reinforce each other mutually in this circle and give witness to us of their truth.[208]

This transcendental longing is the fundamental intuition of the human species, the deepest yearning of the human heart. And Jesus' resurrection satisfies it perfectly: proving that the *unsurpassing love* of a God who would make the supreme sacrifice to save us *is* the Ultimate Reality; and revealing that we can live with him forever— that *our true home* is the *infinite ecstasy* of his *perfect love.*

But how do we know the resurrection wasn't just invented to fulfill this hope?

Maybe the disciples' own transcendental longing deluded them into thinking he was risen when he really wasn't.

Maybe the resurrection is simply a fantasy projection of their deepest wishes.

As we've seen, the historical evidence completely rules this out. The disciples' drive for immortality could have expressed itself in a number of different ways, *but not in the kind of resurrection they describe.* It wasn't even on the radar screen.

(Intriguingly, though, the mode of Jesus' resurrection, with its surprising and previously unimagined transcendent qualities, fulfills their—and our—transcendental longing far more perfectly than their prior "finite" notions of life beyond the grave ever could. The promise it points to far exceeds their wildest dreams.)

Remember Elvis? No one is willing to stake his or her life on the claim Elvis is alive. Jesus is the only person in history where the evidence is strong enough that the claim is seriously entertained; strong enough that people have staked and even given their lives for this claim.

So we have to reckon with the very solid and straightforward historical facts of an empty tomb and transphysical appearances—and the larger historical context that coheres so well with them—and try to make sense of them in light of this transcendental longing at the heart of our human experience.

But how do we know our transcendental longing isn't just wishful thinking?

That the reality it points to actually exists?

Robert Spitzer has recently completed an exhaustive analysis of the philosophical arguments surrounding this transcendental longing. He's found that most transcendent philosophers believe we can't desire something we're not aware of, at least tacitly. However, everything in our experience is limited, conditioned, restricted, finite, and woefully imperfect. When we are beckoned, therefore, from deep within our psyche to seek perfect love or infinite joy, this goes beyond anything we could have learned or discovered from this finite reality. This "transcendent horizon" supersedes the physical world and the categories it's capable of producing—*we could never derive our transcendental longing from this world*. It's *completely foreign* to everything we experience in this finite and totally imperfect reality.

So how did we get it?

One possibility is that it's programmed into the physics, chemistry, and/or biology of our brains. However, this isn't likely because, "quantum physics, macroscopic physics, chemistry, and biology are all conditioned by contingent and finite structures." It seems, then, that the only option is that it comes from a transphysical source. It comes from something that isn't restricted by the inherent limitations of all that surrounds us and all that we are.[209]

Spitzer illustrates this point with the example of love. Have you ever noticed how easily we find fault in the ones we love most? We are painfully aware of love's imperfections, never fully satisfied with a love that is less than perfect. But how can we so easily see the imperfections in love without having an awareness of what perfect love is like? And more to the point, if every experience of love we have is imperfect, where did we ever get this expectation that we should be loved perfectly? We certainly didn't learn or apprehend it from those around us. "It seems that it is intrinsic to us—prior to our experiences of love in the world around us."[210]

Being "intrinsic to us," somehow "prior" to our experience of this world; being *so thoroughly programmed into us*, the most likely conclusion is that the reality our transcendental longing points to— the domain of perfect love—must surely exist. Without the infinite horizon of a perfectly loving Being—i.e., God—to generate and fulfill it, we'd never have such a longing in the first place.

Spitzer adds another clue to support this conclusion. It's our penchant for asking: "why?" We do it all the time. But behind this simple question lies a remarkably complex phenomenon. To be able to ask "why, why is this thing the way it is and not some other way?" is to be aware that particular manifestations of reality aren't the only possibility. We can somehow readily conceive that reality could be some other way, but isn't. This is a profound ability. And yet, children (many times to their parents' consternation) do it so naturally. It seems to be pre-programmed into our psyche.[211]

Spitzer points out that philosophers since the time of Plato have acknowledged that we could never ask why if we didn't have some kind of pre-consciousness of what we seek to know. Otherwise, we would never seek to know anything beyond what is given to us in our experience.[212] So we couldn't ask why unless we had some kind of tacit awareness of other possible unrealized ways reality could be. We'd have no idea things could be other than they are. It would never occur to us to ask why.[213]

When we ask why—why reality isn't some other way; especially, why it's not the way we think it *ought* to be; why it isn't like our notions of perfection tell us it *should* be—we manifest an *awareness of an alternate reality that we don't have any natural basis for.*

Why *do* we ask why?

Why do we presume that things could or even *should* be different?

It's a presumption that is totally ungrounded and actually quite audacious. Based on all our accumulated experience, the only thing we should ever presume, the only thing we have a basis, a right to presume, is that the way things are—woefully flawed, broken, and imperfect—is the only way they could be.

It is what it is.

But we don't. And the reason we don't is because *we already have in mind a perfect version of reality we have no worldly experience or knowledge of.*

It is what it is, but against all reason, we think it should be different, and in a significantly better way, a perfect way.

Where did we get all this?

Again, it is difficult, if not impossible, to explain this penchant for asking "why?" if we did not have some tacit awareness of an alternate, perfect reality radically different from our own.

And this awareness is only possible *if the corresponding reality exists.*

Back to the example of love: "It seems that this innate awareness must come from a source that is commensurate with the effect it produces within us, a source that is perfect love itself."[214]

Life is hard…then you die.

Yes, but…we don't accept death as part of the natural course of things. We don't accept imperfection as normal. We *expect* immortality. We *expect* to find perfect love, beauty, truth, justice, and goodness.

Where did we ever get the notion that death, instead of just being the way things are, is really the great intruder?

Where did we ever get these ideals of perfection—ideals that we're convinced are the way things *should* be—that are so completely foreign to the only reality we know?

The best way to explain this transcendental longing which is so basic, so intrinsic to our nature and which defies naturalistic explanation, is that it must be pointing to that ultimate reality which is our true home.

And, like nothing else, the resurrection of Jesus satisfies this yearning for that true home we have felt destined for all along.

The striking correspondence between such a well-attested event and the transcendental hope which it *fulfills so perfectly* makes such an event exactly the kind of thing we would expect to happen.

# Too Good Not to be True

Everybody loves a good story. From kindergarten children gathered around to hear a fairy tale, to Shakespeare, the opera, Broadway, or the movies, we love a good story. The one thing we love more than a good story is a happy ending. Not the sappy, saccharine, all-too-predictable kind (even though these still have surprising power to move us—how many of you have ever welled up at one of those corny romantic movies? Come on now, tell the truth!). But one that rings true, that deals with the complexities and vicissitudes of life and still turns out right.

Why are we such suckers for romantic movies, even, at times, for those corny and totally predictable endings?

Why were the Rocky movies so popular? Not to pick on Rocky, but they weren't exactly cinematographic genius. But that's the point: even though the acting was sub-par and the plotline predictable, they drew millions.

Why do we watch these movies over and over again even though we already know the ending? Boy meets girl; boy loses girl; boy wins girl back; boy and girl live happily ever after. Unlikely hero experiences tragedy; loses partner at hands of evil villain; suffers humiliating defeat; comes back to save the world against insurmountable odds. Nerd tortured by bully; beats bully at his own game; becomes high school hero; wins girl.

Deep in our being this plot of happily-ever-after, good-guy-winning, justice-prevailing, love-conquering-all, is *indelibly written*. Yes, there are other very compelling stories that don't end well—tragedies. But we have a decided preference for happy endings. We find them irresistible. This is the way things should turn out, the way we like it, our ideal, our fantasy.

And most of all, we hope against hope that our story, the drama of our lives, has a happy ending. The happiest of endings, in fact, where, in the cosmic drama, good defeats evil; love, hate; life, death.

I recently heard a best-selling novelist talk about her approach to writing. She explained her strong preference for happy endings in all she reads and why it's the only way she writes. Life is hard enough, she explained. Why add to the hardship? Writing is fantasy after all. I think we'd all agree.

If we could write the story of our lives, we would all write happy endings.[215]

I'm a Yankee fan. Being a Yankee fan can be boring. Over the years they have been enormously successful. Winning becomes old hat. Rooting for the hapless Mets is much more exciting. When they win it's a pleasant surprise! (No offense to my Mets friends.)

But the reason I became a Yankee fan had nothing to do with their winning ways, their celebrated history. I became a Yankee fan as a young kid in the mid-1970's. At the time they were terrible. Only the Cleveland Indians were worse, but not by much. Back in "the day," that was really bad. The Indians were the Mets of the American League!

But then the Yankees mounted incredible comeback after incredible comeback in the late 70's to win two World Series. For me the ultimate was 1978 when they did the unthinkable, coming back from fourteen-and-a-half games out in August to win the Pennant. Then in the World Series, they lost the first two games and had to travel to Los Angeles for the next three. Everybody wrote them off. They were done. No team had come back from such a deficit. Especially facing three away games. And yet they did.

That's why I love the Yankees.

The one thing we like better than a happy ending is a comeback story, which, of course, is a happy ending in itself. We love rooting for the underdog. Against all odds. And when that comeback happens as a result of getting back what was lost—like just about every love story ever conceived!—it's even better. That narrative of something good somehow being tragically lost, but then wonderfully restored and somehow better than before—transformed—is the *happiest* of happy endings.

The resurrection is *the* ultimate comeback story.

*The* happy ending.

It's as real and gritty and tragic as it gets. Yet, it's our greatest fantasy.

In the cosmic battle, love wins the decisive victory, defeating our greatest nemesis, death itself. Perfect love proves to be the logic, the meaning, and the power of the universe. The stories we tell, the narrative arc of our lives, are all relentlessly driving toward this moment.

You can't write a better script!

But no one at that time could have ever imagined or invented such a script—in their context it was simply inconceivable. Women as the first witnesses. A dead messiah. Jesus himself predicting a different ending. The resurrection of an individual before the end time. And so on. The story is solidly historical.

And yet, with all its unlikely, quirky, inconceivable details, *it turns out to be the greatest story ever told.*

No one wants to believe a fairy tale. Too much is at stake. I know that the whole thing seems too good to be true. Like the dreams I had of my dad after his death. But even the most skeptical analysis of the historical evidence makes it harder not to believe than to believe.

And at the same time, metaphysically, the narrative arc of our lives—of life itself!—prepares us for just this kind of story and for it being the ultimate truth about who we are.

Much is made these days in scholarship about the power of narrative, of story. Most now acknowledge there is something *fundamental* to the place of story in our lives. It is the way we think, the way we process and make sense of our world. Stories define us and our reality. They are central to human existence.

*We are "storied" beings.*

As such, they somehow speak to the *nature of the universe*, the way it is structured and ordered. And of all the stories we tell, the epic, cosmic struggle between good and evil is the most central.

*Lord of the Rings* author J.R.R. Tolkien believed this was a major clue to the nature of ultimate reality. As Timothy Keller notes:

Tolkein's famous essay "On Fairy Stories" argues that there are indelible, deep longings in the human heart that realistic fiction cannot satisfy...What we call "fantasy fiction" is massively popular and continues to be consumed by audiences numbering in the billions. The enduring appeal of stories that represent these conditions is unquestionable. But why? As a Christian, Tolkien believed these stories resonate so deeply because they bear witness to an underlying reality. Even if we do not intellectually believe that there is a God or life after death, our hearts (in the Christian view) sense somehow that these things characterize life as it was and should be and eventually will be again. We are so deeply interested in these stories because we have intuitions of the creation/fall/redemption/restoration plotline of the Bible. Even if we repress the knowledge of that plotline intellectually, we can't not know it imaginatively, and our hearts are stirred by any stories that evoke it...

If Jesus Christ was really raised from the dead—if he is really the Son of God and you believe in him—all those things that you long for most desperately are real and will come true. We will escape time and death. We will know love without parting, we will even communicate with nonhuman beings, and we will see evil defeated forever.[216]

"We can't not know it imaginatively."

This instinct permeates every fiber of our being and it becomes irrepressible in the face of a good story. And the gospel story is *the* story, the meta-narrative, to which all these other stories point. They are just a faint glimpse into its spell-binding glory. As Tolkien himself says: "...there is no tale ever told that men would rather find was true..."[217]

217

There is no greater love than God giving his very life to save us. No greater victory than the defeat of death itself.

That's why, like none other, this story has the power to make our hearts soar. We have an *irrepressible intuition* that tells us this story, which represents the ultimate victory of good over evil, love over hate, life over death, is *the* cosmic drama at the heart of our existence. There is something so right and true about it.

But how do we know it's not all just fiction and fantasy?

As Tolkien believed, the most reasonable conclusion it is so deeply imbedded in our psyche is that it *is* the reality we inhabit. It is *the* "narrative arc of our lives."

We live in a world where reality writes so few happy endings—just watch the evening news! So why does the archetypal myth at the heart of human imagination exercise such a *decided preference for the good?*

The raw material for the stories we tell is the reality we experience. Yet this reality is totally ambiguous, a messy mixture of good and evil, love and hate; and one where death is, as far as we know, the all-predictable and irreversible termination of our existence. If this were all there were to it, we'd naturally predict that the stories which captivate us would be thoroughly ambivalent: in some, good would win out in the end; in others, evil would be victorious.

But they aren't at all. Against all evidence to the contrary, they clearly and consistently move in the direction of justice, truth, goodness, life and love. They completely fly in the face of reality as we know it. And this betrays that we do indeed have a tacit awareness of the *deeper* cosmic narrative which is *really* at play.

Which, in turn, reveals who and Whose we really are.[218]

Our desire for *the* happy ending isn't some fairy tale. Rather, it's an accurate intuition of the plot, the storyline, of the universe. It reveals what the universe is up to. And the resurrection of Jesus, the most unlikely, bizarre story, one that no one would ever think to invent, turns out to be the ultimate happy ending, the greatest comeback story of all time, the most amazing transformation possible, fulfilling our cosmic fantasy to a tee.

It's too good *not* to be true.

## Of All People

Have you ever noticed that in just about all the stories we human beings tell, all our "mythology" ancient and modern, there is virtually always a hero, a savior figure. Be it Hercules in Greek mythology, David in the Old Testament, Luke Skywalker in Star Wars, or just about every drama on TV, the cosmic drama of good versus evil is played out in a way that the hero saves the day. However flawed or quirky the hero may be, he or she always finds a way, either through superior wit or strength or sheer determination or even—like my favorite, Inspector Clouseau in the Pink Panther movies—comic ineptitude, to save the day.

Have you ever wondered why this theme is so popular?

It's because all these smaller dramas play out *our fundamental need and deep-seated desire for an ideal savior.*

Even in the political spectrum, despite a consistent track record of bitter disappointment, we keep looking for some great leader, usually a presidential figure, to save us from the mess we're in. Sometimes we even demagogue them (e.g., Trump), elevate them to messianic-like status (e.g., Obama), or, ironically for Americans, treat them like royalty (e.g., the Kennedys).

In the midst of the Los Angeles riots, riots which were sparked when the officers accused of beating him were exonerated, Rodney King famously implored: "Can't we all just get along?" It was an agonized plea that resonates deep within the core of our collective being. If we could all just get along, we would eliminate all the strife and heartache that ails us as human beings. We would achieve what we all so desperately want.

Over the years, a litany of songs, books, preachers, politicians and cultural icons have made the same plea: Give peace a chance. Make love not war. Let there be peace on earth and let it begin with me. C'mon everybody, just love one another. Kumbaya!

But the world is still a mess.

*We* are still a mess.

To Rodney King's question: *No! We can't all just get along.*

No matter how hard we try, no matter how much sense it makes, no matter how badly we all want it, we can't find peace in our world. We can't find peace with our neighbors. We can't even find peace within ourselves. If we're honest, it's not only other people who can't just get along. *We* can't just get along either!

If you're not convinced, go for a drive. Just a few minutes in traffic can bring out the ugliest side of humanity in others—and ourselves!

Or ask yourself this simple question: are all your relationships perfectly harmonious? Thought not.

When you see a group photo, whose picture do you look for first? I look for mine first, too! It may be vanity or self consciousness or a little of both, but we almost universally look for ourselves.

How many of your thoughts are about others—and not simply as it relates to you—versus how many of your thoughts are *just about you?* It's a totally lopsided ratio: we are *consumed* with thoughts about ourselves—how do I look; how am I coming across; how is this person treating me; am I going to be safe; what do I want for lunch; and so on.

We are far more self-absorbed than we should be.

We constantly fall short of who, deep down, *we know we are meant to be;* of living up to our full potential as human beings. As Paul says: "I do not understand my own actions. For I do not do what I want, but I do the very thing I hate."(Romans 7:15)

We wish we could be more loving and compassionate and forgiving and gracious and kind. But we constantly blow it. No matter how hard we try—and many times we don't even try—we can't seem to get this "being human" thing right.

In fact, when we do try, we often make it worse. If we fail, we rationalize, blaming others, our past, our parents. It's always somebody else's fault. The devil made me do it! But even when we succeed, we boast. Whether we say it out loud or not, we become even more self-focused by thinking how "good" we are. (Of course, you aren't all that good when you go around thinking how good you are!)

Along with G.K Chesterton, when he famously responded to a London newspaper editorial asking: *"What's wrong with the world?"*, if we were truly honest, we'd have to say: *"Me!"*

Humanity is broken. We are broken. And we can't fix it. We can't fix ourselves. We need someone to save us, not just from the evil we encounter daily around us, but from our part in it.

As if this isn't bad enough, we are riddled with angst, acutely aware of how vulnerable we are to all kinds of suffering and pain. And acutely aware of how small and insignificant we are, especially in this scientific age. The cascading frontiers astronomers and physicists continue to shatter with ever-new discoveries revealing just how big and expansive our universe is are truly fascinating. But they're also incredibly *depressing*: who are we that anyone out there should care? We are *so* tiny and alone in such a vast, cold universe, it leaves us with an acute feeling of cosmic loneliness.

Moreover, many of our days are spent in abject tedium, ruts and routines that leave us profoundly bored with life, searching for that missing piece to make us whole. We often live lives of quiet desperation, with no greater meaning or fulfillment in sight.

And then there's death. The ultimate enemy. An enemy which is the source of so much of our angst, and therefore, so much of our self-absorption. Without the fear of death, think how free we'd be— much of our egocentricity would just melt away. We are completely powerless, completely overcome in the face of death.

Einstein is purported to have said that the ultimate question is whether the universe is friendly or not. From our collective experience, we'd have to say a resounding NO! In the end, our lives seem to be *spectacularly* meaningless, just a fleeting blip on the cosmic radar screen.

We desperately need someone to save us from death. We desperately need someone to save us from our existential angst. And we desperately need someone to save us from ourselves.

Jesus is one of the most impressive figures of history. And what makes Jesus most remarkable, surpassing all others, even history's other greatest figures, is his radical love. There was a beauty, truth, and goodness to his life that towers over the rest. So much so that those who knew him could make the claim that he never sinned. If anyone was pure goodness it was this man.

Utter humility, extravagant mercy, prodigal grace.

The man for others, loving with breathtaking abandon, *literally* pouring out his life.

Pointing to Jesus, even Hinduism calls Christianity the religion of love par excellance. The life he lived, the love he embodied, was truly sublime. (As we saw above in Part II, there is little doubt historically that Jesus lived such an exceptional life—his "crazy" love wasn't a fabrication of the later gospel writers; it defined who he was.)

In 1989, the Menendez brothers killed their parents in cold blood. It was a gruesome crime. From prison, some twenty-eight years after the murders, they did a series of interviews about the circumstances leading up to the crime. Consistently, the one thing they wanted people to know is that this crime *didn't reflect who they are.* Whether their abusive father drove them to it, or they were just immature, spoiled rich kids who made a foolishly tragic mistake, they wanted the world to know that they deeply regretted what they did and that, despite it all, they *really are good human beings.*

With the rare exception of someone like Hitler, everyone wants to be perceived as "good." Everyone feels the need to justify their actions, no matter how heinous, in order to say they are good. How many times do fallen politicians, notorious criminals, or celebrities caught in some scandal go on TV to try to "rehabilitate" their image. To explain why they did what they did in order to maintain that "deep down" they really are good people. That they just made a mistake, or are being misunderstood, or were driven to what they did by forces outside of their control, like the psychological trauma of growing up in a dysfunctional home, or, as in the case of the Son of Sam serial killer, David Berkowitz, by demonic power (literally claiming that the Devil made him do it!).

Even 9-11 mastermind Osama Bin Laden believed—no matter how transparently warped it might be—that what he was doing was good, that he was fighting the good fight, "being a good person."

Some deep and undeniable impulse within tells us that this is what we should be. And we will do all kinds of mental gymnastics to get ourselves and others to believe that we really are good despite all evidence to the contrary. Psychologically, we need to see ourselves as good people because somehow we know—we really know!—that this is essential to who we are as human beings. However short we may fall of this ideal, there is an overwhelming impulse that tells us this is what we were meant to be.

In light of this, Jesus fulfills the potential, the purpose, the "goal" of human life like no other. He was the one *fully human* being, *living the ideal we all aspire to.* Even those who don't believe in him, who don't think he was in any sense divine, admire him for this. Whether it's the "being your best self" of pop culture, the "self-actualization" of the psychologists, or the noblest aspirations of secular humanism, *we are all striving in some way to be what Jesus was.*

The day after winning the 2017 Masters Golf Tournament, Sergio Garcia was interviewed by Charlie Rose.[219] Winning the Masters was undoubtedly the greatest success of his golfing career and, arguably, his life. During the interview he talked about his "team," which included his fiancée and family, and the vital role they played in his victory. He said that they have made him a better golfer, but *more importantly,* they've made him a better person.

Being a better person trumps being one of the best golfers in the world.

How often do people at the pinnacle of success, be they professional athletes, celebrities, business tycoons, or whoever, say the same thing? No matter how much success they've attained in their given field, they almost universally agree that the most important thing is being a better person, a good human being.

How many eulogies inevitably emphasize how kind, giving, and selfless the deceased was? In the end, when all is said and done, this is what matters. Not what they accomplished in life. Not how much money, success, or fame they amassed. But what kind of positive impact they had on others. How good they were.

The greatest success any of us can have is to be a success at the greatest enterprise of all: life. To be a good person.

And this is exactly what Jesus did, to perfection.

The life he lived is *the* ideal human life.

We love it when our modern heroes and role models—celebrities— prove to be "nice guys" or "gals." We fawn over the ones who will spend an afternoon at the children's hospital visiting sick kids, or who dedicate their spare time to a charity for under-privileged youth. When we hear stories of someone running into one of these "stars" and the star takes time to talk like a regular person, we gush over them. As high as we exalt them, we want our celebrities to be down-to-earth, relatable, and most of all, humble. The main reason so many are enamored with Pope Francis is this very thing. He treats the highest office in the Church and one of the most powerful in the world as an opportunity to serve, especially the least, and not to be served.

I've had the chance to talk to a couple of people who met Mother Teresa when she was alive. The most remarkable thing about her, they each separately said, is that she made you feel like you were the only person in the room; like you were the one who was special; like *you were the saint.* Even with all the attention focused on her, with all the crowds and media pressing in, she was totally focused on the person in front of her.

What makes Pope Francis and Mother Teresa such compelling figures is the way they reflect Jesus. Washing someone's feet has become the metaphor for humble service. When Jesus did this for his disciples it was a shocking display, far too humiliating for someone in his position. Yet this radical humility defined his life. It was his M.O.

Was any person as humble as Jesus, especially if his claim to be God is true?

And if he is who he claims to be, his death on the cross *saves us in the ultimate possible way.* He's won the decisive battle of good versus evil. Not only does he save us from our human brokenness, from our self-absorption and all the strife and heartache it creates, he saves us from death itself, our ultimate enemy. And he does all this in the most heroic, self-sacrificing way possible: *by laying down his life.*

According to Christianity, in our self-absorption, we have completely rejected God. Alienation from Him is the cause and the essence of our brokenness. But on the cross, God willingly *absorbs* all the pain and heartbreak our rejection causes so that we might be reconciled to Him, assuring us—in the most complete way possible, the only way we can *completely trust*—that He loves us no matter what, even if we kill Him! This is our salvation, if we accept it: reconciliation with the Source of our being.

And in the resurrection, where God transforms the incomprehensible suffering of the cross into a stunning and unimaginably greater glory, he reveals that all of our suffering, no matter how overwhelming or mystifying, will be transformed in the same way. He won't just put an end to it. He will somehow *use what we've suffered* to create an unimaginably greater glory for us in eternity.

If God, what Jesus has done means the universe is friendly beyond all imagining. By taking on the fullness of our humanity, God is *irrevocably* united to us. By giving *Himself* to us and for us, He's bound Himself to us for all eternity. We are absolutely *not* alone in the universe. We are profoundly loved by the Power behind it all. Our lives have supreme meaning. We're infinitely significant to Him, and in Him, we're ultimately safe and secure.

This blessed assurance overcomes and obliterates all our cosmic loneliness, existential angst, quiet desperation, and fear of death, and in turn, frees us from the bondage of our addiction to self. If God, Jesus saves us from all that ails us most as human beings, all that we most desperately need saving from, and in the most sublime way possible, sacrificing *himself* for us.

Has anybody done it better?

Famed *The Vampire Chronicles* author Anne Rice knows a thing or two about supernatural heroes and villains. In a note to her readers, who are quite familiar with all her characters, she writes: "After all, is Christ Our Lord not the ultimate supernatural hero, the ultimate outsider, the ultimate immortal of them all?"[220]

By all accounts, Jesus *is* the ultimate savior figure.

But it's not the kind of story we'd tell. We like to see our heroes exalted, successful, triumphant. In short, winners. We prefer royalty to be met with pomp and circumstance, to roll out the red carpet. We want our celebrities all made up and dressed to the nines, beautiful, strong, surrounded by paparazzi and adoring fans. And power, the ability to impose their will, is essential. People are heroes to us because they use their unique position and power for good. They overcome evil; they aren't overcome by it!

The people of Jesus' day were no different. They found his crucifixion absurd and scandalous. Their heroes would never die so shamefully. No savior would be so weak, so *pathetic.*

To them the cross was the great stumbling block to belief.

This is such an odd way to save the world. Not by power and might, but by vulnerability and humility. God crucified. Humiliated. Defeated. A complete and total loser. And yet, there is something so right, so perfect about it. With all our images of beauty, from supermodels to natural wonders, none compares to that of sacrificial love. Think of the emergency responders running into those towers on 9-11.

Is there anything that evokes greater awe and admiration?

Nothing can compare to the beauty of God Himself sacrificing His life for us. It is the most "awesome" act imaginable: perfect love incarnate dying to save us. Though no one would ever create this kind of savior figure, it turns out that Jesus couldn't be more heroic. *All our aspirations for the ideal hero who saves us in the ultimate way find their fulfillment in Him.*

Of all people, Jesus is *the* ideal archetypal hero we've been looking for all along. He stands out in history not only as having lived the most beautiful, loving and fully human life, but also—if his claims are true—as the one who achieves the salvation we are most desperate for, defeating sin, evil, and death.

And he does it in the most heroic way, laying down his own life.[221]

Of all people, if there was one person we would most expect to be raised from the dead, it would be Jesus, the one who most fully embodies the human ideal; the one who is the ultimate savior figure.

And once again, in an astonishing correspondence that no one could have orchestrated, of all people, this man has the only credible claim to have conquered the grave.[222]

## Why Only a BODILY RESURRECTON Will Do

Imagine what it would be like to live forever on this planet. Imagine you could be permanently resuscitated after death or live on in an endless cycle of reincarnations. That would be *a fate worse than death*: to experience the eventual, never-ending boredom of living in this finite world forever; or to have to go through all the pain and suffering of a lifetime over and over again through each reincarnation.

Now imagine what it would be like to have your soul liberated from your body at death. Imagine that this was the whole point of life after all: to escape this frail and limited earthbound existence. As appealing as this might be, all we've experienced in this life, all we've become, all we are, *would be in vain*. Our disembodied existence would have no connection to this life whatsoever.

Let me explain.

We are "embodied" beings. All that we know and experience happens through our bodies. Our bodies are *essential* to our personal identity, to who we are and how we relate to one another. As Richard McBrien observes: "We are human insofar as we are oriented toward others. And our orientation toward others is made possible and necessary by our bodiliness."[223] In a disembodied reality, we'd lose all this.

So it matters—enormously!—whether there's a relationship, a "continuity," between this life and the next. If there's no connection, no continuity, then there's *no meaning* to this life. It's just a colossal waste, a random cosmic detour subjecting us to all sorts of trials and tribulations for no good reason. Why would we have us go through this life if there's no point to it all? Why couldn't we just start out in that next disembodied state to begin with?

More to the point, what *kind* of God would put us through all this pain and misery for no good reason? He'd have to be cruel and reckless.

And if there's no connection, no continuity, then our best moments in this world amount to nothing. None of it remains part of us, including the people and relationships that matter most. It's like the expression: "What happens in Vegas, stays in Vegas." What happens on earth, stays on earth. In other words, *you won't see your loved ones in heaven.* What kind of a God would so callously discard the experiences and relationships that matter most to us in this world? Also One who is cruel and reckless.

Even worse, without some kind of personal identity—which is what our embodied existence provides—eternity will be utterly loveless, because love can only exist between "persons." And an eternity devoid of love means that the supreme source of our joy and fulfillment has no place in it. As Keller explains, if in eternity our disembodied souls blend into some kind of greater (divine) consciousness, like drops of water in the ocean—as Eastern religions teach and much New Age thought speculates—then we simply melt into an *impersonal* spiritual reality. We lose our individual identity. We are no longer a self. And this would make eternity love-less, since only persons can love. If, after death, we aren't personal beings, beings in possession of a personal identity, beings with a *self* consciousness, we will lose the thing we want most—love.[224]

If there is some other kind of joy in eternity, something other than love, it just proves the point—it has nothing to do with this world and the supreme joy and meaning love has here: so why would God put us through this life? And how could he so easily dispense of all that defines and delights us most as human beings?

The same applies if the point of this world, this embodied existence, was to *learn* some "lesson" for a disembodied eternity—it can't have anything to do with love, since an eternity devoid of personal identity is still an eternity devoid of love.

The "transphysical" resurrection of Jesus wasn't simply a return to this life through resuscitation or reincarnation. It was a transformation to the transcendent sphere. To a place of infinite being and bliss. To a mode of existence where *the limitations our earthly bodies impose no longer apply*.

But Jesus' resurrection also involved the transformation and perfection of the earthly body, the transformation and perfection of all that is good in this life to the transcendent level. Which means there is a real continuity between this life and the next: our "embodied" experience has some *profound connection to our eternal destiny*.

This life really matters. It has eternal significance.

It also means that the experiences and relationships of this life aren't just discarded or forgotten, but *infinitely transformed, healed, and perfected*. The things that make this life most worthwhile and satisfying, the people and relationships we treasure most, remain but with this one difference: all the hurt and pain involved in them is utterly vanquished; what was so wonderful about them, infinitely magnified.

Eternity isn't loveless. Totally the opposite, it's *love's perfection*.

And all of this means that *God isn't cruel and reckless*.

Continuity and transformation. Of all the ideas humans have envisioned of immortality, this is the only one that takes the continuity between this life and the next seriously and at the same time, offers a vision of immortality that is truly transcendent. It is the only way this life has meaning and the next life is ultimately satisfying.

As Luc Ferry points out: "For the Buddhist, the individual is but an illusion, something destined for dissolution and impermanence; for the [Greek] Stoic the individual self is destined to merge into the totality of the *cosmos*; Christianity on the contrary promises immortality of the individual person: his soul, his body, his face, his beloved voice—as long as he is saved by the grace of God."[225]

And as N.T. Wright concludes: "The resurrection, in the full Jewish and early Christian sense, is the ultimate affirmation that creation matters, that embodied human beings matter."[226]

Among all the available options, this is the only one that truly works. It's the only one that keeps God's goodness, wisdom, and love intact; the only way God could be a God of love and not cruel and reckless!

At the same time, this vision of immortality, the only one that provides perfect continuity and transformation, comes about in a way that is historically unprecedented. No one could have guessed it; or would have wanted to—it's the Edsel of Immortality! Historically, it is such a *radical departure* from the other prevailing views of the time, it can only be explained by an encounter with one who has been resurrected in a way no one expected or could have conceived.

"Transphysical" resurrection is the least natural, and in many ways, at least on the surface, the least attractive vision of immortality available. Perhaps this is why so many, Christians included, continue to opt for some variation of disembodied immortality. Yet, "transphysical" resurrection is the only viable, meaningful, and intelligible vision of immortality possible; the only way embodied human beings matter.

So, the only *truly satisfying vision of immortality* originates from a historical event *that no human would ever think to invent.*

Once again, the correspondence between historical event and metaphysical reality is striking.

## Conclusion: Coincidence Unlikely

In this chapter, without presupposing the existence of some kind of Higher Power, Rational Intelligence, or God, but by simply examining the metaphysical reality we inhabit, we saw that there is good reason—actually four good reasons—to believe that the resurrection of Jesus, with its substantial historical evidence, isn't just logically possible, but philosophically probable. The absolutely unique historical claim enjoys an *astonishing correspondence* with four different yet powerful philosophical arguments.

Our metaphysical environment *begs* for just such an event to take place.

In the next chapter, we will take this a step further. After outlining the formidable evidence for the existence of God based on recent trends in science and philosophy, we will presuppose that God exists.

Philosophically, if there is a "God," the resurrection moves from being a strong probability to a logical necessity.

# CHAPTER

# 9

# The Logic of the Universe

*Presupposing God: A Slam Dunk*

LIFE IS HARD...THEN YOU die.

Antony Flew was one of the most influential philosophers of the twentieth century. He was also an ardent atheist. In fact, nobody advanced the cause of atheism in the last century more than Flew.

Since the aftermath of the Enlightenment, the arguments about God's existence, both pro and con, remained fairly stagnant. That is, until Flew came along. Not only did he raise cutting-edge arguments that rattled theists (those who believe in God), he forced those same theists to think more deeply, which, in turn, produced powerful new arguments for the existence of God.

As philosopher Roy Abraham Varghese observes: "It is not too much to say that within the last hundred years, no mainstream philosopher has developed the kind of systematic, comprehensive, original, and influential exposition of atheism that is to be found in Antony Flew's fifty years of antitheological writings. Prior to Flew, the major apologias for atheism were those Enlightenment thinkers like David Hume and the nineteenth-century German philosophers Arthur Shopenhauer, Ludwig Feuerbach, and Friedrich Nietzche."[227]

However, to everyone's great surprise—including Flew's!—he became a believer late in life. I'll explore the major reasons for his conversion more fully in a moment because they represent major developments that have *fundamentally shifted* the so-called "God debate," developments which routinely get drowned out by better publicized but far less compelling arguments (most notably, those advanced by Christopher Hitchens and Richard Dawkins). But for now, just know that he became a believer because of recent advances in science and some of the very philosophical arguments that were constructed to respond to *his* atheistic critiques.

Based entirely on this new evidence and rigorous logic, Flew reversed himself and came to believe there is a rational intelligence behind the universe:

> Why do I believe this, given that I expounded atheism
> for more than a half century? The short answer is this:
> this is the world picture, as I see it, that has emerged
> from modern science...But it is not science alone that
> has guided me. I have also been helped by a renewed
> study of the classical philosophical arguments.[228]

Flew adds that for him, belief in God is not just a reasonable position to take, something deduced or inferred by a given line of argumentation, but the *undeniable conclusion* from the vision of reality *science* is now giving us. As we'll see below, the reality of a divine intelligence "emerges from the conceptual heart of modern science and imposes itself on the rational mind."[229]

Flew is not alone. As Michael Licona notes: "During the past forty-five years, many scientists and philosophers have discovered volumes of data from recent advances in astrophysics and molecular biology that they believe imply an intelligent creator and designer of our universe who purposefully intended the existence of life on earth." This includes many *leading* philosophers.[230]

We've been told over and over again that modern people are abandoning faith in God. That developments in science and technology are making belief in God naïve and simplistic. That faith is nothing more than a primitive superstition or psychological defense mechanism humans can now evolve beyond. That as the world becomes more educated, more steeped in the scientific worldview, *atheism is the natural result.* As if faith and science are diametrically opposed; belief and reason, self-contradictory. Most people simply assume that belief in God is in rapid decline. The media and pop culture tend to reinforce this assumption.

As it turns out, however, the vast majority of people throughout the world, including America, share Flew's position. Worldwide, the overall number of believers is expected to *increase* in the coming years. Even among those living with a modern, scientific worldview.

Belief in God is showing no signs of decline.

Sociologists Peter Berger and Grace Davie report that the majority of sociologists who specialize in the study of religion have abandoned the so-called "secularization thesis" which said that, as societies become more modern, belief in God would inevitably decline. Based on the empirical data, they now agree that belief in God does *not* decline with modernization.

Instead, the data shows that, long-term, it's not religious populations that are in decline, but secular ones. A 2015 Pew study predicts that in forty years those who don't believe in God (atheists and agnostics) or hold any religious affiliation will *decline* from 16.4 percent worldwide to 13.2 percent. This has lead University of London professor Eric Kaufmann to speak of "the crisis of secularism", in which the decline of secularism and liberal religion is inevitable.[231]

In America, only 4% of the population call themselves atheists. That's the same percentage as it was in 1944![232] God's demise has been grossly overstated. Moreover, the anticipated decline in religious belief as cultures modernize and become more educated simply hasn't happened. If anything, the trend is in the opposite direction.

234

Studies of Americans have shown that the more educated you are, the *more likely* you are to attend church regularly. There seems to be some positive correlation between education and belief in God.[233]

As Harvard Psychiatrist Armand Nicholi points out: "Freud thought that the human race would someday outgrow the need for belief—especially as the masses became more educated. In fact, according to a recent Gallup poll, although more Americans are more educated today than ever before, more also believe God plays a direct role in their lives than ever before."[234]

A 2008 Pew Forum survey found that among those with graduate degrees only 8 percent reported being atheist. A whopping 92 percent believed in God, or an impersonal or universal spirit, 79 percent believed in miracles, and 74 percent believed there was life after death.[235] Even among physical scientists, polling has revealed that almost 40 percent believe in a personal God—presumably that number would be higher if belief in some kind of impersonal being were included. It's only among elites, specifically members of the National Academy of Sciences, that the number drops, and precipitously so, to only 7 percent who believe in a personal God.[236] Overall, however, the statistics show that higher levels of education don't necessarily result in lower levels of belief in God.

Maybe faith and science aren't all that opposed after all.

Maybe belief in God isn't all that unreasonable.

Philosophical objections to the resurrection *hinge primarily on the larger worldview one assumes*. Those who reject it do so primarily because they assume a modern, scientific worldview doesn't allow for the miraculous since there is no rational basis for believing in a "God" capable of performing them.

But if it can be shown that there is some kind of rational intelligence behind the universe, and that this being created us with some purpose in mind, then the case for the resurrection reaches a virtual certainty. It there is a God, then the resurrection of Jesus is not only possible. It's *inevitable*. I'll explain why below.

So, if, like the majority of people on the planet, you already believe there is a God, the argument for the resurrection is practically a slam dunk. If you don't, or if you're not sure what to believe about God, consider the evidence and arguments that changed one of the greatest atheistic minds of all, Antony Flew.

## Following the Logic

When I first studied the philosophical arguments for and against God in college some thirty years ago, I had already rejected the nominal Catholic faith I was brought up on—my real "religion" growing up was baseball: all I really cared about was replacing Thurman Munson as the catcher for the Yankees! Like many my age who confront life's ultimate questions for the first time (What's the meaning of life? Is there a God? What happens when you die?), I was on an all-consuming quest for "the Truth," whatever that meant and wherever it led, even if it was to atheism.

So I was intensely interested in the classic philosophical proofs for the existence of God. But I found that in each and every case—with only one exception that I'll explore below—the objection carried equal weight. They ended up *canceling each other out.*

The whole thing ended in a stalemate.

Later on, when I taught these proofs, I'd watch the same thing happen to my students. Studying them usually left them in a state of confusion, not knowing what to believe.

However, despite a conspicuous lack of press,[237] in the last thirty to forty years there have been *significant, game-changing developments* in the so-called "God debate". Developments that even convinced someone like Flew to reverse his ardent atheism. Because it's worth looking at them in some detail, I'll examine the three areas where things have shifted dramatically.

## Getting a Tune-Up

The first area involves what's known as the argument from "fine tuning." Based on the findings of modern science, it asserts that the universe is so carefully "fine tuned" for human life that it can't be the result of spontaneous and arbitrary materialistic processes but has to be the work of a divine mind. As Flew points out: "It has been calculated that if the value of even one of the fundamental constants— the speed of light or the mass of an electron, for instance—had been to the slightest degree different, then no planet capable of permitting the evolution of human life could have formed."[238]

And as Robert Spitzer adds, the probability of our low entropy universe—which is necessary for life spontaneously emerging— coming into existence on its own "...is about the same odds as a monkey typing Shakespeare's *Macbeth* by random tapping of the keys in a single attempt (virtually impossible)."[239] Spitzer also notes that:

> Fred Hoyle and William Fowler discovered the exceedingly high improbability of oxygen, carbon, helium, and beryllium having the precise resonance levels to allow for an abundance of carbon necessary for life. [Hoyle] compared the emergence of a single cell within the universe by pure chance to "a tornado sweeping through a junk-yard assembling a Boeing 747 from the materials within."
>
> He also compared the emergence of a single protein in the universe by pure chance to a solar system full of blind men solving Rubik's Cubes simultaneously.
>
> The "resonance level" anthropic coincidence was so striking that it caused Hoyle to abandon his former atheism and declare:

237

"A common sense interpretation of the facts suggests that a superintellect has monkeyed with physics, as well as with chemistry and biology, and that there are no blind forces worth speaking about in nature. The numbers one calculates from the facts seem to me so overwhelming as to put this conclusion almost beyond question."[240]

Furthermore, the evidence points to the earth as being *absolutely unique*—the only planet capable of sustaining life, especially in ways that matter to human beings. Scientists have even coined a term for this: the "Anthropic Principle," which says that our entire universe is uniquely fine tuned to give rise to human life on earth. And, despite a strong desire on the part of many scientists to find it, there is absolutely no credible evidence that extraterrestrials exist. In other words, all the data we have suggests that the earth is the only planet where rational, sentient creatures like us exist.[241]

It's as if the entire universe were designed for this!

Even Stephen Hawking admitted that, in the absence of an alternative explanation (see below), "It would be very difficult to explain why the universe should have begun in just this way, except as the act of a God who intended to create beings like us."[242]

This argument from fine tuning is so compelling that those who wish to deny the obvious conclusion—that there is a superintellect behind the physical order—must resort to the *completely speculative* idea of a "multiverse." If there is a multiverse, then the combinations are theoretically numerous enough to allow for the possibility that on one planet in one universe the conditions might exist to arbitrarily and spontaneously create life as we know it.

But presently there is little if no evidence for a multiverse.

It's a speculative idea, a theory that only exists in the imagination of the scientists who postulate it. Flew argues that it is so speculative that it makes the whole idea of rational explanation meaningless. He agrees with Swinburne's blunt conclusion: "It is crazy to postulate a trillion (causally unconnected) universes to explain the features of one universe, when postulating one entity (God) will do the job."[243] In other words, it's a *desperate reach* for those who are unwilling to accept the irrefutable conclusion that a rational intelligence must be behind the one "finely tuned" universe *we do know* exists.

(As I understand it, the evidence that some physicists find for the multiverse comes through developments in "string theory", which is itself a *purely theoretical construct*. Like string theory, the multiverse lies beyond the observable universe. It's all hypothetical. And both—for very different reasons—will likely always remain beyond our capacity to observe, making them, in principle, unobservable. Moreover, to date every proposed multiverse theory has substantial fine-tuning requirements. For example, in the version that includes the idea of "bubble universes", these universes need to be slowly rolled out at a very *precise* rate so that they are spaced far enough not to collide. Furthermore, the latest thinking among the majority of physicists is that the multiverse, if it exists, would have to have a *beginning*—a determination that is not likely to be overturned, as will be shown below along with why this is so significant.)

But even supposing a multiverse does exist, it doesn't explain how *rationally* ordered governing principles arose in the first place. Even if they only occur in one universe out of a trillion trillion, they still require a deeper rationality to account for their existence. In fact, even those who argue for a multiverse acknowledge the need for fine tuning in the expansion of these universes—if not done in a rationally ordered fashion, it would implode upon itself.

The multiverse doesn't negate the need for a rational intelligence behind it all.

And in order to explain the laws of nature, the only real option is a divine Mind.[244]

Fine tuning doesn't just exist in the physics of the universe. It's also in our biology. And here, the evidence for a divine mind may be even stronger. Recent discoveries about DNA—the genetic code—press the question: "How can a universe of mindless matter produce beings with intrinsic ends, self-replication capabilities, and 'coded chemistry?'"[245]

In other words, how can something "mindless" just *happen* to generate something of *immensely greater complexity and sophistication?* Philosopher David Conway argues that purely materialistic causes cannot account for "the very first emergence of living matter from non-living matter. In being alive, living matter possesses a teleological organization that is wholly absent from everything that preceded it." Moreover, materialistic causes can't account for:

> the emergence, from the very earliest life-forms which were incapable of reproducing themselves, of life-forms with a capacity for reproducing themselves. Without the existence of such a capacity, it would not have been possible for different species to emerge through random mutation and natural selection. Accordingly, such mechanism cannot be invoked in any explanation of how life-forms with this capacity first "evolved" from those that lacked it.[246]

Atheists are forced to argue that these life-forms just spontaneously arise through purely materialistic causes. But this utterly fails to explain the most remarkable feature of these life-forms: "...these genetic instructions are not the kind of information you find in thermodynamics and statistical mechanics; rather, they constitute semantic information. In other words, they have a specific meaning. These instructions can be effective only in a molecular environment capable of interpreting the meaning in the genetic code. The origin question rises to the top at this point."[247]

Nobel Prize-winning physiologist George Wald originally believed that life came about spontaneously. But later, he changed his position to believe that there must be a preexisting mind responsible for its complexity:

> How is it that, with so many other apparent options, we are in a universe that possesses just that peculiar nexus of properties that breeds life? It has occurred to

me lately—I must confess with some shock at first to
my scientific sensibilities—that both questions might
be brought into some degree of congruence. This is
with the assumption that mind, rather than emerging
as a late outgrowth in the evolution of life, has existed
always as the matrix, the source and condition of
physical reality—that the stuff of which physical
reality is constructed is mind-stuff. It is mind that has
composed a physical universe that breeds life, and
so eventually evolves creatures that know and create:
science-, art-, and technology-making creatures.[248]

It is here, with these recent discoveries about genetics, that the
case for fine tuning becomes practically irrefutable. Flew concludes:

What I think the DNA material has done is that it
has shown, by the almost unbelievable complexity
of the arrangements which are needed to produce
(life), that intelligence must have been involved in
getting these extraordinarily diverse elements to work
together. It's the enormous complexity of the number
of elements and the enormous subtlety of the ways
they work together. The meeting of these two parts
at the right time by chance is simply minute. It is all
a matter of the enormous complexity by which the
results were achieved, which looked to me like the
work of intelligence.[249]

Only an infinite Intelligence could produce such "end-directed,
self-replicating" life.

# Being Rational About It

The second area of proof that changed Flew's mind has to do with new insights and philosophical arguments about human consciousness and rationality. Scientists are basically at a loss to explain their existence through purely materialistic processes. They are stumped, for example, in explaining how the capacity to do complex mathematics or abstract philosophy developed as an ability that helped our ancestors survive. As a matter of fact, a few prominent scientists and philosophers have acknowledged that this is the greatest challenge to a materialistic worldview, to atheism. As Varghese points out:

> The reality of rationality cannot be evaded with any appeal to natural selection. Natural selection presupposes the existence of physical entities that interact according to specific laws and of a code that manages the processes of life. And to talk of natural selection is to *assume* that there is *some logic to what is happening in nature (adaptation)* and that we are *capable of understanding this logic.*(my italics)[250]

It's a stunning fact and one we routinely take for granted: we are able to think logically, abstractly, and self-reflectively, and moreover, we do it in a universe that abides by ordered processes we can predict and understand. In fact, *this is the basic presumption modern science is based upon.*

Without it, science couldn't function.

However, nothing in the physical world—the domain of science— can adequately explain the existence of this consciousness and rationality. They require a non-physical source that is endowed with similar but immensely greater capabilities. Varghese again:

> Although the new atheists have failed to come to grips with either the nature or the source of life,

consciousness, thought, and the self, the answer to the question of the origin of the supraphysical seems obvious: the supraphysical can only originate in a supraphysical source. Life, consciousness, mind, and the self can only come from a Source that is living, conscious, and thinking. If we are centers of consciousness and thought who are able to know and love and intend and execute, I cannot see how such centers could come to be from *something that is itself incapable of all these activities.* Although simply physical processes could create complex physical phenomena, we are not concerned here with the relation of simple and complex, but with the origin of "centers." It is simply inconceivable that any material matrix or field can generate agents who think and act. *Matter cannot produce conceptions and perception. A force field does not plan or think.* So at the level of reason and everyday experience, we become immediately aware that the world of living, conscious, thinking beings has to originate in a living Source, a Mind.(my italics)[251]

Because they come so naturally to us, because we use them so effortlessly, we usually fail to see how unusual and amazing our rational faculties are. As Varghese continues:

Beyond consciousness, there is the phenomena of thought, of understanding, of seeing meaning. Every language reveals an order of being that is innately intangible. At the foundation of all of our thinking, communicating, and use of language is a miraculous power. It is the power of noting differences and similarities and of generalizing and universalizing— what philosophers call concepts, universals, and the like. It is natural to humans, unique, and simply mystifying. How is it that, from childhood, you can effortlessly think of both your dog Caesar and dogs in general? You can think of redness without thinking of a specific red thing (of course redness does not exist independently, but only in red things). You abstract and distinguish and unify without giving your ability to do these things a second thought. And you even ponder things that have no physical characteristics, such as the idea of liberty or the activity of angels. This power of thinking in concepts is by its very nature something that transcends matter.

If there are those who dispute any of this, consistency demands that they stop talking and thinking. Every time they use language, they are illustrating the all-pervasive role of meaning, concepts, intentions, and reason in our lives.[252]

How does a purely physical universe produce such intellectually oriented creatures, and then behave in such a logically consistent way so as to allow us to unlock its mysteries?

How did we ever get to be "centers of consciousness" who can think self-reflectively and then rationally choose our way in the world?

How did we ever develop the capacity to think in such (genetically useless) abstract terms which invariably drive us to ponder life's great mysteries, relentlessly seeking to "make sense" of it all—why are we meaning-seeking creatures in the first place?

How is it that we are so curious about matters, such as philosophy and art, that don't seem to have anything to do with our survival as a species?

As Vatican astronomer and physicist Paul Mueller puts it:

If you buy into scientific materialism, you take it for granted that energy and matter are the only things that exist. But then you find yourself in the odd position of having to think that the "human phenomenon" is a rather odd and special exception to the universe. On that assumption, human thinking, feeling, willing, loving, and so forth, have to be seen as strange and atypical phenomena in the universe. On that assumption, we end up having to see ourselves as being a very strange and special "outlier" in a universe that is nothing but matter and energy.[253]

How does matter and energy produce such a phenomenon? It can't.

The only logical way to explain the human phenomenon is an origin of comparable dimension, one that lies beyond matter and energy; one that has analogous, even if radically superior, capabilities of thinking, feeling, willing, and loving.

There is an old medieval argument for the existence of God that says something greater cannot come from something lesser. Therefore, the source of human life must be an intellect at least as great, if not greater.

The fact that I am writing this sentence and you can comprehend it means we are rational beings. And the only thing that can account for this remarkable and undeniable fact is a supremely rational being who is responsible for human consciousness and rationality.

## Beginning With a Bang

The third thing that changed Flew's mind about God are recent scientific discoveries that support and advance the classic cosmological proof for God's existence. Simply put, this proof says that something cannot come from nothing. Since every created thing is contingent on something else, some prior cause, there must ultimately be some non-contingent reality, some uncaused cause or first cause that is responsible for everything else. Creation is evidence of a creator. As philosophers have always recognized, this argument is foolproof as long as there is a beginning point.

If the universe has a beginning, then an uncreated divine Being must stand behind it.

That's why the major objection to the cosmological proof has been to argue something called "infinite regress": time moves eternally backward just as it moves eternally forward. In other words, *there is no beginning point* because time is infinite in both directions, past as well as future. The material universe, therefore, has always existed and therefore requires no first cause.

It never came to be. It just is.

As I mentioned above, when I first studied the proofs for God in college, there was one where the objection didn't completely cancel the argument out. This was it. The cosmological proof seemed to frustrate philosophers in a way none of the others did. Their strongest rebuttal, the best they could come up with—infinite regress—is *unbearably counterintuitive.*

Think about it for a second. Time marches on, relentlessly. It's always moving forward, in one fixed direction. It doesn't go backward one day, then forward the next. Or back for a million years and then forward a million. Time, of course, is a human construct, but it accurately measures the constant and predictable movement— the progression and evolution—built into material reality. Things grow and decay; they don't regress and return to their original state. Trees decomposing on the ground don't suddenly "recompose" and become a healthy, thriving tree again. We don't grow older for a while and then go backward, returning to our youth, eventually becoming infants again. Despite our infatuation with movies like *Back to the Future* and the idea of time travel, overwhelmingly and without exception, all the empirical data indicates that time only moves in one constant, unrelenting direction: forward.[254]

It is grossly speculative, therefore, to posit backward movement when nothing empirical supports this. It goes against all observation, intuition and common sense.

It is *manifestly unintelligible.*

For example, do you remember learning about planes in math class? (Sorry to bring up bad memories!) You had to draw the little arrow at the beginning and end of the line to indicate it continued infinitely in both directions. Although quite abstract and hard to imagine, in theory, it's perfectly intelligible. Even if it's hard to picture, the idea a static line might extend without end in either direction makes sense theoretically.

But time is *dynamic* and with a specific *directionality*. It *evolves* and *progresses*, always moving forward. So on what grounds, then, can the argument be made that it moves or even just extends backwards infinitely? Material reality, the only reality we know and have data for, only moves in one direction. There is no basis, therefore, to posit infinite regress.

However, even if time is infinitely regressive, the simple existence of matter still requires some non-contingent cause, some explanation for its being. For me, this was the true flaw with the critique of the cosmological proof. How does something come from nothing? How is it that anything exists at all? Why is there something instead of nothing?

None of the responses philosophers proposed had a good answer for this.

Creation—existence itself—is something that begs for an explanation. To just accept it as a brute fact seemed incredibly irrational. Even if a self-existing, "eternally static" universe is theoretically conceivable, or even logically possible, the odds against it are enormous. It seemed to me vastly more logical and probable that there had to be some uncaused cause responsible for it all.

Flew himself was one of those philosophers who dismissed the cosmological proof by arguing infinite regress. But eventually, as a theist he came to admit the flaw in this critique: "In response to these approaches, Leslie asserts that 'the existence even of an infinite series of past events couldn't be made self-explaining through each even being explained by an earlier one.' If there is an infinite series of books about geometry that owe their pattern to copying from earlier books, we still do not have an adequate answer as to why the book is the way it is (e.g., it is about geometry) or why there is a book at all. The entire series needs explanation…the universe is something that begs an explanation."[255]

So, infinite regress doesn't negate the fact that *something cannot come from nothing*. As Spitzer argues:

> It does not matter whether one postulates an *infinite* number of caused causes (realities awaiting causation to exist), because an infinite number of hypothesized realities awaiting causation to exist is collectively still awaiting causation to exist—it is literally an infinite amount of nothing, and an infinite amount of nothing is still nothing. Therefore, there must be at least one reality that does not have to await causation to exist—a reality that exists through itself (an uncaused cause)— in order to have *anything* real.[256]

Even if time is an infinite spectrum, moving eternally backward— as unfathomable and unlikely as that is—as well as eternally forward, the bare fact that anything exists at all begs for an explanation. It requires an uncaused cause.

*"An infinite amount of nothing is still nothing!"*

However, recent scientific discoveries about the origins of the universe, big bang cosmology, are rendering all this speculation about infinite regress mute. The best evidence *overwhelmingly points to a beginning.*

As Flew recalls, the two books in which he most fully developed his reasoning for being an atheist were written prior to the latest developments in big bang cosmology. When, in the 1980's, the contemporary scientific consensus was becoming clear, he admitted to being embarrassed because "it seemed that the cosmologists were providing scientific proof of what St. Thomas Aquinas contended could not be proved philosophically; namely, that the universe had a beginning."[257]

Even as an atheist, Flew maintained that if the universe had no beginning, then there was no need to explain its existence. It was simply a "brute" fact. However, if there was a beginning to the universe, that would change everything. It would be necessary to ask what produced that beginning. He realized that, if the big bang theory proved true, it would have a huge impact on the question of God: he, and any other rational person, would have to ask what produced this beginning. Flew notes that even Stephen Hawking agreed on this point, admitting in A *Brief History of Time:* "So long as the universe had a beginning, we could suppose it had a creator.[258]

Those scientists who don't like the inevitability of this conclusion have adopted completely speculative concepts, like the multiverse, in response. As with the fine tuning argument, they provide a convenient way out.

Flew marks this move: "Modern cosmologists seemed just as disturbed as atheists about the potential theological implications of their work. Consequently, they devised influential escape routes that sought to preserve the idea of the multiverse, numerous universes generated by endless vacuum fluctuation events, and Stephen Hawking's notion of a self-contained universe."[259]

Theoretical physicist and former ABC News science correspondent Michael Guillen notes the same move: "As an aside, I can't resist mentioning that compared to the increasingly complex and mystical...hypotheses astronomers are taking seriously these days—multiple universes, imaginary time, dark energy, and so forth— the much-maligned hypothesis of God can hardly be considered bizarre anymore. Indeed, even though scientists will never admit it... given the peculiar new direction astronomy is taking, I believe God is fast becoming the much-sought-after *simplest explanation of all!*"[260]

And as John Lennox points out, some of these scientists have not been shy about their motives. In 1927 Georges Lemaitre first proposed the groundwork for the big bang theory, namely, the idea the universe was expanding. Sir Arthur Eddington taught Lemaitre at Cambridge and was duly impressed with his work. But later on he made this revealing remark: "Philosophically, the notion of a beginning of the present order of Nature is repugnant...I should like to find a genuine loophole."

Lennox also cites the case of Sir John Maddox who, in the 1960's, was fiercely resistant to further evidence for the big bang:

> For him, the idea of a beginning was "thoroughly unacceptable", since it implied an "ultimate origin of our world" and gave those who believed in the biblical doctrine of creation "ample justification" for their beliefs...
>
> ...Maddox was hostile to the notion of a beginning precisely because the Genesis creation model clearly entailed such a beginning, and he did not welcome scientific confirmation of that model. However, his protests had to give way when confronted with the evidence. The discovery of the galactic red-shift and the cosmic echo of creation, the microwave background, confirmed the obvious prediction that the biblical account implied—there was a beginning to space-time.[261]

Despite protests and the speculative theories they produce, the *strongest (empirical) evidence physics has produced to date points to a beginning*, and therefore, to some kind of supernatural (i.e., beyond the natural, contingent order) first cause to bring it about.

But even if science can one day show that we do live in a multiverse (which, most agree, is highly improbable since any postulated mutliverse lies beyond our ability to observe empirically and likely always will), the scientific evidence still points to a beginning.

The Second Law of Thermodynamics is a fundamental tenet of science. This is what Albert Einstein said about it: "A law is more impressive the greater the simplicity of its premises, the more different are the kinds of things it relates, and the more extended its range of applicability. [Entropy] is the only physical theory of universal content, which I am convinced, that within the framework of applicability of its basic concepts will never be overthrown."[262]

Regardless of whether we live in a multiverse or not, Spitzer explains how this basic law of physics makes a first cause necessary. According to the second law of thermodynamics, in isolated systems, entropy always stays the same or increases. In the universe as a whole, then, entropy will continue to increase until the universe eventually runs down. If the universe existed infinitely, then, like a perpetual motion machine, it could never wear out. The amount of available energy in the universe would have to remain constant. But this is impossible according to the second law of thermodynamics. The only way this law could hold true in an infinitely existing universe is if we found ourselves in a state of maximum entropy (because "sometime" back in eternity the universe would have already completely run down) where no energy was available—which is obviously not the case since I'm moving my fingers to type this sentence![263]

So, before the universe began wearing down, before it began moving from order to disorder, there had to be a previous point in time where the availability of energy and order in the universe was at a maximum. There had to be a *beginning*.

Sptizer points to another key insight of modern physics that corroborates this conclusion. It's the basis of the Borde-Vilenkin-Guth (BVG) proof. In our universe, a relative velocity cannot exceed the speed of light. Since we know that relative velocity decreases as the universe expands, at some point in the distant past all relative velocities had to be close to the speed of light. That would be the point where our universe couldn't go back any further. It would be the beginning of the universe.

This would hold true for a multiverse as well. As long as there is a finite maximum velocity (whether that's the speed of light or something else), there has to be a beginning. How do we know every multiverse would have to have a finite maximum velocity? Because if physical energy could travel at infinite velocity, it would mean that it could exist everywhere at once in the space-time continuum. But then incompatible forms of energy would be simultaneously occupying the same points in the continuum. Which is impossible. Matter and antimatter, for example, can't do this. Neither can electrons and protons. Therefore, even multiverses (if they exist) must be governed by finite maximum velocities, meaning that they, too, would have to have a beginning.[264]

But what about Hawking's theory of spontaneous creation from nothing, that "nothing" being the law of gravity?

Spitzer responds: "Something physical, such as a false vacuum of a quantum field, is *not* nothing, because the quantum condition through which the false vacuum occurs is *something*. This can be compared to my bank account. Just because it has a zero balance does not mean that the bank account and the bank do not exist."[265]

Besides, all this does is push the question back one step further. "If proposals like that of Hawking and Mlodinow lead us only to transphysical purely intelligible realities (like the law of gravity) without the necessary condition for their existence, then it seems that physics is pushing us closer and closer to a transphysical act of thinking, which…[is the Creator of everything else.]"[266]

The existence of gravity, or whatever other means of spontaneous generation of the universe are proposed, still begs for an explanation. How did *it* come to be?

As Keller observes, without God:

> either original matter sprang from nothing…has always existed without a cause, or there is an infinite regress of causes without a beginning. Each of these answers takes us out of the realm of science and the universe we know…for science knows nothing of beings or physical processes that spring out of nothing or that have no beginning.[267]

From a purely scientific standpoint, then, the *empirical* evidence—the true currency of science—points to a beginning of the universe, which implies a non-contingent (i.e., uncaused) cause to bring it about.

In the end, Flew changed his mind about God because he concluded that the evidence which has emerged from science in the last thirty years or so, along with the strongest philosophical arguments marshaled to explain this evidence and respond to objections like his, supports belief in a personal God, or in his words: "...an agent of intentional actions."[268]

Ultimately, the best evidence and logic led Flew to agree with other theists that: "God created the world so as to bring into being a race of rational creatures."[269]

## The Mind of God

But why? If the best scientific evidence and strongest philosophical arguments lead to the conclusion that there is a rational being who has created rational creatures for some grand purpose, what is it?

What is *the logic of the universe?*

In the movie *Castaway* Tom Hanks plays the part of a man who is stranded on an island for four years after his plane crashes. Eventually he is rescued. But during his years as a castaway, he "makes" a friend: a Wilson volleyball he finds in the debris of the plane's wreckage. Appropriately enough, he names him "Wilson." And he begins an imaginary dialogue.

Over time he develops a "relationship" with Wilson. In fact, Wilson becomes so dear to him that, when he builds a makeshift raft in an attempt to escape the island, he takes Wilson with him. And when Wilson is swept out to sea during this attempt, he even risks his life to save him, collapsing in tears when he can't.

He risks his life to save a *volleyball!*

The day after this happens, a passing cargo ship rescues him. But without Wilson's "friendship," he never would have been able to keep his sanity. Without Wilson, he never would have been able to survive. He needed "someone" to keep him from going insane from the suffocating, even lethal, effects of loneliness.

Loneliness kills![270]

Although the movie was a fictional account, it was based on extensive research about people caught in a similar situation. And as such, it speaks a profound truth about who we are as humans: we are *intensely social* beings.

We are made for relationship.

We really can't survive without it.

For time immemorial, writing has been a dreaded chore for teenagers. And for the teachers like me giving a writing assignment, an epic battle of wills. The agonized groans. The endless negotiation. The indignant and eloquently argued protests. (If only they saved some of that eloquence for the paper!)

And the inevitable question of ultimate concern: how *long* does it have to be?

But about ten years ago, everything changed. Something mystifying happened. Those same students who would organize a revolution, wage a crusade, or fight to the death just to get out of writing a one-page essay, were now writing non-stop and with an intensity and passion few novelists possess.

They were writing far more prodigiously than any teacher ever asked them to!

What was the reason for this tectonic shift? *Texting.*

But why? What's so appealing about texting?

It's *just writing* after all. Not to mention that when all this started, texting was an arduous task. The original cell phones, the flip phones, didn't have a full keyboard. You had to hit the number that corresponded with one of the three letters you wanted to select and then file through until you got it.

And yet, with my own two eyes, I witnessed kids gleefully working this clumsy keypad for *hours on end*. In fact, getting them to put their phone away was harder than taking a lion cub from its mother!

How do you explain this? Actually, it's simple. Texting is all about social interaction (even though many would argue it has diminished authentic, that is, personal, face-to-face interactions). So no matter how painful the act of writing is, teenagers who did everything humanly possible to get out of it now eagerly embrace it with reckless abandon, losing themselves in this previously dreaded chore for hours on end.

That's how much they crave connection with their peers.

In fact, this is the power of social media. It's why we're so addicted to it; why it consumes so much of our time and energy; why it has become so dominant in our culture; why people will even risk their lives just to send a text (some studies are now showing that texting while driving is every bit as dangerous as drunk driving, if not more so).

We *crave* connection.

Have you heard of the so-called Harvard Happiness study? It's one of the most comprehensive studies ever done. For over seventy-five years and counting, Harvard researchers have followed a diverse group of 724 men—most of whom have died by now—and their families trying to determine what makes for happiness. Is it success, achievement, wealth, power, fame? Or as most would anticipate, some combination, some ideal mix of these and perhaps other factors?

What the researchers found surprised them. It turns out there is *one single, glaring and consistent* thing that determines how happy you are: relationships. And not just having a number of relationships, but the quality of those relationships.

In fact, if you have just one person you can count on, one person in your life who you know will be there for you through thick and thin, even if the relationship isn't perfect, even if it has its ups and downs, this, according to this large, long-term Harvard study, determines more than any other factor *by far* your health and happiness.[271]

Love is what we crave most. Nothing else comes close. Nothing else can satisfy our deepest longings. Nothing else can give us true happiness. So if there is some logic to the universe, some point to it all, some purpose a rational being has in creating us, it must involve love.

Love is the only thing that makes sense of life.

Deep down, *love is where the meaning is found.*

*Love is what we're made for.*

And as Robert Spitzer asks: Why else would the Creator bring "beings meant for love" into being unless God Himself is loving? "If the Creator is not loving, then the creation of 'beings meant for love' seems absurd...Could the Creator be any less loving than the 'loving nature' He has created?" Indeed, if God *is* love, then creating beings who are not only capable of love, but only fulfilled in love, makes perfect sense.[272]

Despite debuting over twenty years ago, the movie *Jerry McGuire* remains popular today because of its many memorable lines, like (who can forget): "Show me the money!" In the movie's climactic scene, Jerry McGuire (played by Tom Cruise) bursts into Dorothy Boyd's (played by Renee Zellweger) house and delivers a long, rambling speech. When he *finally* finishes, Zellweger responds with what is probably the movie's most memorable line: "You had me at hello." But before she does, Cruise passionately proclaims his love for her with a line that has to be a close second: "You complete me!"

*You complete me.*

Anyone who's married knows how true this is. When you find that right person, when you find your soul mate, you walk off into the sunset happily ever after. They really do complete you.

Okay, all the married couples can pick themselves up off the ground now from laughing so hard! Of course this *isn't* true. No finite, fallible human being can ever complete us.

And yet...and yet, *we routinely expect they will.* One of the most powerful notions in our culture is that when you do find the right person, you *will* walk off into the sunset and live happily ever after. That they will be that "missing piece" you've been looking for all along. That they will complete you. In fact, the longing for a love that will complete us is the deepest longing of the human heart.

But, if no finite, earthly love will ever satisfy our restless hearts; if no imperfect, human love can ever fulfill us, then we weren't made for just any kind of love.

We were made for an *infinite* love. For a *perfect* love. For a *supernatural* love.

For the kind of love *only God can give us.*

He alone completes us.

So the reason He created us must ultimately be for His perfect love, *for a relationship with Him*; which, of course, has a lot to do with the way we relate to and love one another.

I recently came across an intriguing study that was done on a group of people making an Ignatian retreat. Ignatian retreats involve prolonged periods of silence. This solitude affords participants the opportunity to focus intently on their relationship with God. As a result, many report very pleasant and/or intense experiences of "communing" with Him, which, in turn, results in a heightened sense of well-being. The study revealed that retreatants usually showed significant increases in levels of dopamine, which is to be expected since dopamine is normally correlated with a sense of well-being.[273]

More and more, studies like this one are showing similar results. There seems to be a strong correlation between faith in God and a deep sense of peace and happiness. There also seems to be a strong correlation between faith in God and physical and mental health. Those who believe in God, in particular, a personal God who cares for them, tend to live longer, have better health, experience less anxiety and depression, are more psychologically "functional" and report being "happier" than average.

In *Can a Smart Person Believe in God*, theoretical physicist and former ABC News science correspondent Michael Guillen concludes: "According to science: godliness (generally in the form of traditional Christianity and Judaism)—what I'm calling SQ [Spiritual Quotient]—is good for us, *demonstrably* good, both mentally and physically. Compared to the average population, high-SQ people appear to: heal faster from illness and surgery; recover more easily from alcohol and substance abuse; cope better with stress, trauma, and emotional loss; be less likely to suffer from depression; and be more likely to feel happy and optimistic."[274]

Harvard psychiatrist Armand Nicholi concurs:

Several years ago I conducted a research project exploring Harvard University students who, while undergraduates, experienced what they referred to as "religious conversion." I interviewed these students as well as people who knew them before and after their conversion. Were these experiences an expression of pathology, i.e., isolating and destructive, or were they adaptive and constructive? Did these experiences impair or enhance functioning? Results published in the *American Journal of Psychiatry* stated that each subject described "a marked improvement in ego functioning, [including] a radical change in life style with an abrupt halt in the use of drugs, alcohol, and cigarettes; improved impulse control, with adoption of a strict sexual code demanding chastity or marriage with fidelity; improved academic performance; enhanced self-image and greater access to inner feelings; an increased capacity for establishing 'close, satisfying relationships'; improved communication with parents, though most parents at first expressed some degree of alarm over the student's rather sudden, intense religious interest; a positive change in affect, with a lessening of 'existential despair'; and a decrease in preoccupation with the passage of time and apprehension over death."[275]

In short, according to the metrics of psychology, post-conversion they were significantly more functional and well-adjusted.

All this research suggests that a relationship with God produces a significant improvement in quality of life and a profound sense of well-being; which is exactly what you'd expect if this is what we are really made for.

Only God completes us.

This is why he created us.

*This* is the logic of the universe.

(It isn't the place to get into how this all works: how love, ontologically, requires free will; how only the concrete ambiguities of this earthly life can provide the necessary conditions for the real freedom required to respond to God's love, or not; how our response to his love determines our eternal destiny, and so forth. But suffice it to say, this fundamental insight about love being the logic of the universe can be fully worked out in a perfectly consistent and rationally compelling way.)

## What's a Loving God to do?

So how does all this relate to the resurrection?

If there is a divine mind behind the universe, then the philosophical objection to the resurrection melts away. Not only is the resurrection possible, it becomes *a logical necessity*, something a God of perfect love *must* do. Since statistically most people reading this already believe in some kind of intelligent creator—or hopefully have been convinced by reading this section!—let me explain.

First of all, if there is a God, then, by definition, he/she/it can do anything. The higher power responsible for the laws of nature can certainly disrupt them at will. Since miracles, also by definition, suspend these laws through some kind of supernatural intervention, they must be *logically possible*.

Even one that violates death.

Admittedly, such instances are rare. And notoriously hard to prove. Whether something is miraculous or not is usually the subject of endless debate. But even if no one can prove any specific miracle has ever happened, if you accept the very well- supported premise of a rational creator, *the miraculous is always a theoretical possibility.* Even if you maintain that this higher power wouldn't ever want to intervene in creation once it's set in motion (the Deist approach), you must at least admit that such a creator has the capacity to do so. Otherwise, he wouldn't be the all-powerful creator!

So if, as the evidence strongly suggests, God exists, the main philosophical objection to the resurrection, the a priori assumption that miracles can't happen, doesn't hold true. As Antony Flew admitted when he was still an unbeliever: "Certainly given some beliefs about God, the occurrence of the resurrection does become enormously more likely."[276]

It's bias against the supernatural which prevents the most people from accepting the resurrection. *But this bias isn't well-founded.* As we've seen, on purely rational grounds, it is significantly more probable that the supernatural does exist. And if you remove this bias, all bets are off; the miraculous is just as possible as not. What becomes decisive is the historical evidence, which, in the case of the resurrection, is quite powerful.

More to the point, if God were to intervene, the resurrection is the one way above all others we'd expect Him to exercise miraculous power. What better way is there for God to reveal His perfect love and power—the *sublime love* of the cross conquering the *ultimate enemy* of death? What better way is there for God to reveal that we were created to *live eternally* in fellowship with Him?

The resurrection is the one miracle *most essential to His purpose in creating us.*

The one miracle He would be *most likely to perform.*

Or, to put it another way: with so many religions to choose from, with so many prophets and gurus running around, with so many people claiming to have the truth, how are we to supposed to know who God is or why He made us? We find ourselves in a state of confusion, *which a loving God wouldn't leave us in.* As *the* supermiracle, an event that stands out from all others as unequivocally supernatural, the resurrection clearly reveals who God is and why He made us.

The resurrection is *precisely how* a God of perfect love *would* supernaturally intervene.

Second, if love truly is the logic of the universe, then this means God *has* to intervene in creation in ways remarkably similar to Jesus. Bette Midler had a huge hit years ago called "From a Distance." The song poignantly depicts God watching over us from a distance. That image pulled on our heartstrings: what a comfort to know that God is lovingly watching over us!

But if you think about it, if it's true, it isn't comforting at all. *It's our worst nightmare.*

Any God who just watches the tragedies and misery of this world in such a detached way is *totally indifferent*. What parent could watch their child suffer without agonizing alongside them? A distant God *doesn't really care at all about us.*

If God truly loves us, then He has to agonize alongside us. He has to become *personally* involved. He has to experience human suffering. And the only way to do this is by taking on human flesh, taking on all the limitations and vulnerabilities of being human.

A God who hasn't suffered as we do, who doesn't *suffer with us*, isn't a God of love.

Thus, a loving God *has to become one of us.*

And to be truly human, He has to feel the terror and dread we feel in the face of death. He has to share in our mortality and die an actual death.

At the same time, if He really loves us, He must reveal Himself to us, *personally*. He can't remain distant, aloof, hidden. To leave us in the dark about who He is would not only be cruel, it would also *completely undermine His purpose in creating us.*

How can we love a God we have no real, personal knowledge of?

Knowledge and love are profoundly and inextricably intertwined; intimacy is only possible through a deeper knowledge of the beloved. You can't really love someone who is distant and detached. You can't really love someone who remains hidden (metaphorically speaking) behind a mask. You can't really love someone who doesn't reveal their true self to you.

Actually, this is putting it too negatively. Love doesn't just *have* to make itself known. Real love *wants* to make itself known. When something really good (or bad) happens to you, what's the first thing you want to do? If you're like the other seven billion of us, you want to share it with those you love most.

*Love's deepest desire is to share itself with its beloved.*

To reveal itself. To be intimately close.

A loving God wants to reveal Himself to us in the deepest possible way.

But it's impossible to have this kind of intimacy with some far-off transcendent being, some abstract divine mind, some generic rational intelligence. It's like trying to have a relationship with the quadratic equation. Even if you're a mathematician who happens to admire its beauty, its elegance as a theorem, you wouldn't want to go on vacation, share your deepest thoughts, or whisper sweet nothings to it!

The only way God can be intimately close to us, can be truly *loveable*, is if He makes Himself known in a warm, personal, relatable, tangible, concrete way.

In other words, if He becomes human and dwells among us.

Also at the same time, even though our broken human condition is the result of us rejecting Him and His way of love—our addiction to self—a loving God must enter into our predicament in order to call us back to Himself, to save us. He can't pursue us with his overwhelming presence and power because that would strip us of our freedom, our capacity to love him in return. He has to pursue us in all the lowliness and humility of a meek and gentle human being who woos and invites us back with love—the beauty of his life poured out for us—and leaves us the option for true reconciliation.

Moreover, by experiencing the deepest depths of human vulnerability on the cross, He willingly absorbs all the pain our rejection causes Him, which makes it possible for Him to forgive and redeem us.

So in order to suffer with us, reveal Himself to us, and save us, God has to take on our humanity, even to the point of death. But that means He must also rise from the dead. Otherwise no one would know that *He* was God; no one would know that God suffers with us; no one would know that God has revealed himself to us personally; no one would know that God has come to save us—in the wake of Jesus' tragic death, only the resurrection could show that he wasn't just any ordinary mortal, but truly divine.

The resurrection is absolutely necessary to reveal that, in Jesus, God *has* come among us, that God has done the very things He must do if He really loves us. The resurrection is integral and *indispensable* to His loving plan for us, *to the logic of the universe.*

And in the process, by defeating death the resurrection also reveals, as nothing else could, that this love is *the* power and, therefore, *the* reason behind the universe. It reveals why we're here and what happens when we die, our meaning and our destiny.

By revealing a suffering God, an intimate God, a saving God; a God whose love ultimately conquers all, even death, the resurrection is the *necessary fulfillment of God's loving design.*

Third, if the logic of the universe is love, this is exactly what the God of Jesus Christ is all about:

--Christian faith says that God is a Trinity, a God whose very being is three persons loving each other from all eternity; that the very *essence* of God *is* love. (Since love can only exist between persons, a solitary being can't *be* love.)

--It says that God, in the Incarnation, gave up all the prerogatives of divinity, all the glory and ecstasy of heaven, in order to fully embrace the human condition, even to the extent that *He willingly suffers with us.*

--It says that, in an excruciating death on the cross, the Atonement, *God sacrificed his life to save us.*

--And it says that God's offer of salvation is *sheer grace*, that it can't be earned through moral effort, or any other way—like it's some kind of commercial transaction or conditioned on something we do—but that it can only be freely received the way a child (ideally) is loved by their parents.

In these ways and many more, Christian faith points to a God of unconditional love *more clearly, deeply, and uniquely than any other religion, philosophy or worldview.*

It's through Jesus, after all, that the world first learns of an unconditionally loving God. That's why, as the great scholar of world religions Huston Smith points out, even Hinduism views Christianity as the religion of love (or path to God through love) *par excellance.*[277]

And, as many other scholars have noted, love is central to Christianity in a way that it isn't to any other worldview. The other major religions all value love and a number of them depict God as loving. But love isn't the central reality by which everything else is defined. And having a close, intimate relationship with God is out of the question. Only in Christianity is a profoundly personal relationship with a personal God not only possible and permissible, but it's why we're here. It's the ultimate point of existence.

Antony Flew never became a Christian. But he admitted that Christianity is the best candidate to be the revelation of the God he came to believe in: "As I have said more than once…If you're wanting omnipotence to set up a religion, it seems to me that this is the one to beat!"[278]

In a universe centered in love, no other worldview comes close to the Christian narrative in capturing and revealing this truth. Christianity corresponds to ultimate reality more closely than any other worldview: a God of perfect love *has* to do the very things Jesus did and *be* the very kind of God Jesus revealed.

If, deep down, love is where the meaning is found—if God *is* love—then *Jesus embodies and reveals this God like no other.*

In fact, nothing could prove God's love more than the fact that He became human, suffered, and died for us. The cross is love's perfection: the total giving of Godself to us; the furthest extent to which God's love can go; the ultimate expression of His love.

What more could God do to prove His love for us?

There is *no greater love.*

And that's why this is *exactly* what God *must* do in order to love us *perfectly.*

Unlike anyone else who's ever lived—no one else comes close— Jesus stands out as the sublime embodiment of God's love. *Jesus is everything a perfectly loving God must be.* Which means he must be this God come among us.

So, it's only natural to expect that he would rise from the dead.

## The Philosophical Upshot

Michael Licona has observed that: "Since most philosophers and theologians agree that a miracle has occurred when the event has a divine cause, recognizing that an event is a miracle is much like recognizing something is the product of an intelligent designer... We may recognize that an event is a miracle when the event (1) is extremely unlikely to have occurred given the circumstances and/ or natural law and (2) occurs in an environment or context charged with religious significance. In other words, the event occurs in a context where we might expect a god to act. The stronger the context is charged in this direction, the stronger the evidence becomes that we have a miracle on our hands."[279]

Historically and metaphysically, it's hard to imagine a context more charged in this direction than the events surrounding Jesus' life.

Metaphysically, we are wired for transcendence, longing for the happy ending, searching for the ultimate savior, craving a truly satisfying vision of immortality, designed for perfect love; all of which is best explained, not as a figment of our imagination, but as a deep intuition, an innate awareness, of the *ultimate reality we inhabit.*

This is what we were made for.[280]

But death threatens all of this, especially the love which is at the center of life. Relationships are the thing that makes life most meaningful. As Keller observes: "Death removes them one at a time over the years, stripping you down and down. Finally, it comes for you and removes you from the loved ones remaining. Almost by definition, real love wants to last; it never wants to part from those we love. Death strips us of everything that makes life meaningful... it is our ultimate enemy."[281]

Death turns our world upside down. But the resurrection turns it right side up. A world in which Christ rises has supreme meaning. His way of life, his love, isn't just some nice philosophy or beautiful pattern to emulate, it's the ruling force of the universe.

This is the only way life makes any sense.

The only way our deepest longings are fulfilled.

As Morton Kelsey says: "The resurrection tells us that at the heart and center of the universe love is reigning. Something deep within us resonates with this radical view of the nature of things in spite of all the evidence to the contrary."[282]

And at the same time, historically, the claim that someone has risen from the dead has only been seriously made for one person: Jesus. Not one of the criminals crucified alongside him. Not Elvis. Not Ghandi or MLK. Not even Abraham, Moses, Buddha or Muhammad. Only with Jesus is there *enough evidence for the case to go forward.*

On top of this, in Jesus we find a *staggering convergence of independently verifiable historical facts:* forgiving sins and teaching with divine authority, introducing an otherworldly ethic, performing miracles in a manner and to a degree no one else ever has, speaking of himself as the unique Son of God the Father, living so exquisitely that those who knew him would claim he never sinned, dying as the only one who can reconcile us to God, and then, of course, the tight sequence of empty tomb and appearances. And these facts all come together in such a completely coherent way that they inevitably lead to the conclusion that he is God.

As it turns out, he is *the one person in all of history* we would most expect to rise from the dead.

In the end, then, we are left with a *stunning correspondence between these historical facts and the complete fulfillment of all our metaphysical longings:* for immortality, infinite joy, perfect love; for good vanquishing evil; for the ultimate savior to make all this happen; and for a vision of eternity that incorporates both continuity and transcendence.

And more impressively, if there is a divine mind behind it all, which, as we saw, is nearly irrefutable, we are left with an *absolutely unique correspondence between these historical facts and the logic of the universe:* without rival, Jesus completely embodies a God who made us for his perfect love; Christian faith matches the logic of the universe perfectly.

If there was one event in history that these longings and this logic would tell us to expect, it is this: Jesus' resurrection.

Life is hard…then you die…but then you can rise again with Jesus.

# SUGGESTIONS FOR
# GOING DEEPER

Collins, Francis S., *The Language of God: A Scientist Presents Evidence for Belief,* New York, NY: Free Press, 2006.

Davies, Paul, *God and the New Physics,* New York, NY: Simon and Schuster, 1983.

Davies, Stephen T., *Risen Indeed: Making Sense of the Resurrection,* Grand Rapids, MI: Eerdmans, 1993.

D'Souza, Dinesh, *What's So Great About Christianity,* Carol Stream, IL: Tyndale House, 207.

Flew, Antony, *There is a God: How the World's Most Notorious Atheist Changed His Mind,* New York, NY: HarperOne, 2007.

Guillen, Michael, *Can a Smart Person Believe in God?* Nashville, TN: Nelson Books, 2004.

Keller, Timothy, *Making Sense of God: An Invitation to the Skeptical,* New York, NY: Viking, 2016.

_____, *The Reason for God: Belief in an Age of Skepticism,* New York, NY: Riverhead Books, 2008.

Lennox, John C., *Gunning for God: Why the New Atheists are Missing the Target,* Oxford: Lion Books, 2011.

McGrath, Alister and McGrath, Joanna Collicutt, *The Dawkins Delusion? Atheist Fundamentalism and the Denial of the Divine*, Downers Grove, IL: InterVarsity, 2007.

Nicholi, Armand M., Jr., *The Question of God: C.S. Lewis and Sigmund Freud Debate God, Love, Sex, and the Meaning of Life*, New York, NY: Free Press, 2002.

Spitzer, Robert, *The Soul's Upward Yearning: Clues to Our Transcendent Nature from Experience and Reason*, San Francisco, CA: Ignatius Press, 2015.

# CONCLUSION: WHAT DO YOU REALLY WANT?

## I Mean, What Do You Really, Really Want?

HAD JUST GIVEN A brilliant Easter sermon—if I do say so myself!— and was greeting people after the service when one congregant came up and told me, "Great sermon, Pastor. You gave us some powerful reasons to believe Jesus really rose from the dead." Like most churches on Easter, there were a lot of people who only come once a year. So I felt great satisfaction at giving such an inspiring and convincing sermon.

Then he asked, "But if the evidence is so good, why don't they believe it?", implying that most of them left completely unconvinced!

Despite bursting my bubble, it was a great question.

*If the evidence is so overwhelming, why doesn't everyone see it this way?*

Several years ago, I heard the true story of a woman who was invited to a Bible study by a friend. Over the course of several weeks, the group examined the evidence for the resurrection. The woman didn't believe in Jesus, but she was open to hearing the evidence. Faithfully, she came to every session. At the end of the study, her friend asked her, "So, what do you think?" She responded, "Oh I'm convinced Jesus rose from the dead now." Elated, her friend (rhetorically!) replied, "So you believe in him now?"

"Oh no, absolutely not. If I did that I'd have to change my whole life and *I don't want to do that.*"

It was a very honest response. Intellectually, she accepted it was true.

But she didn't *want* it to be true.

Often, consciously or not, this is what drives our evaluation of the evidence. We may not be fully aware of it or openly acknowledge it the way this woman did, but—*as it should be*—this is ultimately the determining factor: our will. Which is probably why so many don't even bother to look at the evidence in the first place.

Deep down, they don't *want* it to be true.

Recently, the announcer on a Christian radio station I listen to from time to time was reporting on a survey that was done to see why so many kids who grow up in the church renounce their faith in college. The assumption going in was that they encountered superior intellectual arguments that crushed their inferior beliefs. To the contrary, the survey revealed that it wasn't the intellectual arguments that swayed them—even though many admitted that they would use this as an excuse to mask the real reason.

The majority of those surveyed candidly revealed that the main reason they abandoned their faith was because they *wanted to live in a way that wasn't consistent with these beliefs.* They wanted to be free from the morality their belief system called for, especially—many honestly confessed—around drinking and sexual mores (activities that naturally present intense temptation in a college context). In other words, renouncing their faith had far more to do with their will than with reasoned argument and evidence.[283]

Let me be clear. I'm not trying to make a moral judgment or saying that there aren't a good number of people who genuinely struggle to find the evidence convincing. Many have a hard time reconciling Christian faith with a rational, scientific worldview—this is one of the main reasons many other young people cite for rejecting belief in God, and the main objection this book is intended to answer.

But given the glaring absence of compelling alternative explanations; and given the many who a priori reject the possibility before examining the evidence; and given the many who admit, oftentimes after finally coming to faith, that what held them back wasn't the intellectual argument, it's a simple fact: the ultimate factor in coming to believe the resurrection is desire.

Do you *want* it to be true?

Over the years, Dr. Phil has featured a number of people on his program who've been "scammed" by online posers who pretend to be interested in a romantic relationship. It's called catfishing. On one show a woman appeared who sent one of these "catfishers" 187,000 dollars! She was in complete denial that her Facebook boyfriend wasn't really who he was pretending to be.

So Dr. Phil showed her his license and passport, both of which clearly didn't match who he was posing to be. Dr. Phil also had a private investigator locate the man's address. Again it didn't match his claims. The investigator even found other victims of the scam. But, in the face of this tsunami of evidence, she still insisted that her boyfriend was legitimate. The audience groaned in exasperation every time she'd give some ridiculous rationalization to explain the clear facts being presented to her.

She so badly wanted it to be true, she refused to accept any evidence to the contrary.

It blinded her to the obvious conclusion.[284]

Often we are so invested in a particular position or worldview that we can't see the plain evidence before us. People tend to believe what they most want to believe. We see what we want to see. Our biases and desires skew our interpretation of the evidence.

Of course, *this can be just as true of those who believe.* Those who want the resurrection to be true can just as easily see evidence that's not there. Or find weak arguments compelling.

So how do you keep your biases from slanting the evidence?

Many believe that we can't overcome them. That our presuppositions are so deeply, even subconsciously, ingrained, our motives so complex and difficult to unravel, our perspective so limited by our particular time, place, and culture that we can't escape our subjective biases.

Scholars often refer to this as our *horizon*: we can't see beyond it.

In fact, the Postmodern world in which we live has been dominated by the notion that all truth is subjective. That either there is no absolute truth or, if there is, we can't know it. That our respective horizons prevent us from comprehending any larger truth beyond the boundaries they impose. Our *personal truth* is the only truth we can know for sure. What's true for me, what's true in *my experience*, is all I can trust and may not be true for you.

To make matters worse, there's something called "confirmation bias," which is defined as the tendency to seek out information that confirms your already held beliefs and reject anything that conflicts with them. Education doesn't diminish confirmation bias. Experiments have shown that it is just as prevalent among highly educated individuals.

Unfortunately, the contemporary political climate has accelerated the intensity of confirmation bias at an alarming rate. You may not remember the *Phil Donohue Show*. It last aired over twenty years ago. But it was one of the last places where people on opposite sides of an issue *actually talked to each other* face to face. Where they actually had to *thoughtfully engage* each other's viewpoints, often requiring them to re-think their position.

Nowadays, we tend to only listen to voices that reinforce our own position without ever considering views we're uncomfortable with: conservatives only listen to people like Rush Limbaugh and Fox News; progressives to NPR and CNN. Confirmation bias magnifies the effect of the limitations our horizons impose. What chance do we have of overcoming our horizon if we aren't even willing to listen to other perspectives in an open and rational way? [285]

## Over the Horizon

I don't want to downplay the significant role our horizons and confirmation biases play.

But they *aren't* insurmountable.

A good illustration of this is the recent officer-involved shootings of African Americans. If you're white you tend to presume the police officers acted appropriately. Cops are the good guys after all. And you tend to only accept information that reinforces this view.

But if you're black you probably presume they're racist and acted maliciously. A sad history of abuse, "the talk," and your own interactions with the police have understandably led you to be suspicious of cops. And the only voices you trust are those who provide support for this view.

Each perspective contains some element of truth. Most police officers only use deadly force as a last resort and in situations where they feel their lives threatened. But sadly, racism is alive and well in our country, even among many whites who believe we aren't racist, who are blind to the subconscious and structural biases that affect our attitudes and behavior. We are often oblivious to our racial biases and the systemic privileges that come with being white in America. This includes police officers, who aren't immune to it. On top of this, our history is littered with cases where the police *have* acted abusively with a strong racial component.

However, in each incident, there are *facts that can be established with a high degree of certainty*. An individual's horizon may influence how they interpret these facts, but even people who come with radically different experiences and presuppositions can agree that there is *a truth* about what happened and, provided a thorough and transparent investigation is done, that this truth can be known.

No one maintains that there are two completely different sets of objective facts.

The shared presumption is that something objectively true happened, and if people work hard and honestly enough, if they consider all the evidence, if they sincerely try to see things from the *other perspective*, they can agree in substance on what it is despite their biases—otherwise, why discuss and deliberate over it as much and as passionately as we do!

The limited lens of one's subjective perspective, their horizon, doesn't necessarily doom them from knowing the truth with a *reasonable certainty*, so long as they make the necessary, and at times uncomfortable and arduous, effort to find it.

In fact, this is essentially the position of the emerging philosophical approach, known as "critical realism," that most scholars (including most biblical and historical scholars) have adopted. While multifaceted and complex, in essence critical realism tries to strike a balance between the older Modernistic, (logical) positivistic view that objective reality is totally knowable and accessible to all, and the resulting Postmodern skepticism that maintains subjective limitations prevent us from knowing anything in a truly objective way. Simply put, it says that despite the limitations our horizon imposes, we can apprehend objective reality in a fairly accurate and trustworthy way, provided we are aware of our biases and diligently work to move beyond them. [286]

So what's required to do this?

Basically two things: *openly admit your desires, biases, and presuppositions* and *consciously pursue the truth above all else.*

First, if you work to identify the limitations of your horizon, and then readily admit them, they lose their grip: it is far less likely that you will unwittingly succumb to them. This admission forces you to question your motivations. It forces you to take a second, third, and fourth look at evidence and arguments that conflict with your position. It forces you to doubt your doubts about alternative views. It forces you to admit you may not be right and, therefore, to adopt a position of *humility*. Above all, it forces you to subject your judgments to *external critique*, to allow other people and/or viewpoints to challenge your own.

And this enables you to take the critical step: to genuinely see things from another perspective; to have true *empathy* for an opposing position. When I was teaching and we were going to debate a topic in class, before letting students express their own view, I often had them defend the opposite position. They hated it. But, since they were being graded on how well they did it (!), they had to work to fully understand, embrace and promote a perspective they didn't share. Whether or not they changed their view, this usually enabled them to see the issue in a whole new light.

Ultimately, if you can learn to *sympathetically* and *compellingly* articulate an opposing position as well or better than those who hold this position, then you are starting to see it from their perspective, significantly weakening the power horizon exercises.

Or as Michael Licona, who has wrestled with the question of horizons as they relate to the resurrection more thoroughly than any other scholar, puts it: "Historians must allow themselves to understand and empathize fully with the horizon of the author/agent and, furthermore, *allow themselves to be challenged fully by that horizon to the point of conversion.*"(my italics)[287]

Vigorously defending an opposing perspective can bring you to that point.

I've found that the best way to transcend your horizon is to "try on" an opposing view for a period of time. Wear it for a while. In other words, see the best in it and give it every benefit of the doubt as being true. Then imagine it as your own view. This creates real empathy and admiration. When you can genuinely see the merit and beauty of another perspective, even if you think it falls short in the end, you are beginning to overcome your horizon.

For example, I don't think that the world's major religions are equal paths the same God. But I wish they were. As a modern American living in a pluralistic culture, this idea is *very* appealing to me, more appealing than having to accept where I think the evidence actually leads: namely, that Christianity is the fullness of truth. It also suits my philosophical bias better: a loving God would never privilege one group or religion over another. I am very attracted to the idea that the world's religions are just different paths to the same God! So much so, that when I was younger, I "wore it" for a long time, happily adopting it as my own view.

Moreover, having studied these religions in depth in college, having "tried them on" even to the point of contemplating conversion to several of them, I still see the compelling beauty of each. I am still profoundly enriched by what they've taught me. So even though I was raised Catholic in a culture profoundly shaped by the Western, Judeo-Christian worldview, this gives me *reasonable confidence* that my horizon isn't determining my evaluation of the evidence. And furthermore, the cultural Catholicism I grew up with really isn't anything like what, in college, I discovered the essence of Christianity is. This reassures me that, in ultimately finding the other world religions to be less compelling, I didn't just revert back to the familiar confines of my horizon.

Second, consciously pursuing the truth above all else means making the truth your *ultimate desire*, above every other preference and inclination. Which can be agonizingly complex, trying to sift out a pure desire for truth from other powerful motivations deep in our psyche. But it can be done, at least to a significant degree. The key is a *relentless* willingness to go wherever the evidence takes you, even if it challenges you to the core, even if it leads to a conclusion you don't really want to reach (you know you're on the right track when this happens!).[288]

N.T. Wright suggests a helpful way to think about this, proposing love as the perfect analogy for discerning the truth. Someone in love gives sustained attention to their beloved. They're radically open to their beloved and all the ways their beloved might change their life. In fact, they delight in the thought! Similarly, if we love the truth, we'll give it sustained attention and be radically open to how it might change us. Captivated by its beauty, we won't resist where it's leading us, thereby breaking down the biases that hold us back. And just as with a beloved, the more attentive and open we are, the more the truth will begin to reveal itself to us.[289]

Conversely however, the truth won't reveal itself unless we are intensely focused, pursuing it with all our heart. And it won't reveal itself unless we are radically open, willing to leave everything to follow it. A casual or half-hearted approach won't do. Neither will a wavering heart. The truth only reveals itself to those who, above all else, truly love and, therefore, abandon themselves to it.

The fact that people often do arrive at some truth that is inconvenient, disruptive, or just plain hard for them to accept, is a good indication that our horizons, and the desires they implant, can be overcome. You can *willingly* choose to override what you really want, your willful desires and worldview preferences, with a deeper desire to know what's true.

If the truth is what you really, *really* want, you can find it.

Lee Strobel is a good example of how this can be done. The *last* thing in the world he wanted to believe was the resurrection. But, admitting this bias, he pursued an in-depth search anyway.

A graduate of Yale Law School, he's an award-winning journalist and for many years was the legal affairs editor for the Chicago Tribune newspaper. He is a highly intelligent, analytical, and very, *very* skeptical man. One day, his wife came home and announced that she had become a Christian. Strobel was an avowed atheist. He believed Christianity was a mythical delusion built on a false legend about Jesus. He wanted to prove his wife wrong. That way, they could go back to the happy life they knew before.

So he launched his all-out investigation.

Applying the training he received at Yale Law School and his experience as a legal affairs editor, he says he "plunged into the case with more vigor than with any story I had ever pursued." He read books, interviewed experts, analyzed history, explored archeology, studied ancient literature, and for the first time in his life, picked apart the Bible verse by verse.

> I'll admit it: I was ambushed by the amount and quality
> of the evidence that Jesus is the unique Son of God.
> As I sat at my desk that Sunday afternoon, I shook my
> head in amazement. I had seen defendants carted off
> to the death chamber on much less convincing proof!
> The cumulative facts and data joined unmistakably

toward a conclusion that I wasn't entirely comfortable in reaching.

Frankly I wanted to believe that the deification of Jesus was the result of legendary development in which well-meaning but misguided people slowly turned a wise sage into the mythological Son of God. That seemed safe and reassuring: after all, a roving apocalyptic preacher from the first century *could make no demands on me.* But while I went into my investigation thinking that this legendary explanation was intuitively obvious, I emerged convinced it was totally without basis...

In light of the convincing facts I had learned during my investigation, in the face of this overwhelming avalanche of evidence in the case for Christ, the great irony was this: it would require much more faith for me to maintain my atheism than to trust in Jesus of Nazareth!

...What's more, my journalistic skepticism toward the supernatural had melted in light of the *breathtaking historical evidence that the resurrection of Jesus was a real, historical event...*

The atheism I had embraced for so long buckled under the weight of historical truth. It was a stunning and radical outcome, certainly not what I had anticipated when I embarked on this investigative process. But it was a decision compelled by the facts.(my italics)[290]

We can overcome our horizons if we want to, if we freely admit our biases and pursue the truth with all-out abandon. But when it comes to the resurrection, this only pushes the question back one step further: why doesn't everyone who has *genuinely sought to overcome their horizon* see how good the evidence is?

## The Simpler the Better

William of Ockham was a fourteenth-century Franciscan monk and philosopher. He proposed an idea, known as Occam's razor (a misspelled attribution), that has won widespread acceptance, even in the scientific community, because of how efficient and accurate it's proven to be. Briefly put, Occam's razor says that the simplest explanation for any set of phenomena is usually the correct explanation. (Some challenge the validity of this principle, and there certainly are all kinds of qualifications that need to made about its use, but most recognize its empirical merit—when applied, it seems to hold true.)

With the resurrection, the simplest explanation is a true miracle. Metaphysically, in contrast to all the other speculative constructs, like the multiverse, God is the simplest explanation for the emerging scientific evidence; meaning, we most likely live in a universe where the miraculous is a real possibility. And historically, in contrast to all the other convoluted alternatives, the fact Jesus rose bodily from the dead is the simplest explanation for the phenomena of empty tomb and appearances; meaning, it most likely qualifies as one of those rare instances of a miracle.

In fact, a clear majority of biblical scholars, including some of the most skeptical, agree on the basic facts under-girding Jesus' resurrection: the disciples found his tomb empty and, shortly thereafter, believed that he appeared to them risen from the dead. What many (roughly a quarter) question is, on the one hand, the nature of these appearances—that they are anything more than a delusionary experience—and, on the other hand, that they constitute a true miracle—for philosophical reasons, they don't think miracles are possible; if anything "supernatural" happened, therefore, it had to be just some kind of a fluke.

Throughout the course of this book, we've seen that the unprecedented nature of the appearances and the subsequent faith they generated makes some kind of delusion virtually impossible—the disciples must have seen an embodied, albeit glorified, Jesus, *objectively* "out there" in the real world.

We've seen that the historical context, the multiple and astoundingly unique things Jesus said and did, for example, his miracles, "sinlessness," otherworldly ethic, acting with divine authority, exhibiting a divine self-consciousness, etc., offer abundant and powerful corroboration for the resurrection as a true miracle—it wasn't just some kind of strange and inexplicable anomaly (which is all we'd conclude if it happened to anyone else), but rather, it *uncannily* coheres with his *divine pedigree*. It happened in a historical context that was "charged with religious significance," a context where we'd expect just such a miracle.

And we've seen that the philosophical bias against the miraculous, and especially the resurrection, is not only unfounded, but instead, tilts far in the opposite direction—metaphysical arguments can be mounted that strongly suggest the resurrection, and the latest scientific evidence (combined with the corresponding philosophical arguments) weighs heavily in favor of the existence of a God who would have to intervene in *just this way* in order to fulfill his loving design. Thus, the metaphysical context also makes just such a miracle highly likely—if you press the findings of astrophysics and molecular biology over the past forty years or so to their logical end, Jesus embodies everything ultimate reality must be.

Applying the tried and true measure of Occam's razor then, it seems quite evident that the resurrection as a true miracle is the most probable explanation of the evidence, even to the point of virtual certainty. However, like most of the knowledge we possess, it can't be proven with one-hundred percent certainty. And that means there is still room to find the case lacking.

The threshold of proof isn't high enough to compel universal belief.

But why? If there really is a God who truly raised Jesus from the dead, why doesn't he make it abundantly clear for all to see?

Doesn't the fact that it isn't this clear undermine the whole thing?

Doesn't the fact that intelligent people who've worked to overcome their respective horizons can disagree about the evidence for the resurrection mean it can't be true?

## Free to be Me

Earlier, I posed a question that is often asked: why didn't Jesus appear to those who didn't believe in the resurrection? Like Caiphas or Pilate. There I answered by saying he did, at least to a few. But there's a second part to that answer. He didn't appear to those who were *unwilling* to believe in him, those who didn't ultimately *want* to believe in him, because *that would override their freedom.* If they saw him risen, they would be overwhelmed by the evidence and have no other choice but to believe.

It wouldn't be their loving response to him.

And this would fundamentally undermine the freedom in love that is at the heart of the Christian worldview. Love can't be forced. It can only be freely chosen. God wants a real relationship with us, which can only happen if we really want one with Him too.

Richard Swinburne explains:

> the whole point of the human drama on Earth [is free will]. For this purpose, we saw that God must put a certain "epistemic distance" between himself and human beings...If he shows himself only to chosen witnesses, then they can tell others about it. As a result, others will have quite a bit of evidence of what God has done and taught, which they can utilize to make themselves fitted for God's friendship; but they will still not have the overwhelming evidence that would make free choice impossible.[291]

For God to compel belief—whether by Jesus appearing to those who didn't want him to be Lord, or by providing overwhelming and irrefutable evidence for modern skeptics—is to undermine the whole purpose for life on earth: the free response that love requires. So the fact that some very sincere and reasonable people don't see how compelling the evidence for the resurrection is doesn't undermine the Christian worldview at all.

Instead, *it affirms it.*

The resurrection is the definitive proof of Jesus' divinity. If risen, he is Lord of the universe and wants to be Lord of your life. If not, you don't have to reckon with him. You can just admire him as a wise teacher, compassionate sage, or fiery prophet. Or dismiss him as a terribly misguided, misunderstood, or mythological figure. But he has no claim on your life, no reason to be the all-consuming love of your life.

In the end, what we choose to believe reflects our deepest desires. So according to Christian faith, in the final analysis, our response to the resurrection has to be driven by *what we want most to be true.* Whether we want a God like this to be true. Whether we want him to be the all-consuming love of our lives.

As Mark Link says: "And this is as it should be...Jesus does not reveal his identity so clearly as to leave no doubt about it. Nor does he keep it so hidden that the open-hearted searcher will miss it. He satisfies both possibilities."[292]

Anyone who really wants to see *will see.*

With a loving God, this is how it should be. How it has to be.

Of course, in talking about the will, I'm not saying that someone has to have the desire for the resurrection to be true to find the evidence convincing. They only need to be open to the truth, open to the possibility, *open to the implications of the resurrection for their life.*

I readily admit that when I first came to this evidence, deep down I didn't want it to be true. As I've already shared, I preferred to believe several of the other religions I was studying in college. I was far more attracted to them. In comparison, I found Christianity exceedingly more complex and demanding.

I still do.

While the promise the resurrection holds far and away surpasses anything else, it would be *easier* for me to believe all religions are just equal paths to the same God; easier for me to live according to *my* will, not His; easier for me not to have to deal with the church and all its flaws.

Sometimes my skepticism offends believers who think a pastor should be naturally inclined to blindly believe in every reputed supernatural occurrence. It upsets them that I don't share their enthusiasm over an alleged angelic intervention in their lives; or some shrine they tell me about where people were supposedly healed; or how God "miraculously" answered some prayer of theirs. I scoff at these kinds of reports. (Not out loud, of course. I am a pastor after all—I'm supposed to be polite! But in my mind, I'm completely cynical and that usually shows by the fact I don't react as enthusiastically as I would if I really believed what they were telling me.) I find it very difficult to believe these kinds of things are anything more than coincidence and circumstance, wishful thinking and well-meaning delusion.

(Just to be clear, *with qualification*, I do believe God answers prayer and intervenes in our lives—if we want Him to—but I *only* believe this because I first came to believe in the resurrection.)

And when it comes to my biases, I'm reactionary. I tend to go to the opposite extreme just to ensure I'm not succumbing to them. Yes, I'd like to believe the things Jesus promises. I'd like to believe that when we die there is a paradise we can live in forever. I'd like to believe there is a God out there who really loves us. But the last thing I want is to be naïve, to believe in a fairy tale, *to be duped!* Especially if I'm going to stake my life, and possibly my eternity, on it. Santa Claus and the tooth fairy turned out to be myths, so why wouldn't I expect the same of the resurrection?

It's every bit as fantastic.

But despite my every inclination not to believe, the one thing I did (and still do) want most was to find the truth—wherever it led, whatever the cost. When I first took a serious look at the resurrection in college, I reluctantly came away with a conclusion similar to Strobel's: it was much harder not to believe than believe.

Since that time, I've gone at the question again and again, often as a result of encountering some new claim or counterargument, always open to the possibility it isn't true (at times, wishing for an *easier* life, hoping it isn't!). But every time I go deeper, often pursuing some credible sounding objection, I end up finding more evidence. Even in the process of writing this book, pursuing a possible objection led me to evidence I'd never seen before.

And while I have come to find that there is nothing better than a relationship with Christ—it's more than worth the demands and challenges—without the evidence, I would never trust he's real.

My only challenge to you, the reader, the only thing I ask, is that you approach this evidence with the same openness and tenacity. If, at the end of the day, you find it intellectually unsatisfying or truly don't want it to be true, fair enough. But just be sure that there aren't other forces—like the limitations of your horizon, unfounded biases (philosophical and otherwise), moral preference (lifestyle changes it might call for), the comfort and convenience of the worldview you've already adopted, etc.—driving you from a conclusion you would otherwise find true and be willing, therefore, to stake your life on.

Be sure it's what you really, *really* want!

## The Exhilarating Rush of Reason

"There was an atheist couple who had a child. The couple never told their daughter anything about the Lord. One night when the little girl was five years old, the parents fought with each other and the dad shot the mom right in front of the child. Then the dad shot himself. The little girl watched it all. She then was sent to a foster home. The foster mother was a Christian and took the child to church. On the first day of Sunday school, the foster mother told the teacher that the girl had never heard of Jesus and to have patience with her. The teacher held up a picture of Jesus and said: 'Does anyone know who this is?' The little girl said, 'I do, that's the man who was holding me the night my parents died.'"[293]

You may have heard this story before or read it on the Internet. I don't know for certain whether it's true or not. I seriously tend to doubt it. But that doesn't matter. It points to a reality many people have found to be true. Because Jesus is risen, they claim, you can have a personal encounter with him. By faith, you can experience his risen presence right now. And in this way know he truly is risen from the dead.

I confess that this suggestion wouldn't have worked for me before I saw the evidence. How do you know you're *actually* experiencing Jesus and aren't just having indigestion, or didn't just drink too much caffeine! Or that you're not experiencing Allah, Nirvana, or some other spiritual reality—every major religion makes similar claims about experiencing God, the Absolute, or Ultimate Reality. Without the objective evidence to back it up, I would've simply concluded it was just autosuggestion, a biochemical reaction, or some kind of generic spiritual experience.

But in the end, coming to terms with the reality of the resurrection *is* a matter of faith. Obviously, I think the evidence is so overwhelming that I'm largely convinced by it alone. However, many—perhaps too many to be mistaken—claim to have experienced the risen Lord in their lives in a way that leaves no doubt he's alive. Many have done this as a result of being led to this final step of faith by the proof itself.[294]

Ultimately, this is where all the evidence leads: to an act of trust that is confirmed by a real encounter with the risen Lord. Such knowledge can never prove to anyone else it is true. But for the one who experiences it, *it is more real than the air they breathe.* As Augustine put it: "God is the One Who is more intimate to us than we are to ourselves."[295]

Yes, in the end, belief in the resurrection requires a leap of faith, an act of trust.

*But it's not a big leap at all.*

In fact, it's only a small step to faith.

The proof is so compelling it doesn't really require much faith at all.

Back to Lee Strobel: "Yes, I had to take a step of faith, as we do in every decision we make in life. But here's the crucial distinction: I was no longer trying to swim upstream against the strong current of evidence; instead I was choosing to go in the same direction that the torrent of facts was flowing. That was reasonable, that was rational, that was logical."

After describing his conversion he concludes: "There was no lightning bolts, no audible replies, no tingly sensations. I know that some people feel a rush of emotion at such a moment; as for me, however, there was something else that was equally exhilarating: there was the rush of reason."[296]

The exhilarating rush of reason.

This is what I felt when I first examined the evidence. And it's what I feel every time I explore it more deeply. As one who needs to *see to believe*, this is the only way I could have faith in the resurrection and faith in Jesus.

When you consider the sheer cumulative effect of the historical evidence—just four or five pieces of the evidence listed in Part I would be enough to deem the resurrection credible, but there are at least *twenty-five*...

When you consider how *desperate* all the alternative explanations are...

When you consider how *uncannily* the resurrection fits into the larger historical picture surrounding the figure of Jesus...

When you consider how it fulfills the *transcendental longing* at the core of our being like nothing else could...

When you consider how uniquely and perfectly it corresponds to the *logic of the universe*...

That exhilarating rush of reason comes flooding in!

# APPENDIX I

## The Bright Light of Eternity or Just the Operating Table?

*Near-Death Experiences as Possible Corroborating Evidence*

'M EXTREMELY SKEPTICAL ABOUT so-called life-after-life or near-death experiences. They are far too subjective to be trusted. How do we know that those who report having these experiences are actually seeing the bright light of eternity? As some studies suggest, the euphoria many of them report feeling may simply be the natural rush of adrenaline the body produces as it goes through the dying process. The bright light many report seeing may just be the bright light of the emergency room or operating table, where an abundance of these experiences happen. There's no way to know. It's all in the mind of the beholder.

By contrast, the resurrection is a public, objectively verifiable event.

However, I've recently come across some evidence that *may* provide objective corroboration for *some* reported near-death experiences and in a way that *possibly* provides additional confirmation for the resurrection. (Emphasis on "may," "some," and "possibly"!) In no way is this evidence necessary or on the same level as the evidence and arguments for the resurrection presented in this book.

It is merely—*if* true—the proverbial icing on the cake.

The evidence I'm referring to comes from Robert Spitzer, who has done an in-depth analysis of the scholarly literature on near-death experiences. He presents this evidence in *The Soul's Upward Yearning*, pointing out three intriguing and possibly probative ways *some* near-death experiences can be verified.

First, some of those who report having a near-death experience happen to be blind from birth. Of these, roughly eighty percent are able to accurately describe people and phenomena that they shouldn't be able to—not only have they never seen them before, *they've never seen before!* And yet, despite having no prior experience of sight, much less any visual access to the specific attributes they report, they describe them in detail, as only a seeing person could. How can this be explained if they didn't have a genuine sensory experience which transcended their blindness?

Second, in some cases, while clinically dead, people are able to accurately describe phenomena occurring around them; for example, the procedures medical personnel are performing to revive them, things their loved ones are saying and doing, etc. At times, some are even able to produce detailed knowledge about things *far outside the room they're in.* Being "dead," they should have no conscious awareness of anything at all, much less of phenomena that are outside normal sensory awareness, phenomena that the "living" people in the same room can't access.

The most interesting example Spitzer cites is of a woman who could describe a shoe sitting on a third floor window ledge outside the hospital. Not only did she somehow know it was there, but she described certain details that were only noticeable close up, such as a worn little toe. These details could only be verified when the psychologist who did the interview *crawled out on the window ledge* and saw the shoe, exactly as described.[297]

In many of these instances, it is certainly possible that such knowledge could have been derived, innocently enough, through ordinary means, akin to "sensory leakage." Scientific studies on paranormal experience have revealed that without being aware of it, people often access knowledge through ordinary means and then later report it as if extraordinary.

But in cases like the woman above, there doesn't seem to be any way this could have happened: the information she reported, with exquisite detail, was completely inaccessible to her, even prior to her near-death experience. She would have had to been the one to place the shoe on the ledge, or have viewed it with some kind of high powered telescoping device prior to her near-death experience, to know what she knew; neither of which, as far as investigators were apparently concerned, happened.

And third, in many near-death experiences people claim to encounter deceased loved ones. In some cases, they accurately report previously unknown data supposedly given to them by these deceased relatives and friends. When vetted, it seems as though this data could not have been accessed any other way.[298]

A case in point is the only near-death experience I'd ever found remotely credible. Many years ago, I heard about a teen whose girlfriend died in a car accident where he was at fault. He was also seriously injured in the accident. When he got out of the hospital, he went to see the girl's mother and told her he had had a near-death experience. He wanted to assure her that her daughter was in heaven.

He also told the mother he had seen her sister. The sister had died when they were both young girls, long before the teen was born. When she scoffed at this report, he gave her a message from the sister. It was something the two girls never shared with anyone else, a secret just between the two of them, a secret she had forgotten about long ago, after her sister died. When he told her, she became convinced that the whole thing must be real. The only way he could have known this secret is if he actually saw and talked with her sister during his near-death experience.

(The reason I'm not completely convinced even by this example is that there is still a remote possibility that the mother unwittingly shared this secret during an ordinary conversation that the boyfriend was somehow privy to—either he was present or his girlfriend, her daughter, passed it along—and then completely forgot that she had let this memory "slip out.")

It's important to note that Spitzer doesn't claim that all or even most of the near-death experiences that are reported are real or can be verified. Some may be faked, imagined or delusional (or, demonic, if you believe such a reality exists). But he does emphatically submit that those which happen to fit into these three categories can't be explained any other way; they are *verifiably* transcendent experiences.

*If* these experiences are what they purport to be, then they may provide limited corroboration for the resurrection. The kinds of things people report during them *bear an uncanny resemblance to a distinctly Christian understanding of the afterlife.* Based on the body of commonly reported data, this is Spitzer's evaluation: "…the reports about the loving being of light, the presence of Jesus, the love and joy of the deceased, and the presence of paradise closely parallel the revelation and Resurrection of Jesus Christ."[299]

In two key ways, therefore, they would corroborate resurrection faith. First, they would show that eternal life is real and that, in contrast to other alternative understandings of what it is like, it is actually consistent with the mode of Jesus' resurrection—people retain their personal identity and are able to relate to one another in a real, albeit indescribably transformed, way. In other words, love is the essence of eternal life.

Second, these reports are fully consistent with all that Jesus taught and stood for, especially his revelation of a God who has ultimately created human beings to share in His love, if they choose to, and his revelation that *He* is this God come in person with unsurpassing love to save us.[300] In other words, they are fully consistent with everything

Jesus—unparalleled by anyone else—was and even indicate that he is reigning in heaven as the risen Lord.

Thus, *if* real, these near-death experiences constitute an independent witness to Jesus' resurrection and to the divinity his resurrection implies.

I want to reemphasize that none of this evidence from near-death experiences rises to the same level as the evidence surrounding the resurrection of Jesus; personally, I don't put much stock in it. But, it does potentially provide some limited confirmation of the resurrection, and for that reason, may help some to find it more credible.

So, if all this helps, great.

But if not, if any of this is problematic for you, please ignore it.

It's not essential to the argument.

(One quick note: As I mentioned above, Dale Allison is a scholar who has recently compiled an impressive array of examples of veridical apparitions from the dead. Visions of the deceased are well known throughout history. But these "ghost-like" appearances are easily dismissed as some kind of dream or delusion. Allison, however, points to a small number of these apparitions which, seemingly, can be verified objectively. Though fundamentally different from Jesus' appearances, the examples he's elucidated are suggestive that the dead live on in a way roughly parallel to Jesus' victory over the grave. And, like near-death experiences, *if* real, this could potentially provide another avenue of corroboration for the resurrection.

Since this is a fairly new proposal which hasn't yet been thoroughly subjected to scholarly review, and since the sample is so much smaller than veridical near-death experiences, at this point these apparitions can only very tentatively be held up as possible further support for the resurrection.

For more on this, see Michael Licona, *The Resurrection of Jesus*, pp. 625-629 who gives a quick overview of Allison's findings, and then on pp. 634-639 analyzes these findings, especially the marked differences between these veridical apparitions and Jesus' appearances.)

# APPENDIX II

## Shrouded in Mystery

### *The Shroud of Turin: Tangible Proof of the Resurrection?*

I T WAS THE MID-1980's—NOT too long after I first looked at the evidence for the resurrection and, as a result, took my "leap of faith"—when I stumbled upon a book about something called the Shroud of Turin. I had never heard of it before. But I quickly learned that it purports to be the actual burial cloth Jesus was wrapped in immediately following his crucifixion, before being placed in the tomb. Much more intriguing, it contains a mysterious image, supposedly of Jesus' dead body, that many believe provides proof of his resurrection.

First surfacing in 1349 in Lirey, France, the Shroud is a large linen cloth, roughly 14 feet 3 inches by 3 feet 7 inches. Running the long way is a faint, discolored (brownish-yellow) image of a man, both front and back, who seems to have died by crucifixion. In addition, it contains real human blood stains which are consistent with the scourging, crowning with thorns, crucifixion, and thrusting of a spear into the side that Jesus experienced during his passion.

Many think the crowning with thorns and wound in the side were unique to Jesus: although it is possible one or both were done to other victims of crucifixion, ancient records indicate that only scourging was a common practice, and then, only in certain crucifixions. So the unique combination of these three elements—scourging, crowning with thorns, and spear in the side—significantly increases the likelihood it was Jesus.

Moreover, the blood stains flow around the wounds and along the body in a way that is entirely realistic, something almost impossible to duplicate without an actual body suffering the actual wounds of a crucifixion with this specific combination of elements in place.

Lastly, there are a number of scorch marks covering the Shroud. For a short time, it was kept in a monastery in Chambery, France. In 1532 a fire broke out there that nearly destroyed the Shroud. The scorch marks were caused by exposure to the heat of this fire. At that time the Shroud had been evenly folded and stored in a metal box. As a result, the scorches occurred around the edges of these folds. To repair the damage, new material was sown in, including a new backing cloth. When the Shroud is fully laid out, the repaired areas now appear as darkened, diamond-shaped, symmetrically-spaced markings in the areas around the folds.

In 1578 the Shroud came to Turin, Italy, where it has remained ever since and has often been put on public display.

The book I picked up summarized the results of the 1978 Shroud of Turin Research Project (STURP) investigation. A team of accomplished scientists were given a unique opportunity to subject the Shroud to a number of tests. Many on the STURP team were skeptical it was anything more than a medieval forgery and completely confident they would quickly identify the substance(s) and process used in creating it. But to their surprise, it defied explanation.

They couldn't determine how the image was made.

No known method, ancient or modern, could explain it.

Some of the tests they performed only seemed to add to its mystery. For example, when they applied something called VP-8 imaging—designed originally to analyze x-rays and subsequently used in modeling the surface topography of Mars and the moon—the Shroud produced a nearly perfect 3-D image. This *isn't supposed to happen.* Under this process, two dimensional images—paintings and photographs—always result in a completely distorted image. The anomaly points to an anatomically perfect image, something an artistic forgery couldn't produce: the image could only have been made by a real body.

In the end, the STURP team concluded that the Shroud was almost certainly a first-century object from the region around Jerusalem and that it contained real human blood. Although they couldn't explain what produced the image on it, they speculated that it had to be caused by some kind of light—not heat—radiation. A number of the researchers came away convinced it was the burial Shroud of Jesus, with some who'd been agnostic or atheist even abandoning their skeptical worldview. After reading this book, I was seriously contemplating whether the Shroud might just be physical evidence of Jesus' resurrection.

But only a couple of years later, in 1988, carbon 14 dating seemed to show that the Shroud was no more than seven or eight hundred years old, most likely originating in the mid-1300's. *Case closed: it was, after all, just a medieval forgery.* I was slightly disappointed when I heard these results—even if unnecessary, it would've been nice to have physical confirmation of the resurrection—but I moved on, not giving the Shroud a second thought.

As expected, Shroud research came to a screeching halt. It remained dormant for the next few years. But then something surprising happened. A number of scientists began calling the validity of the carbon dating into question. It turned out there were a number of significant errors and oversights during the sampling process, and normal, well-established protocols weren't carefully followed.

Originally, testers were supposed to take samples from seven different places. But inexplicably, they only removed a single small strip from a questionable part of the cloth. Not only did this go against the previously agreed-upon method for testing the Shroud, it violated basic protocols normally used in the carbon dating process.

Even common sense dictates using more than one spot.

In another violation of normal protocol, experts who were on hand to test and analyze the sample being taken in order to avoid gross errors, such as the selection of dyed material, never did so. In fact, it was later shown that the area this single sample was taken from was a darker area, making it likely that it is of a different chemical composition than the main part of cloth. In other words, the sampled material wasn't from the original Shroud. It was probably from material sewn in to repair the Shroud at some later point.

And lastly, the sample wasn't properly cleaned, another "best-practice" of carbon dating that was inexplicably ignored and leaves open the possibility that contaminants were present.

All this makes the process suspect.

Any one of these omissions could result in a significant distortion of the dating. Indeed, a 1993 examination of the sample showed there were contaminants on it that likely skewed the dating. And further testing in 2005 revealed the presence of a dye on the sample strip. This indicates that the sample *was* taken from an area of the Shroud which had been repaired, not the original material.

Beyond these serious problems with the testing process, there are other reasons to doubt the 1988 results. As many have pointed out, the 1532 fire undoubtedly subjected the cloth to added carbon. This would invariably distort any carbon 14 dating, even if only by a few hundred years. But that was never taken into account.

Also, because material was sewn in to repair the Shroud after the fire, the possibility exists that this "new" material, and not the original fibers, was mistakenly selected. If protocol had been diligently followed, it could ensure this wouldn't happen. But it wasn't.

And lastly, the Shroud has been handled multiple times and subjected to many different elements over the years. Simple contamination from these other sources could significantly alter the dating. Again, appropriate cleaning measures would have prevented this from being a problem.

Most important, as experts in the field admit, carbon dating is not infallible. On rare occasions it's even been known to yield future dates! Even when everything is done right, results can be wildly inaccurate. In fact, when archeologists encounter dating that defies other solid time markers, they ignore the results, chalking them up to some kind of unidentified anomaly.[301]

Since the 1988 carbon dating, new dating methods and techniques have been developed that show the Shroud is far older than the carbon 14 results indicate. While these new methods still need further review by the scientific community before being fully accepted and endorsed, so far they've held up under such scrutiny and therefore appear reliable.[302]

The upshot of all this critique is the need for another round of carbon 14 testing.

The 1988 results are simply too flawed to be trusted.

Recently, in the summer of 2018, another challenge to the Shroud's authenticity has emerged. A study published in the "Journal of Forensic Sciences" presented the results of experiments applying Bloodstain Pattern Analysis (BPA) to the bloodstains on the Shroud. It concluded that they aren't consistent with ancient crucifixion, with the details of Jesus' death and burial.

In other words, the figure on the Shroud *can't* be Jesus.

While many jumped to the conclusion that this proves the Shroud is a fake, that is far from clear. For one thing, the experts are deeply divided. A number of them question the methodology of these experiments. Tests were done on a mannequin and a live person, but not a cadaver. Only a cadaver would have the realistic characteristics of a body following death.

Neither a mannequin nor a live body is *scientifically equivalent.*

Moreover, no experiment, even on a real body, could replicate all the unique variables at play as a body is removed from a cross, placed in a burial cloth, and then transported. No experiment can precisely replicate the exact blood pressure and blood viscosity near the time of death, especially as these are variously affected by trauma, depending on the individual. No experiment can replicate all the unpredictably unwieldy movements of a recently deceased corpse as it's taken down from a cross and bound up in a cloth—it's impossible to account for all the possible different ways a body might be contorted in the process. No experiment can replicate the actual interactions between cloth and body as it was carried away, how it might have shifted or moved in transport and how the cloth rubbing against the flesh might have affected the blood-flow.

All these *dynamic* variables can have a significant impact on blood-flow.

Other experts challenge the validity of BPA itself. BPA has proven problematic in criminal cases, leading some forensic experts to disavow it. The jury's out (pardon the pun) whether it should be used at all. Until certain it is a valid forensic tool for contemporary use, it shouldn't be used on ancient artifacts where the challenges are manifoldly greater.[303]

But perhaps the most compelling reason for questioning the results of this study, as well as the 1988 carbon dating, is the substantial evidence for the Shroud's authenticity *neither address.*

Whether this new forensic study is validated or not; whether new carbon 14 testing happens or not, the Shroud exhibits other phenomena that neither the BPA analysis nor the carbon dating results can explain, phenomena that place it *squarely in first-century Palestine.* Furthermore, the image itself still presents an *insuperable puzzle* that no forensic analysis or dating can resolve. And many believe these are the most important factors for determining its authenticity. Here's a brief overview:

--Out of the STURP investigation, world-renowned botanist Max Frei identified a number of pollen grains from the Shroud that are unique to Palestine, a few of which, based on sedimentary layers near the sea of Galilee, are likely to be two-thousand years old.

--Ancient burial practices often included placing coins over the eyes of the deceased. Detailed analysis has revealed that the facial imprint on the Shroud has coins over the eyes that were minted by Pilate in Judea in 29 A.D.!

--The man on the Shroud bears all the earmarks of ancient crucifixion, including details that weren't known in the Middle Ages but have come to light through twentieth-century investigations. Medieval crucifixes, as most today, depict Jesus with nails through the hands. However, as forensic studies have shown, a nail placed through the hand would never support the weight of a body: it would rip right through the flesh between fingers. Ancient crucifixion was through the wrist. No medieval forger—no one from the third century on, for that matter, when crucifixion ceased to be used—would know this. And yet, the wounds on the Shroud appear around the wrists, not the hands.

--The image itself remains utterly baffling. To date, there is no natural explanation for it. Ever since Secondo Pia first took his famous picture in 1898 revealing that it is a perfect photographic negative, the image has been a scientific enigma. The fact that it is a perfect photographic negative means the image is *evenly present throughout*, even on areas where the cloth did not touch the body. (Like a blanket, it wouldn't evenly come in contact with every area of the body.) Excluding the blood stains, the image is three dimensionally correct and anatomically perfect. In other words, it was formed after the blood congealed—some good amount of time *after* the body was laid in it. By the way, the blood is a positive image.

Moreover, the image is superficial, only marking the very tips of the cloth's fibers. And on the half of the cloth containing the image of the front of the body, the forward facing portion (not the image of the back), it is also a double image: it appears both on the top uppermost surface and, in a much fainter way, on the back surface, but remarkably, *not on the fibers in between!* Incidentally, the front and back surfaces correspond to one another with anatomic precision.[304]

There is no known chemical process that can account for all this. The best guess is some kind of *intense burst of vacuum ultraviolet radiation*. It had to be light and not heat radiation; otherwise, it would

301

have scorched the area between the front and back of the image and not just the surface areas.

One of the most stunning features of the Shroud is that you can make out the skeletal structure of the hands, almost like an x-ray. To some researchers, this suggests that the upper part of the Shroud collapsed *through* to the lower, as if the body was transparent at the time the image was made—if it hadn't, only the outside of the body and no internal structure would appear. This leads these researchers to speculate that the burst of radiation must have emanated evenly throughout the body because the body didn't prevent the collapse of the cloth. In other words, it lost its solidity at the moment of the radiation burst. And this would explain how the uppermost surface of the fibrils were discolored without scorching them. It would also explain the double image.[305]

There is nothing known that would be capable of producing this effect naturally. Even the most sophisticated machines developed to date cannot replicate the intensity required for such a phenomenon: the exceedingly high amount of power required in such an infinitesimally small amount of time can't be matched by any ultraviolet light source presently available.[306]

Some of those who've investigated the Shroud have suggested that only a supernatural source such as the resurrection could produce this effect. If they're right, *if* the Shroud is authentic, then it is, remarkably enough, a *tangible* piece of corroborating evidence for the resurrection.

But there are a lot of "if's."

*If* it's a first-century relic; *if* it's Jesus' actual burial cloth; *if* the image was produced miraculously. As with near-death experiences, *the Shroud can't be considered part of the formal case for the resurrection.*

And it doesn't need to. The evidence for the resurrection stands on its own.

However, unlike near-death experiences, the Shroud can be verified in a publicly observable way. In fact, it has to be if it's going to be considered authentic. It has to pass the test of empirical, scientific inquiry, which, so far, it has. As a result, *if* substantiated, it can be considered objective evidence Jesus rose from the dead.

While personally I think the case for the Shroud is stronger than near-death experiences, I wouldn't stake my life on it the way I have on the evidence for the resurrection. But I must admit that the insuperable mystery the Shroud presents makes a supernatural origin the most likely explanation.

So if you do find all this compelling, the Shroud can serve as an additional, and quite remarkably, *tangible* corroboration of evidence that already rises to the level of virtual certainty.

(For a quick overview of the evidence for the Shroud's authenticity, see *The Son Rises* by William Lane Craig, pp. 62-67. For the best in-depth overview to date, including the detailed scientific explanations investigators base their conclusions on, see *God So Loved the World*, Appendix I, by Robert Spitzer.)

# ACKNOWLEDGMENTS

To Danielle Travali, Barbara Liu, and Kathy Colello: thank you for all your help in the editing process and making me a better writer. Any mistakes or lack of eloquence in the text are purely the result of my own (ill-advised!) revisions of your revisions.

To Jan Kardys: without your help I would never have had the courage or knowledge to pursue publishing this book. You have always been an awesome cousin; you are also a wonderful writing consultant. For all your gracious assistance and warm hospitality, for all the books you gave me to read about writing a book, for your wonderful writers' conferences, and for repeating answers to questions I asked a hundred times over, thank you, thank you, thank you.

To all my family, friends, former students and parishioners: in innumerable ways that you probably weren't aware of, you have supported, encouraged, and inspired me to bring this book into being.

Last but not least, to all the baristas at the Starbucks I frequent: thank you for providing me with the endless cups of coffee that enabled me to bring this book to completion.

# ENDNOTES

1. Here's a quick rundown of the facts: first, these so-called "analogies" to the resurrection are based on dubious sources. In most cases they post-date Christianity, meaning that, if anything, *they borrowed from—or "plagiarized"—the Christian story*, not the other way around. While in some cases (probably only three to five) it is true that these myths do pre-date the Christian era, there is absolutely no evidence or hint of any "dying and rising god" myth circulating in first-century Palestinian Judaism, which makes it highly unlikely that Jesus' disciples could have known about them. Second, the supposed parallels with the gospel narratives of the resurrection turn out to be superficial if not outright spurious. *They aren't really parallels at all.* For example, in the most popular version of the oft-cited Osiris parallel, the goddess Isis takes pity on Osiris after he is killed by his brother who chopped his body into fourteen pieces and then scattered them around the world. She goes in search of his body parts and, finding only thirteen of them, gives him a proper burial. Subsequently, Osiris is given the status of a god in the netherworld—hardly a parallel to Jesus' resurrection or exaltation! Third, these myths are usually connected with the fertility cult of ancient paganism which, using the metaphor of physical life, is focused on the death and rebirth cycle of nature, not humanity. They're not at all about the resurrection of a human being, but about the change of seasons and the hope for a rich and fruitful harvest. That's why the god in question dies and "rises" at the same time every year, most often in conjunction with the harvest; which is in direct contrast to Jesus' *once-off, unrepeatable* resurrection. Fourth, and most decisively, these stories are always and everywhere presented as tales. *No one actually thinks someone has truly come back from the dead. Indeed, no one telling or hearing these stories would ever stake their life on such a claim.* This is in stunning contrast to the very real historical claim at the core of Christian faith that a particular, well-known person has actually come back from the dead, and to the eyewitnesses of this event, who were willing to give their lives for the truth of this claim. In sum, the nearly universal consensus among scholars is that these not-so-analogous "parallels," most of which are too late to have influenced the Christian story anyway, are merely myths, usually tied to pagan fertility rites, that have nothing to do with the actual, historical resurrection of a human being. No one would have mistaken them to be anything else. See N.T. Wright, *The Resurrection of the Son of God* (Minneapolis, MN: Fortress Press, 2003), pp. 80-81.

2. Raymond E. Brown, *The Anchor Bible: The Gospel According to John XII-XXI* (New York, NY: Doubleday, 1970), pp. 998-1000, 1031-1033.

3. Richard Bauckham, *Jesus and the Eyewitnesses: The Gospels as Eyewitness Testimony* (Grand Rapids, MI: Wm. B. Eerdmans, 2006), pp. 49-51.

4. Also: "The divergences…, properly understood, demonstrate the scrupulous *care* with which the Gospels present the women as witnesses…

   "It is natural to suppose that these women were well known not just for having once told their stories but as people who remained accessible and authoritative sources of these traditions as long as they lived. Which women were well known to each Evangelist may have depended on the circles in which that Evangelist collected traditions and the circles in which each woman moved during her lifetime." See Bauckham, *Jesus and the Eyewitnesses*, pp. 49-51 for the full explanation.

5. Morton Kelsey, *Resurrection: Release From Oppression* (Mahwah, NJ: Paulist Press, 1985), p. 76.

6. Raymond E. Brown, *The Virginal Conception and Bodily Resurrection of Jesus* (New York, NY: Paulist Press, 1973), p. 119.

7. Ibid., p. 121.

8. Ibid., p 126, f. 216.

9. Scholars have detected a few hints of early tradition within the texts themselves. Here are two: In Luke 24:12 there is an independent tradition of the story found in John 20:2-10 of Peter and John running to the tomb after the women discover it empty. But in Luke, the beloved disciple is not named and does not join him. Peter goes *alone*. However, a mere twelve verses later (v. 24) Luke says that "*some* of those who were with us went to the tomb and found it just as the women had said." Because it disagrees with verse 12, scholars point out that Luke must be using earlier traditions that he is not free to change and, therefore, harmonize. In other words, he is faithful in recording these separate traditions just as he received them. Moreover, the fact that v. 24 agrees with John's account that more than just Peter went to the tomb, indicates that this version of the story is most likely the earliest tradition, probably reflecting eyewitness testimony to the event.

   Second, the first appearance of Jesus to Mary Magdalene is found in three independent streams of tradition—Matthew, Mark's lost ending, and John— which means it must *pre-date* all three. And in Matthew it is awkwardly placed—the women have just been instructed by the angelic interpreters to go tell the disciples Jesus has been raised and will appear to all of them together, when Jesus, seemingly *unaware of the angels' announcement*, suddenly appears to them on the way. If Matthew felt free to modify the tradition, he certainly would have done so more seamlessly, not making it look like Jesus and the angelic interpreters can't get their act together! Again, this indicates that Matthew is dependent upon an earlier tradition *he is not free to change.* And the most likely reason he isn't free to change it is that this tradition is authoritative *eyewitness testimony* to the event.

10. Brown, *The Virginal Conception and Bodily Resurrection of Jesus*, pp. 113-114. Or, as one ingenious scholar has argued, according to common Roman practice, either the soldiers left the body on the cross for the wild beasts to devour, or they barely covered it in a shallow grave that wild dogs would easily unearth and consume. Either way, not too long after crucifixion, the body would be unidentifiable. See John Dominic Crossan *Jesus: A Revolutionary Biography* (San Francisco, CA: HarperCollins, 1994), p. 154. One of many insurmountable problems with this theory is that in Palestine this kind of practice, especially around Passover in the holy city of Jerusalem, would constitute such a grave offense to Jewish sensibilities—the exposed or improperly buried corpse of a dead man was believed to be a curse on the land—that riots would have inevitably ensued, something the Romans desperately sought to avoid. This makes it highly unlikely the Romans would have followed their common practice. Indeed, avoiding an uprising is probably the reason Pilate put Jesus to death in the first place. Moreover, there is solid extra-Biblical evidence that the Romans allowed for the proper burial of corpses in Jewish occupied territories. For this evidence and more on the problems with Crossan's theory, see the alternative explanations to the resurrection in Chapter 3.7.

Also, hear the observation of one of the most critical and widely respected historical Jesus scholars of our day: "...the primitive Passion Narratives lying behind our Gospels, a primitive pre-Pauline formula, and some kerygmatic speeches in Acts all unite in affirming a particular aspect of Jesus' death: he was buried. Putting together the glancing statement in the laconic creed Paul cites in 1 Cor 15:4 ("he was buried"), the references to Jesus' burial in Acts (2:29-32; 13:29), and the stories of Jesus' burial contained in the quite different pre-Marcan and pre-Johannine Passion Narratives (Mark 15:42-47; John 19:38-42), we can see, from the criterion of multiple attestation of independent sources, that, from the earliest days, the Christian movement believed that Jesus had been buried, whatever the precise circumstances." John P. Meier, *A Marginal Jew: Rethinking the Historical Jesus, Volume V* (New Haven, CT: Yale University Press, 2106), pp.251-252.

11. Raymond E. Brown, *The Death of the Messiah* (New Haven, CT: Yale University Press, 2008), p. 1240.

12. Ibid., pp. 1213-1241.

13. "No canonical Gospel mentions the washing of Jesus' body, and that would probably have been the most basic service that could be rendered to one who

309

had died on a cross and would be covered with blood. (Mishna *Oholot* 2.2. specifies that blood on a corpse is unclean.)" Ibid., p. 1244.

14. Ibid., pp 1244 and 1246.

15. Brown, *The Virginal Conception and Bodily Resurrection*, p. 114.

16. Brown, *The Death of the Messiah*, pp. 1240-1241.

17. Ibid., p. 1241, f. 86.

18. "Moreover, the Christian memory of Joseph of Arimathea…would be rather pointless unless the tomb he supplied had special significance." Brown, *The Gospel According to John*, p. 976.

19. Kelsey, *Resurrection: Release From Oppression*, p. 84-85.

20. Wright, *The Resurrection of the Son of God*, p. 643.

21. "It is unlikely that early Christians would have invented out of the blue a story of their leader's apostasy and denial of Jesus, if that had not happened… "…[or] made up the story of the disciples hiding in cowardice…" William Lane Craig, *The Son Rises: The Historical Evidence for the Resurrection of Jesus* (Eugene, OR: Wipf and Stock Publishers, 1981), p. 77.

22. Frederick Dale Bruner, *Matthew: A Commentary, Volume 2: The Church Book* (Grand Rapids, MI: Wm. B. Eerdmans, 2007), p. 790.

23. Ben Witherington III, *The Gospel Code: Novel Claims About Jesus, Mary Magdalene and Da Vinci* (Downers Grove, IL: InterVarsity Press, 2004), p. 74.

24. Wright, *The Resurrection of the Son of God*, p. 608.

25. Brown, *The Gospel According to John XIII-XXI*, p. 976.

26. Wright, *The Resurrection of the Son of God*, p. 638.

27. On the verisimilitude of guards placed at the tomb, Brown observes that: "Tomb violation was not unusual in antiquity, usually in search of treasure; but the present instance would involve the transfer of a corpse. That was done occasionally for honest reasons (to move the recently deceased to a better tomb) or dishonest reasons (for sorcery or magic), and the suggested motivation of the disciples (deception) in the charge before Pilate falls into the later category. That Pilate's help could plausibly be enlisted to prevent a tomb violation designed to create a superstitious devotion is seen from an inscription that has had a fascinating history…" He goes on to explain that some think this inscription was provoked by the events surrounding Jesus' tomb. It warns that anyone who tampers with a tomb will be subject to trial and severe punishment. This reveals that the Romans would have considered tomb violation a very serious crime and possibly could have taken action to pre-empt it in the case of a subversive figure put to death by the State, like Jesus. For more on this, see Brown, *The Death of the Messiah*, pp. 1292-1294.

28. Someone might counter that their motive was the later (after they died) fame they anticipated receiving: they would be forever honored as heroes of

the faith. But this falters on three counts. First, it's predicated on the idea that they would be in some kind of everlasting state where they could enjoy their fame. But their firm belief in this everlasting state was based entirely on Jesus having been resurrected. If they knew he hadn't risen, why would they ever think they would live on to enjoy this post-mortem fame? Second, in their time the church was a tiny band of marginalized rejects. How could they ever have foreseen the dominance it would achieve, a dominance which would be necessary for their names to go down in posterity? And third, their hoax involves outright deceit. Even if they had some other reason to presume they'd find themselves in a post-mortem state, how could they ever think this deceit was noble and laudable; that it was deserving of honor and admiration? The only consequence they would have reason to expect in an after-life is shame and punishment.

29. Carl E. Olsen, *Did Jesus Really Rise from the Dead? Questions and Answers about the Life, Death, and Resurrection of Jesus* (San Francisco, CA: Ignatius Press-Augustine Institute, 2016), p.122, f. 19.
30. Brown notes a possible Jewish polemic against the early church: "Even if the criminal were king of kings, he may not be buried in the grave of his fathers, but only in that prepared by the court." Brown, *The Death of the Messiah*, p. 1210. The mention of king of kings may be a veiled reference to Jesus since it is a title early Christians gave him. If it is, then it's also a *sarcastic* remark about the unlawful status of Jesus' corpse, mocking this *supposed* king of kings who couldn't even be buried in his family grave because *he was a criminal!* However, in the process, it also acknowledges that Jesus' body was buried in a tomb approved by the legal authority of his day, namely Pilate. While inconclusive, if this were directed at Jesus, it is a further admission that his opponents knew of his burial in a well-known tomb.
31. Did the early church preserve these burial clothes? Are they what later becomes known as the Shroud of Turin? It's an intriguing possibility, but probably impossible to prove. There is more the Shroud of Turin in Appendix II below.
32. Brown, *The Virginal Conception and Bodily Resurrection of Jesus*, p. 124, f. 210.
33. Brown, *The Death of the Messiah*, p. 980.
34. Craig, *The Son Rises*, p. 75.
35. Most scholars agree that there's no good reason to deny that Pentecost was the date of some kind of memorable, perhaps inaugural, public proclamation of the early "kerygma" (preaching of the primitive gospel narrative, specifically, the death and resurrection of Jesus). Luke would have no reason to invent the dating of a special missionary event at Pentecost—which celebrated the giving of the land to Israel—since there's no symbolic connection between the two.

It's not a feast that has any relevant meaning or special symbolic import for Christian faith. Moreover, whatever else they think he may have added or embellished, many scholars detect Luke using very primitive traditions of the kerygma in recounting the story. This indicates that what lies at the core of the Pentecost story is a genuine memory of the kerygma being publicly proclaimed in a large setting for the first time.

36. James Martin, *Jesus: A Pilgrimage* (New York, NY: Harper One, 2014), p. 370.

37. Raymond Brown lays out a number of factors that would have contributed to remembering the site. From the fact that James, the brother of Jesus and leader of the Jerusalem church, would have naturally had a family interest in the tomb, to an increased interest in that period for venerating the tombs of prophets and martyrs (the Maccabees' tombs are a good example), there is good reason to think that there would be a living tradition of the memory of the site. He suggests that the later mishnaic text *Berakot* 9.1 provides evidence for this attitude: "When a place is shown where wonders happened in Israel, say, 'Blessed is the One who wrought wonders for our ancestors in this place.'" For more, see Brown, *The Death of the Messiah*, pp. 1280-1281.

38. Martin, *Jesus: A Pilgrimage*, p. 370.

39. Ibid., pp. 325-326.

40. Dan Bahat, "Where Was Jesus Buried?", in *Jesus: The Last Day*, ed. Molly Dewsnap Meinhardt (Washington, DC: Biblical Archeology Society, 2003), p. 125.

41. Wright, *Resurrection of the Son of God*, pp. 707-708.

42. Joseph A. Fitzmyer, *A Christological Catechism: New Testament Answers* (Ramsey, NJ: Paulist Press, 1981), p. 76.

43. See Lee Strobel, *The Case for the Real Jesus: A Journalist Investigates Current Attacks on the Identity of Christ* (Grand Rapids, MI: Zondervan, 2007), pp. 148-149, for another good example. He cites a 2007 Discovery Channel documentary making a similar claim. In 1980, archeologists had discovered ossuaries with the names "Jesus, son of Joseph", "Matthew", "Mary", "Judah, son of Jesus", and another "Mary". Since DNA tests showed the remains in the Jesus and second Mary ossuaries were not related through the same mother, the documentary speculated that the Mary in question was Magdalene, and that this was Jesus' family tomb. However, the archeologists who made this discovery reached no such conclusion. Aware of how common these names were, even in combination, they knew how extremely unlikely they were to be the skeletal remains of Jesus of Nazareth. Strobel provides a good analysis of just how common these names were and the statistical improbabilities involved.

44. Brown, *The Death of the Messiah*, p. 1210.

45. Wright, *The Resurrection of the Son of God*, pp. 694-695.

46. Geza Vermes, *Jesus the Jew: A Historian's Reading of the Gospels* (London: Collins, 1973), p. 41.

47. Brown, *The Gospel According to John XIII-XXI*, pp. 971. He adds: "And obviously the appearances that were reported would be those made to the more important figures known by Christians, for example, Peter, the Twelve, and James; appearances to women and to minor disciples would be put into the background and would not form part of the kerygma. The important Palestinian communities of Jerusalem and of Galilee might retain the memory of appearances with local associations. If at the stage of preaching recalled by Paul the geographical location of an appearance was not a matter of import, this factor would become important when the evangelists tried to fit appearances into a continuous narrative beginning with the empty tomb in Jerusalem. At times the story that came to an evangelist may have had a fixed locale that he preserved; at other times he may have adapted the story and made it fit into a locale dictated by his purpose in writing. It is no accident that Luke and John xx favor the tradition of appearances at Jerusalem. John has stressed Jerusalem in describing the public ministry of Jesus; and Luke (ix 51, xiii 33) made Jerusalem the goal of Jesus' life and the place from which the Christian message was to spread to the world (xxiv 47; Acts I 8).
"Thus the divergency as to locale and sequence found in the Gospel narratives of the post-resurrectional appearances of Jesus is not necessarily a refutation of the historicity of those appearances but may be the product of the way in which and the purpose for which the stories were told and preserved."

48. Witherington III, *The Gospel Code*, p. 75.

49. For more on the restraint they show, see Wright, *The Resurrection of the Son of God*, p. 612. To read The Gospel of Peter for yourself, see "The Gospel of Peter", in *Documents for the Study of the Gospels*, eds. David R. Cartlidge and David L. Dungan (Minneapolis, MN: Fortress Press, 1994), pp. 76-79.

50. Wright, *The Resurrection of the Son of God*, p. 611.

51. As documented by the Roman historian Tacitus. See Craig, *The Son Rises*, p. 29.

52. There is some question about which disciples were actually put to death for their faith. How many of the *original eyewitnesses* to the resurrection were persecuted and/or killed for their belief in it—or at least lived with this threat so that they were *willing to die* for this belief? It's a great question because the argument presented here hinges entirely on the fact that those original eyewitnesses were willing to give their lives. If it can't be shown they were—or at least a significant number of them were—the argument falls apart.
Tradition holds that all the Twelve Apostles were put to death—minus Judas, of course—with the possible exception of John, who was supposedly exiled on the island of Patmos. However, much of this tradition is historically suspect.

But, there is solid evidence—some of which is extra-biblical—that at the very least Peter and James among the Twelve, and Paul, James the brother of the Lord, and Stephen were all martyred. (It's possible Stephen may not have been a witness to the resurrection, but it's more likely that he was. We don't know for certain, but his significant leadership role in the early church—one of seven "deacons" second only in rank to the Twelve Apostles—is much more intelligible if he was one of the many unnamed witnesses who saw Jesus risen.)

Moreover, we know there were periods of systematic persecution of the early church by several Emperors, most notably Nero, who reigned during a time when a good number of those original witnesses were still alive and likely targeted. Nero scapegoated Christians—as the most detested underclass in the Empire, they were an easy mark—for the burning of Rome in 64 A.D., a fire many believe he set so he could rebuild the city and name it after himself. Historical records show that Christians suffered brutally. (see the previous endnote for one example)

But the best evidence is found within the New Testament itself. As scholars generally agree, many of the oldest texts are written to communities of first-generation Christians experiencing persecution that could become intense at times and even deadly. These texts contain numerous exhortations, admonitions, and allusions not to give up the faith and deny Jesus, especially in the face of the very pressing reality they could lose their lives for it. Undoubtedly, these texts reflect the situation many of the eyewitnesses to the resurrection found themselves in.

Furthermore, there are numerous allusions to the *actual* martyrdom of Jesus' original followers. In Luke 21:16, for example, Jesus tells his disciples that *some of them standing there will be put to death for proclaiming his Name*. Writing in the generation after those disciples lived, Luke never could have recorded this if it wasn't an accepted fact that some of them *had* died for their faith in Jesus, "some" implying more that just Peter and James. Similarly, in Mark 10:30 Jesus tells the disciples they will endure persecution as a result of leaving everything to follow him. And just a little later, when James and John ask to sit on thrones at Jesus' right and left side when he comes into his kingdom, Jesus turns around and asks them if they are ready to drink out of the cup he is to drink from and to be baptized in the bath he is about to receive—both euphemisms for his impending suffering and death on the cross. When both respond that they are willing, Jesus predicts *they will*. (Mark 10:38-29) Again, if it weren't well known that the Twelve *had* suffered such persecution with *at least* some of them dying a martyr's death, these passages never could have been recorded—especially since they were being held up as the model for Christians of the following generation not to give up their faith in the face of the persecution they were experiencing.

Beyond the Twelve, we don't know much about most of the original apostles. (The term "apostle," which simply means "sent" or "one who is sent," was a term used to designate those who had seen Jesus risen from the dead.) There is no reliable chronicle of the suffering the upwards of five-hundred other eyewitnesses might have experienced for their faith. That only develops through later tradition, much of it being legendary. The one apostle we do have a lot of information about is Paul. But if his experience was typical of the other apostles, which it almost certainly was—we can naturally imagine that anyone engaged in a similar ministry of preaching the gospel in that culture would have endured the same kind of reaction—the constant threat of suffering and death for the gospel was indeed the *norm*.

In II Corinthians 11:23-33, Paul gives the most extensive list of his persecutions: numerous imprisonments; countless floggings, five times with thirty nine lashes; beaten with rods three times; stoned once; and "often near death" as he describes it. He talks about all kinds of hardships and traveling dangers he willingly endures in order to proclaim the gospel—traveling, especially by sea, which Paul does numerous times, was particularly perilous back then. And he mentions one specific instance in Damascus where, unbelievably, even to him, he escapes *certain death* at the hands of King Aretas.

More significantly, he also notes that *other ministers* of Christ are experiencing the same fate. In I Corinthians 4:9-13, he compares the relatively safe Corinthian church to the *lot of the apostles, i.e., those other eyewitnesses to the resurrection.* These apostles, among whom Paul considers himself a member, are deemed last of all, he says, because God is allowing them to endure intense hardship and persecution for the sake of the gospel. He then uses a poignant description: the apostles are like those sentenced to death, doomed to die in the arena, i.e., *to be fed to the lions!* Whether he intends this literally or not, the insinuation is the same: *death is an ever-present reality for those apostles who dare to proclaim that they saw Jesus risen from the dead.* In I Corinthians 15:30, Paul mentions the fact that "we" are facing the constant threat of danger, "every hour." In the surrounding passage, he's quite explicit that belief in the resurrection is the only thing that could possibly motivate anyone to endure this threat.

In I Thessalonians 1:6, Paul reminds the Thessalonians that they received the word with joy *in spite of persecution.* Most of the Thessalonians believed on the basis of the testimony Paul and other eyewitnesses gave to having seen Jesus risen. They didn't witness it themselves. But this statement implies that those eyewitnesses who proclaimed the gospel to them were *already* being persecuted for sharing their testimony.

And from prison, while facing the imminent prospect of death for continuing to preach the resurrection, Paul tells the Philippians (1:21-23) that he would *prefer* to die because that would mean he would be with Christ. Paul certainly wasn't alone in this sentiment. It reflects the same calculus the other apostles were surely making: certain of the resurrection, they preferred death because it brought the ultimate reward, being with Christ.

Actually, Paul himself provides the earliest evidence that the apostles were persecuted. Before becoming a disciple, Paul admits, with profound regret, that *he persecuted the church violently!* (Galatians 1:13) And that he was *conspiring with others* to do so in what appears to have been a fairly organized enterprise (see Acts 8:1-3; Acts 9:1-7, where Paul receives letters from the high priest and then proceeds to travel with two others to carry out his "murderous threats" in Damascus). He even assisted in the death of the first Christian martyr, Stephen, by guarding the cloaks of those who were stoning him. If the information Luke provides in Acts about Paul's persecuting activity can be trusted—and there's little reason to doubt it—then Paul persecuted Christians up to the point of death, imprisoning many (Acts 22:4-5), tried, under the threat of persecution, to get them to blaspheme by denying Jesus, and cast his vote in agreement as they were being condemned (Acts 26:9-11). Given that Paul's conversion happened only several years after Jesus' crucifixion, a fairly robust and systematic persecution must have begun soon after Jesus' death. Many of the "victims" of this persecution had to be those original eyewitnesses to the resurrection. Evidently, right from the start, there was a group of people, including Paul, intensely committed to the destruction of those proclaiming resurrection faith. Undoubtedly, then, martyrdom was a very real threat for those who claimed to see Jesus risen.

So, there is abundant evidence that for the first disciples, the constant threat of persecution and martyrdom was a pervasive reality. It was dangerous to be a follower of Jesus! And this is the essential point. Even if many or all of the original eyewitnesses weren't put to death for proclaiming Jesus risen from the dead (although many probably were), *they believed they could be.* In fact, given that, based on the resurrection, they were proclaiming outright blasphemy—that Jesus was Yahweh's equal—it's hard to imagine how those first followers *wouldn't be harshly persecuted.* However far the tradition can be pressed, there is no doubt that those first Christians, including the witnesses to the resurrection, experienced the *constant threat of martyrdom,* and that some of them actually died for their belief.

53. Huston Smith, *The World's Religions* (New York, NY: Harper Collins), pp. 331- 332.
54: Bruner, *Matthew: A Commentary Vol. II*, p. 775. "I think Chrystostom put what is involved here plausibly: 'How could [the disciples]…have been able

to persuade the multitude? By saying what? By doing what?...Seeing him yet alive and merely seized, they had fled: and after his death were they likely to speak boldly in His behalf, unless He had risen again.' (89:1:525-26). Henry, too, 436, calls the leaders' suspicions groundless because when the disciples 'had not the courage to own him while he lived,...it was not likely that his death should put courage into such cowards.'"

55. Martin, *Jesus: A Pilgrimage*, p. 274.

56. Gary B. Habermas, "Mapping the Recent Trend Toward the Bodily Resurrection Appearances of Jesus in Light of Other Prominent Critical Positions", in *The Resurrection of Jesus: John Dominic Crossan and N.T. Wright in Dialogue*, ed. Robert B. Stewart (Minneapolis, MN: Fortress Press, 2006), pp. 79-80.

57. As quoted in Lee Strobel, *The Case for Christ: A Journalist's Personal Investigation of the Evidence for Jesus* (Grand Rapids, MI: Zondervan, 1998), p. 247-248.

58. Islam maintains that the Quran is *the* standing miracle. That there is no way Muhammad, an illiterate, uneducated nomad, could produce something as profound as the Quran; and, that this is a public document which can be tested to see its clearly revelatory character. But many have read the Quran, including myself, and have failed to see its *supposedly transparent* divine origin. Although it contains a clarity and beauty all its own, there is nothing that innovative or profound—i.e., clearly revelatory—about it. It isn't at all self-evident. In fact, as Pope John Paul II so effectively argued, Islam, as revealed in the Quran, is *regressive*, pulling back from the radical innovations of Christian faith to something more akin to Judaism. It is more of a devolution, a return to something more tame and familiar, than a revelatory leap forward. Just think of the Trinity, as one quick example, versus traditional (Monistic) monotheism which Islam zealously embraces, adamantly backing away from Christianity's "heretical" innovation. See John Paul II, *Crossing the Threshold of Hope* (New York, NY: Alfred A. Knopf, 1994), pp. 92-93.

To be fair, Islam does say that the Quran can only be fully appreciated in its original language, Arabic. Much like the *emotive effect* of a Martin Luther King speech, the rhythm and poetic character of the words *create an impression and yield an insight no translation can capture*. This might be true. The Quran may be exceedingly more powerful and illuminating in Arabic. But why would God reveal himself in such a restricted way? Most of the world doesn't speak Arabic and never will. So *how can this constitute a public, universally verifiable truth claim?* If God's intent is to reveal himself to the world, as Islam agrees it is, why would he conceal himself so severely from those who don't speak Arabic? The answer is, he wouldn't.

Moreover, the resurrection, if it happened, is *manifestly supernatural.* No one can deny its objectively phenomenal character. It *is* self-evident. Coming back from the dead in a glorified body is unquestionably the miracle of all miracles, something only God could do. Whether the Quran, even when read or heard recited in Arabic, has a supernatural character or not is a matter of *subjective interpretation.* (see endnote 62 below for a good illustration) Whether Muhammad could have produced it on his own or not remains debatable. In the end, it is left to the eye of the beholder, which proves nothing.

59. Craig, *The Son Rises*, p. 94.

60. Timothy Keller, *The Reason for God: Belief in an Age of Skepticism* (New York, NY: Riverhead Books, 2008), p. 212.

61. Craig, *The Son Rises*, p. 48.

62. Michael Licona relates this example: "The Qur'an provides a test for people to verify its divine origin: gather the wisest people in the world and call upon the *jinn*, which are similar to demons but without necessarily all the negative connotations, and try to write a surah, or chapter, that's as good as one in the Qur'an. The implication, of course, is that this can't be done.

   "...One person who speaks Arabic wrote what he calls *The True Furqan*, in which he maintains the style of the Qur'an in Arabic but with a message that's more Christian than Islamic. Some Muslims heard a portion of it read and were convinced that it was the Qur'an! One scholar in Arabic dialects told me that some of the classical Arabic in *The True Furqan* was much more beautiful than anything he had read in the Qur'an. So I guess the test has been passed." As cited in Strobel, *The Case for the Real Jesus*, p.129.

63. In comparing Jesus to other messianic figures of his day, Wright notes that resurrection wasn't a private event. It wasn't something someone could claim—no matter how disappointed they were at the death of a leader they had pinned all their hopes on—without publicly verifiable evidence to back it up. He suggests that the only reason the Christians could make a claim no one else dared to make is because they could produce that evidence. N.T. Wright, *Who Was Jesus* (Eerdmans, 1993), p. 63 as quoted in Keller, *The Reason for God*, p. 216.

64. There are some impressive exceptions. For example, the child in the movie *Heaven is for Real* claims to see his grandfather, who he never knew. But instead of describing him as an old man, at the age he died, he describes him as he looked in his thirties. How would he know this if he didn't see him in heaven?

   Still, there is no guarantee that he didn't access this information somewhere else. Even though the family maintains he never saw or could have seen a picture of his grandfather at this age, they may be mistaken. Experiments involving sensory leakage, among other things, caution against too easily accepting what are genuinely made but potentially erroneous claims. For more on near-death experiences and the possibility of some that can be verified, see Appendix I.

65. To date, the scientific community has found no credible evidence of paranormal phenomena. Theoretical Physicist Paul Davies provides a good example from his own research: "Proponents of so-called paranormal phenomena claim that the human mind can actually exert forces on distant matter. Presumably such forces are unknown at the reductionist level: they are not nuclear, gravitational or electromagnetic. The most direct illustration of these psychic forces is in the spectacular cases of remote metal bending, where the subject appears to deform a metallic object by mind-power alone, without physical contact. The author has devised an extremely stringent test of this phenomenon using metal rods sealed inside glass containers from which the air has been replaced by a secret combination of rare gases to preclude tampering. In a recent trial of arch-metal benders not one was able to produce any measurable deformation." Paul Davies, *God and the New Physics* (New York, NY: Simon and Schuster, 1983), pp. 225-226.
For a concise overview of the phenomenon of clairvoyance in particular, that also gives the relevant references to a number of major studies done through the years on paranormal phenomena in general, including short quotations from each which poignantly summarize their findings, see Wikipedia, "Clairvoyance", accessed October 20, 2016, https://en.m.wikipedia.org/wiki/Clairvoyance.

66. For instance, there are cases where so-called "mediums" have been exposed by savvy interviewers. Aware of how these "mediums" can manipulate information, the interviewer withholds key facts they require to produce "extraordinary" knowledge, like something only the family of a deceased loved one might know. These "mediums" rely on ordinary knowledge that they derive through clever tactics: taking guesses, asking leading questions that divulge more than people realize, and playing on the person's vulnerability, namely their deep-seated desire to have the medium be right so they might communicate with a deceased loved one or at least know they've attained life after death. No supernatural knowledge is being revealed, only the manipulation of ordinary facts. The 1993 PBS NOVA episode *Secret of the Psychics* provides some excellent example. The way the host, magician James Randi, is able to frustrate two well-known Russian psychics, among others, is particularly illustrative.

67. Robert Spitzer, *The Soul's Upward Yearning: Clues to Our Transcendent Nature from Experience and Reason* (San Francisco, CA: Ignatius, 2015), pp. 190-195.

68. "...historians do not picture the early missionary context as one in which widespread reports of resurrections similar to that of Jesus were common. Quite to the contrary, the early Christian missionaries confronted misunderstanding and even conflict. In her history of Christian theology, Margaret Miles identifies a conflict regarding the role of the body in claims of immortality: 'Belief in the resurrection of body seemed at best misguided, at worst an ignorant superstition, a confusion of two very different beliefs, immortality of the soul and resurrection of the body...Against the Platonic teaching that the soul is naturally immortal, Christians insisted that immortality of the soul was a gift from God, and that it was insufficient without the resurrection of the body.' In sum, what the early Christians were saying about Jesus and about our future did not fit with widespread beliefs about what happens after we die." Ted Peters, "The Future of the Resurrection", in *The Resurrection of Jesus: John Dominic Crossan and N.T. Wright in Dialogue*, ed. Robert B. Stewart, p. 161.

The most ancient and enduring view of life after death in both the Jewish and Greek world was an abode of the dead Jews called Sheol and Greeks knew as Hades. While notions of this abode remained vague, by and large it was depicted as a dark, murky, shadowy place under the earth. Everyone automatically entered it at death and then remained there permanently with only some kind of limited consciousness. Needless to say, it was a depressing and regrettable state.

The predominant understanding of life after death in the Jewish world of Jesus' day was the general resurrection, where all the dead would be raised bodily together on the last day. Speculation about the resurrected body varied widely. It could be depicted as closely resembling the present earthly body or, as in Daniel 12:2-3, a dazzlingly bright figure shining like the stars (whether this was meant literally or just metaphorically, in order to convey the idea that it was no longer subject to corruption or decay, is unclear.) But the glue that held all this speculation together was the notion that the body would be restored, and therefore bound, to the re-created physical world of the space-time realm. The person who was resurrected would easily be recognized as the person who had lived before.

Influenced by Hellenistic philosophy, another popular idea that most Jews were familiar with was a disembodied immortality where the soul would live on separate from the body in some kind of paradise. The true essence of the person, which is pure spirit, "escapes" all the limitations of embodied, earthly existence and dwells blissfully forever in the heavens. By the way, this closely aligns with the predominant modern view of life after death. Seeing created, material reality as a blessing, and not as bondage, most Jews rejected this idea but did end up incorporating it into their understanding of the intermediate state between death and the final resurrection. They determined that, at death, the soul or spirit is liberated from the body to go to some kind of heavenly resting place while it awaits the final resurrection, at which time it re-inhabits the earthly body. While the embodied state of resurrection remained the goal, this "interim" holding state prior to the general resurrection was purely spiritual.

Some in the pagan world espoused a form of transmigration where a person's soul could reincarnate into a different body. Again, the person who came back to life would look exactly like every other living person, having a real, finite, earthbound body subject to decay. Although they didn't adopt it, many Jews would be familiar with this belief.

The Hebrew Scriptures say very little about the after-life and only in the later texts do they present a positive view of it. Most of the Old Testament simply presumes the existence of Sheol. See Wisdom 33:6, Job 10:21, 17:13-16 for descriptions of this completely depressing, semi-conscious, murky netherworld. The earliest positive notions of the after-life come in the eighth century B.C. in Hosea 6:1 ff. and 13:14, which are probably just using resurrection language metaphorically. But these verses would later be interpreted as referring to the actual general resurrection of the dead. Similarly, written in the sixth century B.C., the famous dry bones passage of Ezekiel 37 is clearly a metaphor for Israel's return from exile. But later it gets interpreted as a literal resurrection text. Psalms 49 and 73 give a vague and formless hope of life after death in the form of justice for the righteous beyond grave. Isaiah 26:19 and 53:10-12 speak explicitly of triumph over death for the Servant of Yahweh. Whether or not this was originally intended only as a metaphor, it soon came to be understood literally. The first intentionally explicit mention of the resurrection comes in the second century B.C. in 2 Maccabees 7:14. This verse says that the martyrs will be vindicated by God who will raise them in the general resurrection on the last day. Around the same time, Daniel 12:2-3 says that the righteous will shine like the stars forever. This probably means in the final resurrection.

By Jesus' day, several views dominated the Jewish landscape. The Pharisees represented the majority perspective. They looked forward to a final resurrection and likely held that the righteous who die prior to this last day live with God in some disembodied existence while awaiting the more blessed state of resurrection. The Sadducees believed there was no life beyond the grave. (That's why they're sad you see!) The Essenes believed that the final judgment which inaugurated the general resurrection was imminent. A popular symbol for eternal punishment—Hell—was Gehenna. This was the garbage dump in Jerusalem where waste was burned in a perpetual fire. It was originally a Pagan site for human sacrifice and later became the place where dead bodies were burned. For the most thorough, up to date review of all the varied notions of immortality in Jesus' time see N.T. Wright, *The Resurrection of the Son of God*, Parts I-III, pp. 3-583.

69. Brown, *The Virginal Conception and Bodily Resurrection of Jesus*, p. 86, f. 147.

70. See Daniel 12:2-3. For a similar depiction with a Christian twist, see Revelation 1:12-16. In *The Resurrection of the Son of God*, pp. 604-607, N.T. Wright highlights the stark contrast between these common conceptions and the portrait of Jesus in the gospels. The implication is obvious: the gospel writers couldn't have invented or imagined such a strange portrait.

71. N.T. Wright, *Simply Christian: Why Christianity Makes Sense* (New York, NY: HarperOne, 2006), p. 113.

72. Craig, *The Son Rises*, p. 121.

73, Wright, *The Resurrection of the Son of God*, p. 477.

74. See Wright, *The Resurrection of the Son of God*, p. 612 for his definition of "transphysicality" and an exposition of how unique this depiction is: one searches in vain for any precedent or prophesy *and* any subsequent example. The notion of "transformed physicality" is utterly unique and, especially because first-century Palestinian Jews had a number of other well-established, sensible, and far more appealing notions, presses the question: where did they get all this?

75. Brown, *The Virginal Conception and Bodily Resurrection of Jesus*, p. 73.

76. Ibid., pp. 85-92.

77. Wright, *The Resurrection of the Son of God*, p. 478. See Chapter 7 for Wright's full analysis of the "spiritual body" Paul is talking about in I Corinthians 15, especially as he responds to those (shrinking number of) scholars who deny Paul means a physical body. In Greek, the phrase Paul uses for "spiritual body" is a technical term not found elsewhere. At the very least, Paul means a real body—the contemporary, mainstream, and exclusive meaning of the word he uses for "body"—which is reinforced by the very physical images he uses to describe it: first fruits, seed, sun, new clothes, etc. However, in this "New Creation," Paul indicates that this body will be even more robustly physical. And most exceptionally, it will be animated by the Spirit: though more physical (real? solid?), it will be transformed to the eschatological sphere—immortal, incorruptible, and not effected by space and time. For Paul, Jesus is clearly the model for Christian resurrection: the "spiritual body" he envisions will resemble Jesus' resurrected body. This is why what he says about it is so vital to understanding what Paul (and the other eyewitnesses) saw when the Jesus appeared to them.

78. Joseph A Fitzmyer, *The Gospel According to Luke X-XXIV* (New York, NY: Doubleday, 1985), p. 1539.

79. Wright notes the same phenomena in the narrative description of Jesus' appearance in John's gospel. He appears as a real, tangible, physical person—he even cooks breakfast!—but John implies that there is some odd, indescribable feature that is throwing the disciples off. Wright points out that when John says no one dared to ask him "who are you?", the Greek verb used there is the rare *exetazo*. It implies much more than simply asking. It means something more akin to "press with a question", to "scrutinize, examine, enquire." Why? What is it about him that fully allows his disciples to grasp that this is the same Jesus they've known all along, yet at the same time perplexes them so? And in a way that can't quite be put into words? The scene is truly bizarre. They seem to want to examine him as if he is some kind of science experiment, a new discovery, a strange element they'd never encountered before. In one sense, they are depicted here looking at Jesus the way someone who never saw a meteor before would quizzically look at one that just fell from the sky.
    John also says they were afraid to press their question. This too is puzzling. What were they afraid of? Wright suggests that, in this strange sequence, John has retained something of that "primal moment of simultaneous recognition and puzzlement" which they could only express as a question they dare not ask; and that all this confirms how unusual and unprecedented the phenomena associated with Jesus' appearances must have been. Wright, *The Resurrection of the Son of God*, pp. 678-679.
80. Michael R. Licona, *The Resurrection of Jesus: A New Historiographical Approach* (Downers Grove, IL: IVP Academic, 2010), p. 413, f. 455.
81. Wright, *The Resurrection of the Son of God*, p. 696.
82. Ibid.
83. In *The Resurrection of the Son of God*, N.T. Wright further emphasizes this point. Why did the early church tell "this kind of story", which has no precedent or parallel? That they did requires a historical explanation. And the only satisfactory one involves an empty tomb followed by transphysical appearances.(597) The appearances of Jesus are nothing like the many visions connected with Jewish biblical, prophetic, apocalyptic or mystical traditions where figures appear in blinding light or dazzling radiance, surrounded by clouds, in heavenly scenes, etc.(604) Why don't they depict Jesus shining like a star, the way Daniel (12:2-3) depicts those who will be vindicated into heavenly glory? "Many of those who sleep in the dust of the earth shall awake, some to everlasting life, and some to shame and everlasting contempt. Those who are wise shall shine like the brightness of the sky, and those who lead many to righteousness, like the stars for ever and ever." This would have been an all-too-obvious precedent. No, Jesus' appearances do not in any way resemble the kinds of visionary experience Jews of that day were conditioned

to expect. Something else, namely a "transphysical" resurrection, is required to explain the nature of the appearance stories.(609)

84. See, for example, Exodus 19:9-25, Isaiah 6:1-8, Ezekiel 1:1-28, Daniel 7:9-14.
85. Wright, *The Resurrection of the Son of God*, p. 704.
86. Gary Habermas, *Mapping Recent Trends*, in *The Resurrection of Jesus: John Dominic Crossan and N.T. Wright in Dialogue*, p. 79.
87. Craig, *The Son Rises*, p. 97.
88. Most scholars judge those few gospel texts that have Jesus talking about his resurrection as being composed after the fact: the gospel tradition puts these words into Jesus' mouth, in part, to soften the embarrassment surrounding the fact that he didn't foresee the unusual way he would be vindicated.
89. Jesus says: "...for I tell you that from now on I will not drink of the fruit of the vine until the Kingdom of God comes."(Lk 22:18); and, "Truly I tell you there are some standing here who will not taste death until they see that the kingdom of God has come with power."(Mk 9:1); to the high priest's question whether he is the Messiah, the Son of the Blessed One, Jesus says: "I am; and you will see the Son of Man seated at the right hand of the Power and coming with the clouds of heaven." (Mk 14:62) These sayings, which most scholars agree are authentic, point to what Christians call the Second Coming. There isn't, in these authentic sayings, any hint of Jesus' resurrection. Yet, each implies that his vindication will take place in the lifetime of those he is speaking to. Similarly, in the parable of the wicked tenants (Mk 12:1-12), Jesus talks about his eventual vindication before those who put him to death without any reference to his resurrection.
Referring to Jesus' anticipation of an immediate Parousia (i.e., Second Coming), as reflected in texts such as Mark 14:62, John 14:3, and I Thessalonians 4:16-17, Raymond Brown suggests that: "Mark 14:25 and Luke 23:42-43 are other passages that would be more intelligible if Jesus expected immediate victory in the kingdom after death. All this would fit in with a theory that Jesus did not know precisely what form his victory over death would take. One might conjecture that as a Jew he spoke of this victory in terms of the imagery of Dan 7 which he used to reflect on the Son of Man. In fact, however, the resurrection took place after his death, and the Parousia has remained in the future."(53) "'Future Son-of-Man Sayings' i.e., passages that speak of the Son of Man returning from heaven in the future in order to judge the world or raise the dead are found in all the Gospels, as well as in postulated preGospel sources. Many scholars maintain that they were the earliest Son-of-Man usage to take shape in the tradition; and we saw... the possibility that they stemmed form Jesus' own self-reflection on Dan 7. The original connotation may have been that when Jesus would come back, he would fulfill the Danielic description of a "son of man" (human being)

324

to whom the Ancient of Days would give all power and judgment."(111-2) Raymond E. Brown, *An Introduction to New Testament Christology* (Mahwah, NJ: Paulist Press, 1994), pp. 53, 111-112.

90. Wright essentially comes to the same conclusion via his own innovative approach: based on a *metaphorical reading* of Jesus' apocalyptic sayings—he argues very persuasively that this is how they were originally intended to be read—Jesus saw his future vindication exclusively in terms of being the Son of Man exalted at the *general resurrection in the age to come* where he would be revealed as the Messiah, put an end to evil, establish the kingdom of God in full force, execute judgment, and finally, be enthroned alongside Yahweh. Wright, *Jesus and the Victory of God* (Minneapolis, MN: Fortress Press, 1996), pp.517-519, 642-645.

91. For a detailed exposition of this view, see Wright *The Resurrection of the Son of God*, pp. 476-478.

92. Ibid., p. 478.

93. Wikipedia, "The Edsel", quoting author and Edsel scholar Jan Duetsch (no citation provided), accessed April 8, 2016, https://en.m.wikipedia.org/wiki/Edsel.

94. Craig, *The Son Rises*, p. 116.

95. Bauckham, *Jesus and the Eyewitnesses*, p. 505. The one obvious exception to this is the story of Emmaus. (Luke 24:13-35) It appears highly embellished. Here, Luke *is* acting like a good ancient historian, teasing out one very important implication of the resurrection: the risen Jesus is still present to the nascent church in the breaking open of scripture and the breaking of the bread, their Eucharistic celebrations. But aside from dramatizing this point, Luke retains the same essential elements found in the other appearance narratives: the doubt of the disciples; the failure to recognize Jesus in his risen appearance; the thoroughly embodied nature of his risen form; Jesus' ability to appear and disappear; and the bewildered astonishment when they do recognize him and try to comprehend the completely unprecedented nature of his appearance. Luke uses this raw material—this historical core—to make his point, to reveal what the resurrection, in one important way at least, means to the early church; namely that, because Jesus rose, he is still with them when they gather in his Name.

96. Wright, *The Resurrection of the Son of God*, pp. 599-602.

97. Ibid.

98. Ibid., pp. 602-604.

99. Wright goes on to show that all four accounts agree in key details: the time the women went to the tomb, early morning on the first day of the week following Jesus' crucifixion; that Mary Magdalene was one of several women who went, with Matthew, Mark, and Luke agreeing that one of the other women was

325

named Mary as well; that there was a stone rolled across the front of the tomb, but the problem it presented was resolved without the women having to do anything; and that an unusual stranger, identified as an angel in a couple of the accounts, spoke to the women about what had taken place. In addition, several of the accounts agree on other key details: in Matthew and John, Jesus appears first to Mary Magdalene, and in Matthew to the other Mary as well (Incidentally, a number of scholars believe that one of the later endings added to Mark contains early, independent tradition of this first appearance of Jesus to Mary Magdalene); Matthew, Luke, and John have the women go tell the disciples what they've seen; Luke and John add that Peter and another disciple go to see the tomb for themselves.

Wright also makes the point that the gospel writers, as anyone giving different accounts of the same event, including contemporary historians in that day such as Josephus who, between the *War* and the *Life*, gives different accounts of events in which he was involved, are capable of highlighting—often for dramatic effect—different aspects of the story. For example, upon hearing the women's report, Luke (24:12) has Peter going to see the tomb alone. But a mere twelve verses later (24:24) he can report that, according to the two disciples on the road to Emmaus, there were several disciples who went. So some of the differences in the story, such as which women went to the tomb, aren't an insurmountable obstacle to thinking they are substantially historical. Ibid., pp. 612-13.

100. For specifics see N.T. Wright, *The New Testament and the People of God* (Minneapolis, MN: Fortress, 1992), pp. 172-81, 307-20, and especially the helpful summary on pp. 319-320. Another good overview is found in Brown, *An Introduction to New Testament Christology*, Appendix I, pp. 155-161. In *The New Testament and the People of God*, pp. 171-181, and *Jesus and the Victory of God*, pp. 481-86, Wright references many of the most significant contemporary would-be messiahs: in the 40's B.C. Judas ben Hezekiah led a revolt and was killed; in 4 B.C. a certain Simon, ex-slave of Herod the Great, and Athronges both separately led independent messianic movements; in 6 A.D. Judas the Galilean led a revolt; in the 40's A.D. Theudas, who claimed to be a prophet, and Tholomaeus were both executed for leading independent insurgent movements; in the 50's A.D. Eleazar ben Deinaeus and Alexander were ringleaders of another rebellion; during the Jewish War, 66-73 A.D., Menacham, John of Gischala, and, perhaps the most notable, Simon bar Giora all led revolts with strong messianic overtones; and finally, the last major revolt in 135 A.D. was led by Simeon ben-Kosiba (Bar-Kochba="son of the star") who the venerable rabbi Akiba called the Messiah.

101. Strobel, *The Case for the Real Jesus*, p. 102. The *only* notion of suffering associated with the Messiah was the so-called "messianic woes", a period

of intense suffering for God's people, and perhaps, all the earth, that some thought would precede his coming. *But in no way would the Messiah himself suffer.* Many believed the Messiah's coming would lead to the "age to come," the time of the general resurrection. But the real proof-test for the Messiah would be Israel's liberation from pagan rule. Most thought he would accomplish this through some great military victory which would establish his kingship and usher in God's reign. This would be the messianic age of perfect peace and justice envisioned in Isaiah. Among all the variations of messianic belief, there was a core set of shared expectations: the resounding triumph of the Messiah, justice for Israel, control of the land, and a gloriously restored Temple. None of which happens through Jesus! See Wright, *The New Testament and the People of God*, p. 320 for more.

102. Wright, *The Resurrection of the Son of God*, pp. 559-560.

103. Ben Witherington III, "Biblical Views: Making Sense of the Unlikely Easter Story", in *Biblical Archeology Review* 37:2, March/April 2011, p. 30.

104 As Richard Bauckham points out: "The image of God the sovereign Ruler on his majestic throne high above all the heavens was so dominant in Second Temple Judaism that the notion of divine self-degradation to the lowest human status could easily have seemed quite inconceivable." Richard Bauckham, *Jesus and the God of Israel* (Grand Rapids, MI: Eerdmans, 2008), p. 54.

105. As quoted in Timothy Keller, *Making Sense of God: An Invitation to the Skeptical* (New York, NY: Viking, 2016), p. 244. Keller finds this quote in Richard Bauckham, *Jesus: A Very Short Introduction* (Oxford: Oxford University Press, 2011), p. 108.

106. Keller, *The Reason for God*, p. 217.

107. In fact, many who make this argument recognize that if those first Palestinian-Jewish disciples believed in Jesus' divinity, then the resurrection is the only way to explain it. So, to avoid the obvious conclusion, they argue that belief in his divinity is the result of later Hellenistic influence during the second and third Christian generations, when those first disciples were long gone. Moreover, those who argue Jesus' divinity was an innovation of later generations often point to the council of Nicea—some three hundred years after Jesus' death—as the point of full-blown development of this gradually evolving idea. At the popular level, the result of all this scholarly speculation is that many just assume the council of Nicea invented Jesus' divinity!

But, if anything, *Nicea is a step backwards from the earliest Christology.* It confuses and obfuscates the clear confession of Jesus' full divinity that is expressed in the earliest sources, the confession of faith of those first disciples. In *Jesus and the God of Israel*, Richard Bauckham has done an exhaustive and groundbreaking study of Christology in a Jewish context. He very effectively argues that, according to the contemporary mindset of Second Temple Judaism, the way Jesus is included in the divine identity would be the clearest and most exalted way to talk about his divinity. *No higher way would be possible.* In other words, in their context, those first disciples could not have believed in and expressed Jesus' divinity more fully or clearly. Citing the widespread and early Christian attribution of Ps 110:1 to Jesus, Bauckham states: "Jesus, seated on the divine throne in heaven as the one who will achieve the eschatological lordship of God and in whom the unique sovereignty of the one God will be acknowledged by all, is included in the unique rule of God over all things, and thus placed unambiguously on the divine side of the absolute distinction that separates the only Sovereign One from all creation. God's rule over all things defines who god is: it cannot be delegated as a mere function to a creature. Thus, the earliest Christology was already *in nuce* the highest Christology. Only the one who alone is eternal in the full sense can be the creator of all things and sovereign Ruler of all things. When this uniquely divine eternity is attributed also to Jesus, it is clear that the early Christians knew precisely what they were doing in Jewish theological terms when they understood Jesus to participate in the creative work and the eschatological rule of the one God."(234-235)

So, as early as we can trace, those first Christians maintained that Jesus shares the attributes unique to the divine identity, that belong to God alone: Creation, Sovereign Rule, eschatological lordship and exaltation, and eternity. From a first-century Jewish perspective, there would have been no more explicit way to express Jesus' full divinity, the fact that He is God. At Nicea, when the very clear Jewish understanding is translated into the concepts of Greek philosophy, categories of nature and essence, this is diluted by separating out what he does and who his is, which in turn, opens the door to understandings that actually diminish the full divine identity Jesus has in the New Testament. *Nicea is not a step forward in exalting Jesus as God. It is actually a step backward, confusing the much clearer confession of the earliest Palestinian Christian community.*

108. This is Hurtado's comment about the state of scholarship: "Some earlier history of religions researchers apparently found it difficult to reconcile this [evidence that indicated Jesus was worshiped alongside Yahweh in the earliest Aramaic-speaking Palestinian community] with their notions of what could be expected of Jewish Christians. Thus they attributed the origin of the cultic veneration of the risen Christ to a later stage of the Christian movement and invoked the influence of pagan cults as the cause. This is a sad example of a supposedly rigorous historical enterprise, though not the only case of a triumph of preconception over evidence." Larry Hurtado, *One*

*God, One Lord: Early Christian Devotion and Ancient Jewish Monotheism, Third Edition* (New York, NY: Bloomsbury, 2015), p. 131.

As evidence, Hurtado offers this example: Paul had numerous clashes with other believers over issues in the churches he writes to. He found many of their views problematic and defective. Moreover, he had major conflicts with some Jewish Christians over how the mission to the Gentiles should proceed. But, remarkably, "nothing in Paul's letters indicates any awareness that his fundamental view of Christ was unique or that he had made any serious innovation in the way Christians before him had regarded the exalted Jesus… Indeed, the Pauline letters may enable us to catch glimpses of Christian belief and devotion from the first few years of the church"

Paul's conversion probably took place sometime between 32-35 A.D. Immediately from that point on, within the first few years of the church, he had contact with Christians in Damascus, Jerusalem, and Antioch (Galatians 1:17-23), a significant geographical spread. So, the understanding of Jesus he was familiar with "was impressively broad in geographical extent and went back to within a few years of the beginning of the church. Actually, we must conclude that Paul's acquaintance with Christian beliefs went back even earlier than his Damascus road experience, for he must have obtained some familiarity with Jewish-Christian devotion in order to have been moved to persecute Jewish Christians for their beliefs (Gal. 1:13; 1 Cor. 15:9). In Paul, then, we have not only an important Jewish Christian in his own right but also one who was familiar with, and discloses aspects of, the devotion of Jewish-Christian groups of the most primitive period of Christianity. Paul, whose own faith was decisively shaped within the very first few years of Christianity, and in contact with believers familiar with the earliest Christian groups in Palestine, gives the impression that the exalted status he accorded to the risen Jesus was reflective also of the faith of those who 'were in Christ' before him (Rom. 16:7).

"Thus, Paul's own letters, the earliest literary access to Christianity afforded to us, provide strong evidence that the period in which to seek the decisive beginnings of the veneration of Jesus is not at all late but extremely early, easily with in the first decade of the Christian movement. They also indicate that the setting for the origin of Jesus veneration is within Christian groups led by, and at least initially comprised mainly of, Jewish Christians, including Aramaic-speaking groups in Palestine." (4-5)

Another, lesser-known way scholars have attempted to explain belief in Jesus' divinity is by arguing that the Judaism of first-century Palestine had become *syncretized*. That is, by the time of Jesus, the influence of the surrounding Hellenistic, polytheistic culture had so infiltrated Jewish thought that the pure monotheism of orthodox belief had been corrupted and diluted. Jews

329

were in continual contact with belief systems that included a pluralistic pantheon of gods and "divine men" and began to incorporate elements of them into their own beliefs. In particular, scholars point to a multiplication of intermediary figures (e.g., angels) who act on behalf of Yahweh and seem to share in His authority, and the personification of traits that mediated God's presence and activity in the world (e.g., Wisdom). As a result, with their strict monotheism "softened" by these developments, the members of the incipient church had ready-made options for speaking of a divinized mediator. In this context, even if it was a novel move, they could easily assimilate belief in Jesus' divinity alongside Yahweh.

But here again, Hurtado (along with other scholars, most notably Richard Bauckham) offers decisive evidence that this wasn't the case at all. To the contrary, Jewish monotheism was as strong, pure, and fierce as ever, and it would never tolerate even the slightest hint of any rival to Yahweh. As one example, in the literature, these intermediary figures are depicted doing God's bidding not because they share in His divine authority, but rather, mimicking the "lords", the ruling authorities, of that culture, to accentuate God's exalted status: Yahweh is too great to deal with mundane things— He uses servant figures to accomplish His will instead of doing it Himself. Thus, monotheism is heightened and intensified through these figures, not diminished.

Hurtado devotes much of *One God, One Lord* to surveying the relevant evidence. See especially Chapter 1 and pp. 49-41, 68-72, 85-95, and 144-157. Most scholars now concur with his conclusion.

109. The reasons scholars give include: the poetic quality of the passage, which stands out from the prose Paul uses in the rest of the letter; what they detect to be an Aramaic substratum, i.e., the Greek seems to have been translated from an underlying Aramaic text or oral tradition; and the fact that it doesn't fit the context—Paul is using it to make a very different point, namely that Christians should behave like Christ, which is not the main point of the passage—Jesus' exaltation is.

110. Avery Dulles, *Apologetics and the Biblical Christ*, p. 68, as quoted in Mark Link, *The Seventh Trumpet: The Good News Proclaimed* (Valencia, CA: Tabor Publishing, 1978), p. 194.

111. To which he adds: "Nor does Christology seem to be a point of contention between him and (say) the church in Jerusalem. Despite regular assumptions and assertions, there is no historical evidence for an early 'Jewish Christianity' which (like the later 'Ebionites') denied any identification between Jesus and Israel's God." N.T. Wright, *Paul and the Faithfulness of God* (Minneapolis, MN: Fortress Press, 2013), p. 649.

112. Ibid., p. 709. For the full quote: *"None of this seems to have been a matter of controversy within the earliest church.* This indicates, against the drift of studies of early Christology for most of the twentieth century, that what we think of as a 'high' Christology was thoroughly established within, at the most, twenty years of Jesus' resurrection. In fact, to employ the kind of argument that used to be popular when it ran in the opposite direction, we might suggest that this Christology must have been well established even sooner, since if it had only been accepted, say, in the late 40's we might have expected to catch some trace of anxiety or controversy on this point in Paul's early letters at least. And we do not. The identification of Jesus with YHWH seems to have been part of (what later came to be called) Christianity from more or less *the very beginning.* Paul can refer to it, and weave it into arguments, poems, prayers and throwaway remarks, as common coin. Recognizing Jesus within the identity of Israel's One God, and following through that recognition in worship (where monotheism really counts), seems to have been part of 'the way' from the start."

113. The evidence for the highest Christology (i.e., estimation of Jesus' divinity) being early is extensive. In addition to the examples already cited in this chapter, here's a sampling of several other good examples: the story of Jesus walking on water, which is found in both Mark (6:45-52) and John (6:16-21), is clearly a theophany, or manifestation of God. Jesus is *revealed as God,* saying and doing what only Yahweh can. As John Meier has shown, the primitive story underlying the gospel tradition predates both gospels, going back at least to the early 60's, but probably much earlier. John P. Meier, *A Marginal Jew: Rethinking the Historical Jesus Volume II* (New York, NY: Doubleday, 1994), pp. 905-933. The same is true for the story of Jesus calming the storm (Mark 4:35-41 and parr.), where the amazed disciples ask "Who is this?" Since Jesus has done what *the Old Testament says only God can do,* the implied answer is: God! This too is an early story that predates the gospels it's recorded in. In a passage found in Matthew (11:27) and Luke (10:22) that sounds a lot like a number of sayings in John, Jesus says: "All things have been handed over to me by my Father; and no one knows the Son except the Father, and no one knows the Father except the Son and anyone to whom the Son chooses to reveal him." Jesus, the Son, has an intimate knowledge of the Father *that only God can have.* Most scholars judge this saying to have been derived from what is called the "Q source," which most also believe is one of the earliest traditions behind the gospels, a tradition firmly embedded in the first Christian generation. Its similarity to many Johannine sayings has puzzled scholars because most posit that John's high Christology is the result of it being the last gospel written. The fact that a saying which is most at home in a Johannine context is found in one of the earliest traditions

331

means that John's high Christology wasn't a late development, but rather, appears, at times, in the earliest strata of gospel tradition. According to most scholars, the saying where Jesus laments over Jerusalem, found in Matthew (23:37-39) and Luke (13:34-35), is also derived from "Q." There Jesus speaks as the covenant God who has been calling Israel back to himself long before he was ever born. *He speaks as the Eternal One.* In Matthew 28:18-20, which is written during the second or third Christian generation, but is thought by scholars to contain a baptismal formula from an earlier period, Jesus tells the disciples to baptize using *the Name* of God. But the Name they are to use, the true Name of God, isn't Yahweh. It's now revealed as *Father, Son, and Holy Spirit.* In other words, Jesus the Son, along with the Spirit, possesses the same divine Name, and therefore, divine identity and status as the Father. In Matthew, Mark, and Luke, John the Baptist says, in fulfillment of prophesy, that he has come to "prepare the way of the Lord." The two prophetic texts he is alluding to are Mal 3:1 and Is 40:3. In them, "the Lord" who is coming is Yahweh himself. But in the gospels, this is *applied to Jesus.* In all four gospels, Jesus' words and authority supersede Torah, the very *word of God.* In all four gospels, Jesus replaces the Temple as the Shekinah *presence of Yahweh* with his people. In all four gospels, Jesus forgives sins *as only Yahweh* can. This is just a sampling of the evidence that the earliest Christology was the highest Christology. Much more could be added. (For more on Jesus as Yahweh's personal presence, see Wright, *Jesus and the Victory of God*, pp. 644, 646, 653)

114. Over the past twenty years, the widespread view among scholars that the understanding of Jesus' divinity developed from an incipient form in the earlier writings of the New Testament to a full-blown confession in the later writings (most admitted there were clear affirmations of Jesus' divinity right from the beginning, such as we saw in Philippians 2:6-11, but that the clearest expressions came later) is being rethought and overturned.

Scholars have finally paid attention to the Jewish background of the New Testament (largely overlooked, as many modern scholars now admit), and this "is quite rightly having a revolutionary effect on gospel Christology, where, in place of the older view that the synoptics had a 'low' Christology and John a 'high' one, the truth is dawning that Mark, Matthew and Luke have just as 'high' a Christology as John, only expressed in a way for which earlier generations of scholars were unprepared." Wright, *Paul and the Faithfulness of God*, p. 1045.

115. In other words, the earliest texts of the New Testament give just as full and robust an affirmation of Jesus' divinity as the latest. Mark, the first gospel written, is a perfect example. Richard Bauckham contends that Mark consistently presents Jesus acting not simply as God's agent, the way the

Messiah was expected to, but as one who, from the Jewish perspective, does what is properly reserved for God alone. One of the clearest indications of this is in 14:62 where Jesus tells the High Priest that he will see him sitting at the right hand of the Power. As is evident by the High Priest's response, who tears his robe in outrage at hearing such blatant blasphemy, this can mean nothing less than that Jesus shares the unique identity of God who alone exercises the cosmic rule over all things. Bauckham, *Jesus and the God of Israel*, p. 265.

116. Wright, *Paul and the Faithfulness of God*, p. 710.

117. Bauckham, *Jesus and the God of Israel*, p. 57-59. Ironically, it's *under the influence* of Hellenism, which many older scholars (most notably Rudolf Bultmann) argued was the catalyst for belief in Jesus' divinity, that the clear and unequivocal confession of Jewish Christianity is muddied and diminished, the exact opposite of what these older scholars maintained happened.

118. Avery Dulles, *Apologetics and the Biblical Christ* (Paramus, NJ: Newman Press, 1963), p. 71.

119. Brevard S. Childs, *Biblical Theology of the Old and New Testaments: Theological Reflection on the Christian Bible* (Minneapolis, MN: Fortress Press, 1993), p. 321.

120. Brown, *An Introduction to New Testament Christology*, p. 112.

121. Wright, *Simply Christian*, p.113.

122. Karl Rahner, *Foundations of Christian Faith: An Introduction to the Idea of Christianity* (New York, NY: Crossroad Publishing Company, 2013), p. 274.

123. Brown, *The Death of the Messiah*, pp. 1093.

124. Ibid., pp. 1094-1096.

125. Wright, *The Resurrection of the Son of God*, p. 709-710.

126. Charles L. Quarles, "The Gospel of Peter: Does It Contain a Precanonical Resurrection Narrative", in *The Resurrection of Jesus: John Dominic Crossan and N.T. Wright in Dialogue*, ed. Robert B. Stewart, p. 210, f. 49. Also see Brown, *Death of the Messiah*, pp. 1208-1211.

127. Brandt Pitre, *The Case for Jesus: The Biblical and Historical Evidence for Christ* (New York, NY: Image, 2016), p. 239, f.19.

128. Wright, *The Resurrection of the Son of God*, pp. 709-710.

129. William Lane Craig, "Wright and Crossan on the Historicity of the Resurrection of Jesus", in *The Resurrection of Jesus: John Dominic Crossan and N.T. Wright in Dialogue*, Robert B. Stewart ed., p. 147.

130. Wright, *The Resurrection of the Son of God*, p. 709.

131. Stephen T. Davis, *Risen Indeed: Making Sense of the Resurrection* (Grand Rapids, MI: Eerdmans, 1993), pp.80-81.

132. Wright, *The Resurrection of the Son of God*, pp. 697-701.

133. Strobel, *The Case for the Real Jesus*, p. 143.

134. Ibid., p. 142.

135. As quoted in John C. Lennox, *Gunning for God: Why the New Atheists are Missing the Target* (Oxford, England: Lion Books, 2011), p. 214.

136. For a devastating critique of this theory, see Wright, *The Resurrection of the Son of God*, pp. 701-706.

137. Licona, *The Resurrection of Jesus*, p. 522.

138. Craig, *The Son Rises*, pp. 132-133.

139. Ibid., pp. 116-117.

140. Ibid., pp. 112-113.

141. Wright, *The Resurrection of the Son of God*, p. 699.

142. Ibid., pp. 80-81.

143. Licona, *The Resurrection of Jesus*, p. 148.

144. Hurtado, *One God, One Lord*, pp. 104-105.

145. William Lane Craig, "Wright and Crossan on the Historicity of the Resurrection of Jesus", p. 139.

146. Bruner, *Matthew: A Commentary, Vol. II*, p. 785.

147. Craig, *The Son Rises*, pp. 84-85.

148. Blank, Blinzer, Bode, von Campenhausen, Delorme, Dhanis, Grundmann, Hengel, Lehmann, Leon-Dufour, Lichtenstein, Manek, Martini, Mussner, Nauck, Rengstorff, Ruckstuhl, Schenke, Schmitt, K. Schubert, Schwank, Schweizer, Seidensticker, Strobel, Stuhlmacher, Trilling, Vogtle, Wilkens. Craig adds: Benoit, Brown, Clark, Dunn, Ellis, Gundry, Hooke, Jeremias, Klappert, Ladd, Lane, Marshall, Moule, Perry, J.A.T. Robinson, Schnackenburg. I would add John P. Meier, Joseph Fitzmyer, Ben Witherington, and N.T. Wright to the list.

149. Habermas, "Mapping the Recent Trend Toward the Bodily Resurrection Appearnaces of Jesus in Light of Other Prominent Critical Positions", in *The Resurrection of Jesus: John Dominic Crossan and N.T. Wright in Dialogue*, Robert B. Stewart ed., p. 91.

150. See Appendix II for more about the Shroud. Several years ago I attended a brilliant lecture on the Shroud. It was given by a nun who was also a biochemist. For an hour and a half she didn't even mention the Shroud. Instead, she dazzled us by taking us through every conceivable image-formation method known to human beings throughout history. In the last few minutes she showed a picture of the Shroud. She concluded by pointing out that, with all the knowledge science has amassed, no known method can account for how the image it contains was formed. It remains a tantalizing mystery.

151. Wright, *The Resurrection of the Son of God*, p. 689.

152. Ibid., pp. 691-692.

153. Kelsey, *Resurrection: Release from Oppression*, p. 174.

154. Keller, *The Reason for God*, p. 219.

155. Wright, *The Resurrection of the Son of God*, pp. 707 and 710.

156. The only evidence Aslan offers for this conclusion is the historical record of contemporary messianic movements. In fact, this context is what drives his entire thesis: there were many would-be messiahs in Jesus' day and they all could be characterized as zealots; Jesus led a messianic movement; Jesus must have been a zealot. In other words, this is how Jesus must have been because this is how *every other* would-be messiah was. Because zealots are fiercely nationalistic, they would never teach people to love their enemy. Hence, Jesus couldn't have meant "love your enemies" in a universal way.

But this is a circular argument: Aslan chooses to omit data that contradicts the historical portrait he's *already* decided is right. *He sees in Jesus only what his (preconceived) zealot prism allows him to see.* However, as contemporary scholarship is demonstrating more and more, one of the primary reasons Jesus is so noteworthy is that he doesn't fit neatly into this context. In so many ways, he is radically unique, so unlike the Judaism that precedes and the Christianity that follows him. In fact, this "discontinuity" or "dissimilarity" is one of the most reliable criteria scholars use for judging what is historical. The more sharply something stands out from its context, like the very radical command to "love your enemies," the more likely it is to be historical. For his treatment of "love your enemies," see Reza Aslan, *Zealot: The Life and Times of Jesus of Nazareth* (New York, NY: Random House, 2014), pp 120-121. In contrast, John Meier, *A Marginal Jew: Volume IV*, pp. 528-551, provides the most thorough analysis of this saying to date, including abundant citations of other scholars and their estimation of this teaching.

Indeed, even the Jesus Seminar, a group of fringe scholars who deny that most of what is recorded in the gospels goes back to Jesus, concluded that Jesus taught "love your enemy." In ranking the sayings most likely to go back to the historical Jesus, they voted it *third highest.* And, as they put it, to love your enemy means you have *no* enemies—quite un-Zealot like! The Jesus Seminar, *The Five Gospels: The Search for the Authentic Words of Jesus* (New York, NY: Macmillan Publishing Company, 1993), pp. 145-147.

157. Aslan, *Zealot: The Life and Times of Jesus of Nazareth*, pp. 102-109. Another example is that Jesus didn't die as a martyr to revolution. More and more scholars are inclined to regard the traditions surrounding the last supper and the garden of Gethsemane, where Jesus agonizes over his impending death, as historically credible. Because of the scandal and embarrassment they create—for example, in the face of death, Jesus isn't heroic, the way Greek heroes and Jewish martyrs always are, but instead, pleads not to have to die—it is difficult to explain these traditions any other way. But these traditions also indicate that Jesus believed he was dying to accomplish his Father's will by

335

establishing a new covenant through his blood. He is no mere martyr, but rather, the mediator of this covenant.

158. Aslan, *Zealot: The Life and Times of Jesus of Nazareth*, p. 176. For how this "creed" came about: "In ancient Israel, the right hand was a symbol of power and authority; it signified a position of exaltation. 'Sitting at the right hand of God' means sharing in God's glory, being one with God in honor and essence...

"In other words, Stephen's Son of Man is not the kingly figure of Daniel who comes 'with the clouds of heaven.' He does not establish his kingdom on earth 'so that all peoples, nations, and languages should serve him' (Daniel 7:1-14). He is not even the messiah any longer. The Son of Man, in Stephen's vision, is a pre-existent, heavenly being whose kingdom is not of this world; who stands at the right hand of God, equal in glory and honor; who is, in form and substance, *God made flesh.*

"That is all it takes for the stones to start flying.

"Understand that there can be no greater blasphemy for a Jew than what Stephen suggests. The claim that an individual died and rose again into eternal life may have been unprecedented in Judaism. But the presumption of a 'god-man' was simply anathema. What Stephen cries out in the midst of his death throes is nothing less than the launch of a wholly new religion, one radically and irreconcilably divorced from everything Stephen's own religion had ever posited about the nature of God and man and the relationship of one to the other. One can say that it was not only Stephen who died that day outside the gates of Jerusalem. Buried with him under the rubble of stones is the last trace of the historical person known as Jesus of Nazareth. The story of the zealous Galilean peasant and Jewish nationalist who donned the mantle of messiah and launched a foolhardy rebellion against the corrupt Temple priesthood and the vicious Roman occupation comes to an abrupt end, not with his death on the cross, nor with the empty tomb, but at the first moment one of his followers dares suggest he is God."(168-169)

159. Hurtado, *One God, One Lord*, p. 172. Hurtado cites several reviews of his work which acknowledge the impact it has had. Now, the majority and still growing opinion is that Jesus was worshiped and given the status of divinity by the earliest Palestinian-Jewish group of disciples. As Andrew Chester notes: "The clear (though not unanimous) scholarly consensus is that, despite all the problems it creates for our understanding of early Christianity, a Christology that portrays Christ as divine emerges very early, in distinctly Jewish terminology and within a Jewish context." And, "...it is difficult to make sense, for example, of Phil 2:6-11 except on the basis that it is assumed and expected that Christ will be acclaimed and worshipped in the same way as God (and that this will itself be to the glory of God); and Hurtado makes

a sustained, cumulative case for there being some kind of cult of Christ in Christian circles in Palestine as well as in the Pauline communities." Andrew Chester, "High Christology Whence, When and Why?" *Early Christianity 2* (2011): 22-50 (citing 38-39).

After a large-scale review of his work, Crispin Fletcher-Louis concludes: "The onus is now on those who would argue against Hurtado's view that a high Christology is a very early, essentially Jewish and widespread, if not a thoroughgoing, feature of earliest Christianity."(Crispin Fletcher-Louis, "A New Explanation of Christological Origins: A Review of the Work of Larry W. Hurtado," *Tyndale Bulletin 60* (2009): 161-205 (citing 165).

160. Hurtado, *One God, One Lord*, p.122

161. Ann Rice, *Christ the Lord* (New York, NY: Ballantine Books, 2006), pp. 329-330.

162. Wright, *Jesus and the Victory of God*, pp. 81 and 86. For more on the impact of these changes and the present state of historical Jesus scholarship see Chapter 3 in this same book; Wright, *Paul and the Faithfulness of God*, pp. 1044-1045; and Robert Spitzer, *God So Loved the World: Clues to Our Transcendent Destiny from the Revelation of Jesus* (San Francisco, CA: Ignatius Press, 2016), pp. 71-74, 270.

163. Wright, *Simply Christian*, p. 99.

164. Keller, *Making Sense of God*, pp.230-231. Also see Wright, *The Resurrection of the Son of God*, p. 596. As one of, if not the, foremost scholars of his generation, Wright essentially declares that the heyday of form-criticism is over. While in vogue from the 1920's-1970's, it has lost its appeal for most modern scholars. They now recognize that the agendas of the original form critics were what drove the project. As a result, the basic assumptions that under-gird form-criticism are seriously flawed. It isn't trustworthy as a tool of scholarship.

165. For more see Bauckham, *Jesus and the Eyewitnesses*, pp. 264-271.

166. Carmine Gallo, *Talk like TED: The 9 Public-Speaking Secrets of the World's Top Minds* (New York, NY: St. Martin's Griffin, 2014), pp. 139-142.

167. Ibid., pp. 225-226.

168. Bauckham, *Jesus and the Eyewitnesses*, pp. 330-335 and 341-346.

169. Ibid., p.346.

170. Because we so often associate eyewitness testimony with legal proceedings, we assume it is all equally vulnerable to error. But the nature of eyewitness testimony in the gospels is substantially different. In court, periphery details are essential. And the research shows that these are among the things that are least likely to be remembered accurately. However, for the gospels, the gist of the events, their essence and meaning, is primary. As Bauckham observes, what leads psychologists to question the accuracy of the testimony

of eyewitnesses in legal proceedings is substantially different from the kind of eyewitness testimony provided in the gospels. The witnesses to Jesus aren't concerned with peripheral details, but rather, as participants in the events and not mere bystanders, their focus is presenting the essence of what happened. Moreover, they aren't trying to remember and identify faces they first observed (often briefly) during unexpected, rapidly unfolding, stress-ridden events.

Bauckham shares Alan Baddeley's assessment of this phenomena: "[M]uch of our autobiographical recollection of the past is reasonably free of error, provided that we stick to remembering the broad outline of events. Errors begin to occur once we try to force ourselves to come up with detailed information from an inadequate base. This gives full rein to various sources of distortion, including that of prior expectations, disruption by misleading questions, and by social factors such as the desire to please the questioner, and to present ourselves in a good light." Alan Baddeley, *Human Memory: Theory and Practice* (revised edition; Hove: Psychology, 1997), p.222.

Bauckham also quotes Gillian Cohen as she sums up her survey of the psychological studies this way: "In daily life, memory successes are the norm and memory failures are the exception. People also exhibit remarkable feats of remembering faces and voices from the remote past, and foreign-language vocabulary and childhood experiences over a lifetime. As well as such examples of retention over very long periods, people can retain large amounts of information over shorter periods, as when they prepare for examinations, and sometimes, as in the case of expert knowledge, they acquire a large amount of information and retain it for an indefinitely long time. Considering how grossly it is overloaded, memory in the real world proves remarkably efficient and resilient." Gillian Cohen, *Memory in the Real World* (Hillsdale: Erlbaum, 1989), p. 222. So, unlike courtroom testimony, the scientific research on memory supports the contention that *in substance, in essence*, the gospels could and likely do record accurate historical data about Jesus.

171. The "twist" is that the Samaritan is the *hero* in the story, the one who acts in the most compassionate and "God-like" way. Jews detested Samaritans more than any other group, even going so far as to use "Samaritan" as a pejorative synonym for "demon possessed." In their culture, you couldn't say anything worse about someone! If Jesus just wanted to emphasize compassion for the neighbor—the way we usually interpret the parable—or even simply love of enemy, he would have had a Jew be the hero and help a Samaritan left for dead by the side of the road. His point is far more profound: to love his way, God's way, we must see the divinely created goodness, the image of God, even in those we detest the most.

172. Incidentally, there is some question whether Dr. Drew was refused treatment at the hospital he was first brought to and whether that treatment could even have saved his life—he simply may have lost too much blood to be revived. It seems that people at the time made this presumption because, in the segregated South, it *was* a widespread practice to turn black patients away. Both the film I saw as a child and the book my student showed me presented this presumption as fact, and that's how it entered my memory.

173. As cited in Keller, *Making Sense of God*, pp. 231-232.

174. Bauckham, *Jesus and the Eyewitnesses*, pp. 354-355.

175. In Michael R. Licona, *The Resurrection of Jesus: A New Historiographical Approach* (Downers Grove, IL: InterVarsity Press, 2010), p.204. See pp. 201-208 for more on this dramatic turn and, in addition, an interesting, and quite eclectic, sampling of scholars who believe the gospels were either written by eyewitnesses or by those who used eyewitnesses as their sources. Licona notes that even the hyper-skeptical Elaine Pagels argues that the gospel of John, the last to be written and, therefore, often dismissed as the least reliable historically, has significant eyewitness testimony behind it. In fact, many scholars now recognize that John, for all its theological embellishment, contains some of the oldest and most reliable traditions among all the gospels.

176. Wright, *Jesus and the Victory of God*, p. 87. This is Wright's summary of the present state of historical Jesus scholarship: "The much vaunted 'normal critical tools', particularly form-criticism, are being tacitly (and in my view rightly) bypassed in the search for Jesus; enquiry is proceeding by means of a proper, and often clearly articulated, method of hypothesis and verification… much of the impetus for form-critical, and redaction-critical study came from the presupposition that this or that piece of synoptic material about Jesus *could not* be historical; in other words, that *an historical hypothesis about Jesus could already be presupposed* which demanded a further tradition-historical hypothesis to explain the evidence. If, however, a viable alternative historical hypothesis, whether about Jesus or about the early church, is proposed, argued out, and maintained, the need for tradition-criticisms within the search for Jesus (to say nothing about its undoubted value in other historical enterprises) could in principle be substantially reduced and altered in shape. This is exactly what happens in the hypothesis of (say) Sanders and Meyer: all sorts of things in the gospels which, on the Bultmannian paradigm, needed to be explained by complex epicycles of *Traditionsgeschichte* turn out, after all to *fit comfortably within the ministry of Jesus*."(my italics)

177. Meier, *A Marginal Jew: Volume V*, pp. 240-253.

178. The Greek word used here, *epiginoskei* emphasizes the "really." The emphasis is on *truly* knowing, in the deepest sense possible: no one truly knows the Father like the Son; no one knows the Father as profoundly and intimately

as the Son and visa versa. The reason this passage is so fascinating (and frustrating) for scholars is that it doesn't sound like the rest of the prose in what are known as the Synoptic Gospels, Matthew, Mark, and Luke. Idiomatically and thematically, this verse, the so-called "Johannine logion," is more at home in the Gospel of John. However, it appears in both Matthew and Luke via a common source scholars call "Q." Most scholars think Q is one of, if not the, oldest traditions contained in any of the gospels. Since most also think John is the last gospel written and that this accounts for its lofty prose and its evaluation of Jesus as being on a plane with God the Father, it is baffling how a saying that can be traced to such an early stage of the tradition—making it significantly more likely to come from Jesus himself—could have such a high estimation of him. However, as we've already seen, developments over the past twenty years are convincing many scholars that this high evaluation of Jesus existed right away, and therefore, the "Johannine logion" is just further evidence of this fact.

179. Robert Spitzer, *God So Loved the World: Clues to Our Transcendent Destiny from the Revelation of Jesus* (San Francisco, CA: Ignatius Press, 2016), p. 63. If Jesus' image of an unconditionally loving God doesn't blow your mind, it's only because we're so use to hearing it. It's been stripped of all its wild and shocking magnificence, beaten down into just another pious platitude.

Generally, the Eastern religions teach that God is impersonal, an energy or a force. Since love is only possible between "persons," you can't have a close, personal relationship—or any kind of "relationship" at all—with this kind of God. (As an intriguing aside, however, the largest of the four paths to God in Hinduism, Bhakti Yoga, sometimes referred to as "theistic Hinduism", and the largest of the two strains of Buddhism, Mahayana, sometimes called "popular Buddhism", conceive God in personal and loving terms: in other words, they stray from the purity of an impersonal divinity that lies at the core of both traditions. Even though neither approaches the kind of radically loving God Jesus reveals, this is another powerful indication—see Chapters 8 and 9 for more—that the intuition of and longing for a personal God is a universal impulse.) Islam teaches that Allah is loving, compassionate, and merciful. However, the greatest sin in Islam is "shirk," or association; that is, confusing or associating anything too closely with Allah. This includes having a close relationship with Him. There is a healthy distance that humans must keep in order to respect Allah and avoid "shirk," this greatest of all blasphemies. Allah wants surrender, not a close, intimate, loving relationship. He created us to honor and serve Him, not to be in close fellowship with Him. Islam, after all, literally means "peace," the peace that comes from surrendering the will to Allah.

The closest anyone comes to this radical innovation of Jesus are notions of God's gratuitous love found in the Old Testament, especially Hosea 1:2-11 and 3:1-5. But the Old Testament understanding differed in three significant ways. First, God's unconditional commitment was to the nation of Israel, not each and every person; it was corporate, not individual. Second, there were conditions or limits to Yahweh's covenantal love. There was a point at which it could be withdrawn, at least for a time. That's what exile was all about. In fact, in Hosea God tells the prophet to marry a prostitute not, as it first seems, to assure Israel of His unconditional love, but to *shame Israel for its infidelity*—the image of a prophet of God "yoked" to a prostitute would be so disgusting and grotesque that it would provoke the nation to reconsider it's idolatrous and shameful unfaithfulness to Yahweh. The entire book is a prophetic warning that God will withdraw His covenantal love and protection if Israel continues in its disobedience. It's written to shock the nation out of its stupor before it's too late. And third, within the overall context of the Old Testament, the image of God that emerges and dominates is a *significant departure* from the radically intimate, warm, and unconditional love of Jesus. Yahweh, whose overwhelming presence inspires dread more than love, whose holiness creates distance more than intimacy, is more frequently depicted in terms of strict justice. (That's why it *isn't* a good thing to see the face of God! No fallible, profane human being can be in his holy presence and live.) He is a God of justice more than love. As a holy God, He has little tolerance for sin and is often seen punishing it swiftly and severely. And arbitrarily. Forgiveness, especially for the most heinous sins, is never assured. When David commits adultery and murder, he is relieved to find that Yahweh will spare his life, something that usually doesn't happen for such capital offenses or such egregious sinners. (If you doubt any of this, read through the Old Testament and see what kind of overall impression you get about Yahweh.) Indeed, this is why Jesus' contemporaries found him and his image of God so scandalous and revolting. If he wasn't presenting something so far out of the mainstream, if his teaching and praxis weren't such a radical departure from traditional belief, they wouldn't have found him so offensive and problematic. To many, especially the religious leaders charged with safeguarding the Old Testament tradition, the free forgiveness Jesus practiced, his association with sinners, his understanding of God as an intimately close Father, and the unconditional love of God he taught were outrageously heretical and a major factor in their rejection and condemnation of him. In other words, Jesus never would have been so controversial or gotten himself crucified if his view of Yahweh was anywhere close to the Old Testament view—clearly demonstrating that the Old Testament view wasn't anywhere close to the radically, unconditionally loving God Jesus presented and embodied. This also

341

explains why many of Jesus' most beloved parables, e.g., the Good Samaritan, the Prodigal Son, were the ones that scandalized his contemporaries most.

180. What about Buddha? Didn't he emphasize compassion as the ultimate value? Not really, and certainly not to the extent Jesus did. While he highly valued it, compassion wasn't his main emphasis. Escaping the cruelty of this world through Enlightenment was. That's why, while he critiqued the brutally hierarchical Caste System, he never directly challenged it or tried to undo it. Instead, in his teaching about transmigration, "no-soul", and the path to Nirvana, he effectively led people to accept their fate in the Caste hierarchy and focus entirely on being liberated from the *illusion* of suffering which so often stemmed from their state in life. In effect, compassion was more a means to achieving Nirvana than a reality to be sought for its own sake. It was a penultimate value.

But weren't democracy and our democratic ideals born in ancient Greco-Roman culture? Only partially and in a woefully *undemocratic* manner! Democracy was only for the educated elite. As much as it enfranchised some, the hierarchical social order of the Greco-Roman world excluded and oppressed many more. The so-called Household codes, which were alive and well at the time of Jesus, are a good example of this. Women, slaves, and children all had their subservient place in this hierarchy. These codes, however, were subsequently subverted and eventually undone by the church as it advanced Jesus' radically new ethic throughout the Roman Empire in the intervening centuries.

And what about Judaism? Didn't the Torah command care for the foreigner, for the poor? To an extent it did. But Judaism still overwhelmingly saw wealth as a blessing for faithful behavior and poverty as a curse for sin, otherwise known as retributive justice. For all practical purposes, a person's worth, their value, was still largely based on their position in the social order. Just look at the way women and children were viewed, not to mention slaves and the lower classes: more as property than people, their worth being determined by the free male adults in their life. And the few passages that talk about treating the foreigner compassionately are more than balanced by those that see all pagans—non-Jews—as godless and therefore substantially inferior, even to the point that intermarriage with them was forbidden and, in extreme cases, like "the ban" (e.g., Joshua 8:24-29), they were to be eradicated from the land, i.e., put to death! See Exodus 23:20-33 for some very explicit language about the pagans as enemies of Israel and Yahweh, and the need, and intention of Yahweh, to drive them from the land. The God of Israel tended to be quite exclusive. You had to be Jewish—and male—to be truly blessed and enfranchised. It is true that Israel's chosen status was for the purpose of being the light to the nations, God's instrument in saving the world. But that's not a major emphasis. More often, God is depicted as exclusively Israel's God, taking sides over and against the pagan nations. There are rare glimpses of a more universalistic impulse, such as in Isaiah and Jonah. But this is worlds apart from Jesus' radical inclusivity that brings this impulse to the fore and dresses it with relentless mercy. Once again, if in any way Jesus' teaching comfortably conformed to the ideas of his day, he wouldn't have been such a controversial figure. No one would have thought he was so subversive. No one would have thought to crucify him!

For more on the revolutionary ethic Christianity introduced and how these ideals (unconsciously) pervade our modern (Western, democratic) worldview, see Keller, *Making Sense of God*, pp. 43-45, 188.

181. At least as far as his culture allowed—they couldn't preach or teach because women weren't allowed to speak in public before men, especially if that involved preaching or teaching. But in every other way, Jesus treated them as full-fledged disciples. And when the opportunity presented itself, as in the case of the Samaritan woman, he did instruct them to publicly proclaim his name. Moreover, if the resurrection happened, the first person he chose to appear to from the dead *was a woman*, Mary Magdalene.

See John Meier, *Jesus: A Marginal Jew: Rethinking the Historical Jesus, Volume III* (New York, NY: Doubleday, 2001), pp. 73-80 for a solid exposition of Jesus' attitude toward women as disciples. Meier reveals how shocking it would have been in that culture for Jesus to have had women followers. It would have aroused intense suspicion and caused tremendous scandal. Which leaves little doubt that this was indeed Jesus' practice and that it was extremely unusual if not absolutely unique.

182. The only image of God that comes close, at least among the major world religions, is that of Judaism. However, as previously noted, the unconditional faithfulness of Yahweh is not given to individuals but reserved only for the nation as a whole. And, there are some sins that cannot be forgiven—that's why David is so grateful God lets him live after committing adultery with Bathsheeba and murdering Uriah her husband. It's not a given that God would forgive such "capital" sins. Normally He didn't. Moreover, all sin had to be atoned for. That's the whole purpose behind the Temple and its sacrificial system. You had to make up for what you did. You had to pay the debt you owed. There was no such thing as "free forgiveness." Finally, Old Testament grace is arbitrary: David is forgiven for two capital offenses, while Saul isn't forgiven his lesser offenses. God seems to play favorites, loving and forgiving based on preference and whim, e.g., Cain and Abel, Esau and Jacob, Joseph and his brothers. So while this is "grace" in some severely restricted way, it is in stark contrast to the totally unconditional, free forgiveness Jesus offered to any and all who would receive it.

183. Richard P. McBrien, *Catholicism* (San Francisco, CA: Harper and Row, 1981), p. 520.

184. Jesus' mother Mary was, of course, declared sinless by the Catholic Church. But this is a conclusion of later church doctrine—centuries later!—not history. Buddha made a similar impression on his contemporaries, but with three notable differences: first, in Eastern thought, sin is understood as an illusion (Maya), not a moral failure. Second, for a number of reasons—such as the fact that the sources for his life are so far removed, written a hundred and fifty years or so afterward—there is little historical evidence that his contemporaries viewed Siddhartha achieving the same kind of perfection Jesus' contemporaries attributed to him. And third, Buddha rejected any notion that he was divine or had attained a level of perfection that would indicate he was. In a famous exchange, one of his disciples is speaking in lofty and glowing terms about his master's wisdom and lifestyle. Buddha takes him to task, asking if he knows of every other sage who's ever lived; if he can be certain that there is none greater than he. Implicit in his rebuke is a denial that he has achieved some kind of superior perfection of life; he is rejecting any insinuation that he might be without fault. See Houston Smith, *The World's Religions*, p. 90. Buddha adamantly denied he was a god, and thus sinless; which happens to be much more palatable in Eastern thought anyway: there have been multiple incarnations of Brahman (God). This is distinctly opposed to Western thought, notably in Judaism and Islam, where it is ontologically impossible for God to become human. And distinctly opposed to Jesus, who, if often only in veiled ways so as not to short circuit his ministry by being put to death for blasphemy, encouraged people to understand that he was divine.

185. Theissen and Merz, *The Historical Jesus*, p.290 as quoted in Richard Swinburne, *The Resurrection of God Incarnate* (New York, NY: Oxford University Press, 2003), p. 86.

186. See Meier, *A Marginal Jew: Volume II*, pp. 777-788.

187. Ibid., p. 630.

188. Brown, *An Introduction to New Testament Christology*, p. 63.

189. Ibid., p. 65. See Brown's larger discussion of Jesus' miracles, including the most notable examples of the other miracle workers scholars have discovered—Hanina, Honi the Circle-Drawer, and Apollonius of Tyana—along with helpful sources for further study, pp. 60-70. Also see Spitzer, *God So Loved the World*, p. 192, who elaborates more fully on the same point found in Brown that is noted here. For a detailed analysis of contemporary miracle workers see Meier, *A Marginal Jew: Volume II*, pp.576-601.

190. Spitzer, *God So Loved the World*, p. 206.

191. Wright, *Jesus and the Victory of God*, pp. 623, 644-653. While this point is more speculative than the other data in this overview—the jury is still out on whether the majority of scholars will follow Wright in this—it puts the pieces of the puzzle together in a more cohesive fashion than any other explanation to date. It has greater explanatory power in accounting for what Jesus thought he was up to and who he thought he was, especially in claiming so many divine prerogatives for himself. Two highly regarded historical Jesus scholars provide support for key parts of Wright's view, especially the fact that Jesus saw his ministry, in particular his exorcisms, bringing about the final defeat of Satan/evil—which implies an extraordinarily high self-estimation—and that Jesus was absolutely unique in this. For more, see Gerd Theissen and Annette Merz, *The Historical Jesus: A Comprehensive Guide* (Minneapolis, MN: Fortress, 1996), Chapter 9, especially pp. 257-259.

192. Keller, *Making Sense of God*, p. 237.

193. Wright, *The New Testament and the People of God*, pp. 399-400. In addition: "We could press this point another way. Suppose that Jesus had been known to have been a person of bad character. If, for example, he had been a known drunkard or philanderer, or if he had had the reputation of preaching for personal financial reward, then the whole idea that his death on a Roman cross had somehow, through his coming to life again, achieved significance of whatever sort for the lives of others, let alone the crowning significance attached to those events in the New Testament, would simply be laughable. If, again, he had simply been a teacher of great timeless moral platitudes, it may be doubtful whether he would have been crucified in the first place; but even if we get over that hurdle, we may be sure that his death, even if followed by a strange resurrection, would not have been understood as his life's greatest achievement, but rather its sad curtailment. Any resurrection that might be claimed for such a figure would hardly carry the meaning that Israel and the world were now renewed. It might at best be the occasion for yet more teaching, perhaps now including stories about a life 'beyond'... But let us suppose that...Jesus had done and said certain things which led people, in however muddled a fashion, to believe that somehow their god was achieving his purpose in and through his work. In such a case, the beginnings of post-resurrection belief in the saving significance of his death...is far more credible."

194. Once again, the one possible exception being the Buddha. Since Buddha is the closest and only real alternative candidate, let me specifically reiterate why he doesn't qualify. Buddha adamantly rejected any attempt to make him divine—he himself was thoroughly agnostic about God anyway. Jesus, on the other hand, implicitly made this claim for himself before anyone else ever did and affirmed, cryptically at least, those fleeting insights or

accusations (blasphemy) that glimpsed or hinted at his divinity. Moreover, the earliest written sources for Buddha's life are much later, upwards of a hundred and fifty years after his death. Contrast this with the gospels, which are written thirty to seventy years after Jesus' death, and which we know contain sources from an earlier period, sources which include those who knew Jesus personally and still acclaimed him as sovereign Lord. And lastly, the Eastern concept of God is radically different: not the utterly transcendent, completely other, personal being of the West, but the imminent, pantheistic force that permeates material reality, including some residual presence in every human being. To claim Buddha was divine (i.e., attained the kind of divine consciousness a select few others—avatars—were already believed to posses and for which all humans are ultimately destined) is categorically different than saying he is the absolutely unique incarnation of the one and only, holy God who exists outside of creation and, by definition, transcends space and time.

195. By the way, this is where *all other alternative reconstructions of the historical Jesus fall short:* they fail to explain how, in light of the resurrection, the early church so rapidly developed this particular belief in Jesus' divinity. One of the strongest indications that the Jesus of history is, in substance, the Jesus of the gospels is that he had to be doing the sort of things the gospels record, namely, claiming divine prerogatives for himself, in order for those who believed he rose from the dead *to conclude that this meant he was Lord*—even if, during his public ministry, they were utterly mystified by it all.

The resurrection is certainly necessary to account for this claim, but it's not sufficient. If he were merely a sage, prophet, zealot, cynic, teacher of moral truth, or whatever else, even believing him risen from the dead, they never would have come to the conclusion he was divine. Their belief in Jesus' divinity also required that he had lived a life fully consistent with it. This is the *only way* to *fully* account for the fact that those who knew Jesus personally could acclaim him, virtually right after his death, to be God in the flesh. And this, in essence, is the kind of life the gospels record him living.

For the detailed evidence Jesus was in fact worshiped as God alongside Yahweh by these first Christians almost immediately after his death, see Hurtado, *One God, One Lord*. Hurtado also offers a similar analysis about the historical Jesus: during his public ministry he must have made the kind of (completely unique) impression that would generate worship after the resurrection. In other words, he had to be saying and doing the kinds of things the gospels record. (120-122)

196. The various incarnations of Brahman (God) in Hinduism are categorically different. For one thing, with the exception of Buddha, there is no certainty that any of the others were actually historical figures. For example, there is no

historical evidence Krishna ever existed. The vast majority of scholars think he is a mythological character and the Bhagavad-gita is a work of fiction. And if some were real people, there is absolutely no historical evidence those individuals believed they were divine or that anyone else did until much later, certainly not in the wake of, or even first few generations after, their deaths. Remember, the writings about Buddha come one hundred and fifty years or so after his death. And even if they are reliable, they record Buddha emphatically denying any attribution of divinity to himself. Moreover, the concept of divinity is radically different in Eastern cosmology: *the line between divine and human is blurred*. Everyone has an element or "piece" of divinity within and is ultimately destined to be completely unified—deified—in the end, the individual soul melting into the larger World Soul, who is God. Indeed, the whole point of Hindu religious practice (the four yogas) is to discover the divine within. This divinity, Brahman, is completely un-definable, the All in All, a totally esoteric ultimate reality. Scholars and devotees argue whether Brahman is pantheistic, or not, whether Brahman is personal, or not, whether Brahman is polytheistic, or not. But they universally affirm that, while Brahman somehow transcends existence itself, Brahman is in all things and all things are in Brahman. In some profound, inexplicable way, then, we are all Brahman, or a part of it. So the incarnation of Brahman (known as an avatar) isn't the transcendent, wholly other, personal God taking on finite flesh in an utterly unique and solitary life, but the full manifestation of the (impersonal) divine being/consciousness across a number of lives (there are disagreements about how many avatars there have been—the number has ranged from seven to twenty two, with contemporary Hindu thought reaching a consensus of ten—actually nine past and one expected to come), which is more or less the destiny all humans will eventually achieve. Thus, there is no real parallel between the Hindu and Christian concepts of incarnation.

197. Swinburne, *The Resurrection of God Incarnate*, p. 202.
198. R. Douglas Geivett, "The Epistemology of Resurrection Belief", in *The Resurrection of Jesus: John Dominic Crossan and N.T. Wright in Dialogue*, Robert B. Stewart ed., p. 96.
199. Kelsey, *Resurrection: Release from Oppression*, pp. 94-95.
200. Meier, *A Marginal Jew: Volume II*, pp. 519-520.
201. Lennox, *Gunning for God*, pp. 221-222.
202. Ibid., pp. 176-177.
203. Link, *The Seventh Trumpet*, p. 82; Meier, *A Marginal Jew: Volume II*, pp. 515-516.
204. Licona, *The Resurrection of Jesus*, pp. 624-639.
205. Meier, *A Marginal Jew: Volume II*, p. 520

206. Rodney Starks, *America's Blessing: How Religion Benefits Everyone, Including Atheists* (West Conshohocken, PA: Templeton Press, 2012), p. 109.

207. Philip Yancey, *A Skeptics Guide to Faith: What It Takes to Make the Leap* (Grand Rapids, MI: Zondervan, 2009), pp. 38-39.

208. Rahner, *Foundations of Christian Faith*, p. 275.

209. Spitzer, *The Soul's Upward Yearning*, pp. 95-96.

210. Ibid., p. 143.

211. Ibid., p. 97.

212. Ibid., p. 122.

213. Ibid., p. 125.

214. Ibid., pp. 147-148.

215. Stephanie Evanovich, Keynote speaker at the 2015 Unicorn Writer's Conference, August 15, 2015, Manhattanville College, Purchase, NY.

216. Timothy Keller, *Preaching: Communicating Faith in an Age of Skepticism* (New York, NY: Viking, 2015), pp. 175-176.

217. Keller, *Making Sense of God*, pp. 173-174.

218. See also Spitzer, *The Soul's Upward Yearning*, pp. 79-82 who goes on to note that this archetype of the cosmic battle of good and evil appears universally in the dreams of very young children in a way that they could not learn from the outside world.(87) This leads him to conclude: "Our attraction to and love of myths comes from within us—or better, from the presence of God within us—inviting us into His noble mission, into Himself, and into His destiny."(90) The best way to explain the prevalence and power of this innate archetype is as pointing us to the ultimate reality for which we were made.

219. "Charlie Rose", Connecticut Public Television, Channel 24-2, show airing on April 10, 2017.

220. Rice, *Christ the Lord: Out of Egypt*, p. 338.

221. Moses and David save Israel from foreign domination and oppression, but *not* evil and death. Muhammad, Buddha, Confucius, and Lao Tzu were primarily teachers—none of whom sacrificed their life to save anyone. Nor did they do anything to bring about—to affect—the promise or transformation they taught about. No one of these figures ever claimed to be God Himself. No one of them ever claimed to be the One who saves. Several of them specifically disavowed it. Furthermore, no other figure, no warrior, rebel, activist, philosopher, scientist, prophet, political leader, etc., has actually saved anyone from the ultimate power of sin, suffering, evil, and death. And with the possible exception of a few who are on the lunatic fringe, no one has ever *claimed* to be able to save anyone in this way. Jesus stands alone as the only potentially legitimate, ultimate savior figure. He believed his mission to be the ultimate defeat of evil, the decisive victory over Satan—which means that he was claiming to save us from suffering and death.

In fact, one contemporary writer attributes the remarkable spread of Christianity across Africa over the past century to just this. Lamin Sanneh, a Yale scholar who specializes in the study of African Christianity, concludes that Jesus, unlike any other, fulfills this longing for an invincible savior who can free human beings from the power of evil and death. Keller, *Making Sense of God*, pp.149-149.

222. Another way to look at this is by asking: what if Elvis or Einstein or JFK or Buddha was the only person for whom the claim they rose from the dead could be seriously made? If their resurrection vindicated and validated the kind of life they lived, what kind of universe would that suggest? Depending on who the claim was made for, it would be one where talent or intelligence or political savvy or charisma or enlightenment mattered most. Actually, it would be a world much like our own, where these things are already paramount. But it would be a world far from ideal, far from what is most essential to our humanity. Certainly not the kind where perfect love ultimately reigns and where being fully human—loving one another—is the point. With Jesus, however, this is exactly the kind of universe that is implied; the kind of universe that aligns perfectly with our deepest longings and what we (self-evidently) seem to be designed for.

It must be said that the only person who comes close to Jesus as an ideal savior figure is Buddha, who was renowned as much for his compassion as his enlightened being. However, the differences between the two are mammoth. Buddha was completely agnostic (he remained silent whenever his follows asked him about God, viewing the question as completely irrelevant) and categorically rejected any notion that he was a god. He would be horrified both at the idea of *bodily* resurrection and that God would become *incarnate* to save us: he was all about escaping fleshly existence. For him, love wasn't the point. Enlightenment (Nirvana), which frees you from the finite domain, was. And Enlightenment isn't about being fully human, but about detaching yourself from the bondage of human existence, from the illusion of suffering. Moreover, he didn't die a sacrificial death, and, over and over again, emphatically renounced all notions that he was some kind of savior figure. He simply presented himself as a guide, as one who was sharing the Truth he had discovered, a Truth anyone else was capable of achieving on their own. Only much later does one strand of Buddhism (Mahayana) turn him into a savior figure. Furthermore, he had a radically different understanding of life beyond physical death, one where love is not the ultimate value. In sum, Buddha wasn't the man for others—his life defined by love—as much as he was the man who *woke up*—waking up being a metaphor for enlightenment. In contrast, Jesus' life was, in every way, defined by his sublime love.

Logically, if there is some point to life, it must involve fulfilling the purpose for which humans are made, i.e., being fully human. And love is how we reach our fullest human potential—compassion is the essence of *humanitarianism* after all. Jesus embodies this as no other person ever has. So he is by far the most logical candidate for resurrection: if there was one person who walked the face of the earth that we would expect to rise, it would be him.

223. McBrien, *Catholicism*, p. 1150.
224. Keller, *Making Sense of God*, p.167.
225. Luc Ferry, "The Victory of Christianity over Greek Philosophy," in *A Brief History of Thought: A Philosophical Guide to Living*, trans. Theo Cuffe (New York: Harper Perennial, 2011), pp. 85-86.
226. As quoted in Licona, *The Resurrection of Jesus*, p. 638.
227. Roy Abraham Varghese's preface in Antony Flew, *There is A God: How the World's Most Notorious Atheist Changed his Mind* (New York, NY: Harper Collins, 2007), p. ix.
228. Ibid., pp. 88-89.
229. Ibid., p. 112. See page 91 for a similar statement: in a complete reversal of his atheism, Flew now thinks that the soundest *philosophical* explanation for the many new phenomena uncovered by modern science is that we live in a rational universe that had to have sprung from a divine Mind.
230. Licona, *The Resurrection of Jesus*, p. 157.
231. As cited in Keller, *Making Sense of God*, p. 24.
232. Rodney Stark, *America's Blessing: How Religion Benefits Everyone, Including Atheists* (West Conshohocken, PA: Templeton Press, 2012), p. 29: "...the percentage of Americans who are atheists hasn't changed in the past sixty years. Four percent told the Gallup Poll in 1944 that they did not believe in God, exactly the same percentage as in the Baylor National Survey of Religion in 2007." A larger percentage, roughly sixteen percent, don't positively affirm any kind of belief in God, but this includes agnostics—those who claim they aren't sure whether God exists or not, and/or who claim that we can't ever know one way or another, i.e., the evidence is too ambiguous to be certain. An atheist says they are sure that there is no God.
233. Keller, *Making Sense of God*, pp. 9-10, cites a Pew study which shows that the assumed decline in faith as modernization increases hasn't happened. In *America's Blessing*, pp. 72-73 and 133-143, Stark shows that, in a statistically significant way, higher rates of church attendance are actually correlated to *higher* levels of education and achievement.
234. Armand Nicholi, *The Question of God: C.S. Lewis and Sigmund Freud Debate God, Love, Sex, and the Meaning of Life* (New York, NY: Free Press, 2002), pp. 54-55.

235. Licona, *The Resurrection of Jesus*, pp. 159-160, f.92. He also cites a 2007 Tobin and Weinberg study that found 65 percent of professors in secular universities believe; only 8 percent report being atheists.

236. Michael Guillen, *Can A Smart Person Believe in God?* (Nashville, TN: Nelson Books, 2004), p. 20. Also see p. 24 where he cites a 2003 Harris pole of post-grads, 85 percent of whom say they believe in God.

237. Most people are familiar with Richard Dawkins and Christopher Hitchens. But the more highly respected atheists, like Thomas Nagel, Sam Harris, and Terry Eagleton, frequently find their arguments embarrassing to the atheist position: they are unsophisticated, vacuous, and significantly flawed, often knocking down strawman arguments and attacking superficial caricatures of belief instead of the more valid considerations. The arguments mounted here, the arguments which shaped Flew's thinking, confront the deeper challenges posed by these more respected atheists and their far weightier arguments.

238. Flew, *There is a God*, p. 115.

239. Spitzer, *The Soul's Upward Yearning*, p. 312.

240. Ibid., p. 316.

241. Francis S. Collins, *The Language of God: A Scientist Presents Evidence for Belief* (New York, NY: Free Press, 2006), pp. 67-78. Collins also points out that all these steps in the formation of the solar system are so well described by physics that they are unlikely to be revised. In other words, unlike the many other upheavals of prevailing theories seen in the physical sciences over the last number of decades, these observations about fine tuning are firm and, even if we gain additional information, there is little chance they will change. See Guillen, *Can a Smart Person Believe in God?*, pp. 121-123. See also Guy Consolmagno and Paul Mueller, *Would You Baptize an Extraterrestrial?...and Other Questions from the Astronomers' In-box at the Vatican Observatory* (New York, NY: Image, 2014), pp. 252-254. Despite their unflinching and enthusiastic openness to the possibility of extraterrestrial life, they show that, to date, there is absolutely no credible evidence it exists. However, if discovered at some point, on pp. 254-286 they discuss in detail the implications extraterrestrial life would have for belief in God and the special place humans have in His creation. In opposition to those who claim that the discovery of extraterrestrial life would create major theological problems for theism in general and especially Christianity in particular (where God becomes human), they provide a thorough and compelling response. The existence of intelligent, sentient, extraterrestrial life is completely compatible with the loving God of Christian faith. Collins also happens to concur with this conclusion.

242. As quoted in Collins, *The Language of God*, p.75.

243. Flew, *There is a God*, p. 119; Richard Swinburne, "Design Defended", *Think* (Spring 2004), p. 17.

244. Ibid., p. 121.

245. Ibid., p. 124.

246. David Conway, *The Rediscovery of Wisdom* (London: Macmillan, 2000), p. 125.

247. Flew, *There is a God*, p. 129.

248. George Wald, "Life and Mind in the Universe," in *Cosmos, Bios, Theos*, ed. Henry Margenau and Roy Abraham Varghese (LaSalle, IL: Open Court, 1992), p. 218.

249. Flew, *There is a God*, p. 75.

250. Roy Abraham Varghese, "The 'New Atheism': A Critical Appraisal of Dawkins, Dennett, Wopert, Harris, and Stenger", Appendix A in Flew, *There is A God*, p. 167. Keller notes how atheist philosopher Thomas Nagel thinks that the existence of human consciousness is the greatest challenge to atheism. Materialism is hard-pressed to explain why reality is filled with rationally-minded, self-conscious human beings. Keller then goes on to remark: "…it is very hard to explain how the ability to do complex mathematics and abstract philosophy was a capacity that helped our ancestors survive. Steven Pinker, a convinced materialist, has been forced by these arguments to agree. He is not sure why these capacities developed." Keller, *Making Sense of God*, pp. 222-223.

251. Ibid., p. 183.

252. Ibid., pp. 176-177.

253. Guy Consolmagno and Paul Mueller, *Would You Baptize an Extraterrestrial?… and Other Questions from the Astronomers' In-box at the Vatican Observatory* (New York, NY: Image, 2014), p 280.

254. The Theory of Relativity has fundamentally challenged our notions of space and time: it appears that time is variable, depending upon speed and gravitational forces. The faster you go, especially as you approach the speed of light, the more time slows down. But this is a question of rate, not direction. There is still a sequential "before/after." Things still "progress," moving forward, but just at a slower or faster rate. As Paul Davis states: "…earlier-later ordering relation is an objective property of time…" Paul Davies, *God and the New Physics* (New York, NY: Simon and Schuster, 1983), p. 137. In fact, many physicists now think that the reality we call time only *begins* with the introduction of space and matter at the Big Bang, meaning that it can't be infinitely regressive.

Especially when it comes to Quantum Mechanics, modern physics often relies on mathematical descriptions of phenomena that are *profoundly counterintuitive*, but which prove to give a more accurate account of reality.

Thus, any argument about regressive time being counterintuitive is vulnerable to critique on the grounds that we can't rely on intuition in these matters. On this basis, a number of physicists would argue that time could be, and indeed is, infinitely regressive. While this *may* turn out to be true in the matter of time (although the more prevalent thinking regarding Relativity, namely that time has its origin with matter and space in the Big Bang, would rule this out), the mathematical formulas used to describe these counterintuitive realities betray a profound rationality; they can, quite elegantly, capture reality in a logically consistent and meaningful way, with a kind of semantic content, albeit through "numerical" abstraction. And this deeper rationality provides compelling evidence for a divine mind. Simply put, where did the exquisite order these elegant formulas are capable of consistently describing so accurately come from? For more on this see Davies, *God and the New Physics*.

255. Flew, *There is A God*, pp. 144-145.
256. Spitzer, *The Soul's Upward Yearning*, p. 323.
257. Flew, *There is A God*, p. 135.
258. Ibid., pp. 136-137. Darwin also came to the same conclusion, at least at one point during his life. (There are questions about where he eventually landed. At another, later point he seems to have considered himself an agnostic. Some speculate that the death of his young daughter adversely affected his faith; others point to persistent doubts he had about historical revelation, the existence of different religions, the nature of God, and so forth.) As quoted by Flew: "[Reason tells me of the] extreme difficulty or rather impossibility of conceiving this immense and wonderful universe, including man with his capability of looking backwards and far into the futurity, as the result of blind chance or necessity. When thus reflecting I feel compelled to look to a First Cause having an intelligent mind in some degree analogous to that of man; and I deserve to be called a Theist." Flew also points to some of the most prominent voices in science today who follow this same rationale: scientists like Paul Davies, John Barrow, John Polkinghorne, Freeman Dyson, Francis Collins, Owen Gingerich, and Roger Penrose to philosophers of science like Richard Swinburne and John Leslie.(106)
259. Flew, *There is A God*, p. 137.
260. Guillen, *Can a Smart Person Believe in God*, p. 77. Guillen also notes the dramatic shift in thinking regarding both the big-bang and fine-tuning: "Since the mid-twentieth century, however, that scientific view has changed by 180 degrees, and in the process, come into greater agreement with the essence of Genesis 1:1 in two profound ways. First, it now appears that the cosmos did indeed have a definite beginning: starting with a 'big bang,' it sprang into existence *out of nothing* (what scientists call *a quantum vacuum*).

Second, there appears to be stunning evidence the universe came into being not accidentally, but in accordance with some master plan.

"Astronomers have coined various catchy phrases to describe the million-and-one details about the cosmos that seem too good to be random. One of them is *the rare earth hypothesis*, meaning the earth looks to be not just another planet, one among billions and billions, but a world unique in ways that really matter to us...

"Even the late great cosmologist and Uncertain Atheist Sir Fred Hoyle, whom I had the pleasure of knowing during my years at Cornell, felt compelled to admit it. In his book *Intelligent Universe*, Hoyle says, 'The probability of life originating at random is so utterly miniscule as to make it absurd'...

"Hoyle calculated that the chances of Randomness creating a single protein molecule by accident were about as tiny as a sightless person solving Rubik's Cube.

"Put another way: he calculated Randomness would need about *three hundred times* the age of the earth to create a single protein molecule by accident. That amounts to about 1.3 trillion years! Considering that scientists currently estimate the entire universe to be only 13 *billion* years old, that doesn't leave nearly enough time for Randomness to have pieced life together from scratch, by accident." pp. 121-122.

261. Lennox, *Gunning for God*, pp. 29-30.
262. Gerald Holton and Yehuda Eikana, *Albert Einstein: Historical and Cultural Perspectives* (Princeton: Princeton University Press, 1997), p. 227.
263. Spitzer, *The Soul's Upward Yearning*, pp. 301-302.
264. Ibid., pp. 295-296. In light of the BVG proof, the only way for physicists to avoid the obvious conclusion of a beginning is to posit an "eternally static" universe. A perfectly stable universe could be infinite and require no beginning. However, on pp. 298-300 Spitzer addresses the insurmountable logical contradiction involved in arguing for an eternally static universe, the only possible exception to the BVG proof.

In order to transition from whatever state pre-existed the big bang (quantum gravity of string theory, for example) to the state that follows which we inherit (described by General Relativity), an eternally static universe would have to accommodate the decay of moving from one state to another. But this would mean that it must be metastable. It would have to go from a perfectly stable state of maximum entropy to the complete reverse, initiating a state of entropy. In which case, it is no longer perfectly stable. It is impossible for it to be, by definition, perfectly stable, but at the same time, metastable, i.e., *not perfectly stable*.

On this basis, Spitzer then concludes that physics is coming close to proving a beginning of the universe. He then quotes Vilenkin to the same effect: "It is said that an argument is what convinces reasonable men and a proof is what it takes to convince even an unreasonable man. With the proof now in place, cosmologists can no longer hide behind the possibility of a past-eternal universe...There is no escape, they have to face the problem of a cosmic beginning." Alexander Vilenkin, *Many Worlds in One: The Search for Other Universes* (New York, NY: Hill and Wang, 2006), p 175.

265. Ibid., p. 307.
266. Ibid., p. 310.
267. Keller, *Making Sense of God*, p. 218.
268. Flew, *There is A God*, p. 150.
269. Ibid., p. 93.
270. There is mounting evidence that loneliness and social isolation have debilitating, and, at times, deadly effects, and on both mental and physical health. You may have noticed the trend among popular health professionals, like Dr. Oz, in emphasizing healthy relationships right alongside diet and exercise as key factors in a healthy lifestyle.

But what about hermits? In other words, how do you explain people who intentionally isolate themselves and seem to thrive mentally, physically, and spiritually? People like St. Antony, who preferred to be alone in the dessert? They feel (and would often share or write about) a heightened sense of connection and companionship through their communion with God. In their minds, they are never alone. They've found the ultimate relationship. And in any case, many hermits continued to have social interaction: people often sought them out for their spiritual wisdom. Virtually all modern "cloistered" movements are communal, providing the best of both worlds.

271. Liz Mineo, "Good Genes are Nice, but Joy is Better", *The Harvard Gazette* (April 11, 2017) https://news.harvard.edu.story. Also see the outstanding TED talk by psychiatrist Robert Waldinger, the fourth director of they study. With over thirteen million hits and counting, it's become a YouTube sensation.

272. Spitzer, *God So Loved the World*, p. 58.

273. "The Terrible Teens", *More2Life*, show broadcast April 5, 2017 on Sirius XM 130 EWTN Global Catholic Radio Network, https://www.ewtn.com/radio/weekday.

274. Guillen, *Can a Smart Person Believe in God?*, p.149. He also writes: "...consider the recent explosion of scientific research on the subject. In 2002, sociologist Byron R. Johnson and his colleagues at the University of Pennsylvania's Center for Research on Religion and Urban Civil Society wrote an article titled 'Objective Hope,' in which they evaluated 669 studies published to date in peer-reviewed journals. The vast majority of the studies—anywhere from 65 to 97 percent of them—show that spirituality (generally in the form of traditional church- and synagogue-going Judea-Christian

godliness) is associated with a long list of physical, mental and emotional benefits: lower levels of hypertension, depression, suicide, sexual promiscuity, drug addiction, alcohol abuse, and criminal delinquency, plus higher levels of academic achievement and feelings of well-being, hope, purpose, meaning, and self-esteem—as well as a longer life span." p. 5. See pp. 149-151 for a more detailed breakdown of research results.

275. Nicholi, *The Question of God*, p. 80. See also his conclusions on p. 94. Additionally, he discusses research done on Harvard students revealing the significant positive effect of a spiritual worldview for dealing with depression. And on p. 103, he talks about Freud's lament that those holding a religious belief demonstrate higher gratification—Freud lamented this both because it contradicted his theory that belief in God is pathological, and thus leads to less gratification, and because he could never bring himself to believe in God and experience this gratification for himself.

276. Licona, *The Resurrection of Jesus*, p.115.

277. Smith, *The World's Religions*, pp.32-33. As an aside, Christianity is the only truly worldwide religion. As technology continues to shrink our world and people are becoming more and more exposed to other religious traditions and worldviews; as Christianity enters into the marketplace of ideas along with all the other great religious and philosophical traditions, more people are choosing it over any other worldview. Unlike the other major religions, it has transcended the limitations of culture to reach into almost every corner of the world. Surely this says something about its ability to address life's ultimate questions in the most satisfying way, especially in accounting for the supreme place love holds in human life. See Keller, *Making Sense of God*, p.148, and Dinesh D'Souza, *What's So Great About Christianity* (Carol Stream, Illinois: Tyndale House Publishers, 2008), pp. 9-10 for more and some of the statistics.

I also need to point out that the idea that God *is* love has so infiltrated our culture that most people have no idea where it originated. In the popular understanding, it has become a truism that, fundamentally, all religions, or at least the major world religions, teach that God is love; that this is the fundamental belief all religions, deep down, hold in common. But this is simply not the case. The notion that God *is* (unconditional) love, and all this implies, is unique to Christianity. And, even though culturally much of its full Christian meaning has been distorted or diminished, because we have so thoroughly assimilated it into our thinking, few are aware of what a radical innovation—what a revelation!—this teaching was when Jesus first introduced it.

One final note: if your experience of Christians or Christianity has not been good; if Christians or the church have hurt you or been unbearably hypocritical or failed to authentically live this ideal of love, it breaks my heart. I am so sorry. But this isn't because Jesus or the faith he revealed has failed. It's because sinful human beings and/or a humanly flawed institution has utterly failed to live up to its own creed and let you down. That doesn't diminish the damage that may have been done. It is totally unacceptable, and it embarrasses and infuriates me that we in the church so often cause so much pain. However, I would plead with you not to let any person or institution, even the church, get in the way of your relationship with God. He is good; we are not.

278. Flew, *There is A God*, p. 157.

279. Licona, *The Resurrection of Jesus*, p. 163.

280. By the way, I wholeheartedly agree that without the philosophical presupposition that there is some creative intelligence behind the universe, the idea Jesus rose from the dead is absurd. However, it's far more probable than not that there is a divine mind responsible for the universe. And our transcendental longing provides strong corroboration for this reality.

It's hard to explain why we have this transcendental longing if there is no God or infinite horizon to fulfill it. It can't be explained through any materialistic cause, in particular, as an effective mechanism for evolutionary development. Instead, it works against adaptation. It constitutes a significant distraction. Constantly contemplating the grass that is greener on the other side means that you'll be less motivated to take care of the grass on this side. Dreaming about "pie in the sky by and by" takes the focus off of this life, seriously compromising human progress. Indeed, calling it the "opiate of the people (masses)," Marx complained that preoccupation with this longing (religion's panacea of God and heaven and the like) undermined human progress by leading people to accept forms of oppression and alienation they would otherwise fiercely resist. It distracted them from focusing on improving their lot in life, their survivability, and kept them from thriving as stronger, more capable, better-adapted individuals.

This longing also can't be dismissed as a group adaptive response, providing some kind of benefit for the larger population; for example, in making people more altruistic, willing to make sacrifices that benefit the larger group because of some kind of perceived transcendental reward. Evolutionary biologists are in almost universal agreement that selection operates on the individual, not on the population at large. Therefore, any altruism this longing might produce can't be explained as an adaptive response oriented toward group benefit. See Francis S. Collins, *The Language of God: A Scientist Presents Evidence for Belief* (New York, NY: Free Press, 2006), pp. 27-28.

When people have one foot in this world and one in the next, they are less attentive to this life and all the problems it presents. Believing that things will eventually be set right in the world to come, they are more apt to fatalistically accept the imperfections of this world. The loss of productivity this causes severely undermines the communal good (which Marx also sought to correct by railing against this "opiate of the people"). Think of all the good, all the medical breakthroughs, for instance, that would have happened already if people weren't continually allured by the perfections of another world, being preoccupied, for example, with devoting hours on end to religious activity; "wasting" their time, lives, and potential contributions to human thriving worshiping a non-existent entity.

In addition, this longing often propels people to forfeit their lives more easily. The promise of an eternal reward encourages people to give their lives as martyrs, to save strangers (clearly not an adaptive response), or to let go more easily when faced with an existential threat, such as a serious and potentially terminal diagnosis—it doesn't make sense to fight for survival when there's a far better reality waiting on the other side. And, the awareness that things are not as they ought to be—the by-product of this longing—is a significant source of angst, depression, and despair. It weighs us down and can even become immobilizing, adversely affecting our health, even leading to suicide. Not a very effective mechanism for survival and adaptation!

Ultimately however, even without the metaphysical probability that God exists, the case for the resurrection, though not as strong, is still quite compelling. In other words, in a metaphysically neutral environment, one where it is just as likely God exists as not (a fifty-fifty probability), the resurrection can be judged "very certain." If you remove any philosophical bias in either direction, the historical evidence provides a relatively high degree of probative certainty. This is the conclusion of Michael Licona in *The Resurrection of Jesus*. He starts from a position of neutrality regarding bias for or against the existence of God, and then analyzes the evidence according the historical bedrock, i.e., the bare minimum data that scholars of every stripe agree upon. From this hyper-critical approach, and in a way that turned out to surprise even him, he is able to conclude that the resurrection, as a true miracle—a supernatural event caused by a God—is very certain.

281. Keller, *Making Sense of God*, p. 163.
282. Kelsey, *Resurrection*, p. 93.
283. For a different kind of exposition of this phenomena, see Jim Spiegel, "Unreasonable Doubt," *Christianity Today: Volume 55, Number 1* (Carol Stream, IL: Christianity Today International, January 2011), pp. 48-49. Spiegel points out that many intellectuals dress their moral preferences (or immoral lifestyles) up with rational objections to belief in God. He cites the famous case of philosopher Mortimer Adler who, after being baptized at the age of 81, admitted that the real reason he resisted religious faith for so long was because he didn't "want to live up to being a genuinely religious person." (I could add the many testimonies I've heard from people who say almost the

exact same thing post-conversion: though they presented it as intellectual doubt—and no doubt they did have genuine and valid questions of faith—the real resistance was to some kind of lifestyle change.) This also cuts the other way: sometimes people cling to an unreflective faith because of psychological hang-ups or fears, social factors, conditioning, family pressure, and the like. Generally, those who believe and those who don't aren't cool and detached about the question. Our willful desires, moral and psychological factors, have a lot more to do with it than we think.

284. "Scammed and Stupid", *Dr. Phil*, WWLP, Channel 22 Springfield, show airing July 29, 2013.

285. See Christine Herman, "A Lesson in Listening," *Christianity Today: Volume 61, Number 5* (Carol Stream IL: Christianity Today International, June 2017), p. 42 for a good exposition of this phenomena.

286. Licona, *The Resurrection of Jesus*, p. 612.

287. Ibid., p. 60.

288. For a more detailed discussion of Critical Realism as I'm applying it here, see Wright, *The New Testament and the People of God*, pp. 32-46. Also see Licona, *The Resurrection of Jesus*, pp. 50-62 for a more in-depth approach to transcending horizon and bias. He proposes six tools which include: attention to method, making the individual's bias and method public, peer pressure, submitting ideas to unsympathetic experts, accounting for the relevant historical bedrock, and detachment from bias. While he intends this for use by professional historians, i.e., scholars, much of it can be fruitfully applied to a personal quest for truth.

289. Wright, *The New Testament and the People of God*, pp. 45 and 66.

290. Strobel, *The Case for Christ*, pp. 264-266. I've thoroughly enjoyed reading Strobel's work. I think his conclusions are usually right on target. And I know many people who have come to faith as a result. But as a hard-core skeptic, I wouldn't have been convinced by the arguments he presents unless I had seen the deeper evidence under-girding these conclusions for myself. To be fair, his methodology seems to be to rely on the authority of scholars who are trusted experts so as not to overwhelm people by going into all the in-depth evidence. As one who is trying to find that balance between enough versus too much, I appreciate his approach. However, I've talked to a number of people who've found this approach lacking and who need to see that evidence for themselves. So, by citing him here I am in no way suggesting that his approach is sufficient for the hard-core skeptic, or that what he presents is all there is to the evidence—I hope this book has shown that there is so much more to it—even though he has done amazing things in giving many people good reason to believe.

291. Swinburne, *The Resurrection of God Incarnate*, pp. 172-173.

292. Link, *The Seventh Trumpet*, p. 194.

293. Author Unknown. This story was first brought to my attention circa 2000 when a student shared it with me to use as a prayer in class. They found it on the internet and printed off a copy to bring in to school. As any internet search reveals, many have tried without success to track down its origin and establish whether it's true or not.

294. As I've said, I'm completely cynical about visionary experiences. So I hesitate to include this note. But, there is a phenomenon in the Muslim world that is difficult to dismiss. In recent years many Muslims—by some counts, upwards of ten thousand (and this figure may be grossly underestimated because there might be many more who never report having such a vision for fear of persecution)—have been seeing visions of Jesus who reveals himself as God. These are faithful Muslims who are horrified at first because this is outright blasphemy—there is only one god, and Allah is His Name. And because to accept them as true and become Christian could easily get them killed. But they are so powerful, so real to those who receive them, that they are compelled to convert and publicly confess Jesus as Lord. The frequency of and the consistency in these visions—it happens almost exclusively to scrupulously faithful Muslims; those receiving them are terribly reluctant to accept them as true; the nature of the encounter is very much the same, etc.—combined with the radical and dangerous conversion that results is hard to explain as anything other than genuine. Again, I usually dismiss this kind of thing. But I'm having a hard time doing so. If they are real—still a big if—this is a good and dramatic example of encountering the Risen Lord. Most encounters are far more subtle.

295. Paraphrase from Book 3, Chapter 6:11 of *The Confessions of Saint Augustine* (New York, NY: Doubleday, 1960), John K. Ryan ed., p. 84.

296. Stobel, *The Case for Christ*, p. 269.

297. Spitzer, *The Soul's Upward Yearning*, pp. 191-192.

298. Ibid., pp. 194-195.

299. Ibid., p. 202.

300. Ibid., p. 203.

301. Spitzer, *God So Loved the World*, pp. 350-355, 369-371.

302. Ibid., pp. 355-360.

303. Gelsomino Del Guercio, "Is the blood on the Shroud falsified? Study says yes, but expert points out problems with research", *Aleteia* (July 18, 2018) https://aleteia.org/ 2018/07/18/is-the-blood-on-the-shroud-falsified-study-says-yes-but-expert-point-out-problems-with-research/

304. Spitzer, *God So Loved the World*, pp. 382-385.

305. Ibid., pp. 380-381.

306. Ibid., pp. 376-387.

Printed in the United States
By Bookmasters

Printed in the United States
By Bookmasters